# THE FORESTS

WOOD ANEMONE (*Anemone quinquefolia*), common in low open woodlands and at high elevations in Forests of Virginia, flowers from April to June.

SAGUARO or GIANT CACTUS (*Carnegiea gigantea*), amazing Arizona creature, capable of 50-foot heights and 10-ton weights. Buds open at night; as fruits mature they are eaten by doves.

GOLD POPPY (*Eschscholtzia mexicana*), In spring an incomparable mantle that covers desert foothills.

Photographs by Charles Cleveland Johnson

TRAILING ARBUTUS or MAYFLOWER (*Epigaea repens*), a beauty in springtime among evergreens. The small flowers, fragrant as spice, are pollinated by early flying queen bumblebees.

# WHOSE WOODS THESE ARE:

## The Story of the National Forests

BOOKS BY MICHAEL FROME

WHOSE WOODS THESE ARE:
*The Story of the National Forests*

WASHINGTON:
*A Modern Guide to the Nation's Capital*

BETTER VACATIONS FOR YOUR MONEY

# WHOSE WOODS
# THESE ARE: *The Story*
## *of the National Forests*

MICHΛEL FROME

DOUBLEDAY & COMPANY, INC.

GARDEN CITY, NEW YORK

1962

To the inspiring memory of Bernard DeVoto
and Richard Neuberger, who loved and
championed the National Forests

"Stopping by Woods on a Snowy Evening" from *Complete Poems of Robert Frost*. Copyright 1923 by Holt, Rinehart & Winston, Inc. Copyright renewed 1951 by Robert Frost. Reprinted by permission of the publisher and Jonathan Cape Ltd.

*Library of Congress Catalog Card Number 62–8078*
*Copyright © 1962 by Michael Frome*
*All Rights Reserved*
*Printed in the United States of America*
*First Edition*

Whose woods these are I think I know.
His house is in the village though;
He will not see me stopping here
To watch his woods fill up with snow.

My little horse must think it queer
To stop without a farmhouse near
Between the woods and frozen lake
The darkest evening of the year.

He gives his harness bells a shake
To ask if there is some mistake.
The only other sound's the sweep
Of easy wind and downy flakes.

The woods are lovely, dark and deep.
But I have promises to keep,
And miles to go before I sleep,
And miles to go before I sleep.

ROBERT FROST

# Contents

PART ONE

# POETRY AND POLITICS

CHAPTER ONE

# The Hour Was Dusk

The hour was dusk. Evening twilight, the slender, magic fragment of time bordering daylight and darkness.

The plane was late in leaving Los Angeles, as planes will sometimes be in leaving almost anywhere. But it was worth it. Once aloft, I thought I would have waited willingly three days for this view of the spectrum at dusk, ranging from the distant orange-flecked horizon of the limitless sea to the depth of a new night in the East.

Directly below, the Pacific darkened into bluish black. The surfline rose forth into a fine, clear white. Along the curving coast, the concrete freeways were clogged with motorcars by the tens of thousands scurrying homeward to the hills and valleys and beaches. And all across the landscape a million lights erupted into night-shattering colors. They were white lights, red, green, orange and blue, and a variety of combinations. With the last glow of the natural sun, we had reached the parting of the way with all other creatures of the plant and animal kingdoms, who would now follow their own course into the darkness of the planet.

Yet even so, on one visible frontier the lights thinned. Through the pall of smog and incandescent haze within the Los Angeles bowl, I saw the lights weaken, gradually and then more decisively, then stop completely at a border of mountains.

But why? Why should these tiny synthetic sunlights surrender to a natural barrier? When in other directions they climbed to the peaks, crawled across the tops like a conquering army and down to the sea (and even into the sea at Long Beach)? Why, at a time in history when there are takers for the craggiest, remotest corners of southern California and promoters of the driest, unlikeliest deserts, should nature cling to this balance?

Here, from this plane window, I thought, was the essence of all that I had been studying, seeing, living and dreaming for a period of time which seemed ever so long and yet ever so short. Here was the

The National Forest System of the United

Minn.

Wis.

Mich.

Maine

Vt.

N.H

Mass.

New York

Conn.

R.I.

N.J.

Iowa

Ill.

Ind.

Ohio

Pa.

Md.

Del.

Mo.

Ky.

W.Va.

Va.

N. Car.

Ark.

Tenn.

S. Car.

Miss.

Ala.

Ga.

La.

Fla.

*tates, from Alaska to Puerto Rico*

coexistence of people with mountains and back country, mountains and back country which could be transformed into subdivisions and cities any time we choose. Yet they are not, because somewhere in our wisdom Americans have determined that our survival depends to a vast extent on survival of nature and the outdoors.

Thus do we now enter the realm of the National Forests, which are as old as the oldest history and as new and exciting and meaningful as the most creative work of architecture, and perhaps not much more understood than the most current work of art.

The National Forests were born in the West before the turn of the century to protect the woods and streams of high country from decimation by uncontrolled logging, grazing and fire. But the National Forest System has since grown to occupy about one-tenth of the country's land area, extending from snowy Kenai Peninsula in Alaska to the lush Rain Forest of Puerto Rico, and is administered by the oldest conservation agency in the Federal Government.

National Forests cover the sweep of almost every major mountain range, from the Chugach down through the Cascades, the Sierra Nevadas, the Siskiyous and the Coast Range. They delineate the Continental Divide from Montana through Wyoming, Utah and Colorada to the southerly peaks of the Rocky Mountains in Arizona and New Mexico. They are the heart of the Black Hills, the Ouachitas and the Ozarks in the mid-continent. In the East, they embrace the backbone of the White Mountains and Green Mountains, and of the Southern Appalachians through Virginia, West Virginia, North Carolina, South Carolina and Georgia.

Many rivers are born of snows and glaciers and rain within the National Forests. On this sonorous roll call of beloved American streams are the Yellowstone, Platte, Rio Grande and Colorado; the Green, Salmon and Snake; the Klamath and Trinity; the Wisconsin, Current and Au Sable; the Allegheny, Potomac and James, all three flowing from a single forest in West Virginia, called the mother of rivers.

The National Forests fulfill many purposes.

They protect water supplies of hundreds of cities and towns, and furnish irrigation water, flood protection and hydroelectric power.

They afford grazing land, including the precious high summer range, for 2,500,000 sheep and 1,140,000 head of cattle.

14

About a million and a half mining claims, which is substantially much too many, are outstanding on the National Forests.

They are breathing space and playgrounds for city people, who flock to their tens of thousands of picnic tables, camping sites and recreation areas. Their slopes and trails afford 90 per cent of the country's skiing, at famous Tuckerman Ravine, Sun Valley, Squaw Valley, Aspen and a thousand other valleys and bowls.

The National Forests are the home of one-third of our country's big game animals, plus throngs of smaller game, fur bearers and birds. They comprise America's largest and last great hunting and fishing grounds, unblemished by "No Trespass" signs to bar the sportsman's way.

The National Forests encompass 14,000,000 glorious acres of wilderness, a large kingdom of the outdoors located in scattered segments. Roads, logging and the comforts of home are not permitted, yet those who wish to achieve spiritual harmony with elemental America, or to hunt in its bosom, or to study the natural sciences, are welcome to enjoy life the hard way.

The National Forests are much related to the national economy. Hundreds of communities depend on their timber resources to keep sawmills going. In the sale of timber to private loggers, the Forest Service earns $140,000,000 a year for the government. One-fourth of the receipts goes to counties in which the forests are located, specified for use in building schools and roads. In some cases, this is more than would be earned if the lands were, as they say, "on the tax base." This point of income and aid to local communities is often emphasized before Congress to justify Forest Service appropriations. And the whole issue of economics is stressed by some foresters, underscored and reiterated by lumber trade associations and chambers of commerce.

Leave them to their issues; after all, what is a trade association or chamber of commerce without an issue? Without denying the economic role, I prefer to think of National Forests as they express the poetry of the land and the lore of its people. The visual poetry of trees, from the seedling to the giant Douglas-fir and sequoia, and the oldest living creature on earth, the bristlecone pine, which grows in Inyo National Forest, California. Of the changing seasons. Of the sight and smell of wildlife. And of all growing things, from the tiny verbena blooming on the desert floor to the bald eagle soaring above the highest treetop.

15

The trail of Lewis and Clark is emblazoned across National Forests. So are the comings and goings of Indians, loggers, trappers, mountaineers and homesteaders; of people drawn from everywhere on earth, like the Basques, probably the greatest of all sheepherders, and the Chinese, who flocked into Idaho City, Idaho, in the 1860's, when more gold was taken from the stream beds than has been taken from all of Alaska, "coming like crickets on the march, on jackasses and on foot, over ditches, woodpiles and fences and everything else."

History and lore are embodied in the forest ranger, the descendant in spirit of frontiersmen like Jim Bridger and Jedediah Smith. The early ranger was born to the saddle, a cowboy, trapper or woodsman who could shoe horses, throw a diamond hitch, shoot and ride with the finest in the West. He was an outdoorsman who knew the language if not the science of forestry, a brave figure who dared fight fire with the crudest equipment, and to assert his authority when the range wars turned government land into a battlefield.

The vivid history of conservation in America is told in the National Forests. In the seventies and eighties, the stockmen assumed as their domain the prairies; the lumbermen took the forests; and the iron, copper, coal and petroleum giants the mineral fields. In those days, as in our own, wealth was much the common goal. Exploitation of the West was the state of the national mind. Yet from this period were born the John Muirs, Gifford Pinchots and Theodore Roosevelts, who arose to protect the natural resources before they were completely expropriated or depleted.

Down through the years Congress has written a constructive record dealing with National Forests, in reflecting the interests of the people and the ceaseless prodding of scholars, scientists, educators and dreamers. Two Presidents, one Republican, the other Democratic, and both named Roosevelt, distinguished themselves by their appreciation of the National Forests, as well as conservation of all resources. The first Roosevelt established public lands to be protected and used, and we shall meet him in the midst of his battles to do so. Under the second Roosevelt, the Civilian Conservation Corps (CCC) provided the Forest Service with a force of hundreds of thousands of young men and the opportunity to practice the science of forestry on a nationwide scale. They planted two billion trees on denuded and eroding lands. They revegetated overgrazed and overtrampled range, built watering places and fences for cattle, ponds for animals, fish and birds. They improved campgrounds and installed tables and buildings, developed lakes, ponds and bathing beaches which are still in use.

Now the National Forests have entered a new era. One-tenth of the land area of the United States is a much more pertinent mass in our time than in the nineteenth century, when this was a continent of land unlimited. The remotest corner is no longer remote or beyond use, or beyond demand for use, based on needs legitimate and otherwise: for wider highways, dams, power lines, military bases, expansion of cities, timber, grazing, mining, hunting, camping, fishing—and for preservation, which is a use, too.

The pressures have changed and sharpened with time. Unfortunately, forests are viewed too often in the most traditional terms. On one hand, some of those genuinely interested in conservation criticize timber and cattle industries for cutting and grazing practices of Mc-Kinley's day. But the good timberman today is a good conservationist, too, concerned with growing trees as well as cutting them. And the good stockman knows that he must sell his product not by the head or unit, but by the pound; he wants the best utilization of the range over a long period. On the other hand, miners, ranchers and timbermen cling to precedent and the belief that because they arrived first they should determine use of the land.

In 1960 Congress redefined the functions of the National Forests to properly and legally encompass all of their uses. In the next pages we shall observe how these uses are balanced. They must all hang together, yet everybody prefers to be first in line. "We contend that nothing should be given equal priority with watershed protection," declares a spokesman of the National Reclamation Association. The National Forests were established primarily for timber—well, water, too—and should remain so forever, argues the National Lumber Manufacturers Association. "The attitude of the Forest Service has grown hostile to mining over the years," and you can figure for yourself who said *that*.

At the opposite end of the rainbow is the Sierra Club, a group of Western outdoor enthusiasts, decrying "the present preponderant attention given to the production and harvesting of timber resources, to the impairment of other values which are of ascending public importance." The Sierra Club's solution is to exclude "raw-material exploitation," such as logging, from very large tracts, or else. The "or else"? Transfer the land from National Forests to National Parks.

The difference between National Parks and National Forests confuses many people. Park rangers are mistaken for forest rangers, and vice versa. Not that it really matters to the average vacationing family, although it is good to know and the ranger would appreciate being recognized properly. However, beyond the campground or the entry station, the distinction between Park and Forest is scarcely known.

An official government pamphlet, issued jointly by the National Park Service and United States Forest Service, offers a polite explanation of the differences between them. The areas under both jurisdictions, it declares, "exemplify conservation—the wise use of our resources; and both play an important part in the lives of our nation."

In general, National Parks and Monuments have been established to preserve superlative examples of natural beauty or historic significance. Their geological features, plant and animal life are protected; they are outdoor museums, preserving nature and history without infringement of commercial uses.

In Forests, however, the emphasis is on use. Logging, grazing, mining; berrypicking if you bring a basket, which you cannot do in a National Park unless you are a bear. Hunting, which likewise is prohibited in National Parks. Camping, which you *can* do also in a National Park.

The statement, as I said, is politely and cordially worded by the "sister agencies." However, they have had their jurisdictional disagreements. Yellowstone National Park, the first national preserve, was created by Congress in 1872. The National Forest Reserves were established twenty years later, but in 1907 Theodore Roosevelt and Gifford Pinchot transplanted them from the Interior Department to the Agriculture Department. The National Park Service came into being in 1916, as an Interior Department agency, and most National Parks have since been created out of forest boundaries. Now the Park Service would like to assume jurisdiction of additional National Forestlands.

I admire and respect both agencies. It is right that parks and forests should exist. We do need more parkland and conceivably it should come from the National Forests. But these decisions should be based on full public understanding and a wider appreciation of the role of both agencies.

The Park story has been told many times. We are familiar, or at least acquainted with Yellowstone, Yosemite, Grand Canyon, Gettysburg, Independence Hall, points of singular attraction and focus. National Forests are more diffuse. They cover seven times as much land as the National Parks. The largest Park, Yellowstone, covers 1,000,000 acres, but a 1,000,000-acre Forest is middling in size and at least a dozen are larger than 2,000,000 acres. There are other reasons why we are not so well acquainted with forests. The Forest Service has been concerned with fire protection, reforestation, curbing diseases that threaten to wipe out an entire forest or a herd of deer, in short with basic problems of managing the physical estate, rather than accenting public activities.

Now the very concept of forests and forestry is changing. The ranger is not the old-fashioned, solitary figure climbing his lookout tower. Nor is he concerned primarily with harvesting and growing trees, but with the science of the outdoors. The Multiple Use Act of 1960 declares that forest purposes shall be the enhancement of recreation, soil, range, timber, watershed, wildlife, fishing, mining—based on "the most judicious use of the land for some or all of these resources."

Forests are new and exciting, a frontier of unending adventure and increasing importance as cities, like Los Angeles, continue to grow and spread out. Within our forests, young mountains are forming in the geologic growth of America. Old woodlands are succeeded by young woodlands with new breeds of trees produced through the science of genetics. Soon, through research, there may be cloud seeding to dissipate lightning before it strikes into fire; fire fighting by helicopter with new chemical retardants, and possibly logging by helicopter without disturbing the ground surface.

In the course of my travels through the National Forests, I explored many crannies and corners of America, from the scrub-pine and chaparral back yard of Los Angeles to the wildest wilderness, where glaciers grow. I consorted with, drank with and sometimes slept under the stars with rangers, ranchers, loggers, historians, biologists, geologists and fishermen.

Strangely, though, in sitting in my own quiet corner and looking back for the synthesis and meaning of all that I saw, I recall the incongruous incident of spying on the prairie chicken in his mating grounds in the dust bowl along the Kansas-Oklahoma border. A friend in the Air Force had invited me to go along and observe the use of the helicopter in taking the prairie-chicken census. We arrived in a forlorn little town where the main center of activity was the old-fashioned saloon complete with pool table. All night the wind howled and the dust blew. In the morning we helicoptered over the desolate wasteland, stirring up giant, long-eared jack rabbits. The biologist who had come up from the University of Oklahoma was about as excited as a presidential candidate on election night. We landed in the middle of absolutely nowhere, which proved to be the capital of the prairie-chicken world. Once this barren place had been green with grass, but we Americans, in one of our displays of lesser wisdom, cleared the submarginal land, then farmed and grazed and farmed until the top-soil blew away in dry years. The land was given up and left for dead. But to the prairie chicken it was still a setting for yearly romance. The bird flapped about here and there above the dusty dunes and cackled his weird mating call. To the biologist it was sheer music, but at the time I thought, who in the world but the prairie chicken would want the wasteland? Much to my surprise, the answer came forthwith. Through a film of dust two foresters arrived. This land that nobody (but the prairie chicken) wanted had been turned over to the Forest Service. Here it was a question not of growing trees but of growing grass. It was awfully dismal to me, but full of animation to the foresters. "Oh, we've made a lot of progress," one said. "It takes time with this sterile soil. But we're getting it stabilized with hardy bunch-grass so it will stop blowing." The grass looked scrawny and insignificant, but the forester said it was taking hold well. "Come back in a few years," he invited, "and you will see a productive part of America. It will grow hay and pasture, probably with recreation areas here and there." What then, when this land, left lifeless through human abuse, is finally restored to usefulness? And will there still be a place for the prairie chicken, which, like the foresters, did not renounce it?

In a sense, the question which National Forests endeavor to answer is not whether nature can succeed in its struggle to survive on the human planet, but whether we can succeed in our own struggle. When Mrs. Gifford Pinchot spoke at the dedication of the National Forest in Washington State named for her husband, she recalled to her audience that man himself is a natural resource—"Man, without whose energy the energy of coal and oil, of electricity, yes, of atomic energy itself, is inert and meaningless." She was explaining how her husband arrived at the concept and definition of conservation. "Believing, as Pinchot did," she said, "that the planned and orderly development of the earth and all it contains is indispensable to the permanent prosperity of the human race, conservation in its widest sense became, to him, one of the guiding principles through which such prosperity might be achieved. A bold creative affirmation in spiritual and ethical terms, of our faith in the dignity of man as a child of God."

CHAPTER TWO

# The Tree and the Forest

We are heading now for the deep woods to counsel with trees on their home ground. But en route there is apt to be a tree or two growing in an open field and a front lawn, and interest in trees sprouting in surprising places.

The American elm and its problems on Manhattan Island, for example, were found prominently one morning in the editorial columns of the *New York Times*. "The graceful elm may have to go the way of the no longer spreading chestnut tree," the *Times* editor advised, pleading with the Park Department and his readers to act against Dutch elm disease. "For centuries the durable elm has provided us with a great amount of pleasure and shade," he wrote. "It does not deserve our inattention now."

Likewise, the elm became the center of attention in the midst of a Congressional hearing in Washington. Representative Ben Jensen, of Iowa, was questioning a Forest Service officer. What about the elm? he asked. "We had better be finding some way to eradicate Dutch elm disease," Mr. Jensen warned the Forest Service man and everybody within hearing range. "I hope we can, anyway, because it is really going strong and when it gets into your own back yard, you begin to get scared. I have an elm tree in my back yard that is almost fifteen feet around, four feet from the ground. It has a limb spread of about 150 feet. It is a beautiful tree and, believe you me, I am scared for the life of that tree, as many thousands of people are scared today. The elm is a great tree."

The elm (*Ulmus americana*) *is* a great tree, although it may disturb the sensibility of some enthusiasts of its landscape qualities to realize its hard, tough wood is eminently suited for manufacture into furniture, flooring, boxes, barrel hoops and staves. However, a lawn is not a forest. These areas of land serve different purposes, are managed each in its own way, and consequently plants and animals behave differently on them. In a yard, grass competes with trees for moisture

21

and minerals from the soil. The ground is compacted, cutting down aeration to the roots. Water runs off instead of being absorbed. In a forest, trees receive more organic food material because the forest floor isn't raked. The layer of litter and humus contains water like a sponge for the porous soil beneath it. On the other hand, instead of grass, there may be intense competition from plants, shrubs and other trees. In turning always toward the light, as a tree must do to grow, the forest creature rises upward; generally it has no other direction to follow. But a tree growing in the open has light on all sides, and acquires girth instead of height by extending lower limbs from the trunk. Wonderful for shade, but as the forester would say, it is too limby and knotty for timber.

Entering the forest, we find it essentially an association of plants providing food and shelter for a large variety of animal life. The principal characteristic of the forest is the presence of a tree. Linger for a moment with the first tree we encounter. He, or it, is king of the world of plants, just as man is king of the world of animals. Of all 335,000 known kinds of plants, only this marvelous creature can develop a tall, woody stem and stand erect without support. It is normally at least ten feet high and wears a definite crown. If it is nine feet high and not really of woody substance, you are looking at just another plant or shrub, not a tree.

While you stand beneath its branches, look closely at this single fellow, not necessarily to observe that he is made of root, stem, bark, bud, leaf, flower and fruit, but to enjoy him as a neighbor. Surely, he has grown more precious with the years. Once the forest blanketed our continent, but the sweep of civilization has reduced the stronghold of our tree and his companions to narrow, perilous boundaries. Yet we need him for his wood and for his comradeship.

The greatest lyricist of trees, and probably of forests, too, was not Joyce Kilmer but John Muir, who showed that appreciation of trees, like love, ambition and literature, is a thoroughly individual experience. Once he climbed a tree in the heart of California's forest-land. It was in the midst of a windstorm and he described it so:

"The winds go to every tree, fingering every leaf and branch and furrowed bole; not one is forgotten; the Mountain Pine towering with outstretched arms on the rugged buttresses of the icy peaks, the lowliest and most retiring tenant of the dells; they seek and find them all, caressing them tenderly, bending them in lusty exercise, stimulating their growth, plucking off a leaf or limb as required, or remov-

22

ing an entire tree or grove, now whispering and cooing through the branches like a sleepy child, now roaring like the ocean; the winds blessing the forests, the forests the winds, with ineffable beauty and harmony as the sure result.

"We all travel the milky way together, trees and men; but it never occurred to me until this storm-day, while swinging in the wind, that trees are travelers, in the ordinary sense. They make many journeys, not extensive ones, it is true; but our own little journeys, away and back again, are only little more than tree-wavings—many of them not so much."

Anyone falling under the spell of this picture is likely to look for expressions of spirit in trees, which he may not quite find. For example, the procreation of trees bears a degree of similarity to the procreation of animals, even of human beings; that is, through the fertilization by a sperm of an egg in a female ovary. If this is so, and sex in humans reflects a psychic impulse, could it not be so in a tree? Alas, no. The biologist will explain that the tree, even though it is king of the world of plants, stands below the stage of development of the lowest animal. Our tree cannot move to water or shelter. It has no nervous system. It reacts unconsciously and unvarying to stimulus, the process known in botany as tropism.

Nevertheless the tree breathes, drinks water, nourishes itself and transmits qualities of heredity through reproduction. The tree and the forest around it fulfill wonderful natural functions beyond our capability. Moreover, they depict the sweep of evolution, spanning hundreds of millions of years of life on earth.

The forest is a community, or a whole complex of communities, in which millions of living creatures struggle for water, sunlight, soil nourishment, space in which to grow. Some survive as parasites and bandits. Some grow because others die, decay and decompose. The blight of one can be the blessing of another. Others benefit through co-operation or partnership, such as that between the fungus and alga in a lichen, or the tree and fungi whose vegetative portion becomes associated with the roots. Insects and animals benefit plants by carrying pollen. For man's part, the forester and wildlife manager benefit the trees and animals they cultivate and protect.

The lowest forest community is composed of the organisms of the soil: earthworms, ants, termites, bacteria, fungi and simple plant forms which do not contain chlorophyll. Above them are the world of liverworts, living on soil, rock, decaying wood or the bark of trees, mush-

23

rooms, moss, and fern, plants with roots, stems and green leaves that provide a nesting place for birds and food for higher animals like deer. Ferns are among the real enchanters of the forest, growing in 9000 varieties, including tree ferns with immense, lacy leaves such as you will see in the Rain Forest of Puerto Rico. Then the higher level of the plant kingdom, wildflowers and shrubs, capable of producing seeds, interplayed with bees, insects and rodents. Finally, the trees which furnish cover and feed for the larger animals. In an area where fire has taken place you can see this whole process of plant succession, from the ground up.

Trees feed on materials from the forest soil and air. Within tiny cells of their leaves the green pigmentation called chlorophyll absorbs the light waves or energy of the sun. Through the magic process of photosynthesis this energy is combined with carbon dioxide breathed from the air and water drawn through the roots to produce nourishment and growth. It manufactures glucose, a simple sugar, and subsequently carbohydrates. These in turn combine with nitrogen to form more complex foods, which are transported throughout the tree. Then, as we release carbon dioxide in our breathing, the tree "exhales" oxygen as the by-product of carbon dioxide and water vapor; in producing glucose with the use of oxygen, it releases carbon dioxide and water vapor. How magic a process is photosynthesis! After a century and a half of study, science has yet to understand the exact process, let alone duplicate it—the only way in the world to manufacture carbohydrates. Thus far we have learned to compound chlorophyll. The next step would be a historic break-through in biology.

Tree growth is one of the few phenomena on the planet that successfully counter gravity. Roots go down and outward in the soil, but as the forest tree turns to the light it reaches ever *upward* so that leaves can synthesize food. Leafy crowns fill the space overhead, forming the "overstory" of the forest. Ideally, lower branches, shut off from sunlight, die and drop off. Through this self-pruning, the mature tree develops with a long clean trunk, by all odds best for timber purposes, and attractive to the eye.

Openings in the forest are often filled with little trees shooting up from the ground or sprouting from the stumps of old trees which have died or been cut. Some outstrip their companions and reach the sunlight first. Others lag; they become "suppressed" trees, and unless a fortunate break-through design of nature or forest management gives them more light and growing space they will develop unhealthy and crooked, perhaps die out altogether. Thus from beginning to end the life of a tree is a struggle for sun.

Although trees make demands on the soil, they also help to enrich it. The litter, or duff, on the forest floor is composed of fallen leaves, needles, branches, dead tree trunks and other plant remains. Through weathering and the interplay of insects and fungi, they decay and decompose into humus. Humus loosens compact soil—it is soil, providing the porous quality that opens the way for air and water, the elements vital for plant growth. And it combines with the interlacing roots of trees and other plants to influence the flow of streams.

Trees show their growth and age through the addition each year of a coat of new wood cells between the outside layer of the sapwood and the inner bark. This is the all-important cambium layer, through which water passes from roots to crown. You may admire a tree for *all* its magnificence, but only the leaves and cambium layer are alive; the center, or heartwood, is as dead as lumber at the mill. The cambium layer continues dying, reforming new wood on the inner side and new bark on the outer side, and being born anew. The layer it develops is the annual ring, which, once established never changes in size or place. This is detectable by using an increment borer, a kind of corkscrew that digs into the center of the tree and brings forth a slender sliver. Sometimes a scrawny little fellow, looking like a young tree, especially to the untrained eye, proves to be an old-timer with annual rings close together; a case of growing on poor soil or of a stunting disease somewhere in its lifetime.

All trees bear flowers, some with petals and some without, hardly looking flowery at all, as part of the process of reproduction. Most bloom in the spring, the season of romance, or at least of creation, in the forest, when pollen has ripened and its sac ruptures. Flowers are purposefully showy: to attract insects that carry pollen from male to female, and gather nectar or deposit their eggs within the flower at the same time. Other pollen is borne by the wind, alighting on the female stigma and moving into and fertilizing the ovule.

The net result in due time is a seed-bearing fruit. Some trees mature their seeds rapidly and scatter them early in the growing season. Others, like the nut trees, prepare them slowly for fall sowing. Red oaks and most pines take two years to ripen their seeds. The seed in pine is contained between the scales of its fruit—the cone. But in some species of pine the cones remain closed indefinitely. The seeds are freed only by decay of the cone, or a scorching fire, or by a hungry animal looking for food. Seeds of most conifers and other trees like the American elm are light and may ride the winds hundreds of miles from home before coming to rest. Maple seeds are heavier and do not wander from their parents. Nuts, acorns and berries are plucked and eaten by birds and animals but in many cases still reach their way remarkably and safely into the soil via the digestive system. Seeds of walnut, hickory and oak are carried off by squirrels and germinate where they are hidden if the squirrel doesn't eat them first. Most trees produce seed by the thousands, but chances are only one will take root and in its turn bear seed.

There are many hundreds of kinds of trees, divided into families, then subdivided into genera, and again subdivided into species. The oldest tree family is the conifer, which grew abundantly over the earth in the Jurassic Age, 175,000,000 years ago, and which retains a simple floral structure. More than 100 species of conifer, the needle-leaved cone bearer, also called softwood or evergreen, grow in the United States, including pines, firs, spruces, hemlocks, junipers. Conifers are the main strength of America's timber resources, comprising four-fifths of the large, saw-timber trees.

The largest tree family in the United States, the deciduous, also known as hardwood or broadleaf, include oaks, maples, sycamores, elms, all told about 650 species. Within these families are rule-breaking exceptions. Conifers with hard wood (southern pine). Deciduous trees with evergreen leaves (holly, live oak, some magnolias). Conifers which shed their leaves (larch and bald cypress). Douglas-fir, which is not a fir at all. The mixed-up yew, with coniferlike leaves but a berry instead of cone as its fruit.

Then there are the trees of the tropic and desert forests, the palm, yucca and cacti, some without a true cambium layer and others without leaves.

Trees, plants and animals group themselves by environment and react individually to it. If aspen and Englemann spruce were planted on the same plot, aspen might grow one foot in diameter while the spruce grew three inches, but the aspen would live fifty or seventy years while the spruce might live 300 years or longer. Aspen and cottonwood require full sunlight; they come in following fire, then are overtaken by other trees which are shade tolerant in growth and finally outdistance them. These are the "climax trees," which become dominant when a forest is left to natural progression. Douglas-fir may grow on one slope but not on a facing slope, for it is another tree requiring full sunlight.

26

In the desert, where there is plenty of sunlight but not much water, cacti withstand drought by storing water and shedding leaves, if they have any, in dry periods to reduce transpiration, or exhaling. Water is one of the decisive factors in determining which tree grows where. In National Forests of the Southwest, for instance, within two hours you can drive from the desert floor to the subalpine life zone at 7000 feet and on the way pass through a piñon, juniper and chaparral area, with ten to twenty inches of annual precipitation; ponderosa-pine area with twenty to twenty-eight inches of precipitation, and finally mixed spruce, fir and aspen area, about thirty inches of precipitation. There are other important environmental factors: temperature, light and wind, all related to climate; and factors relating to soil, physical and chemical composition, slope, drainage and water.

The modern forester strives to understand all of these. The goal in his managed forest is a healthy, growing environment for man, plant and animal. Timber cutting is a tool toward this end and not just an end in itself. Systematic cutting releases competition and enables the remaining stand to grow stronger. Or it may be employed to open areas where animals can feed. Or a trail, vista or campground for human use. Or there may be no cutting at all: for example, along a streamside, where shade over the water maintains a cool temperature for fish; in places where animals will benefit from cover; in scenic and wilderness areas, where human visitors can experience the beauty of nature.

Virgin forest? If a virgin forest is one in which timber has never been cut, there is little left in the United States. Nearly all of it is in the West and coastal Alaska, with a potential harvest of up to 100,000 board feet per acre. In contrast, few Eastern stands can yield as much as 5000 board feet per acre. The expression of forest "untouched by the hand of man" tends to be misleading. The forests of the National Parks are said to "allow natural processes of growth and decay free play." But this is not completely so. Fire, insect and disease, three basic natural elements, are subject to control, as they must be; to say nothing of the effect of increasing human use. Whether it sounds proper or not from a sentimental point of view, the survival of fragile wilderness areas, which ten years ago had 100 visitors and may have 10,000 visitors ten years hence, depends on the extent to which they are managed as wilderness, with basic minimum improvements such as litter control, primitive campsites, clearing new trails to avoid congestion and planting additional meadows to provide forage for horses.

27

The same is true of wildlife. The survival of many species depends upon manipulation of food and cover. It depends upon hunting as their tribes increase beyond the carrying capacity of the land. Even in National Parks there is systematic reduction of the herds when they grow too large.

The lives of animals are interwoven with the forest. Insects that feed on trees are themselves the food of parasites, birds and predaceous creatures. The woodpecker is a friend of the tree when it feeds on bark beetles. Birds and squirrels plant tree seeds. But deer and rabbits when they are overabundant chew up and destroy a high proportion of young trees. Livestock trample seedlings. Porcupines girdle the trees, eating around the cambium layer; they are the gangsters of the timber forest and, as far as foresters are concerned, it is always open season on the porky.

This point about the porcupine once was published in the press of the Southwest. It evoked an anguished defense of the animal and criticism of the Forest Service from a lady in Albuquerque. Possibly she was wrong, considering the damage caused by the porcupine and that it would take many, many open seasons to eliminate this animal. But certainly her concern is far better than no concern. Our national record on wildlife is not a very proud one, except for a very few species like deer and antelope. Since the arrival of civilization in America, twenty species of wild mammals and birds have been banished to eternity. They are extinct and gone forever from this world. Another sixty or more species of wild birds, mammals and fish have been depleted to the brink of extinction.

To forestall extinction of wild creatures by providing them with food and cover and protection from excessive hunting is a part of the forest purpose, along with timber, water, recreation. Is this a legitimate use of the forest? Should we really be concerned with extinction, that is, beyond the consideration of sentiment? In reply, Ernest Thompson Seton, the naturalist, has recalled the contribution of domestic species, which once were wild, to the advancement of our race. Who can decide which has done more for mankind, the cow or steam engine, the horse or electricity, the sheep or printing press, the dog or rifle, the ass or loom? Take away these inventions and we are put back a century, or perhaps two; but take away the domestic animals and we are reduced to savagery, for it was they who first made it possible for our aboriginal forefathers to settle in one place and learn the rudiments of civilization.

"Now if the early hunters of these, our domestic animals," Thompson Seton continued, "had succeeded in exterminating them before their stock was domesticated, which easily might have been, for domestication succeeds only after long and persistent effort and, in effect, a remodeling of the wild animal by select breeding, the loss to the world would have been a very serious matter, probably much more serious than the loss of any invention, because an idea, being born of other ideas, can be lost temporarily, while the destruction of an organized being is irreparable.

"This is the most obvious economic view of the question of extermination. But there is another, a yet higher one, which, in the end will prove truly more economic. We are informed, on excellent authority, that man's most important business here is to 'know himself.' And since it is established that man is merely a wheel in a great machine called the universe, he can never arrive at a comprehension of himself without study of the other wheels also. Therefore, to know himself, man must study not only himself but all things to which he is related. This is the motive of all scientific research.

"There is no part of our environment that is not filled with precious facts bearing on the 'great problem,' and the nearer they are to us the more they contain for us. He who will explain the house sparrow's exemption from bacteriological infections, the white bear's freedom from trouble that we attribute to uric acid in the blood, or the buffalo's and the flamingo's immunity from the deadliest malaria, is on the way to conferring like immunities on man. Each advance of science enables us to get more facts out of the same source, and if that source of knowledge happens to be perishable, one can do the race no greater harm than by destroying it.

"The Sibylline Books were supposed to contain all necessary wisdom; they were destroyed, one by one, because the natural heir to that wisdom did not realize their value. He did wake up at last, but it was too late to save anything but a fragment. What Tarquin did to the books offered by the Cumaean Sibyl, our own race in America has done to some of the most valuable books offered by nature. Each animal is in itself an inexhaustible volume of facts that man must have to solve the problem of knowing himself. One by one, not always deliberately, these wonderful volumes have been destroyed, and the facts that might have been read in them have been lost.

"It is hard to imagine a greater injury to the world of thought, which is, after all, the real world, than the destruction of one of these wonderful unread volumes. It is possible that the study of 'man' would suffer more by the extinction of some highly organized animal than it did by the burning of the Alexandrian Library. That is why men of science have striven so earnestly to save our native animals from extinction."

Perhaps our feeling will be more finely drawn by observing a threatened species clinging to survival. This leads us to the spawning grounds of the salmon in the National Forests of the Pacific Northwest. Here to witness one of the greatest forces of nature, the return of this anadromous fish to the place where it was born and create a new life in its turn, though it must then die. What guides the salmon? No one can say. Perhaps sight, smell, chemical composition of the water, or temperature. Probably some combination, plus other instinctive forces too mysterious for understanding. But after three or four years in the ocean, the Chinook turns somewhere off the coast of Oregon and Washington, unerring into the mouth of the Columbia River. It is going home.

Once the salmon enters fresh water it is doomed. Its esophagus and stomach constrict so it cannot take food. From here upstream, as far as 800 miles into the mountains, the fish travels and survives on stored energy and the determination to perpetuate its species. Delayed too long at a dam, or at waterfalls or rapids, it may exhaust its energy reserve and die before spawning. But it will die in the attempt.

The Chinooks start entering the Columbia in March, but the peak movement at the famous Bonneville fish ladders near Portland is in April. Around 40 per cent of the fish are heading for the Salmon River, the "River of No Return," in Idaho. Others go north into the Washington Cascades. At first, in the Columbia, our fish averages sixteen miles per day, but later, heading upstream against swift mountain currents, the rate will drop to twelve miles per day.

By June, the salmon arrive in the tributaries of the Salmon River, seeking the headwaters and finding a last sanctuary in a deep hole or under a cut bank. Each fish remains in seclusion until ready to spawn in mid-August. Then the female selects a spot at the head of a riffle and proceeds to dig a large oval shape depression, called a "redd" (adapted from the old expression meaning to clear or clean), by lying on her side and violently flexing body and tail. Once I stood with two friends at the bank of a shallow stream and watched the waters alive with this magnificent expression of nature, redd digging. It began to rain hard but none of us could leave. In the same flapping, splashing and flashing, which stirred far more water than the heaviest raindrops on the rocks, we witnessed the tragedy of dying and the glory of creation. As part of it, the female lays eggs, which the male fertilizes and buries under gravel as the female continues to enlarge the redd and lay more eggs. The process lasts three or four weeks and spawning is complete. Their energy spent and their purpose fulfilled, the adult male and female die within a week or ten days.

New life begins inside the egg immediately after fertilization. In four months it hatches, but the young fish, or fry, remains buried, absorbing nourishment from the yolk sac attached to its abdomen. The Chinook female may lay 4000 eggs, but less than half will wriggle upward alive in early spring; the remainder will have been buried too deeply, may never have been fertilized, or fall victims to aquatic predators. Those who survive start migrating to the sea in autumn, when they are about five inches long, and again in spring after the ice melts. Unlike their parents, who undergo physiological changes and cannot take food after they enter fresh water, the young feed well until they reach the ocean.

How many of them will return as adults to the spawning ground? Probably not more than 1 or 2 per cent. The fish must contend with natural hazards, such as predators and disease, but man has added several more. True, the salmon are aided by the ladders at Bonneville and a new ladder at Dagger Falls in Boise National Forest, but it must also surmount the obstacles of pollution, irrigation canals, sport and commercial fishing, the destruction of spawning grounds as a result of dam construction. At Westport, Washington, the "salmon fishing capital," to show how things go, about 300 fishing boats set sail every summer morning. Each carries ten passengers bound and determined to bring in their limit (three salmon per person). The prevailing local attitude appears to be, "There are lots of salmon in the sea; let's do nothing to reduce fishing pressure until Oregon does it first; and anyway, this is an important local industry." The Idaho picture is not much better. Regulations permit fishermen to take about 50 per cent of the spawners. But pressure is doubling almost every five years and the catch is nearing 100,000 fish a year. Thanks largely to hatcheries, salmon are still running, but there are doubts about the picture beyond the next twenty or thirty years. Maybe the Chinook will find another way out to the sea. Or stay in the forest, where they can swim to cover.

31

# CHAPTER THREE

# Roosevelt Faces the Public Domain

Snow fell on Washington homes and streets the first wintry days of 1905. But the political climate was sizzling and promised to grow warmer long before summer. The hottest spot in town was the White House, where Theodore Roosevelt had taken residence for another four years following his decisive victory in November. Now he was no longer a Vice President called to higher office through McKinley's death, but President in his own right with a mandate to pursue his course full speed.

The day was Thursday, January 5. In the afternoon the President would go to the National Theatre to address the American Forestry Congress. Probably he sat down with Gifford Pinchot to go over the speech he would deliver, a firm but far from hostile appeal to the West to support his program for protection of the National Forests, then still known as Forest Reserves.

In the morning there was much for him to read in the daily paper and in the reports on his desk. One lively headline dealt with a favorite target of his, the meat-packing industry:

BEEF TRUST A BAD ONE
Attorney General Moody Alleges that Control
Of the Nation's Market for Fresh Meat
Is Merciless and Oppressive

It was the other main story that concerned him most, for it related to his activities of the previous day and, in a broad sense, to the greatest battle he was to fight as President:

FRAUDS IN MONTANA
Sen. Heyburn's Denial
He Challenges Anyone to Prove His Implication
In Frauds in Idaho—Sen. Fulton Declares
His Faith in Innocence of
Sen. Mitchell of Oregon

All during the day his Senatorial opponents, notably Mitchell, Heyburn and Fulton, had paraded to the White House to argue the issues of land laws and land frauds in the West with the President and Ethan Allen Hitchcock, his Secretary of Interior. However, the President knew too well the extent to which land grabbing had cleft the Western domain. The hot spot was Oregon. He had already dismissed the U. S. District Attorney there. Indictments were on record, or soon would be filed, against such figures as Senator John H. Mitchell, Congressman John N. Williamson and Land Commissioner Binger Hermann.

The President also had at hand the annual report of Secretary Hitchcock, which tabulated a national total of 55,000 land entries the previous year under the Timber and Stone Act. Referring specifically to Oregon, the report warned: "Should this rate of entry continue during the entire year in that State, it would mean the acquisition in round numbers, of 600,000 acres of timber lands; and if the same activity in that class of entries were extended to other public land States, then before the expiration of two years practically every acre of unappropriated public timbered lands would have been absorbed."

Roosevelt reacted to the challenge of history, in 1905, as he had the first day he took office four years earlier. This period is *his* page in American history, he who pioneered the development and use of the earth and all its resources for enduring good; or, as Senator Robert LaFollette, of Wisconsin, expressed it, "His greatest work was actually beginning a world movement for staying terrestrial waste and saving for the human race the things upon which alone a great and peaceful and progressive and happy race can be founded."

Today many words are spoken in the name of Theodore Roosevelt, his conservation philosophy, his partnership with Gifford Pinchot. The Republican Party, in its platform of 1952, for example, called for a return to their policies by dividing up the public lands—exactly what they did *not* want. To be bipartisan about it, natural resources recur in political platforms of both parties, but in recent years very little of significance has been accomplished beyond conversation. As for Roosevelt, there is at best a vague knowledge of what he really stood for. He is accorded the veneration due a forefather, although in his own time he was distrusted by politicians and championed unpopular causes; he fought the giants of American industry, the railroads, meat packers, power companies and lumbermen.

Of all his achievements, saving the natural resources was the most important, and saving the forests his hardest fight. In this regard, there were two intertwined, yet independent, issues at the outset: land and timber. Let us first explore the land.

Roosevelt arrived on the scene at a time in national growth when there were still frontiers, Western road agents, Indians on the warpath, Bat Mastersons and Buffalo Bills in their prime. But essentially the line of development now extended to the Pacific and the end was in sight for the seemingly limitless bounty of land. Roosevelt was a national President. His mother was a Southerner. He knew and loved the West from his buffalo-hunting, cattle-ranching days (when he lost more money than he made) in North Dakota. More, he was attuned to the ways of nature, as he always would be. In 1903, he combined exploring the outdoors with politicking. Mostly he spoke from the observation platform of his train at villages and hamlets. He addressed the people in his boyish, boisterous, theatrical manner, with short clipped sentences and those choppy gestures of his fists, attacking the trusts in general and railroads in particular. But he took time out for a visit at his beloved Medora, North Dakota, then two weeks for skiing on a late snow in Yellowstone National Park. He went on to California, spending three days in Yosemite Valley with John Muir. The first night, they lay in beds of fir boughs among the giant trunks of the sequoias, listening to the Rocky Mountain hermit thrush and the waterfalls tumbling down the sheer cliffs. "It was like lying in a great solemn cathedral," Roosevelt wrote, "far vaster and more beautiful than any built by the hand of man."

This unique American political figure was equipped to part company with the nineteenth century and to create a new pattern of belief and action for the twentieth. "In the past," he told his generation, "we have admitted the right of the individual to injure the future of the Republic for his present profit. The time has come for a change. As a people we have the right and the duty, second to none other but the right and duty of obeying the moral law, of requiring and doing justice, to protect ourselves and our children against the wasteful development of our natural resources, whether that waste is caused by the actual destruction of such resources or by making them impossible of development hereafter."

In his autobiography he wrote of the beginning of his era: "The relation of the conservation of natural resources to the problems of national welfare and national efficiency had not yet dawned on the public mind. The reclamation of arid public lands in the West was still a

35

matter for private enterprise alone; and our magnificent river system, with its superb possibilities for public usefulness, was dealt with by the Public Government not as a unit, but as a disconnected series of pork-barrel problems, whose only real interest was in their effect on the re-election or defeat of a Congressman here and there."

Land? The man who could get his hands on the largest slice of it was best of all citizens. It was a period not unlike ours, in which affluence, influence and wealth sometimes are confused with virtue. Something like half our forests had passed into private ownership, and the government appeared determined to dispose of the other half. It was frightening to Roosevelt and people like him who were concerned about the future of the country.

Across the West, immense private principalities were growing. A few men aspired through land control to establish new and separate governments where they would be supreme, free and independent of the United States. Which private kingdom was largest and most powerful? In South Dakota, the Homestake Mining Company dominated the Black Hills, if not the entire state. In Montana, Marcus Daly, the copper king of Anaconda and Butte, controlled the mineral wealth by enacting laws to ruin his competition. Then he moved across the Sapphire Range and proceeded to swallow the Bitterroot Valley with cattle lands, sawmills and, incidentally, a great stable of race horses. In Washington State, the Weyerhaeuser Lumber Company arrived from the Lake States in grand style, picking up nearly 1,000,000 acres. In California, Henry Miller, in the heyday of his reign over the cattle ranges, could ride by horse and buggy the entire length of the state and into neighboring Oregon and Nevada stopping each night on his own lands. General Edward Beale, on a smaller scale, owned 200,000 acres in Tejon Valley and controlled 300,000 additional acres of public grazing lands. The railroads were largest of all. The Southern Pacific owned over 10,000,000 acres and held California in the hollow of its hand.

All this developed as the unplanned consequence of some of the country's land laws—5000 of which have been enacted by Congress since the nation began. At first, settlement of the West was dictated by customs. Pioneers squatted along the rivers and creek bottoms, grazing their cattle on surrounding country. As territories were formed, laws were made and land surveyed; land and water were claimed under territory or state laws. But the public domain was property of the nation and subject to legislative control and disposition by Congress alone. It was defined as areas "acquired by treaty, capture, cession by States, conquest or purchase," and in time would encompass the Louisiana Purchase, Red River Basin, cessions from Spain and Mexico, Oregon Compromise, the Texas, Gadsden and Alaska Purchases.

The most important land law was the Homestead Act, the principle of which was advocated twenty and thirty years before the Civil War by Western Congressmen and expansionists like Senator Thomas Hart Benton, of Missouri. Granting public land to a tiller of the soil, he said, was a just exchange for the settler's effort to open the country, defend the frontier and add to the store of public wealth. Man had a "natural right" to the soil, and certainly many aspired to it, from the humble to the most hopefully ambitious. Abolitionist groups opposing the extension of slavery in the territories supported the free-land principle, entangling it in the controversies leading to the Civil War. Nevertheless, when the Homestead Act became effective on January 1, 1863, the same date as the Emancipation Proclamation, the world thought it a highly fitting complement to that declaration for liberty and it was hailed abroad as "the greatest democratic measure of all history."

Under the Homestead Act any citizen could earn 160 acres of the public domain if he would: (a) live on the land five years, (b) make his home on it and cultivate the ground, and (c) pay fees of about $16. Or, he could gain title after only fourteen months by paying a minimum of $1.25 per acre, or about $176 for the entire tract. When he complied with the requirements, the land "went to patent" and became his property.

Other land laws followed. They were designed to encourage, facilitate and reward Americans who would open frontierlands and settle the West.

The Mineral Land Act of 1866 offered free land to spur exploration and development of mineral wealth, as well as settlement.

The Timber Culture Act of 1873 offered 160 acres to any settler who would cultivate trees on forty acres.

The Desert Land Act of 1877 offered land at $1.25 an acre to the settler who would irrigate it.

The Timber and Stone Act of 1878 provided for the purchase of 160 acres of nonmineral land at $2.50 an acre, so that miners and settlers could obtain timber and building materials from supplementary wild lands for use in construction on their sites.

Large land grants were made to the states for educational purposes, and to the railroads and wagon-road companies, in alternate, checker-board sections of one square mile along their routes, "in aid" to finance construction. Railroads benefited most of all. They were given 150,-000,000 acres, much more than all homesteaders combined. The Northern Pacific received almost 40,000,000 acres, an area greater than Pennsylvania, Rhode Island, New Jersey and the District of Columbia.

And last of this series (although many other laws would be passed after it), the "Scripper Act," or lieu-land clause in the Act of June 4, 1897, provided that patented claims within Forest Reserves or Indian Reservations could be exchanged for an equal area of vacant public domain outside. It was passed ostensibly in sympathy to the isolated settler but, as it happened, the wording applied to any owner of land.

In those days the biggest business of the Federal Government in the Far West was giving away public land. The expression "doing a land-office business" came into the lexicon, honestly and honorably, when government land offices were established in all the larger rural centers and everything possible was done to help a citizen get his legal, right-ful quota of the public domain. But very soon land laws were short-cutted and subverted, leading to fraud, land speculation and land thievery. Temper of the times? Perhaps so; perhaps the compelling force of migration was justification for anyone shrewd enough to gain all the land, timber and water rights he could. But in so doing he became a figure in an unending scandal of American history, later to reach its classic proportion in the Teapot Dome case; and, looking into the future, as long as there is public land, chances are somebody will be trying to separate the public from it.

There were many clever techniques of meeting the letter but not the spirit of the law. Since the Homestead Act required construction of a dwelling, the tiniest possible house would be erected, about fourteen by sixteen—inches, not feet. Frontiersmen acquiring 160 forested acres under the Timber Culture Act would cut over 120 acres, leaving trees on the remaining forty. The story is repeated of men who obtained holdings under the Swamp and Overflow Act: they testified to the "overflowed" character of the lands by swearing they crossed them in a boat, but forgot to mention the boat was being hauled behind a wagon. On the other hand, irrigation ditches built under the Desert Land Act often failed to carry any water.

Millions of acres changed hands under the lieu-land clause. It was designed to aid homesteaders, but enabled anyone, lumber companies, railroads, cattlemen, mining outfits, to dispose of cutover lands, worked-out claims and worthless lava beds and take in exchange the most valuable lands they could find on the public domain. The Northern Pacific, under this Scripper Act, made the following selections: in Washington State, 100,000 acres, principally Douglas-fir, worth about $100 an acre; in Idaho, 120,000 acres of white and yellow pine, worth $50 to $100 per acre; in Oregon, 320,000 acres of the finest yellow pine, worth $100 and up per acre. In exchange, they gave back to the government lands worth little or nothing.

Timber in Roosevelt's time was the factor most directly related to this land activity. The lumber industry, having exhausted most choice timber in the East and Lake States, now leapfrogged the Rocky Mountains, which were too steep and rugged for logging, and turned to the virgin forests of the Pacific. Here they found the nation's last great commercial bodies of softwood, old-growth timber—the tremendous Douglas-fir, redwood and white pine forming the heaviest stands of timber in the world.

The Timber and Stone Act proved the best way for the lumbermen to obtain the land they wanted, fully 10,000,000 acres while it remained in force. Remember, it provided for the purchase of 160 acres at $2.50 an acre. The applicant was required to pledge he would not pass on the title to anyone but would use the materials of the land himself. That, however, proved merely incidental.

On the testimony of Stephen A. Douglas Puter, whom we shall presently observe on his appointed rounds as the Oregon "land fraud king," the first deception of note under the Timber and Stone Act was perpetrated by the California Redwood Company in Humboldt County, California, in 1882–83. At that time an applicant was not required to inspect the land he wanted or to show final proof at the land office that he was using it for his own well-being, as stipulated by law. All he needed was to file, taking an oath of citizenship or showing his first papers. The company recruited seamen by the scores, mostly at "Coffee Jack's" boardinghouse in Eureka. Those who were not citizens were transported to the county courthouse for their first papers. Then, about twenty-five at a time, they proceeded to the land office and filed for locations which the company had already chosen for them. Next stop was a notary public, where they sold their claims for fifty dollars each, heading finally back to their ships, the boardinghouse or their favorite saloon.

From then on, lumber companies transported "entrymen" by the trainload. Often they were teachers, delighted to accept a free trip to

39

the scenic Redwood Empire. They swore their new land was for personal use, then proceeded to transfer title to the lumber company which had organized the pleasant excursion. Complicity of land officials was not uncommon: in some cases a claim to a quarter section of 160 acres or even a quarter-quarter of forty acres was stretched for miles, which is how the term "rubber forty" entered the vernacular.

Professional land locators like Puter sprouted like mushrooms. A sure knowledge of timber was the first requisite for success and the ability to recruit entrymen was probably the second. With a trained eye, Puter located stands of larch bearing clear timber 120 feet to the first limb. In other cases he sold land with more than 100,000 board feet to the acre; within ten years its value rose from $3.25 to $150 an acre. The usual procedure was for the land locator to contact rural residents. The farmer, his wife and sons of voting age each "located" 160 acres of land through the agent and secured title. By prearrangement this land was sold immediately to large lumber operators at a small profit, merely an incentive for signing the papers. The entryman looked very broadly at the requirement that he take up the land "for his own use and benefit," considering that the profit he gained in the land transfer was certainly for his own use and benefit.

Or as the newspaper Portland *Oregonian* disclosed, "The cost of 160 acres under the Timber and Stone Act and the accompanying commissions is $415. As many as five members of a family who, it can readily be shown, never had $2075 in their lives, walk up cheerfully and pay the price of the land and the commissions. Under such circumstances, there is only one conclusion to be drawn, and that is, where a whole carload of people make entry under that Act, the unanimity of sentiment and the cash to exploit it must have originated in some other source than themselves."

In 1900, Puter was commissioned by C. A. Smith, a Minnesota lumberman, to locate the finest stands of Oregon timber. In Linn County he found 9100 acres of Douglas-fir, running as high as 300,000 board feet to the acre—the like of which probably could not be found anywhere today. Puter knew he had to act swiftly, since timber cruisers of the Northern Pacific were on the ground, looking for choice areas to select under the Scripper Act. He hired fifty-seven entrymen in Portland, Brownsville, Albany and Roseburg, paid all their expenses, including transportation to and from the land, land-office fees, and an extra $100 each on receiving their deeds. When the railroad learned that Puter had won the race it demanded the fifty-seven claims be withdrawn, since they had not been filed in good faith. Puter consulted with his friend, sometime partner and legal land fixer, Franklin Pierce Mays, little knowing that Mays was employed by the railroad and counseling both sides. Ultimately he agreed to a compromise, surrendering twenty-four claims to the railroad, and holding thirty-three for Smith.

One of his most celebrated operations, the one for which he finally went to jail, was the "11–7" case (Township 11 South, Range 7 East). Puter and his partner, Horace McKinley (who later fled to China one step ahead of Federal agents), now figured to reduce their investment in time and money. "We decided to play fast and loose," Puter confessed in his period of penitence. The timbered site they had chosen was rough, rocky and snow-covered, near the summit of the Cascade Range. This meant the chance of government inquiry was remote and there would be no need to make any of the improvements the law required. Moreover, they elected to use a legal loophole permitting long-time settlers to file and gain title after ninety days, their terms of residence counting as part of the five-year period under the Homestead Law. In this manner they located twelve claims of 160 acres each, using ten local settlers (two filed twice under different names). All their entrymen had to do was file, advertise over a period of several weeks and submit final proof before receiving certificate and patent. The total cost of advertising and filing was $25—without any charge for the acreage.

In the "24–1" case their craft became truly an art, for they eliminated altogether the signatures of living persons as their entrymen. This was possible through the co-operation of an attractive young lady employed at the county office. She was quite devoted to McKinley, and besides, they were paying her $100 per claim. The normal range of payment to officials was $25 to $100 per claim, depending on volume and their influence.

Puter had another ingenious maneuver going in Crook County. There he lined up 108 "dummies" and since their claims had to be advertised for nine weeks in a newspaper nearest the land he also engaged an editor. Thus was the Deschutes *Echo* established on a $50 hand press spiked to a pine-tree stump in the heart of the forest. Puter paid the editor at the rate of $10 per claim, or a total of $1080.

It was Puter, when he turned state's evidence after being trapped himself, who pointed the finger at the venerable Senator Mitchell. He said he had slipped Mitchell two $1000 bills in Washington to cover the Senator's expenses in interceding with Binger Hermann, the Land Office Commissioner, for approval of claims in the "11–7" case.

The Senator was tried for taking money in another instance of land fraud, but Puter was at the root of his troubles. Soon after his indictment, Mitchell arose on the floor of the Senate. It was only a month after his call at the White House in January. He asked to speak on a point of personal privilege. It was very personal. He denounced the land fraud king as a scoundrel of the deepest die. Why, said the Senator, the only reason Puter made "this infamous and false charge against me was for the purpose and with the expectation of saving himself and his convicted partners in crime from deserved punishment."

Besides, the Senator continued, in righteous wrath, "I assert in the most absolute and unqualified manner that any and all statements by any person or persons to the effect that I ever, at any time or place, entered into a conspiracy with all or any of said persons, or they, or any of them, with me, to defraud the United States out of any of its public lands in the State of Oregon or elsewhere, either by false or forged homestead applications, affidavits, or proofs, are absolutely, unqualifiedly, and atrociously false, and I defy my defamers and challenge them to produce any evidence, other than that of condemned thieves, forgers, and perjurers, to sustain any such charges."

Such fervor certainly deserved support. The Oregon legislature rallied quickly with an appropriate resolution. It declared "our continued faith in the honesty, honor and integrity of our Senior Senator, Hon. John H. Mitchell, and that we at this time extend to him a vote of thanks for the twenty-two years of faithful service by him rendered to our State and Nation, and hereby record our hope and belief that his good name and the fair name of our State will be cleared from any charge of any nature whatsoever."

No doubt many persons shared the legislators' hope and belief, but Francis J. Heney was not among them. Heney, incorruptible and fearless, was Special Assistant to the Attorney General of the United States, dispatched from San Francisco with orders to prosecute and clean up the Oregon land frauds. In this capacity, he replaced John J. Hall, a well-known friend of land speculators who in time would be convicted for shielding them. Heney already had Puter in jail; now, in prosecuting Mitchell, he chose not to rely on the land fraud king's talk of $2000 changing hands in a Washington dining room, but on a much stronger case.

Senator Mitchell was tried under a statute which declares it illegal for a Senator, Congressman or other Federal official to receive payment for services relating to any proceeding, contract, claim, controversy, charge or other matter or thing in which the United States is a party. The star witness was Frederick A. Kribs, financial agent for C. A. Smith, who testified that he paid twenty-five dollars per patent to the Senator and produced the canceled checks to prove it. "The payments," said Kribs, "were made to the firm of Mitchell & Tanner (the Senator's law firm), but I, of course, presumed that Senator Mitchell alone was benefited thereby, as he instructed me, when I asked him how I should remit, to make my checks payable to his firm—'for convenience sake,' as he put it."

The trial began June 20, 1905, in Portland. Oratory and resolutions were set aside. On July 3 the jury returned a verdict of guilty. Senator Mitchell was sentenced to six months in jail and fined $1000. The seventy-year-old Senator survived the trial but died soon after as the result of a dental operation.

Puter, in jail, was disturbed. Not at the Senator's death but at the sentence, which was lighter than his own (two years in jail, $7500 fine). He, Puter, had violated the law, but he felt the Senator far more culpable for violating laws he had participated in making. But the wound was healed when the President pardoned Puter after serving seventeen months. After paying the fine, he still had the money he had earned, or gotten, through his land dealings.

The year was far from over. Congressman John N. Williamson, who ran a sheep business at Prineville, on the Crooked River, was convicted along with his partner and the United States Commissioner. The partners had induced about 100 entrymen to file timber claims on 16,000 acres and the Commissioner accepted them. The land, however, had no merchantable timber, but was just about the best summer range, complete with control of springs and water, in Crook County.

Then there was Binger Hermann, whom Roosevelt dismissed as Commissioner of the General Land Office. He was twice indicted and at best typified the pre-Roosevelt philosophy that the way for the government to manage land was to give it away.

Such was the general shape of things in 1905, when Theodore Roosevelt confronted the problem of the public domain. He was not alone, but surrounded himself with purposeful men: James R. Garfield, son of a President, Secretary of Interior; James Wilson, the white-bearded Secretary of Agriculture; Senator Francis G. Newlands of Nevada; Gifford Pinchot, Chief Forester; Charles D. Walcott, Director of the

United States Geological Survey, and Frederick H. Newell, Director of the United States Reclamation Service.

With the help of these allies, he charted a new government course in dealing with public domain. Besides laying the basis for protecting one-tenth of the land area as National Forests, they also were responsible for creating five new National Parks; four great game refuges; fifty-one bird refuges, and of preserving the nearly extinct buffalo. They brought forth the National Monuments Act, which provided setting aside areas other than National Parks, and the Inland Waterways Commission, to save the waterways and their power for public use. Roosevelt established a conservation conference of governors to awaken the states, a National Conservation Commission and a North American Conservation Conference.

As for January 5, 1905, the time was at hand to resolve basic issues of the National Forests. The President lunched and prepared to warm the assemblage at the National Theatre on E Street with his remarks.

# CHAPTER FOUR

# *Pinchot and Timber*

Theodore Roosevelt is the figure most remembered of the conservation crusade early in this century, as he should be. Throughout this period, however, a singular individual in American history, Gifford Pinchot by name, stood at his right. He was the first native-born, trained forester. There was none before him.

But he was even more than the pioneer of an honorable profession.

"Gifford Pinchot," wrote Theodore Roosevelt, "is the man to whom the nation owes most for what has been accomplished as regards the preservation of the natural resources of our country. He led, and indeed during its most vital period embodied, the fight for the preservation through use of our National Forests. He played one of the leading parts in the effort to make the National Government the chief instrument in developing the irrigation of the arid West. He was the foremost leader in the great struggle to co-ordinate all our social and governmental forces in the effort to secure the adoption of a rational and farseeing policy for securing the conservation of all our natural resources.

"He was practically breaking new ground, and taking into account also his tireless energy and activity, his fearlessness, his complete disinterestedness, his single-minded devotion to the interests of the plain people, and his extraordinary efficiency, I believe it is but just to say that among the many, many public officials who under my administration rendered literally invaluable service to the people of the United States, he, on the whole, stood first."

The generations before Pinchot were highly conscious of timber, although their problem was not how to save it but how to cut it most quickly. The early pioneers might have known better, considering forests were no luxury in Europe and already were being managed with an eye toward perpetual yield. Or they could have learned from the Indians, many of whom lived in harmony with natural surroundings and knew the forest was their source of game and food. (But there were plenty of Indians who abused the land, too.) However, trees seemed to extend as an endless sea across the continent. They were useful but barred the way of farms, homes, cities. The more felled, or burned, the better; there would always be more—such was the American philosophy from colonial days until well past the Civil War.

The timber industry began nobly in the beautiful white-pine forest of New England, furnishing masts for the British Navy. The Maine pines were so immense that as many as twenty yoke of oxen were used to haul them from woods to wharves. The best were sent to England as masts, the others sawed into timber to build ships, or forts to protect the lumber supply from the French and Indians. Superb timber was so plentiful around Bangor, "the world's largest lumber market," that sawmill men discarded slabs thick enough to sell as first grade today. When a lumber crew got down to the muddy bottom of a log boom, they set the lower logs adrift rather than wash or handle them while dirty. For many years later the Penobscot Channel would be clogged with waterlogged pine.

Timber demands increased as the country grew and pushed westward. In the 1850's, prairie schooners and canalboats were made of wood, railroads were laid on wooden ties. After the Civil War there were new industries, new cities, new homes, all utilizing wood. Sawmills advanced into virgin regions of the Lake States, which, with New England, formed the backbone of the lumber industry almost to the start of the twentieth century. But as these areas were thoroughly cut over, or on reaching "production capacity," as corporate historians would say, the industry turned to virgin pinewoods of the South and headed across the Rockies to the Pacific States.

By 1890, early in the Pinchot era, forest devastation was underway almost everywhere. Timber operators, despite their "cut and get out" philosophy, were not alone to blame. The entire nation was intent on advancement and self-exploitation. The general feeling was there would always be plenty of wood supply. Although forest fires destroyed as much timber as was cut, they were regarded as beneficial in clearing the land. Notions of second growth and sustained yield were considered foolhardy. Dr. Carl Alwin Schenck, who would establish the first school of forestry before the turn of the century, stated the first rule of his profession was to aid the cutting of trees, and not to assure a continuing crop through silviculture.

Nevertheless there dawned on the American horizon a desire for forest protection. It found expression in the bosom of the noncommercial-minded set of bird watchers and flower growers, scholars and poets afflicted with an irritating determination to nag the public conscience. Among them were Ralph Waldo Emerson; Dr. Wolcott Gibbs, the chemist-physicist who was president of the American Academy for the Advancement of Science; Dr. Charles S. Sargent, director of the Harvard Botanical Garden and editor of *Garden and Forest* Magazine, and Carl Schurz, the German-born Secretary of Interior, who understood the value of forest management from his native land.

The events which set the stage for Pinchot's role began in earnest in 1871, when the nation was shocked by the worst fire in U.S. history, at Peshtigo, Wisconsin, in which 1500 persons lost their lives and nearly 1,300,000 acres were burned. Disturbed by the wave of fire and destruction, the American Academy two years later urged Congress and the states to recognize the need of "cultivation of timber and preservation of forests and to recommend proper legislation for securing these objects." To pursue this program the American Forestry Association was organized in 1875, beginning its long and constructive history. Very early it heeded an appeal from Secretary Schurz. "The waste and destruction of the redwood and the big trees of California," he said, "have been and continue to be so great as to cause apprehension that these species of trees, the oldest and noblest in the world, will entirely disappear unless some means be taken to preserve at least a portion of them." He called on the Association to reverse the tide of public opinion "looking with indifference on this wanton, barbarous, disgraceful vandalism; a spendthrift people recklessly wasting its heritage; a Government careless of its future." He warned further that passage of the Timber and Stone Act would only "stimulate wasteful consumption beyond actual needs."

As public interest developed, the government took its first tentative steps into forestry. In 1876 Congress authorized the appointment of a special agent in the Department of Agriculture to determine the "annual amount of consumption, importation and exportation of timber and other forest products; the probable supply for future wants; the means best adapted to the preservation and renewal of forests; the influence of forests on climate; and the measures that have been successfully applied in foreign countries or that may be deemed applicable in this country for the preservation and restoration or planting of forests." Ten years later added recognition was given, when the Division of Forestry was created in the Department under Dr. Bernhard E. Fernow, like Schurz a German, who would make important contributions to forestry for many years.

In 1891 Congress acted on the recommendations of the American Forestry Association and others to set aside vast areas of timberland. It authorized President Harrison to make withdrawals from the public domain and establish forest reserves. On March 30 he created the first, Yellowstone Timberland Reserve (now the Shoshone and Teton National Forests), of 1,240,000 acres in western Wyoming. The second was the Pike Reserve in Colorado, followed by the San Bernardino and Sierra in California. All told, President Harrison set aside 13,000,000 acres. They were simply closed. Locked up from public use or entry.

This was the beginning, rather than the end of a problem. Now that the government was in the business of running forests, what to do with them? They could hardly stay locked up forever. Dr. Sargent suggested they be administered by the Army. Others envisioned forestry in relation to nature work like landscaping and botany. When in doubt, the best approach is to call on a consultant or conduct a study. In this case, Secretary of the Interior Hoke Smith directed a letter, prepared by youthful Gifford Pinchot (a versatile drafter of letters, speeches and laws throughout his career), to Dr. Gibbs, asking him to appoint a commission of scientific men to consider and report on these three questions:

1. Is it desirable and practicable to preserve from fire and to maintain permanently as forested lands those portions of the public domain now bearing wood growth, for the supply of timber?
2. How far does the influence of the forest upon climate, soil and water conditions make desirable a policy of forest conservation in regions where the public domain is principally situated?
3. What specific legislation should be enacted to remedy the evils now confessedly existing?

There were seven members of the National Forest Commission. Six were venerable and distinguished scholars and explorers. The seventh, listed as "arboriculturist" by profession and Commission secretary by appointment, was only thirty-one. This was Gifford Pinchot.

Pinchot? He was born the last year of the Civil War, in Pennsylvania, where his grandfather, once a captain in Napoleon's army, had settled fifty years before. The family was wealthy and he was able to choose forestry as a career of service rather than as a livelihood. On graduating from Yale in 1889, he set sail for Europe to study at the National School of Forestry in France, where he learned the historic traditions of his profession, dating from the time of Charles the Wise in the fourteenth century. He went on to study under prominent Europeans, notably Sir Dietrich Brandis, from whom he acquired his lifelong belief that forestry cannot succeed without support of people who are the forest neighbors. He was impressed with Swiss government control over cutting on private lands and with the French law requiring owners to reseed their denuded slopes.

When he returned from Europe he was engaged to develop a forest plan for the George W. Vanderbilt estate at Asheville, North Carolina. It took a wealthy, farsighted individual like Vanderbilt to gamble on logging with consideration of the land and a second generation of trees. As for Pinchot, this was his opportunity to prove that forestry deserved a place in America, and that there was more profit than loss in it. He was tall, lean, full-mustached, with eaglelike sharp nose and deep-set blue eyes. Although a single-minded, uncompromising idealist, his manner was affable and he "belonged" in the company of Vanderbilt and others of means who sought his services in the early nineties. In those years he stretched his long legs in many forests, lectured widely and advocated forest conservation.

With this background he started west in the summer of 1896 to rendezvous with the National Forest Commission in the cool reaches north of Flathead Lake, Montana.

He was surprised and delighted to find that John Muir was among those present and would travel with the Commission. Muir, in his late fifties, tall, slender and cordial, already was a legendary Western figure. He lived more outdoors than indoors, perceived the landscape in terms of poetry and science and described his mountain country thus:

"Vapor from the sea; rain, snow and ice on the summits; glaciers and rivers—these form a wheel that grinds the mountains thin and sharp, sculptures deeply the flanks, and furrows them into ridge and canyon, and crushes the rocks into soils on which the forests and meadows and gardens and fruitful vine and tree and grain are growing."

It is not surprising that Muir and Pinchot took to each other at once and were inseparable during the Commission's tour. They pursued different branches of conservation philosophy, one of preservation and the other of use, but they arose from the same root of dedication to nature and the outdoors. Muir had climbed the mountains of the

49

West, like Shasta, unmindful of snow and cold. Pinchot had climbed Mount Marcy, the highest peak in New York, when the temperature was at least twenty-three below zero.

Muir was an early champion of the reserves in California, having written, "We believe our forests under rational management will yield a perennial supply of timber for every right use without further diminishing their area, and what is left now of the forest lands which after being surveyed is found to be unfit for agriculture should immediately be withdrawn from private entry and kept for the good of the people for all time.

"Nearly all our forests in the West are on mountains and cover and protect the fountains of the rivers. They are being more and more deeply invaded and, of course, fires are multiplied; five to ten times as much lumber is burned as is used, to say nothing of the waste of lowlands by destructive floods. As sheep advance, flowers, vegetation, grass, soil, plenty and poetry vanish."

The Commission traveled through Montana, Idaho and Oregon to the Cascade Range Forest Reserve. From Pelican Bay they drove through the forests of the Cascade Range to Crater Lake, while Pinchot listened to Muir and Professor William H. Brewer (of Yale, a scientific explorer of the West). He thought their conversation worth crossing the continent to hear. They arrived at the mighty deep blue lake, surrounded on all sides by high cliffs and majestic forest. The evening was clouded but nevertheless the Commissioners set out for Crater Island. Halfway over it began to thunder. Whitecaps splashed into their overloaded boat and they turned back to shore at the nearest wooded point, to build a fire and dry out drenched clothing. Muir and Pinchot, who were always wandering off, climbed a hundred feet up a ridge and built a fire on a flat rock. When they got back to camp, Muir felt tired but better for the exercise. It rained heavily during the night and all slept in the tent except Pinchot.

The Commission proceeded south through California and across Arizona to the rim of the Grand Canyon, which they reached on September 29. Of this day, Muir wrote: "We all set out for views along the brink of the Canyon through the queer extensive forest of nut pine and cedar. Pinchot and I afoot traced the rim and enjoyed endless changing views; standing with our heads down brought out the colors—reds, grays, ashy greens of varied limestones and sandstones, lavender, and tones nameless and wonderless."

And Pinchot: "While the others drove through the woods to a 'scenic point' and back again, with John Muir I spent an unforgettable day on the rim of the prodigious chasm, letting it soak in. I remember that at first we mistook for rocks the waves of rapids in the mud-laden Colorado, a mile below us. And when we came across a tarantula he wouldn't let me kill it. He said it had as much right there as we did.

"Muir was a storyteller in a million. For weeks I had been trying to make him tell me the tale of his adventure with a dog and an Alaskan glacier, afterward printed under the title of *Stickeen*. If I could get him alone at a campfire— We had left from our lunches a hard-boiled egg and one small sandwich apiece, and water enough in our canteens. Why go back to the hotel?

"That, it developed, suited Muir as much as it did me. So we made our beds of cedar boughs in a thick stand that kept the wind away, and there he talked until midnight. It was such an evening as I have never had before or since.

"That night it froze, but the fire kept us from freezing. In the early morning we sneaked back like guilty schoolboys, well knowing that we must reckon with the other members of the Commission, who probably imagined we had fallen over a cliff. They had done just that, and they told us what they thought of us with clarity and conviction."

Returning East, the Commission voted to recommend the creation of new reserves and of two new National Parks, Grand Canyon and Mount Rainier. Pinchot, however, was far from satisfied. He may have been the youngest member of the Commission, but he knew more about forestry than the other members combined, and he *knew* he did. He urged a strong public statement that the forests were not being taken out of circulation and locked up. He wanted these areas not only put to use but staffed with a corps of professional foresters. The others suggested a loose-knit system of individual forest supervisors or the old idea of placing the military in charge. In any event, President Cleveland accepted the Commission's recommendation and created 21,000,000 acres of Forest Reserve before quietly leaving office ten days later in March, 1897. These were the Black Hills, South Dakota; Big Horn and Teton, Wyoming; Flathead, and Lewis and Clark, Montana; Priest River, Idaho; Bitterroot, Montana-Idaho; Washington, Olympic and Mount Rainier, Washington; Stanislaus and San Jacinto, California; Uinta, Utah.

A host of Western Congressmen rose up in arms. They demanded return of the Reserves to the public domain and likely would have succeeded but for assurance given to the Homestake Mining Company that it could continue cutting timber, free for the taking, in the Black Hills Forest Reserve. As a result, Congress in 1897 defined the role of the Forest Reserves, with a negative twist. "No public forest reservation shall be established," the law declared, "except to improve and protect the forest within the reservation, or for the purpose of securing favorable condition of waterflows, and to furnish a continuous supply of timber for the use and necessities of citizens of the United States."

The Secretary of Interior was authorized to preserve the forests from destruction and to direct the sale of dead, matured or large growth of trees after they had been marked and designated. Under this new law, the first regulated cutting on any land owned by the United States, Case No. 1, was begun in the Black Hills National Forest about four miles southwest of the present village of Nemo. The sale was made to the Homestake Mine early in 1898. Logging was done mainly with horses and a few oxen; then the logs were hauled to a creekside sawmill, where they were sawed into mine props and hauled by railroad into Deadwood and Lead. In the eight-year contract period, 15,000,000 board feet of timber were removed, but the regulation called for leaving two large trees on each acre for seed purposes. The average stand per acre after cutting was about 480 feet per acre, but thirty-five years later was up to 2600 feet per acre. The Black Hills, where once every gulch had its portable sawmill, freighted in by bull team, became the landmark of Pinchot's sustained-yield cutting —with the year's cut not allowed to exceed the year's growth and with the expectation of better timber as the stand improves.

Essentially, the 1897 law still provides the guiding principles, or did until the Multiple Use Act of 1960, for protecting and practicing scientific forestry in the National Forests. There were serious loopholes, concessions to its opponents, in the early act: the 21,000,000 acres of reserve created by President Cleveland were suspended for one year (everywhere but in California), and returned to the public domain and up for claim; the lieu-land clause was thrown in, permitting the trade of poor land for good; large outfits, as well as small settlers, were given almost unlimited right to cut whatever timber they needed. The door was left open to purposes then proper and lawful, such as settlement, prospecting and mining. But most important, the forests were now accepted by Congress on Pinchot's principle of use.

The next year, 1898, he quit his private practice and became Chief of the Division of Forestry, with the understanding he would run it on his own terms. He was never a civil servant in the ordinary sense of the word. To him the Forest Service owes a heritage almost unique in government, of uncompromising morality—in sharp contrast to some of the regulatory agencies whose high officials have made a shambles of their trust. "From the day I entered the Division of Forestry under President McKinley until I was dismissed by President Taft, not one single person in the office or the field was appointed, promoted, demoted or removed to please any politician, or for any political motive whatsoever," Pinchot wrote in his autobiography, *Breaking New Ground*. Following the pattern he established, the Forest Service throughout its history has been independent in spirit and thoroughly loyal.

As one example, there is the story of Frank T. "Cap" Smith, a pioneer ranger in South Dakota who came to the Service in 1902 after scouting for military expeditions, guarding wagon trains and fighting in the Spanish-American War. He retired in 1925 because of ill-health caused by too many fires, but couldn't stand to accept retirement checks without giving anything in return, or being separated from the Forest Service. He kept his badge and marking hatchet and earned his check by serving under the young rangers who succeeded him.

When Pinchot reported for work the Forestry Division of the Department of Agriculture had a total of ten employees. He made the eleventh. Bear in mind, the Forest Reserves at this time still came under the Interior Department. The principal functions of his Division, he found, were providing technical answers to questions about ornamental shrubs, growing mushrooms and preserving elms from decay. This was soon to change. Pinchot rallied round him a group of young disciples. He was "G. P.," a prophet whom it was an honor to serve, a magnetic personality who inspired the most junior staff member to feel he had part in a great work. In stretching the budget, he offered college graduates the title of "student assistants": twenty-five dollars a month and expenses in the field, fifty dollars a month and no expenses in Washington—and it took a stiff examination to qualify. Forestry schools now emerged at the Biltmore estate, Yale and Cornell, turning out trained young men, who chose the career of service rather than a career of money elsewhere, and who seldom left the Pinchot fold once they joined it.

The Division offered free assistance to farmers, lumbermen, state and local governments, anyone who would have it. The offer included working plans for timber cutting, assistance on the ground and copies of technical publications, such as they were. By the end of the first year, 123 requests had come from thirty-five states. Among those Pinchot met through this program was a member of the New York legislature, Franklin D. Roosevelt, who invited the Chief Forester to advise his legislative committee on forests, fish and game, and in this way was introduced to the concept of conservation.

With this stimulus, the Forestry Division started to grow. Pinchot was the unusual type of bureau chief when he had to appear before a Congressional committee; it was said that he could receive any Senator as a guest in his home if he but wanted to invite him. Instead of writing voluminous reports on one phase or another of forestry, he reported on the practical achievements of his Division. Soon appropriations rose from $20,000 to almost $200,000.

But the young men of the Forestry Division had much to learn. When lumberman and forester met in the woods, the one who was in the business of felling trees thought forestry was next door to bird watching, a long-haired thing, or a new outdoor game that would not last. But then he was astonished at how little he really knew about life in the forest, of how trees grow and reproduce. The forester, on the other hand, was ignorant about the practical problems of sawmilling, manufacture and the utilization of trees, which are strongly related to forestry. In the cattle country it was a matter of learning the ways of sheepmen and stockmen, who resented regulation, counting of their stock and limitation on grazing locations.

Stories grew up about the green student assistants. Like the one who, rifle in hand, rushed breathlessly into a lumber camp. "There's a bear on the ridge!" he exclaimed. "Yep," replied the foreman, "I thought I'd have to tie up that old black sow when you came around." The assistant never learned whether it was a sow or really a bear.

In 1900, Pinchot and his associates, Henry Solon Graves, Overton W. Price, William W. Ashe and others, organized the Society of American Foresters, a professional society which today has a membership of 17,000 in the United States and in many foreign countries. In the early days the Society met weekly in the Pinchot home in Washington, 1615 Rhode Island Avenue, NW., and became known as the "Baked Apple Club" because of Pinchot's practice of serving quantities of baked apple, gingerbread and milk. Through Pinchot's invitations, the meetings brought young foresters in touch with leaders of government, including members of the Cabinet and the President himself.

About this time, Pinchot opened a new campaign to create additional Reserves and to bring all government forest work under his division. The General Land Office in the Interior Department, he argued, had not written too good a record in administering the Reserves. For one thing, it had no foresters. There were many good men working for the Land Office, but it was heavily sprinkled with patronage. Many supervisors of Forest Reserves were purely political appointees or worked under political appointees. As an assignment of work, for instance, the supervisors of the Washington and Lewis and Clark Reserves were both ordered to purchase rakes and rake up their dead wood, scattered over some 6,000,000 acres. Besides patronage and nepotism, Pinchot believed forestry could never take firm root in the Land Office because of scandal and its general philosophy of giving away Western land.

It was natural that Theodore Roosevelt and Pinchot should form an alliance when the President took office in September, 1901. They already knew each other quite well. They shared a love of vigorous sports. Pinchot was a member of the Boone and Crockett, the club of big-game hunters founded by Roosevelt, and had counseled with the future President when he was governor of New York. In fact, one evening at the executive mansion in Albany, T. R. suggested they engage in a little wrestling. Pinchot agreed and presently found himself pinned to the mat. "Boxing?" he then proposed. They put on the gloves and this time Roosevelt was floored. Later, Pinchot played tennis, climbed rocks in Rock Creek Park, waded through the Potomac swamps and jujitsued at the White House with the President.

On the day Roosevelt arrived in Washington after McKinley's death he summoned Pinchot and Frederick H. Newell, who had also counseled with him in New York and would be most identified with reclamation of the West. They joined him at the home of his sister, where he asked them to prepare the portion of his first message to Congress dealing with natural resources.

In this address, delivered to a joint session at the Capitol, December, 1901, Roosevelt opened his new era. He would divide the country on the issues but the final outcome would be national unity and growth.

"The forest and water problems are perhaps the most vital internal problems of the United States," the President declared. "The fundamental idea of forestry is in the perpetuation of the forests by use. Forest protection is not an end in itself; it is a means to increase and sustain the resources of the country and the industries which depend on them. The preservation of our forests is an imperative necessity."

But the President made it clear he was not satisfied with their present status. He said:

"The practical usefulness of the National Forest Reserves to the mining, grazing, irrigation, and other interests of the regions in which the Reserves lie, has led to a widespread demand by the people of the West for their protection and extension. The Forest Reserves will inevitably be of still greater use in the future than in the past. Additions should be made to them whenever practicable, and their usefulness should be increased by a thoroughly businesslike management.

"These various functions should be united in the Bureau of Forestry, to which they properly belong. The present diffusion of responsibility is bad from every standpoint. It prevents that effective co-operation between the Government and the men who utilize the resources of the Reserves, without which interests of both must suffer.

"The water supply itself depends upon the forest. In the arid region it is water, not land, which measures production. The Western half of the United States would sustain a population greater than that of our whole country today if the waters that now run to waste were saved and used for irrigation."

The President warned that great storage works were too vast to be undertaken by private effort, nor could they be accomplished by individual states acting alone. Reclamation was a national responsibility, for it would enrich every portion of the country, just as settlement of the Ohio and Mississippi Valleys had brought prosperity to the Atlantic States.

In fulfillment of the Roosevelt program, a reclamation law was passed within nine months. It provided for construction of twenty-eight irrigation projects in the West. The three greatest, Roosevelt Dam in Arizona and Shoshone and Pathfinder Dams in Wyoming, all were begun by 1905.

The fight for the forests was more difficult and took much longer. Too many powerful commercial interests had had their way on the public domain for years, and they were not about to quit for Theodore Roosevelt and Gifford Pinchot. To the contrary, knowing that new Forest Reserves were being created, timber cruisers ranged the West determined to beat the government to the choicest bodies of timber and to claim them for private interests under the Scripper Act, Timber and Stone Act and other land laws. On the Federal side were fifteen

56

of the most rugged Westerners, the courageous boundary men of the Forestry Division, who traveled on horseback and on foot, writing a powerful footnote to history. Most were employed only part of the year, but proudly claimed they could survey 3,000,000 acres per man during the field season. They furnished the first examination and appraisal—rough though it was—of the nation's forest resources. They classified land as arable, pasture, desert, wooded and timbered; they cruised the timber roughly to learn the approximate stand and species, average height, diameter and condition, depth of humus and litter on the forest floor, the effect of fire and streams on the forests. The boundary men moved fast and their surveys were drawn with imperfections but, as Pinchot said, they were competing with "as competent body of land thieves as ever the sun shone on." Which might be interpreted as a compliment to both sides, if you emphasize the word "competent."

Based on the boundary reports to Pinchot and from him to the White House, vast public domain was converted into Forest Reserves, which henceforth could not be claimed under the land laws, except for mineral rights and legitimate settlement. Within six years 132,000,000 acres were set aside in this manner very likely the greatest, most enduring contribution of Theodore Roosevelt to the Republic. He did so in the face of fervent, sometimes violent opposition from many quarters. In Congress, his "executive usurpation" was roundly denounced. Charges were hurled across the legislative chambers that forests were being created in places where no trees grew. "I venture to say," ventured Senator Henry M. Teller, of Colorado, "that a two-horse team could cart off every stick of timber that ever grew or will grow on hundreds and hundreds of acres."

Somewhere in America during this period the corporate soul entered into communication with the corporate mind. It suggested a new, enlightened, long-range look at the Forest Reserves, which were very likely here to stay, whether big business liked it or not. The result was that a number of captains of industry prepared to quit fighting and start joining, or at least living with, conservationists on the basis of forests for use; many others, of course, fought on and are still fighting the whole concept.

In 1905 the second American Forest Congress, summoned by the American Forestry Association, convened in Washington. It was attended by 2000 distinguished citizens, Senators, Congressmen, lumber kings, educators, philanthropists, writers. Among those on the Arrangements Committee were A. J. Cassatt, president of the Pennsylvania Railroad; Fred Weyerhaeuser, of the firm of the same name; John Hays Hammond, the eminent mining engineer; Whitelaw Reid, publisher of the New York *Tribune*; T. J. Grier, Superintendent of the Homestake Mining Company, and Albert Shaw, editor of *Review of Reviews*. The editor of *American Lumberman*, J. E. Defebaugh, who spoke on "The Changed Attitude of Lumbermen Toward Forestry," explained his surprise at finding himself in such mixed company with this little story:

"Papa, where were you born?"
"In Boston, my dear," he answered.
"And where was Mama born?"
"In San Francisco, my dear."
"And where was I born?"
"In Philadelphia, my dear."
"Well," said the little one, "isn't it funny how
we three people ever got together!"

Continued Mr. Defebaugh: "There are present not only men to whom forestry is a science and an occupation, but men whose business is the cutting of the forest and men who are neither lumbermen nor professional foresters, but who occupy high places in our national life and are interested in the forestry movement because it is for the national good."

When the President came to speak he was greeted with great applause, although the seats were not all filled. It was evident that many people were there that day to hear him, for a large number followed him in and left when he was through. Considering current scandals over timbered-land frauds and the involvement of people in high places, this might have been the time for the President to wield the big stick— as he would do another time with the lumbermen. But now he expressed the basic ideology of Gifford Pinchot, which warned of timber famine but sought the co-operation of the West.

"You all know, and especially those of you from the West," the President declared, "the individual whose idea of developing the country is to cut every stick of timber off of it and then leave a barren desert for the homemaker who comes in after him. That man is a curse and not a blessing to the country. The prop of the country must be the businessman who intends so to run his business that it will be profitable for his children after him.

58

"When wood, dead or alive, is demanded in so many ways, and when this demand will undoubtedly increase, it is a fair question, then, whether the vast demands of the future upon our forests are likely to be met. You are mighty poor Americans if your care for the well-being of this country is limited to hoping that that well-being will last out your own generation. No man, here or elsewhere, is entitled to call himself a decent citizen if he does not try to do his part toward seeing that our national policies are shaped for the advantage of our children and our children's children.

"If the present rate of forest destruction is allowed to continue, with nothing to offset it, a timber famine in the future is inevitable. Fire, wasteful and destructive forms of lumbering, and the legitimate use, taken together, are destroying our forest resources far more rapidly than they are being replaced. It is difficult to imagine what such a timber famine would mean to our resources. And the period of recovery from the injuries which a timber famine would entail would be measured by the slow growth of the trees themselves. Remember, that you can prevent such a timber famine occurring by wise action taken in time, but once the famine occurs there is no possible way of hurrying the growth of the trees necessary to relieve it. You have got to act in time or else the nation would have to submit to prolonged suffering after it had become too late for forethought to avail. Fortunately, the remedy is a simple one, and your presence here today is a most encouraging sign that there will be such forethought. It is the great merit of the Department of Agriculture in the forest work that its efforts have been directed to enlist the sympathy and co-operation of the users of wood, water, and grass, and to show that forestry will and does pay, rather than to exhaust itself in the futile attempt to introduce conservative methods by other means.

"I ask with all the intensity that I am capable, that the men of the West will remember the sharp distinctions I have just drawn between the man who skins the land and the man who develops the country. I am going to work with, and only with, the man who develops the country. I am against the land skinner every time. Our policy is consistent to give to every portion of the public domain its highest possible amount of use, and, of course, that can be given only through the hearty co-operation of the Western people."

The emphasis of the Forestry Congress, as well as the principal point of agreement among all factions represented, was a demand to transfer the Reserves from Interior to Agriculture. "It is well," declared

Congressman John Lacey of Iowa, "that when these reservations have finally been delimited and their outlines fixed, that they should be transferred, not to a department whose business it is to pass the title away to individuals, but to a department that will hold on to this land, that will turn it over to succeeding administrations, and that will preserve the sources of water supply of the country in the West, whose future is entirely dependent upon the successful operation of irrigation."

The enthusiasm of the conclave reverberated on Capitol Hill. Within days Congress enacted the Transfer Act and Theodore Roosevelt lost no time in signing it. The stripling Bureau of Forestry was shored up with a new title, United States Forest Service, and later in the year the Reserves would be retitled Forests. On February 1, Secretary of Agriculture Wilson directed a letter to Pinchot, Chief of the Service, enunciating the principle of the "greatest good," now famous among foresters but subject to varying interpretations in this multiple-use era. Wrote the Secretary:

"It must be clearly borne in mind that all land is to be devoted to its most productive use for the permanent good of the whole people and not for the temporary benefit of individuals or companies. All the resources of Forest Reserves are for *use*, and this use must be brought about in a thoroughly prompt and businesslike manner, under such restrictions only as will insure the permanence of these resources. . . .

"In the management of each Reserve local questions will be decided upon local grounds; the dominant industry will be considered first, but with as little restrictions to minor industries as may be possible; sudden changes in industrial conditions will be avoided by gradual adjustment after due notice; and where conflicting interests must be reconciled, the question will always be decided from the standpoint of the greatest good of the greatest number in the long run."

This represented a great victory, but by no means the final battle. Contention over the Forests would begin anew and anew. "Every year," as Theodore Roosevelt observed, "the Forest Service had to fight for its life. The opposition of the servants of the special interests in Congress to the Forest Service had become strongly developed, and more time appeared to be spent upon it during the passage of the appropriations bills than on all other government bureaus put together."

In 1907 a group of Western Senators, led by Senator Fulton of Oregon, staged a battle royal in behalf, they said, of the poor but honest pioneer, who was being denied his rightful opportunity to acquire land. Fulton tagged a rider to the Agriculture Bill depriving the President of authority to establish additional National Forests in five Northwestern states, Oregon, Idaho, Washington, Montana and Wyoming, plus Colorado. California, the traditional friend of forestry, was not included, but even the Northwest was far from unanimous behind Fulton and company. The Portland *Oregonian* editorialized:

"We now perceive that the public land policy, as it applies to tillable land, should be different from the policy that determines the disposition of timber and coal lands. The man who acquires tillable land usually expects to go upon it and make it productive. The man who acquires timberland hopes to sell it to some large corporation. The corporation, founded by men who foresee a scarcity of timber, expects to hold the timberland until it has greatly enhanced in value. The wait may be ten, twenty-five or fifty years, but the certainty of advancing value makes the purchase a safe speculative investment. Much of the timberland goes into the possession of corporations that do not desire it for milling purposes, but expect to make a profit by reason of future conditions of supply and demand. Tillable land goes to the people—timberland to the capitalistic few who expect to levy tribute upon the people who eventually must buy the timber in the form of lumber."

The Agriculture Bill, with rider, was passed by Congress on February 25. The President had until March 4 to sign it into law. He could have vetoed, but Pinchot and he decided on another course. If they must stop creating National Forests they would do so gloriously. It was a Pinchot-type maneuver, which he had probably been preparing to execute for years. The entire Forest Service now undertook to draw and document proclamations covering areas in the six states involved, for which the field force had already gathered the facts necessary. As the proclamations were completed, Pinchot carried them to the White House, where the President signed them without the slightest public (or private) notice. Then they were sent across the street to the Department of State; the seal of the United States was affixed and the documents were kept under cover for the time being.

All told, the President signed thirty-three proclamations. "I signed the last," he wrote, "a couple of days before, by my signature, the bill became law; and, when the friends of the special interests in the Senate got their amendment through and woke up, they discovered that sixteen million acres of timberland had been saved for the people by putting them in the National Forests before the land grabbers could get at them. The opponents of the Forest Service turned hand-springs in their wrath, and dire were the threats against the Executive; but the threats could not be carried out and were really only a tribute to the efficiency of our action."

Characteristically, Pinchot left his post as he had entered: on the wave of the conservation crusade, but this time it was an ebbing wave in government that swept him out. The year was 1910 and William Howard Taft was President. The direct issue revolved around extensive coal lands in Alaska, claimed under public-land laws by a group of Seattle businessmen and about to be sold to a syndicate composed of J. P. Morgan & Company and the Guggenheim mining interests. Pinchot charged the claims were fraudulent and demanded they be nullified by the Department of Interior. In this manner he became embroiled in a much celebrated controversy with Interior Secretary Richard A. Ballinger, although the larger issue was Taft's retreat on all fronts from Roosevelt's resources program.

Any ordinary bureau chief, or even an extraordinary chief who needs the money, accepts as his own the program of his Cabinet officer and the Chief Executive. Pinchot, however, refused to be silent in the Ballinger controversy, but insisted on presenting his case through friends in Congress and the press. Taft, having elected to retreat from the Roosevelt program, replied with Pinchot's dismissal. Those were epochal days, in which reformers, muckrakers and an alert press rallied to support Pinchot. Congress voted to investigate. The Pinchot cause was notably aided by a youthful Nebraska Congressman, George W. Norris, who dared defy the leadership of House Speaker Joseph Cannon (an incident described in *Profiles in Courage*, by John F. Kennedy), and by Louis D. Brandeis, a vigorous private attorney who later would be a Supreme Court justice.

Following the Ballinger controversy, President Taft and his administration distinguished themselves further in the forestry field. The Forest Service budget was slashed. "We were punished, and I mean in every way possible," is the recollection of a veteran of the era. "We had been pointed out time and again by reporters and others as an example of efficiency in government—the one such bureau in the whole Department of Agriculture. Now the administration just went after our scalps. We were in distinctly bad odor with our department as well as with industry."

As for Pinchot, he lived a long, useful and creative life after leaving

Federal service. He became governor of Pennsylvania twice, once in the twenties and again in the thirties, and is remembered for the extensive construction of macadam "Pinchot roads." His heart was always in forestry and conservation, in which fields he influenced Franklin D. Roosevelt. One point he and his allies sought but failed to gain was government regulation of commercial timber cutting as he had seen in Europe. Their efforts, however, stimulated private industry to adopt better practices and to widen the scope of scientific forestry.

Born at the end of the Civil War, Pinchot lived until a year beyond the end of the Second World War. His spirited, social-conscious wife lived on until 1960, and their home on Rhode Island Avenue in Washington continued as a rendezvous of forestry. Once an industry man suggested the parlor discussion consider means of keeping the labor unions of loggers in their proper place. Mrs. Pinchot rose up angrily. "To think such talk against the workingman would take place under this roof," she exclaimed. "Gifford Pinchot is turning over in his grave at this very instant!" She banished the antilabor forester from the house forever.

In 1945, one year before his death, the eighty-year-old Pinchot was visited at the family estate at Milford, Pennsylvania, by two of his "young men" of the Forest Service. They waited for him in his living room. Perhaps, they thought, he is out working on the new forest-management plan of the estate. They were not wearing their uniforms but shrank into embarrassment to see Pinchot, a proud old man, walk down the stairs wearing *his* uniform.

"I have been a governor now and then," he told the Forest Service on the occasion of its fortieth anniversary that year, "but I am a forester all the time—have been, and shall be, to my dying day."

PART TWO

# PROFILE OF SOME
# FORESTS
# AND FOREST PEOPLE

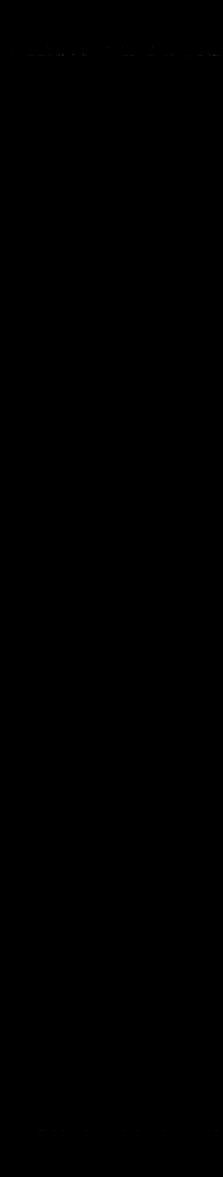

# CHAPTER FIVE

# *Mount Washington and Friends*

I was sitting in the living room at Pinkham Notch Camp and thinking about Europe without prejudice. That is, the word "alpine" had just whistled through the conversation and I thought, "Yes, the Alps." Then I looked around this curious, wonderful, useful building of the Appalachian Mountain Club, which is more than a hut, less than a hotel, and always, regardless of season, enlivened by young people who love the outdoors. They dress for it, and would look at home in the most alpine of European settings. Yet they were obviously proud and happy to be here at Pinkham Notch on the slope of Mount Washington, New Hampshire.

They are rightfully proud. In the fraternity of great mountains, Washington suffers no lack of standing. Western mountains may be much higher and have greater snow depth. The Alps may be the glamorous playground of Europe and a challenge to climbers. But Washington and the surrounding White Mountains have qualities of their own which are hard to match.

Most important, these mountains are loved, enjoyed and protected by people. The White Mountain National Forest is the largest, most visited parcel of public land in New England. And although we think of northern New Englanders as clinging to individualism and the creed of private ownership, in this case they fought for the Federal domain and for the National Forests of the East in general. Today the Appalachian Mountain Club (AMC) and the Society for the Protection of New Hampshire Forests still express the public conscience and encourage the finest of outdoor pursuits, from rugged rock and ice climbing to nature study in family groups. Certainly the unique AMC hut system, a chain of hostels designed for the tramping vacationer who desires cooked meals and a certain degree of comfort, is not duplicated elsewhere.

Mount Washington, elevation 6288 feet, is the highest peak in the Northeast. Picture it as a huge mountain mass with its sides cleft by

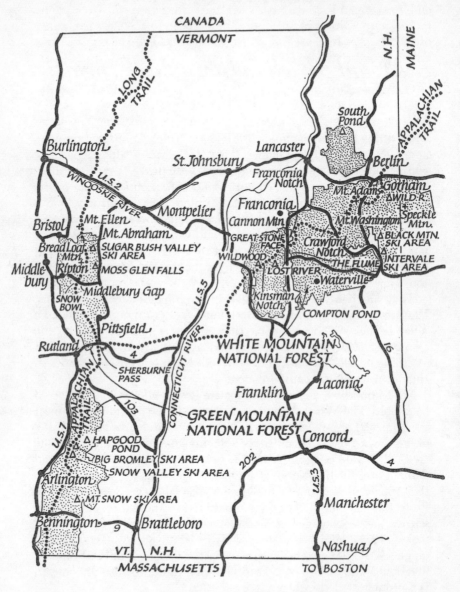

National Forests in New England

four ravines: The Gulf of Slides, Huntington, Raymond's Cataract and Tuckerman Ravine, the great glacial cirque, carved like a mammoth, steep-walled amphitheater. Above them, in the elevation range of 5000 to 5500 feet, are level stretches and grassy meadows, then the broad cone, or summit, windswept, rock strewn, often shrouded in clouds.

The summit lies above timberline, a true alpine zone, with plants, shrubs and mosses typical of alpine and arctic regions. Here, along the ridge of the Presidential Range, you are apt to encounter the most severe weather in America, as severe as any known on this continent south of Alaska and the Yukon. To scale Washington in winter, at its worst, represents a great hazard, challenge and achievement to climbers. Two-thirds of the days between Thanksgiving and Easter are unsuited to ascent; wind and temperature above timberline cannot be judged from the base and usually prove worse than expected. Wind velocities are often more than 100 miles per hour and the highest winds ever recorded, 231 miles per hour, whooshed across Mount Washington in 1934. Temperatures have been measured at forty-six degrees below zero. The combination of high wind and low temperature has such a cooling effect on the human body that physical conditions on Mount Washington are comparable to the worst at Antarctica, although it is much colder there.

Even in summer, storms of incredible violence sometimes arrive unannounced. Quickly the weather approximates northern Labrador's. The temperature dips below zero. Rocks become ice-coated, the freezing fog blinds and suffocates, winds of hurricane force exhaust the strongest tramper. Under these circumstances, mountain safety has become an important activity of the White Mountain National Forest and co-operating state agencies. Over thirty deaths have been recorded in the Presidential Range in the past century, ten during the 1950's; countless more persons have been saved by search and rescue missions, afoot and by helicopter. Some fatalities have resulted from falling ice, rock climbing, ice climbing; one man was crushed to death in a snow hut. But most died of exhaustion and exposure; two persons have frozen to death in midsummer. For these reasons, the AMC and Forest Service urge trampers always to travel with compass and map, and to turn back should the weather switch unpredictably from summer to winter.

The history of tramping in the White Mountains goes back almost a century. The AMC, oldest mountain club in the country, was organized in 1876 "to explore the mountains of New England and adjacent regions, and in general to cultivate an interest in geographical studies." At that time there were only a handful of hiking trails in the mountains. Most regions were wild, most peaks unnamed. With the exception of Mount Washington, the solitude of the Presidentials was disturbed only by the rare visits of timber cruisers or hunters. Washington already was in the vacationer's orbit, with the carriage road and cog railroad. The former, completed in 1861, still extends from the Glen House, an antiquated resort on Route 16, eight miles to the summit. The ascent totals 4700 feet at an average grade of 12 per cent. The railroad rises from the opposite direction, the west side, via Bretton Woods. It was a marvel of its day on completion in 1869— and still is. Maximum grade, thirteen and a half inches to the yard, is steeper than most such railroads in the Alps, and is the steepest outside Europe. At one point the trestle rises about thirty feet above the mountainside. The three-mile trip to the summit takes about one hour and ten minutes. Once on top, half of New England and part of New York State, Canada and the Atlantic Ocean become visible. That is, on a clear day. Otherwise, you may have to settle for the view down into Tuckerman Ravine and to the Lakes-of-the-Clouds Hut across it, and for the cluster of buildings on the summit: Mount Washington Observatory, which opened in 1870 as the first mountain weather station in the world; U. S. Air Force Climatic Projects Laboratory; radio and TV transmitters, and the Summit House, a lunch stop, owned by Dartmouth College. There are such parcels of private land, as the Dartmouth property, the Carriage Road and the cog railroad, but most of Washington lies within the National Forest.

The Summit House is the fourth erected here. The first dates to 1852, when the summit or "tiptop" house, was coming into vogue throughout the New England mountains. Generally it would be reached by horse and buckboard over a tortuous route. "It was a thoroughly hair-raising, bone-rattling experience," reported one sufferer. "Despite the generous advance assurances of certain advertising brochures (which I rather doubted), the carriage road followed a rocky, steep and hazardous course. At one point we went jolting over the crazy scaffolding of a corduroy bridge. Frequently we were close, frighteningly close to deep, yawning ravines."

Perhaps such experiences encouraged mountain enthusiasts to take up tramping. In any event, in 1876 the AMC cleared its earliest trails, notably Lowe's Path, cut by Dr. William G. Nowell and Charles E.

70

Lowe from Lowe's house, in Randolph, 4.5 miles to the summit of Mount Adams. The trails were six to eight feet wide and members either posted signs with the official club "A" along the way or painted "AMC" on the rocks. A dozen years later, in 1888, the first hut, Madison No. 1, was built to provide emergency shelter for climbers on the Presidential peaks.

In the early years of the century, trail construction opened areas now familiar to many White Mountain visitors. In 1914, Carter Notch Hut, the oldest unit still in use, was the first off the Presidential Range and showed broadening public interest in climbing. It cost $1600 to build, twice as much as Madison No. 1, but only a fraction of what it would cost to replace today. The following year the first stage of the Lakes-of-the-Clouds Hut was erected to serve the southern peaks. In 1920 the original Pinkham Notch development was started as a central point to link operations of the three mountain huts. And two years later the legendary Joe Dodge became hutmaster and began his long career as "Mayor of Porky Gulch," serving a constituency of thousands of skiers, climbers and hikers. By the midtwenties the long distance hoofer could cover 300 miles of maintained path and stay at fourteen log shelters. A trail crew of six to ten was taken on each year to work on paths, bridges and shelters, and sign-painter Paul Jenks was turning out 200 to 300 signs a year. Along with weather, wind and time, White Mountain bears contribute to the obsolescence of signs by impolitely chewing them. It could be their way of suggesting, Tramper Go Home.

The Appalachian Mountain Club, like many outdoor groups, has had protection, as well as enjoyment, of the landscape on its mind since its early days. Members observed during their trampings the cause and effect of wasted resources. When Gifford Pinchot developed the concept of conservation, and Theodore Roosevelt popularized it, the AMC was prepared to join in their campaign. It sponsored lectures by Pinchot, advocated the Weeks Bill to create forests in the East and collaborated with other organizations of like convictions.

Forestry in conservation has been the enlightened philosophy of the AMC. It has practiced timber cutting on its own—disposing of slash, clearing firebreaks, thinning crowded stands, salvaging overmature trees and generally improving the value and appearance of its reservations.

"It should not be inferred that we oppose the legitimate utilization of the forest resources of the country, however much we regret the

71

passing of the old-time solitudes," the Club once declared. "A proper use of the forests is wholly desirable, and will tend to their perpetuation. That is forestry. It is the ruthless waste of material, and to the stripping of the timbers from these lands which are of little value for anything but forest growth, that we should stoutly object.

"While the Club urges with others the economic necessities for the establishment of this (White Mountain) national forest, it seems its especial province to put forward the esthetic arguments in the case."

The esthetic arguments again. The viewpoint of the "bird watchers," naturally. A lumber official in Washington warned me about such people. He said they really did not understand forestry and were a pressure group that would subvert the forests into a public playground. That is, subverted from their primary purpose of timber cutting as stipulated in the Act of 1897. This, of course, is precisely what has happened in the White Mountains. At the turn of the century these mountains were the province of large timberland operators, with small areas held by assorted walking clubs, improvement associations and hotel owners. But because of the activities of the AMC and the Society for the Protection of New Hampshire Forests, the White Mountain National Forest has become one of the country's most heavily used recreation areas. And timber cutting has learned to live in a subordinate role. Without bleating about it very much either.

What was it like in the early days? "I have slept under pine trees, which were high, tall, beautiful pine trees when North America was discovered," said the Reverend Edward Everett Hale in 1905, of his native New England, expressing that recurring, disturbing spirit of sensibility. Dr. Hale then was Chaplain of the U. S. Senate, but undertook to lobby for nature nevertheless. "I went up through the same region two years ago with a friend," he continued, "and found my pine trees all gone and sumac and blackberry bushes in their places. It makes a man cry to see it. I have talked with lumbermen who knew where they could find pine trees that had King George's mark on them, because King George, in 1770, valued his New England forests so much that he would not let anybody cut down pine trees without his permission, and he placed on the trees the broad arrow of the English Admiral. Fortunately, he was not able to cut down the trees afterwards. Now we are before Congress because we want Congress to preserve the forests for fifty square miles in that region. I desire that my boy's boy's girls, two centuries hence shall see such pine trees as I saw in 1841."

While he spoke, no less than fifteen logging railroads were at work in the heart of the White Mountains. They hauled virgin spruce, pine and valuable hardwoods out of upper slopes and valleys in large and intensive operations.

Along the steeper slopes, all trees were felled, including the small and useless, so the larger saw-timber logs could roll unblocked downhill to roads built every 100 feet. When tops and branches on the ground became dry, forest fires often destroyed remaining vegetation and humus in the soil. The worst of many fires struck in the dry summer of 1903, burning 80,000 acres—a tremendous land area for a small state like New Hampshire.

New Englanders, and New Hampshiremen in particular, looked for leadership to crystallize their desires to protect the scenic and timber values of the mountains. And so in February, 1901, they organized the Society for the Protection of New Hampshire Forests and, as forester, engaged Philip Ayres, who for the next thirty-four years would contribute a lifetime to conservation in New England and set an example to the nation. He also was president of the Appalachian Mountain Club and was largely responsible for guaranteeing use and access of forest areas by placing them under public or association ownership.

The West already had National Forests in those years, but the East had none. Western Congressmen who opposed National Forests in their own states did not want the idea to spread. Congressmen from states that would not benefit called proposals for new forests "pork-barrel legislation."

Such arguments work both ways. Senator Gallinger of New Hampshire pleaded for "fairness to maintain some forests also in the East." Senator Gallinger said we must "balance river and harbor appropriations going to other sections."

New England had a very strong body of public opinion for forestry among conservation, outdoor and women's clubs. Philip Ayres cited the damage of uncontrolled stream flows, with alternating floods and water shortages, and won over chambers of commerce and business groups. They made league with groups in the Southern Highlands, where farming was almost impossible because of stream and soil erosion, and the mountains had been thoroughly cut and burned over and lay in waste and ruin. Some of these groups wanted preservation and a National Park, others wanted the protection of forestry. But all were agreed that Congress could not delay much longer.

In 1907 the focus switched to the Alleghenies. The great flood caused damage of $100,000,000 in the Monongahela Valley and Pittsburgh, and the chamber of commerce in the Steel City petitioned Congress for National Forests to control the headwaters of the streams in West Virginia.

West Virginia—here was the most tragic land of all, the scene of fires that burned and burned for years, probably more extensively than any fire in history. "The havoc wrought in this section," it was written in 1908, "is calculated to fill a lover of the woods with dismay. There are thousands of acres on which there remains scarcely a tree or vegetation except a rank growth of bracken ferns and club moss." And the Wheeling *Intelligencer* added to the picture: "A few generations ago what is now open plains was as densely wooded as part of the mountain top still is. But tremendous forest fires swept over the summits and the timber and the jungles were burnt, and the dead trunks of trees were broken by the storms of winter, until nothing but a dreary wreck, splintered by storms and blackened by the conflagrations that roll over them, remains to show that forests had once been there. At this time, even trunks of the trees have disappeared, except here and there a log wedged in among the rocks, as though it had been lodged there by the flood of some river."

To the lasting credit of New Hampshire, one of its own introduced the legislation in Congress that brought National Forests to the East. This was John Wingate Weeks, who earned enough money as a Boston broker to purchase a large tract on Mount Prospect above his native Lancaster, where he could enjoy his favorite view of the White Mountains. This tract is now Weeks Memorial State Park, a fitting tribute to Weeks' contribution to forestry. A member of the House when his forest legislation was passed, he was later elected a United States Senator from Massachusetts and in the twenties became Secretary of War and a real power of the Republican Party. In more recent times, his son, Sinclair W. Weeks, was Secretary of Commerce in the administration of President Dwight D. Eisenhower.

In 1910, Weeks and his supporters encountered heavy opposition from Uncle Joe Cannon, the iron ruler of the House. Cannon's position was simple: forests are trees, trees are scenery, and this year the Congress will not waste money on scenery. However, in addition to the New Englanders and Southerners, the Weeks Bill was advocated by the Daughters of the American Revolution, National Association of Manufacturers, American Forestry Association, American Association for the Advancement of Science, and almost everybody but Joe

74

Cannon's home district in Missouri. The bill passed with an appropriation of $11,000,000 for the acquisition of forestlands on the headwaters of navigable streams, which brought it under interstate commerce and resolved a question of constitutionality. A National Forest Reservation Commission, consisting of the Secretaries of Agriculture, Interior and War and two members of each House of Congress, was created to approve all purchases, upon assurance by the Geological Survey that Federal control of lands involved really was needed to protect navigation and the watershed. The Reservation Commission, though little known, is still alive and functioning.

Passage of the Weeks Law laid the basis for establishing the White Mountain National Forest. Land was acquired over the years in 500 separate tracts, ranging from less than one acre to 65,000 acres at an average cost of $7.50 per acre—and there is probably not a single parcel worth less than 100 times as much today. The Forest covers 723,000 acres (45,000 in western Maine, the rest in New Hampshire), or 1130 square miles.

The work of the Society was far from finished with the Weeks Law. There were many areas which had no influence on navigable streams and could not qualify for Federal purchase. It launched a statewide money-raising campaign to save these for administration by the state or by itself—an effort comparable to the widely known "Save the Redwoods" drive in California.

First, the Society rescued Mount Sunapee by purchasing 656 acres for $8000 (and 400 additional acres later). It may seem incredible now on visiting the state park with its ski slopes, hiking trails, playing fields and beautiful view of the Merrimack-Connecticut Valley, but Sunapee was once under heavy logging, despite remoteness and high elevation.

Next, in 1911, supported by hotelmen in Franconia and Woodstock, it started a campaign to buy land surrounding Lost River in Kinsman Notch for $7000. On another front, Crawford Notch was about to be logged of spruce, fir and hardwoods. Together with the AMC, the Society convinced the state to acquire the land, which is today a major recreation area.

Its greatest effort, however, came in the midtwenties, when the entire Franconia Notch was about to be logged. "Buy a tree and save the Notch," became the byword of New Hampshire. Save the Old Man of the Mountains. Save the Flume Gorge. Save Echo and Lonesome Lakes. Within three years 15,000 members of women's clubs,

75

men's clubs, chambers of commerce, outdoor groups and unaffiliated individuals contributed $200,000. The state matched the amount and the cause was won. The Society managed the Notch until 1947, when it deeded all its holdings for the state park.

Other interests of the Society have been to enlarge the State Forestry Department, develop fire protection, wildlife protection, insect and disease control, conservation education in the schools. It furnishes literature and guidance to private landowners on scientific forestry.

Most important, it contributes a point of view and leadership of a type lacking in most states. For example, it has been trying to pinpoint places of botanical interest that should have permanent protection and ownership by local towns. "There is the real necessity of keeping land on the tax rolls," the Society explains. "On the other hand, the right and interest of future generations can be preserved only by the foresight and careful planning of the present generation."

Thanks to the foresight and careful planning of the Society for the Protection of New Hampshire Forests, the Appalachian Mountain Club and the Forest Service, the present generation can enjoy the varied pleasures of the White Mountains.

High in Kinsman Notch, five miles north of Woodstock, the Society administers a 700-acre natural gem of its own, the Lost River Reservation. Here Lost River flows through a series of cavernous potholes, mostly underground, tumbling at one point twenty feet within a cave, and at another point, Paradise Falls, thirty feet in the open air. There is a nature garden of 300 labeled indigenous plants along trails and ladders. During the summer, family groups come to stay in cabins and study nature's ways.

Today the AMC is a substantial institution, with 7300 members in seven chapters and a Boston headquarters (5 Joy Street) housing a library of maps, books and photographs on nature and mountaineering. Most important, in co-operation with the Forest Service, it enables anyone, from children campers and Boy Scouts to family groups and outdoor enthusiasts of all ages, to probe and enjoy the heart of the White Mountains. Its early shelters have now become a network of mountain hostels, opening the way to wilderness travel away from villages, with comfortable lodgings, well-cooked food and the chance to "go light" for a day, a week or all summer. All you need to bring with you are warm hiking clothes, broken-in walking boots, extra socks, shirt, toothbrush and the AMC Guide.

76

The Huts System consists of eight units located one day's hike apart, with the longest distance being five miles. The huts are not lush, plush or posh, and are unsuited for honeymooning since men and women are accommodated in separate dormitories. The meals are completely adequate, if not fancy, with a typical dinner consisting of mushroom soup, goulash or some such meat stew, vegetables, salad, cake and coffee. Rates are very modest: $7.50 for lodgings, breakfast, supper and trail lunch (half rate for children under ten).

The huts are manned by high-school and college students, called "hutmen," who cook and keep house for 15,000 overnight guests yearly. They carry supplies on their backs or on the backs of donkeys, but they like the exercise, such as hiking from the valley in Randolph almost vertically to the Madison Huts. They enjoy the work, too: although the pay is low, 150 youngsters apply every year for an average of fifteen open jobs.

Like air-conditioned chalets, the huts adorn the wooded slopes of New Hampshire's compact wilderness. Each has its distinct attractions. Carter Notch, the easternmost, is handy to trout fishing, as well as bathing, in upper Carter Lake. Pinkham Notch is the only one open all year. Autumn, incidentally, when insects have subsided, is an excellent season for hiking. The Pinkham Camp consists of two heated buildings with bunks for 100 guests in rooms of from two to eight. The Camp lies just off a heavily traveled motor route between Gorham and Jackson, but when the hiker sets out on the Tuckerman Ravine Trail he shortly becomes enveloped in deep, quiet woods. He has left behind the tang of gasoline and smells only the woodsy odor of fir and spruce. Scrambling up the headwall and skirting patches of snow, he finds the popular route up the cone to the summit of Mount Washington. In the area of the Madison Huts, he travels over the highest trail in the East, across the backbone of the Presidential Range. From the hut he can scale the granite walls of Mount Madison, the northernmost peak in the range, elevation 5362 feet. Or hike out the Gulfside Trail and explore the new Great Gulf Wild Area, 5400 acres set aside by the Forest Service in 1959, in which construction, roads and timber cutting are prohibited (although dangerous winds and low temperatures are likely any time of year). The hiker can enter from the west as well, from Franconia Notch to Greenleaf Hut, with full view of the Franconia Range and day trips possible to Echo Lake, Profile Lake and Kinsman Range.

Pinkham Notch is the base for winter activities, mountaineering, ice climbing and snowshoeing. It is only a mile and a half from Pink-

The Hiker's Boulevard from Mt. Katahdin to Springer Mountain

ham to the new Wildcat Ski Area, where Italian-designed gondola cars rise 2000 feet from lower to upper terminal and the start of varying ski trails and slopes for expert, intermediate and novice. But for alpine skiing of the old school, nothing compares with Tuckerman Ravine on Mount Washington itself. There may be no lift facilities in the sun-shaded glacial cirque, but this is the only area in the East where skiing can be excellent as late as May, on granular corn snow, and good even in June. Some slopes are as steep as sixty degrees down the headwall, strictly for the experts. For the convenience of spring skiers, the AMC operates the Tuckerman Ravine Shelter from March 15 to the end of the skiing season, whenever that may be.

Within the National Forest are twelve major camping areas suited to family vacationing, 800 miles of foot trails, 39 lakes and ponds, 650 miles of fishable stream, plus a great many resort hotels around the periphery which you can use as a base for leisurely woodland walks and drives.

The largest campground, Dolly Copp, accommodating 1200 campers, lies six miles south of Gorham in the Pinkham Notch area. It is an excellent base for hiking up Mount Washington, the northern Presidentials and the Carter Range. Perhaps the best camping facilities, however, are at Campton Pond, one of the few areas in the National Forest System with a camping fee (a dollar a night, five dollars a week per party). It is worth the charge. There's fine bathing, too.

The most unusual facility, Covered Bridge Campground, near Conway, is named for the only covered bridge currently protected by the Federal Government. The Forest Service inherited this outdoor wooden heirloom, built in 1859, and maintains it as a reminder of the days before the motorcar and the gas-powered timber saw.

The newest scenic drive in New Hampshire, Kancamagus Highway, crosses the Forest between Lincoln and Conway. Fully completed and surfaced in 1961, it follows the valleys of the Swift River and the Hancock Branch, winding between 3500- and 4000-foot mountains, and climbing high on the flank of Mount Kancamagus. From picnic areas and scenic overlooks there are limitless views of wilderness and tier upon tier of the wooded White Mountains.

# CHAPTER SIX

# Green Mountain Sheep, Potash and People

Vermont—the rocky little state in northern New England. One thinks of it as being tied and bound to past tradition. But Dorothy Canfield Fisher did not believe it so. "If there is one idea which nearly two centuries of no leisured ease and of incessantly shifting economic life have beaten into our collective Vermont minds, it is that human affairs are never unchanging," this lady of letters and wisdom wrote in her book *Vermont Tradition.* "And a very good thing, too, even from the practical point of view. The loss of the past is often anything but a calamity."

Mrs. Fisher's specific references were to the forestland, where potash manufacture and sheep herds once brought prosperity but would have ruined the state in the long run if they had continued.

Living at Arlington, near the western border of the Green Mountain National Forest (a few miles south of the Manchester Ranger Station), she knew her mountains well. And understood them.

"Occasionally one of our big pictorial magazines publishes an article on soil conservation illustrated with horrifying photographs of deeply gullied hillsides, with poor hopeless farm homes clinging to the edges of water-ravaged chasms," she continued. "When we Vermonters turn over such pages, we lift our eyes to our hills and mountains covered to the top with soil-anchoring trees, and feel that nobody need try to tell us that the disappearance of a past way of life is always a loss. Those mossy and forgotten stone walls buried in the midst of forest trees—we let summer visitors muse in mistaken poetic melancholy over the bygone homes which, they assume, used to stand near. It is with cheerful hearts that we climb over them. They served their time well. But their time is not ours. And if, as their builders intended, they had been carefully kept up to hold sheep into mountain pastures, our beautiful home state would have been a desert."

As to their beauty, the Green Mountains in some sections remind one of the Scottish Highlands above Glasgow, with spaths, lochs, moors, the granite Cairngorm Mountains and isolated pastoral towns. Vermont was settled early and arduously by land-hungry pioneers pushing slowly northward and willing to accept, in tight-lipped endurance, encirclement by forests, mountains and Lake Champlain. The Green Mountain Boys have grown into men but are still hardy and independent stock, and insular by choice.

The freedom of the forest, densely covered with white pine, hemlock, maple and oak, was a glorious thing in the early days. From it the pioneers got wood for their houses and farm buildings, fences for their fields, fuel and food, including sugar and syrup which they had found the Indians making from the sap of maple trees. There was freedom, too, in man's relation to wildlife, which had been unknown in England, or anywhere in Europe. Hunting abroad, since feudal days to the present, has not been a right of the people, but is reserved for landowning gentry, and through them for the social upper classes. But in Vermont, the mountaineers, as Mrs. Fisher recounts, felt no inhibition in pulling the triggers of their long squirrel rifles in the forests and open glades. The appearance of a bear caused no panic but "roused the tingling excited enthusiasm of the hunting spirit."

Forest destruction in the course of time took some curious, now obscure turns. Thousands of acres of rocky hillside were clear-cut for farms (much the way modern builders clear-cut their land for subdivisions), although they could not support farming. Then a timber harvest began, gaining tempo with the opening of the Champlain-Hudson Canal in 1823. The towering white pine went first, then the oak, hemlock and spruce. The demand for tannic acid for treating leather took the hemlock with its tannin-rich bark. In addition, Vermont, although we think of it as eternally poor, was enriched with a great woods industry—the manufacture of potash. Potash, known chemically as the alkali potassium carbonate, used in making glass and soap, was derived for many years as the residue after the burning of wood into ashes. In Vermont this became a major industry: the first patent issued by the United States Patent Office went to a Vermonter who had figured a new potash-producing technique. Potash became so important that a bushel of wood ashes outvalued a bushel of wheat and once substituted as a medium of financial exchange during a shortage of currency. Best of all, the woods had to be cleared for settling anyway, so burning the trees and manufacturing something out of their ashes was an added fillip of prosperity.

The potash bubble had to burst because man is always trying to devise a more efficient corkscrew or can opener, or some improvement on almost everything. In this case it proved to be sodium, economically obtained in other places from salt deposits. It rendered potash for industrial purposes obsolete and the day of wood burning for profit was done. The loss, however, was not long lamented. Sheep became the new treasure of Vermont. Flocks of the vaunted Spanish Merino breed, which originated in Africa and had been brought across the Mediterranean by the Moors, were imported and welcomed like the Golden Fleece. The Merinos thrived in the Vermont atmosphere: in pre-Civil War years sheep outnumbered people five to one. At one point the sheep population reached 1,600,000. Long forgotten, except in Vermont, are the wealth and glory these woollies brought the state. They were exhibited all over the world, won gold medals in Europe, were sold at high prices: $800 for an average good animal, as high as $3500 or $5000 for an outstanding ram. The purebreds were sold in large numbers for breeding in many states and distant lands; from Vermont parentage have grown flocks that now graze the American West, the prairies of South America and Australia. But this prosperity was its own undoing, as sheep multiplied elsewhere and had far more room than tiny Vermont in which to increase their tribes. Again, as with potash, the Green Mountain prosperity collapsed. But, as Mrs. Fisher has said, in the final analysis this was the salvation of Vermont; calling to mind the landscape during the height of the Merino era—"It was pictorially lovely, but the erosion-devil must have smiled broadly to see it: those hilly pastures, laced with sweet silver brooks (which when the snows melt or hard rains come always go on a rampage, and gouge out channels down to bedrock), the thin, fine green grass blades, nibbled closer and closer to the earth by the teeth of the ever-increasing flock; the thousands of sharp-pointed little hoofs cutting the covering sod to pieces—the stage was all set for a catastrophe like that which, through goats, has overtaken the Mediterranean countryside, and, through open cultivation, the hill farms of our American Southern mountains."

It was not only sheep that departed the mountains, but people. Vermont's rocky hillside farms were at best low producing; when the West began to call, their attractions could not compete with the rich soils of the Plains States or the adventure of gold in the Far West.

83

With the exodus of farming families for the grain and dairy lands, the back-country farms, which had been cleared and settled painfully, were abandoned and surrendered to nature's ways.

Here, in that unending interplay between man and his surroundings, the forest has been reborn. Where seed trees stood in adjacent woodlands, pine and spruce have reproduced themselves on the abandoned farms. Elsewhere, on old farms, clear-cut potash and charcoal fields, weeds, briers and hardwoods have taken hold. But through forest management and the ecological process of plant succession, better species will take over; they will yield high quality timber—fine maple and yellow birch, spruce and fir at higher elevations—at maturity. Fish and wildlife, from black bear to beaver, are among the beneficiaries; den trees and evergreen stands used by deer as their winter yards are left undisturbed; so are streamside shade trees.

The Green Mountain National Forest is relatively small, but significant. It encompasses the backbone of the range from Mount Ellen, its highest peak (elevation 4135 feet), extending about 110 miles south to the Massachusetts boundary, with a break midway down. Since establishment in 1925, about 220,000 acres have been purchased under the Weeks Law. Much of the 260,000 acres of private land within the boundaries could have been purchased in recent years at a price of five to ten dollars an acre. But while a forester, and a New England forester at that, Sherman Adams, sat close to the seat of power in the White House, Federal policy during the administration of President Eisenhower prohibited the purchase of additional National Forestland. Yet all over the United States pockets of private land within Forest boundaries constitute a troublesome problem: through blighted resorts and tawdry, low-grade amusement areas; billboarded roadsides; fire hazards, and restricted access to the public. If I interpret correctly the government's policy (not too unlike the viewpoint of Truman days, to be perfectly bipartisan) in curtailing land purchases, it was based on two factors: (1) priority spending for more important items like aircraft carriers and guided missiles; and (2) a belief that the government owns quite enough land already. These may be well founded, although some people hold the theory that caring for inner America should be as important as Point-Fouring the world or assaulting Russians and outer space. The land within forest boundaries will never be cheaper and much of it will never be accessible once developed. But if the government *does* own enough land, then the boundaries should at least be redrawn and so defined. And if purchase is ever to be made,

84

it ought to be done while "the price is right" and protection of the Federal estate can be completed.

So much for politics. Vermont forests have more pleasant distinctions. For one, they produce $3,000,000's worth of sweetness yearly in the form of maple sugar and syrup. Vermont leads the nation in this field, thanks to its luxuriant sugar-maple and black-maple trees and the skilled touch of its sugar makers, practicing a centuries-old craft.

It all began with the Indians, who notched a V in the tree bark with their axes and caught the sap in a wooden trough on the ground. It is said they boiled the sap by the simple process of dropping in hot stones. The pioneers, who first learned from the Indians, grew more sophisticated. They used open iron kettles over a fire, continually adding sap as the level in the boiling kettle lowered. They produced a tasty dark syrup, flavored with traces of bark and soot.

Sugar making knows no set schedule on the calendar. The season usually lasts two to six weeks in the period around the end of March or the beginning of April. In those warm days and cold nights the sap rises through the tree. The maple, like the sugar cane and sugar beet, is characterized by an unusually high concentration of sugar, produced within the tree the year before and stored in roots and trunk during the dormancy of winter. Now, with leaf buds swelling and the imminence of spring, the sap is found just inside the bark. The farmer takes to the field, boring a hole two or three inches into the tree about three feet from the ground. Then he drives in a spile, or metal spout, and hangs a bucket beneath it to catch the sap. If the weather is right sap flows all day, and if the tree is large enough, two or even three buckets may be hung below separate openings. Rarely does he tap a young sugar maple, that is, one under forty or fifty years of age. But in this sturdy, stately tree, tapping may go on for years—without seriously affecting the life of the tree or the quality of its wood. One Vermonter reported felling a sugar maple at least 200 years old bearing the marks of a century of tapping.

From the tree the sap is hauled in a metal tank, on a low horse-drawn sled or trailer, or by pipeline in a few places, through the orchards to the sugarhouse. Here the most patient Vermonter, the sugar maker, presides over the storage tank and evaporator. In the narrow-partitioned evaporator, heated by a wood-burning stove, the sap flows around baffles, boiling down into syrup while water vapor escapes through a ventilator in the roof. In the continuing process, the liquid at the farthest end grows thicker and thicker and is drawn off as syrup and new sap is admitted. And all the while the sugar maker tests the mixture, with a combination hydrometer and thermometer, called a "hydrotherm," adding sap as needed to achieve the proper density. Sometimes it takes thirty-five or forty gallons of maple sap to boil down into one gallon of choice syrup. This is one reason Vermont law requires grading and labeling. The best grade is produced from sap of high sugar content, processed, under modern conditions, with scarcely any storing.

Sugar plays a part in the forest glories of autumn, when the hardwoods, the color changers, surge to the forefront of the landscape. In the Green Mountains, the red of maples, the gold of birches, the deep brown of oaks, the purple of dogwood, the yellow of beech and elm interweave for brief weeks with evergreens, before their leaves fall to become part of the carpet covering the forest floor.

Why, really, do forest colors change? The celestial hunters, said the Indians, have slain the Great Bear and his blood dripping on the forest has reddened some trees, while others are yellowed by fat splattering out of the kettle as the hunters cook their meat. No, said New Englanders in times past, discounting such mythology, the frost is responsible.

Modern botany, however, explains it as part of the chemistry of the tree in its preparation for winter—which is likely to begin before there is any frost. In autumn, cool weather slows down the process of photosynthesis, by which leaves have helped manufacture food for the tree's growth. Now their work is done. Chlorophyll compound in numberless tiny leaf cells breaks up into lesser substances. Food remnants are delivered into the tree trunk for storage until they are needed once again in spring. The only substances left in the cells are tiny oil globules, crystals and yellow particles small in number but strong in power to refract sunlight; these give the leaf its yellow color.

Sometimes the cells are laden with more sugar than can be transferred into the tree. Combining chemically with other substances in the leaf, this sugar helps produce many shades of color from the brilliant reddish purple of the dogwood to the austere brown of the oak. Even the conifers, which do not shed their foliage, take on a slight brownish tinge, which reverts to lighter green the following spring.

This is all part of nature's manifest way of facing the change of seasons. In shedding their leaves, broadleaf trees of the North will help their branches to bear snow and ice more easily; yet in the South some broadleaf trees, notably live oak, are practically evergreen. The conifers—pines, spruces, firs and hemlocks? They hardly need a season for leaf-shedding, since their leaves are needlelike or scalelike, and adapt to shedding snow.

While the broadleaf changes color, another process goes on to insure the leaf will drop. A layer of cells develops on the tree side of the stem. Gradually it severs the supporting tissue. When a strong wind swirls around the tree the leaf will be ready to join it and ride off. If no wind arises, the leaf will fall of its own weight, returning to the soil the mineral elements its tree borrowed to grow, and which others will borrow to grow in their time.

Why not proceed now to explore the National Forest? Start from Rutland, between the northern and southern districts. Both districts are crisscrossed with quiet roads, and an occasional modern highway (although no one should ever come to Vermont in a turnpike frame of mind) winding through mountain notches, valleys and villages. The real way, however, to visit a forest or any place worth visiting, is on foot, unless there happens to be a good horse handy. Whether aged or infirm or just out of practice, take inspiration from Hazlitt, who said, "Give me the clear blue sky over my head, and the green turf beneath my feet, a winding road before me, and a three hours march to dinner—then to thinking. It is hard if I cannot start some game on these lone heaths. I laugh, I run, I leap, I sing for joy."

A few miles from Rutland on Route 4, the Rutland-Woodstock Highway, we encounter the Long Trail, "A Footpath in the Wilderness," which extends between the Canadian and Massachusetts borders. The idea of the Long Trail was conceived by a schoolmaster, James P. Taylor, of Saxtons River, who had often hiked Ascutney Mountain with his students of the Vermont Academy. One rainy summer day in 1909, while waiting for the clouds to clear from the summit of Stratton Mountain, he asked himself: "Should the Green Mountain Range continue to be sacrosanct to the spirits of the first 'Green Mountain Boys' and untouchable to everybody else? Sacrosanct to sleep-destroying, food-stealing hedgehogs? Or should the Green Mountain Range enshrine a state-long skyline pathway, as fine as the Ascutney Mountain Trail, connecting Killington Peak with Pico, connecting the Chin of Mount Mansfield with the Lake of the Clouds, connecting one day the Massachusetts line and the Canadian border?"

His idea produced results the following year when twenty-three charter members of the Green Mountain Club pledged to "make the mountains play a larger part in the life of the people" by building trails and providing shelters. After years of trail blazing, the final line in the route between Massachusetts and Canada was opened in 1931. The length of the Trail as now constituted is 255.3 miles. Of this total, eighty miles are within the National Forest and are maintained by the Forest Service. The Green Mountain Club, which now has a membership of 1000, maintains the remaining 175 miles. In addition to the main north-south pathway, there are about eighty-five side trails.

The beauty of the Long Trail is sheer accessibility from numerous roads and side trails, and its appeal to inexperienced trampers as well as veterans. Park your car and start walking. Within five or ten minutes you are removed from the sights and sounds of civilization. Yet there is no danger of getting lost, for the Trail is well marked. Your walk could last an hour or all week. A series of open shelters and cabins are spaced an average 4.2 miles apart. Elaborate equipment is not necessary and essential items, such as blankets, food supplies and cooking utensils, can be bought in Rutland or any of the villages. Tramping along an open summit or in deep woods, the scenery is monotony-free, always changing. A delightful short trip, for example, starts near Mount Tabor village in the southern district, passing ancient charcoal kilns, climbing on an easy grade through a hardwood forest to Little Rock Pond, which reflects the fully timbered shoreline in its clear surface. With shelter and fireplace, this is the ideal spot for sequestered fishing and swimming.

But I suggest starting from the Trail crossing at Route 4, for two reasons. First, here in Sherburne Pass (elevation 2200 feet) you can stop overnight or for a meal at the Long Trail Lodge, a fine, unusual hostelry built by the Green Mountain Club and now well operated by the Treadway hotel company. During the summer a naturalist at the Lodge conducts short nature study and bird walks. Many hiking trips, short and long, can be taken with the Lodge as a base. North into the National Forest to Deers Leap Shelter and beyond to Noyes Camp Pond. South, outside the Forest, across Pico Peak (elevation 3967 feet) and on to Vermont's second highest mountain, Killington Peak (elevation 4241), just five miles from the Pass. Rutland for years claimed Killington was the highest point in the state and it was accorded the honor until triangulations were made from the Chin of Mount Mansfield, showing an elevation of 4393 feet. Nevertheless, the people of Rutland County determined to build the finest summit house in New England. The setting was ideal, for Killington lies in the central area of the Green Mountains, equidistant between the White Mountains and the Adirondacks. In 1879 a handsome frame hotel, stables and other buildings were completed. The hotel prospered for a time but closed its doors around the turn of the century, the end of the summit-house era. Then it was ravaged by storms and hedgehogs until fire claimed it completely in 1916. Today the new Cooper Lodge, just below the summit, is one of the finest camps on the Long Trail, with bunks for sixteen and a caretaker during the summer.

The second reason for accenting Sherburne Pass is that here the Appalachian Trail swings south to join the Long Trail for almost 100 miles to the Massachusetts border. The Appalachian Trail, 2100 miles from Maine to Georgia, ranks among the great boulevards of America. Not because it enables you to travel with mechanical swiftness, but because it places you in the natural world of self-reliance and self-propulsion. Everyone should experience at least a fragment of the Appalachian Trail in his lifetime and the more of it the better.

Here in New England the Appalachian Trail was born, principally in the mind and dreams of Benton MacKaye, of Shirley Center, Massachusetts. Mr. MacKaye studied at Harvard, then entered the United States Forest Service in 1905, Pinchot's time, and remained until 1918, when he became a regional planner. During his career he has contributed his talent to Massachusetts, Connecticut, the Tennessee Valley Authority, Rural Electrification Administration and the United States Indian Service. By modern standards, one might easily compare his merit in the world to the man who can say, "I made $44,000,000 in real estate by the time I was forty-four." About 1918 Mr. MacKaye formulated the project for the mountain footpath from his wanderings in the New England forests, although others had already begun localized trails. In 1922 the first part of the Trail was constructed by hiking clubs of New York and New Jersey in Palisades Interstate Park. New England had much to add with the trail systems of the Appalachian Mountain Club, Green Mountain Club and the Dartmouth Outing Club. In time other clubs were formed farther south. Now these non-professional enthusiasts, through their individual clubs and the Appalachian Trail Conference, supervise and maintain the route with cooperation of Federal and state land agencies.

Starting from its northern terminus at Mount Katahdin, Maine, the Trail traverses fourteen states. Virginia has the longest section, 500 miles; West Virginia the shortest, ten miles below the Potomac River at Harpers Ferry. The Trail embraces eight National Forests (White Mountain, New Hampshire; Green Mountain, Vermont; George Washington and Jefferson, Virginia; Pisgah and Cherokee, North Carolina and Tennessee; Nantahala, North Carolina; Chattahoochee in Georgia, where it reaches its southern terminus at Springer Mountain), two National Parks (Shenandoah and Great Smoky Mountains), state parks and private lands. If you were to walk the entire Appalachian Trail, averaging a brisk seventeen miles per day, it would take you 123 days and nights on the Trail. You would be within 150 miles of half a dozen of the country's largest cities—Boston, New York, Philadelphia, Baltimore, Washington, Atlanta—and cross an occasional motorway, but essentially you would be in wilderness traveling the high country of the East. Your lodgings would be campsites, shelters and cabins such as those on the Long Trail. In Virginia, my own state, there is a very fine system of closed shelters furnished with mattresses and blankets, stove, cooking utensils and dishes. All you bring are food supplies and appetite. Each hut is kept locked, with the key loaned on reservation through the Trail Club.

Having now hiked through the woods a while, let us proceed by other means over the Forest and around the periphery. Vermont is composed not of cities but of villages. Driving south through East Wallingford, Route 8 leads to Weston, tucked away in the hills, with much to offer of village doings. Here are shops specializing in woodcraft, pottery, silver, gunsmithing, clothing and, needless to say, antiques. Just north of the Common the Vermont Guild of Old Time Crafts and Industries operates a water-powered gristmill grinding wheat, corn and rye. During the summer the Weston Playhouse presents a commendable ten-week season. There are half a dozen eating houses in which you are not likely to go wrong. The main attraction is the Original Vermont Country Store, which sells something of everything: New England foods, clothing, handmade bellows, old fashioned cookware, calico dolls, teakettles and cook books. Vrest Orton, who runs the store, is one of the personalities of Vermont; and if you have any questions on the Green Mountain National Forest, he is the authority.

Another favorite village, but city-size of 8000 population, Bennington, lies diagonally across the Forest on Route 7, the Ethan Allen Highway, in southern Vermont. Near here the Americans under General John Stark scored a decisive victory over the British in

1777, an event commemorated by the obelisk Battle Monument, the tallest in the world (306 feet) when it was built before the turn of the century. Well worth noting are the Congregational Church, one of the most beautiful old churches in New England, and the Historical Museum and Art Gallery, displaying pottery, glass, furniture and historical Vermont costumes.

Summer recreation areas are spotted across the southern district. For picnicking, tent and trailer camping, there is Greendale Forest Camp, bordering a mountain stream, five miles north of Weston. For swimming, as well as picnicking and camping, Hapgood Pond Forest Camp, near Peru village, has a 300-foot beach, modern bathhouse, tentsites, tables and fireplaces.

Winter is another story. Vermont has blossomed forth with preeminent ski areas on National Forestland, operated on concession, or "special use" permits. One is Big Bromley, west of Weston, where a new double Riblet chairlift ascends the 3260-foot mountain non-stop in eleven minutes. Two additional switchbacks near the top enable the novice skier to go all the way. Fred Pabst, who operates Bromley, has named his advanced runs Pabst Peril, Blue Ribbon and Avalanche. Pabst knows a good beer when he tastes one, but allows freedom of choice at his new steak house and cocktail lounge. Farther south, at West Dover, Mount Snow has become a major American ski center. The latest development: North Face, an entire area designed for expert skiers, with three steep trails constructed around a glacial cirque leading into the rugged wilderness. The northeastern facing and sheltering ridge should insure late spring skiing. At Mount Snow, you can ski, swim and skate the same day. A heated swimming pool is now open in winter and a skating rink open in summer. Lodgings at inns and motels in the surrounding Dover-Wilmington area provide accommodations for 2400.

In the northern district, Sugarbush Valley, at Warren, is one of the East's most up-and-coming ski areas. The new gondola cars carry passengers to the 4000-foot summit of Lincoln Peak in less than fifteen minutes. Facing the gondola from the opposite side of Sugarbush Bowl is the still newer Castlerock Section, with 5200-foot double chairlift. The Upper Castlerock Trail, serpentine, narrow, with pitches up to forty-five degrees, was built to be tough, a testing ground for skill. In addition, there are T-bar and practice areas for intermediates and novices. Sugarbush has produced a boom in plush lodgings and eating houses, inviting places like Sugarbush Inn, motellike Inferno

91

at the base of the lifts, Mad Bush Chalet, Schuss-Bush Chalet and Fiddler's Green.

This surge in accommodations has more meaning than service to skiers. The National Forestlands of Vermont are not really "on the tax base." Yet they are stimulating a large tax-producing industry, as well as providing outdoor fun for thousands of winter enthusiasts.

The northern district has worthwhile attractions besides skiing. One of the finest scenic stretches lies along Middlebury Gap Road (Route 125). Driving from Hancock village west, first there is Texas Falls Recreation Area, an enchanted wooded picnic grove on the banks of Hancock Branch, with trails winding past the Falls which drop flume-like into a deep ravine. Then, farther west, you drive through dark stands of Norway spruce planted fifty years ago on land owned by Middlebury College. This was part of the immense holdings of Colonel Joseph Battell, flamboyant Middlebury individualist, champion of nature and defier of progress. Despite the general decline in summit houses, he elected to open one at the end of a buckboard road atop Lincoln Mountain in 1899. He was publisher of the Middlebury *Register*, raised prize Morgan horses and owned the Bread Loaf Inn, which he ran more like a house party than a hotel. There were no bellboys, no tipping and frequently no bills. Battell fought intrusion by motorcars, devoting page after page in his newspaper to gruesome accident details, and plainly advising guests that gasoline-powered vehicles were not permitted within three miles. His summit house lasted only a few years; now the upper part of Lincoln Mountain, where it stood, and a dozen other mountains comprise 31,000-acre Battell Forest, which he willed to Middlebury College. And Bread Loaf is headquarters of the Writers Summer School and Conference, held under Middlebury's auspices. As for the town of Middlebury itself, on the west side of the gap, it is perhaps the classic Vermont village, with its beautiful, high-steepled Congregational Church at the head of Main Street, cluster of homes dating to the early 1800's, the Middlebury Inn and the college campus, the oldest in the state and one of the most attractive of the smaller schools. Any time the students feel they need breathing room they have all the Green Mountains at their back door.

# CHAPTER SEVEN

# Pisgah: Dawn of American Forestry

I love to stand on the beautifully landscaped terrace of George Vanderbilt's colossal château and admire the scene of the Blue Ridge Mountains sweeping westward to join the Great Smokies. Then I conjure the youthful, wealthy Vanderbilt standing at the same spot years ago and saying softly, "All this, that my eye can see, is mine."

One would think today that he chose to acquire this mountain kingdom because it was forested as a forest should be, wooded to the summit of Mount Pisgah, and, in his time, free of dwellings built by any other man.

But it was not that way.

When he came here this land was composed of many holdings, largely impoverished farms and logging sites. In many places it was overgrazed by cattle, overcut by lumbermen, burned, slashed and badly eroded.

Then the theory of forestry was placed into practice, for the first time anywhere in the United States. Most trees which now grace the view from the terrace were planted. Others were cut with a plan to replace them with a new generation of trees, as had never been done before.

This was the chosen design of George Washington Vanderbilt, grandson of Commodore Cornelius Vanderbilt and consequently one of the world's richest young men. He arrived here in Asheville, in the western corner of North Carolina, in 1890, after considering many locations on which to build a great country home. He desired one that would compare with the châteaux at Chambord and Blois, surrounded by a landed estate of equal grandeur that would match the Black Forest.

It was not a matter of calculated ostentation. George Vanderbilt

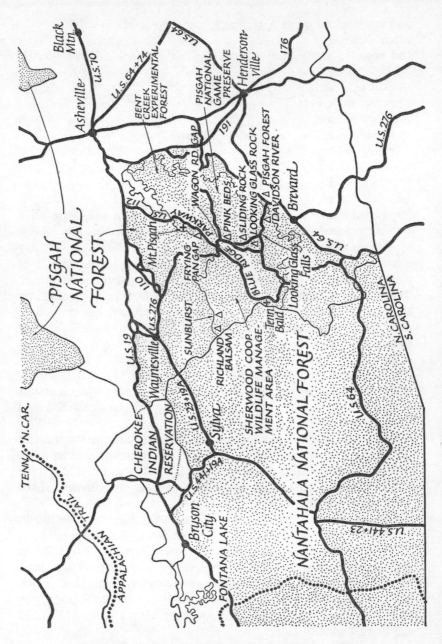

Southern Highlands, Where American Forestry Began

had no need to prove his wealth, although some of the one-room cabin dwelling mountaineers believed the richest man in the world had come to settle in their midst, in his thousand-foot long castle, deliberately to show how poor they really were. But such incongruity worked both ways. One Negro farmer, owner of a small place in the center of the estate, refused to sell out for many times the value of his land. "I have no objection," he would calmly and repeatedly advise the land agents, "to Mr. Vanderbilt as a neighbor."

Vanderbilt was slender, wore a well-trimmed black mustache that made him look like a Frenchman, and was still a bachelor in his early days at Asheville. His primary interests were not hunting, fishing or ladies. As an aesthete of means, he devoted himself to literature, interior design and landscape architecture. Thus, he sought to create a proper environment for his collections of furniture and furnishings, of tapestries, paintings and books. For his estate, he wanted formal gardens close at hand; an arboretum; then naturalistic landscaping; a model farm of the finest domestic animals, and, finally, covering most of his 120,000 acres, a forest in which timber would be managed and harvested, and game protected. He named it Biltmore, from *Bildt*, the Dutch town from which the family's forebears came, and *more*, an old English word for rolling, upland country.

To lay out the estate Vanderbilt engaged Fredcrick Law Olmstead, the slight, lame genius then at the very peak of his career in landscape architecture. Though most associated with the design of public parks, including Central Park, New York, and university grounds, it was he who recommended that forest management be instituted here. To develop the practical plan, he advised Vanderbilt to engage young Gifford Pinchot, lately returned from his study of forestry in Europe and eager to prove it would work in America.

Pinchot arrived in 1891. Initially, he found, the estate covered about 7000 acres of rolling hills and bottomland on both sides of the French Broad River. It was composed of some fifty small farms and ten country places which had been owned by impoverished Southern landed aristocracy. The condition of tree growth was very poor. There were defective, fungus-ridden shortleaf pine and remnants of chestnuts, which must have been the leading hardwood in earlier times. But most had been killed by forest fires set by farmers to improve their pastures.

Then Vanderbilt purchased other land in the mountains, including Mount Pisgah, over a mile high, which someone had named for the

Biblical mountain. ("Get thee to the top of Pisgah," Moses was told, "and lift up thine eyes.") This was to be a great wildlife preserve at a time when there were no game laws to protect wildlife in North Carolina, when deer herds were decimated by uncontrolled hunting with dogs, unregulated timber cutting and repeated burning. Vanderbilt stocked the woods with deer and turkey, and the streams with trout. Their descendants are still thriving. Elk and buffalo were brought, too, but they are all gone. Four game protectors, or wardens, like those of the Black Forest, were hired to tend about 25,000 acres each, cutting trails through the laurel for access and keeping poachers out—when possible. Vanderbilt also built a handsome lodge at Buckspring, on the slope of Mount Pisgah, in the style of a Black Forest hunting lodge. The walls of the lodge were hewn and built from a thousand immense chestnut logs; a wagon road four miles long had to be completed first to haul them up from the valley. The lodge remained in family hands until recent years, when it was presented to the Blue Ridge Parkway, which now runs along this right-of-way. For a time the Park Service considered transforming it into a museum, but decided it would be too expensive a project.

Where the western North Carolina forest had not been cut it was a wonderland to delight the most learned of botanists and the most unlearned of travelers. Flowers and shrubs were everywhere, in the densest woods, the open clearings and on the treeless, tangled heath balds of the higher mountaintops. In early May, after gradual spring thawing of winter's chill, the pent-up forest would come rapidly into bloom. Dogwood arrived to brighten the barren woods, like a milky way, with its profusion of white blossoms. The four large, petallike leaves—chalky white, sometimes pink—surround the true flowers, a small bouquet of greenish white or yellow. The moist ground beneath the dogwood would turn white, too, with snow trillium, the flower of the trinity, bearing three leaflets, three green sepals and three petals, and the curious local name of "Stinking Willy." Another early flower was the pink azalea, which the mountaineers called wild honeysuckle; the blossoms do resemble those of the honeysuckle vine but are larger and more vivid. Soon they were joined by the blazing flame, or fire, azalea, which William Bartram described as "the most gay and brilliant flowering shrub yet known." He said that a long time ago, but anyone who has seen the brilliant Southern Appalachian springtime show of these tall and vigorous shrubs, with their clusters of large, trumpet-shaped orange or red flowers, would agree it is still true.

There were flowers in the branches of tall trees, too. By mid-May the clustered creamy-white blossoms, long, thin and ever erect, of the Fraser magnolia studded the mountain hollows. This giant of magnolias, growing to eighty feet tall, was called the "cucumber tree" by the mountain people because of its small cucumberlike fruit, which swells and opens to scatter reddish seeds. Although magnolias are generally found in warm, humid climates, the hardy cucumber tree adapted itself to the coolness of the mountains.

To the exploring botanist and early forester the genius of the Southern Highlands was in the incredible variety of its vegetation. Here the Fraser magnolia of the South was found thriving on the same mountainside as the red spruce of Canadian forests. Professor Asa Gray, of Harvard, said he encountered a greater number of indigenous trees within the thirty miles west of Asheville than could be observed in traveling from England clear across Europe to Turkey, or from the Atlantic Coast to the Rocky Mountains. On dry, exposed slopes at low and middle elevations Professor Gray met scarlet and black oaks and pines, with some sourwood, black gum and locust. In sheltered coves, with depth of soil, below 4500 feet, he found America's great hardwood timber tree, the fast-growing chestnut, with trunk diameters of nine and ten feet, together with oaks, yellow poplar, buckeye, basswood, ash, sugar maple, beech and cherry. Along streams, lower slopes and ridges up to 5000 feet was the hemlock forest, with a mingling of maples, birches, beech, yellow poplar and holly. At higher elevations he journeyed through the northern hardwood forest, mantled in New England species like yellow birch, mountain ash and red maple, into an island of green Canadian vegetation dominated by red spruce and Fraser fir, or balsam.

The botanist and forester both recognized the great variety and size of trees was due largely to moist, warm winds from the Gulf of Mexico combining with the highest altitude in the East. Fog and cloud would hang in the gaps following rainfall, dripping plant-enriching moisture and making these mountains the region of highest precipitation this side of the Pacific Northwest—higher in precipitation than even the Rockies, with their deep snowfall.

In Pisgah Forest, Pinchot found no less than seventy kinds of trees. He and Vanderbilt considered the Pink Beds, a huge bowl of 20,000 acres, a specially favorite section. It derived its name from the pinkish color of the kalmia, or mountain laurel, called ivy by the local folks. They would ride out in late May or June, when the mountains were tufted with white and rosy laurel. On each shrub tiny teacuplike blossoms clustered with oval leaves at the ends of the twigs. The exposed ridges from rim to rim overflowed with purplish-pink thickets of rhododendron (laurel, in mountaineer lexicon). Where fire had not taken its toll were giant virgin yellow poplar, oak, hemlock, hickory, black walnut and beech.

In 1892 Pinchot began to make working forestry plans. He felt the first needs were to exclude cattle, reduce the fire hazard and conduct improvement cuttings, harvesting old and unsound trees that were shading out young growth.

He discarded the old way of logging. No longer would any and all trees, including young growth, be cut in order to bring out the desirable ones the easiest way, leaving erosion and fire hazard behind. Henceforth, "conservative lumbering" would be conducted in Pisgah Forest to assure a new generation of trees growing to maturity.

As the first process in selective logging, Pinchot and his assistant cruised the timber and chose the trees they wanted cut. These they blazed (that is, branded) with a marked ax bearing the stamp of a Circle V. Part of the immediate goal was to have the timber fall where it would harm the future forest the least. They learned that a sound straight tree could be thrown in any direction, a sound leaning tree anywhere in a half circle. Part of the greater problem was to demonstrate that the added cost of caring for the land was relatively small, for Pisgah was to be the proving ground of theoretical forestry for practical lumbermen everywhere in America.

"I knew little more about the conditions necessary for reproducing yellow poplar than a frog knows about football," confessed Pinchot. He was feeling his way in cutting Big Creek, a deep valley directly under Mount Pisgah. There was no previous record in the United States for comparison. But, after poring over his French and German textbooks, he believed natural reproduction would follow cutting if damage from cattle and fire could be minimized. This was contrary to the lumberman's belief that yellow poplar, or any tree, once logged would not grow lumber again. Pinchot was right. He achieved the first known successful effort to gain natural reproduction of a particular tree through scientific forestry: forty years later he would walk through Big Creek and find yellow poplar growing more abundantly than when he blazed it for cutting.

Lumbering in denser forests, which came a little later, was more complicated. Trees had to be selected with the greatest care, roads had to be built and kept roughly in order. After the better parts of the trunks had been cut into logs and as much of the rest as possible into shingle bolts (round sections of the tree from which shingles are split), they were skidded by mules to the roads, loaded on wagons and hauled to the mill. The mill was a small portable circular with fifty-two-inch saw, operated by a twenty-horsepower steam engine. From the saw the lumber went to the Vanderbilt lumberyard. After the available logs about the mill had been sawed up, the engine was used to run a shingle mill, and when all the bolts had been disposed of, the whole plant was moved to another site. The first year's work in 1893 showed a balance of $1220—plus a growing forest behind it.

The forestry project grew in size and attracted national attention. Secretary of Agriculture J. Sterling Morton visited Biltmore and observed, "Mr. Vanderbilt has more workers and a larger budget for his forestry projects than I have at my disposal for the whole Department of Agriculture." Young men attracted to forestry as a career came to take their places as Pinchot's assistants. Among them was Olmstead's own son, Fritz; instead of following his father into landscape architecture, he followed the magnetic Pinchot into the Forest Service.

Once the Pisgah project was well underway, Pinchot elected to set forth to conquer other fields, continuing here only as a consulting forester. In 1895 he brought in his successor, Carl Alwin Schenck, as chief forester to manage the lumbering operations, experimental areas and planting.

Schenck, who became a legend in the mountains, acted and dressed the Prussian. He was slender, wore a Kaiser Wilhelm mustache. He sported a German forest-service uniform, polished leather boots and spurs, and a feathered Tyrolean hat. It was inevitable that he came to be called The Kaiser.

Schenck was a logging forester first and foremost. "The best forestry," he said, "is the forestry that pays most." This was the basis on which he managed the 112,000 acres of Vanderbilt land under his charge. Possibly he was right, for his time, considering that "conservative forestry" was yet to be sold to the lumber industry.

"Naturally, forestry must be remunerative," he said, "if it is to exist anywhere on a large scale. To that end, the products of forestry, the trees, must command a price sufficiently high to make their production remunerative, and the future of tree investments must look bright and must be reasonably free from reckless competition, forest fires and other hazards.

"Is forestry itself not a business? If it is not, it has no room in a country as businesslike as is the United States. And where in the world of the woods is lumbering not a legitimate part of forestry?"

Despite these commercial pronouncements, he conducted painstaking experiments in forest regeneration. He started in 1895 on the steepest slope, which had been cleared for farming sixty years before and subsequently abandoned. This area and many other worn-out fields, pastures and orchards became outdoor laboratories in which Schenck tested twenty species of hardwoods and twelve of softwoods.

One badly eroded plot, for example, was transformed into a plantation of three species of pine (shortleaf, Norway and Virginia). In another, he tested Douglas-fir, Colorado blue spruce, European spruce, silver fir and white pine and learned that white pine was superior to all in that setting. Elsewhere, in the midst of a hardwood plantation, he planted 5000 white pines, the first two-year-old seedlings on American soil. And on another plot he tried alternating two-year-old white pines raised at Biltmore with four-year-old white pines brought from Germany.

In 1908 he invited lumbermen, foresters, state officials, botanists and newsmen to a three-day Biltmore Forest Fair, showing the results of his work in sixty experimental plots. Eighty-five came. It was a large and enthusiastic rally. "Many of the visitors declared that they have learned more about forestry during the past days than they could possibly have learned in a lifetime had this opportunity not been afforded them," reported the Asheville *Gazette-News*. And Schenck, of course, was proud to show that his lumbering operations were profitable.

Schenck trained many future leaders of his profession at the Biltmore Forest School, which he operated from 1898 to 1913. Students came from all over the country and found him an inspiring teacher. He would lecture three or four hours a day at the little schoolhouse in the Pink Beds. For the remainder of many days the students would be strung out on horseback behind him, traveling full speed while he tended to his duties as forest manager, which he explained to them at frequent stops. The Vanderbilt estate covered 200 square miles and apparently Schenck, with his coattails flapping, was determined to lead his saddle-weary embryo foresters over every mile of it.

The curriculum, however, covered a wide range. Dr. Homer House taught botany. Government and university lecturers came to speak on timber preservation, geology, entomology, zoology, climatology, economics and law. Field studies included forest nurseries, transplanting, surveying, logging, furniture manufacture, fish and wildlife and, of necessity, how to kill and skin rattlesnakes.

Schenck solicited the support of lumbermen for his school but they turned instead to the Yale School of Forestry (originally endowed, ironically, by Gifford Pinchot's parents) and other universities, which thoroughly frustrated the Prussian.

In time, he and Pinchot developed sharp differences. Schenck claimed the "infantile maladies" of American forestry were due largely to agitation led by Pinchot in establishing a distinction between forestry and lumbering. But possibly their primary point of difference was in their judgment of the human species. Recording a trip they made together in the Pink Beds, where they found a number of farmers squatting in the most fertile sections, Schenck wrote, "It dawned upon me that the real owner of Pisgah Forest was not George W. Vanderbilt, but these mountaineers, who were using his property for farming, pasturing, and hunting at their own pleasure. Pinchot apparently took these inroads on the rights of the proprietor for granted. To my own European feeling they were equal to theft and robbery."

Pinchot, on the other hand, noted that Schenck, "being a German with official training, had far less understanding of the mountaineers than he had of the mountains and woods. He thought of them as peasants."

Pinchot was endowed with a consummate faith in people. It was the source of his strength, in the same sense as with Winston Churchill, who would write, "I was brought up in my father's house to believe in democracy. 'Trust the people.' That was his message." Thus, Pinchot, who had heard such a message, too, believed in the mountaineers, despite their impoverishment, backwardness and sheer abuse of the land.

In a way, these mountain folk, through their very mistreatment of the land, were responsible for establishment of National Forests in the East.

Many a mountaineer and his family slept and dwelt in a one-room cabin, which he had built himself, alongside a stream, hugging the mountainside against the wind. He believed in the family as the all-important unit in social life and might have had ten children within this single room. The cabin had one door and no windows, or at best an open window covered with split boards. Within, an open fireplace served as cookstove and furnace. Homespun was the common wear and anyone under the age of nineteen in shoes was either moving to the city or getting married. Hookworm, typhoid and tuberculosis were rife through hills and hollows.

These people, who lived in isolated poverty for generations, started drifting down before the Revolutionary War and in the early 1800's. Some were Scotch-Irish Presbyterians, who left Pennsylvania to find religious and civil liberty. Others came from Maryland and Virginia at a time when those colonies were growing more tobacco than was profitable and only the cheapest kind of labor, that is, slave labor, could make it pay. The yeoman farmer could not compete and drifted farther and farther into the southerly backwoods.

They brought a manner of speech with them, a direct carry-over of old English, almost as it was spoken in the times of Elizabeth and Shakespeare. It survived into our time, a combination of a language hundreds of years old with the freshness of the raw frontier. A bag was a "poke," a comical person an "antic," a sweetheart a "donna," and when a man gave notice of a meeting by word of mouth he "norated." They spoke with a lyric softness and utility of words. "I thought shorely undoubtedly of a sartin hit war so," one might say. Or, "I didn't fault him for hit."

The mountaineer lived off the land, hunting deer, bear, rabbit, squirrel, turkey, and fishing in the streams. He used forest wood for building his log cabin, for his fuel, the butt of his rifle, his furniture and the cover of his still. But he knew little, or absolutely nothing, about care of the land, as he cleared the mountainside to raise corn, fatten and feed his hogs, cattle and mules. After the Civil War, he tried tobacco. It required rich new ground and for a while paid high prices, till the market dropped and the ground gave way, seamed with gullies.

"Ordinary farming on these mountain slopes cannot exist permanently and should never exist at all," Secretary of Agriculture James Wilson warned in his report of 1901, which Theodore Roosevelt transmitted to Congress with a strong recommendation for national Forest Reserves in the Southeast.

"No more than 10 per cent of the land of this region has a surface slope of less than 10 degrees (approximately 2 feet in 10), while 24 per cent of it has been cleared," Secretary Wilson continued. "In this region land with slopes exceeding this cannot be successfully cultivated for any considerable time, because its surface is rapidly washed into the rivers below by the heavy rains, and the same agency leaches out and carries to the sea its more soluble and fertile ingredients."

Already the valley lands had largely been cleared, and the farmers were advancing up the mountain slopes, clearing patches nearly to the summits. They planted a field in corn, grain, then grass, then within five or ten years abandoned it to weeds and gullies. A forest which took centuries to grow perished in less than a decade. Soil which accumulated over a thousand years was cleared, cultivated, abandoned and on the downward road to the sea. From one of these thousands of cleared fields more soil was sometimes removed by a single heavy rain than during the preceding centuries while it was densely forested.

As the streams flowed toward the sea they removed the soil of valley farms, too; they widened and plowed new channels across the fields, damaging thousands of acres of the most productive valley land.

"It is only a question of time, to be measured not in centuries but in years," the Secretary warned, "when, unless this policy is changed, there will be no forests in this region except on the small remnants—say 10 per cent of the whole—where the mountain slopes are too precipitous and rocky to make the cultivation of the land possible, even by an Appalachian mountaineer and his hoe."

This point contributed to the ultimate enactment of the Weeks Law in 1911. For ten years Secretary Wilson's report, in which Pinchot's hand was strongly evident, was a principal source of arguments to bring the National Forests east. It proposed to protect the mountain slopes of the Southern Appalachians within a Forest Reserve, in this way safeguarding the valleys and gentler slopes for cultivation by the native farmer, who would continue to own the bottomlands. Secretary Wilson called it a national problem since, "The dangers growing out of the policy now in force are national in character, as are also the benefits of the policy now advised."

On passage of the Weeks Law, this area outside Asheville was established as the Pisgah Purchase Unit. Five years later two other units, the Mount Mitchell and Unaka, were merged with it. It was not the first National Forest in the East, but was the first one composed of land not originally in the public domain. That is, here for the first time the Federal Government invoked its new authority to purchase private land for the protection of river headwaters and define it as National Forest.

Within Pisgah National Forest, which extends over an area roughly 100 miles long and forty miles wide, the most historic section is the Pisgah Ranger District. More than half its 160,000 acres were given to the government by Mrs. George W. Vanderbilt in 1916, following her husband's death. The remainder was purchased over the years until the late 1930's, mostly from lumber companies, which felt they were quite through with the land after once logging it. The largest tract was acquired from the Sunburst Lumber Company; the National Forest obtained 36,000 acres, while other land and the mill at the town of Sunburst were bought by the Champion Fibre and Paper Company, which is generally highly regarded for its forestry practices.

Today second-growth timber is harvested on land once managed by Gifford Pinchot and Carl Alwin Schenck, without damaging the forest or really interfering with the enjoyment of visitors, who total over a million yearly on the Pisgah District. During May and June it becomes a vast flower garden, rhododendron and azalea, immense kalmia, dogwood, redbud and cucumber magnolia blooming mile after mile. During summer clear, cold mountain streams with numerous cascades and tumbling falls add to the forest beauty, while the cool woods offer a haven to campers. And in autumn the purple haze and blaze of color in the foliage form a panorama to rival New England.

Speaking of camping, or of sight-seeing, one of the choice spots is in the Pink Beds, just off Route 276. It is about eighteen miles from Asheville via the valley of the French Broad River and about the same distance from Brevard. A plaque marks the site of that first forestry school started by Dr. Schenck. You are almost at the base of Looking Glass Rock, a massive forested boulder and a landmark of these mountains. Within a couple of miles you can picnic or swim at Sliding Rock Falls, where youngsters love to slide over the watery rocks. Also nearby, Looking Glass Falls cascades 276 feet over a rocky precipice.

Here, too, you are just below Wagon Road Gap, joining one of the newest links of the Blue Ridge Parkway, which follows the crest of the Blue Ridge Range through highly scenic parts of the National Forest as it journeys westward to the Great Smoky Mountains. Crossing the Parkway onto Route 112, you will reach Frying Pan Campground, over a mile above sea level, the best spot for cool nights and mountain hiking.

If you are not a camper, there is still place for you, and a fine place, too, at Pisgah National Forest Inn, on the slope of Pisgah Ledge, elevation 5120 feet. In lieu of tennis, golf or swimming are the restful atmosphere, excellent American food, prepared by Leslie and Leda Kirschner, and leisurely walking trails through wildflowers and woodland. From here you can climb the summit of Mount Pisgah and see the world—well, five states, anyway.

When the Vanderbilt land was acquired by the Forest Service, it was designated as a National Game Preserve and remained closed to hunting from 1916 to 1932 in order to stock up deer herds. At one period the Forest Service ran a "fawn farm," raising about 200 fawns yearly on bottle feeding. As the herds grew in number, Pisgah deer were made available to game departments in other Southern states and their descendants are now scrambling over the countryside from Virginia to Oklahoma. Since 1932, game hunts have been held for deer, bear and smaller animals every fall, except during a four-year period when a severe epidemic of shipping fever killed about half the deer herd.

Mrs. Vanderbilt shared her husband's interest in the mountains and was drawn to the problems of the mountain people. Observing that most homes had looms, she inspired the establishment of Biltmore Industries in order to widen the opportunities open to them. Their weaving proved successful not only as a craft but as a business venture which is still thriving. Another pioneer in stimulating pride and profit in craftsmanship was Miss Frances Goodrich, a social worker. Early in the century she started Allanstand Cottage in Asheville to bring "healthful excitement" to mountaineer ladies. It became evident to the people, who had hand-hewn and hand-made almost everything they owned, that they could not only use and swap such products, but sell them. Other shops arose. In 1930 the Southern Highland Handicraft Guild was formed to preserve the better traditions and to encourage creative use of materials. It has done these jobs well. Allanstand in Asheville is the Guild's chief display and marketing center; you will not go wrong shopping there for jewelry, wood carving, pottery, wrought iron or weaving. For five days every summer, at the Craftsman's Fair in Asheville, craftsmen set up their looms, benches and wheels en masse to whittle, sew and carve in full public view.

There is another mountain craft deftly practiced, though not in such full view. The character of the country and the character of some of these talented folk being what they are, western North Carolina has ranked for many years high among the moonshine centers of the universe. This probably started when a few of the mountain men considered the yield of their steep land in bushels was mighty poor and decided a measurement in gallons would be more profitable. Or when others allowed that, while they didn't dislike work, exactly, outwitting the law would surely add zest to it. Moonshine, being tax free, has a flourishing market. It costs less than store-bought whisky, if you can stand the taste.

Is moonshine brewed in our National Forest? Ted Seeley, who is now ranger of the Pisgah District, won't say that it is, but won't say it isn't, either. However, during the thirties, one still was discovered by the district ranger about every two weeks. In those days, before galvanized iron pots and portable oil burners, revenuers would track their way in by following telltale wood smoke curling up from the forest. But the ranger (whose functions do not include revenuing) had a silent, unwritten agreement with his constituents not to wreck a still unless he had to. In a way, he hesitated about interfering with the economic life of the community; besides, he knew that his moonshiners might fire the woods if he acted rashly. So whenever the ranger discovered a still he would tack up a sign, "Get this still out of here within ten days."

Speaking of present practices, let us not overlook the Carolina caged-bear routine. Gracing the foreground of the historic gateway to Pisgah National Forest on Route 276 is a roadside souvenir and refreshment stand. Here you can buy a Coke, hand it to a bear through the bars of his cage and watch him drink it. The purpose of his presence is to attract your interest and trade.

Western North Carolina has a variety of such crude attractions. One is the reptile "garden" on Route 19, which everyone who loves wild creatures should see—not because it is good, but to observe how the animals, assorted scraggly deer, a bear and snakes, are cared for. There are the "Twin Yona" (Cherokee for twin bear) caged on the roadside in the Indian Reservation between the National Forest and Great Smoky Mountains National Park. And like displays of wildlife before gift shops and gasoline stations in Maggie Valley.

How are these creatures captured? And how are they cared for? I asked the State of North Carolina for its policy on such things and received a copy of the application for a permit to trap an animal, along with the regulations for holding it legally in captivity. "North

106

Carolina law prohibits the taking of cub bears at any time or in any manner," the State Wildlife Resources Commission advised. "Most of our roadside bears are purchased from Indians who can take them legally on their reservation. The sentiment of the Commission is strongly against keeping bears or any other wild creatures in captivity—outside a zoo." (Responsible persons in the Smokies, however, seriously question whether Cherokee Indians are indeed responsible —or simply are the easiest to blame.)

I discussed this with the Humane Society of the United States. It considers this frightening handful of gas stations, gift shops and zoo-owning North Carolinians as the worst in the country for mistreatment of wild creatures.

Enough of this unpleasantness. Write your Congressman. Write the governor, if you live in North Carolina.

Let us proceed to the Biltmore estate, the remainder of the vast Vanderbilt holdings, 12,000 acres of sheer Southern and worldly glory, commingled to form a showpiece of America. The approach road winds three miles through planted pine, hemlock and hardwoods, rhododendron and kalmia, landscaped by Frederick Law Olmstead. Before the house was built a three-mile spur had first to be erected from Biltmore station to transport construction materials to the site. Then a thousand workmen, including many artisans from Europe, were engaged; they worked five years, 1890 to 1895, cutting and fitting the Indiana limestone and executing the detailed carvings which rise to the peaked slate roofs and lofty chimneys. On the interior, the 250-room house contains a treasure of paintings, tapestries, statuary, porcelain, furniture from early Renaissance through Empire, and portraits by John Singer Sargent of personalities associated with this house.

Part of the estate is occupied by Biltmore Dairy Farms with its 1200 purebred Jersey cattle. George Vanderbilt was interested in improved methods of breeding and brought the finest stock from the Isle of Jersey. At one time sheep, horses, chickens and pigs were raised here, too.

The Biltmore grounds were managed by Chauncey Delos Beadle, who came to work under Olmstead in 1890 and remained for sixty years as superintendent of the estate. His artistic touch is most evident in the Italian garden and its formal aquatic pools; the four-acre English walled garden, and the azalea garden, with specimens which he collected all over the world.

These are probably the finest gardens in America, and perhaps in the whole world. Yes, we are dealing in superlatives. And if the sun must set on these Appalachians, let it set gently while we stand on the terrace, bordered with wisteria and trumpet creeper, and admire the view to the south and west of Pisgah and its healthy, growing forest.

# CHAPTER EIGHT

# *Woody, the Barefoot Ranger*

Ranger Arthur Woody was quite content to stay put in north Georgia, where he could watch trees, wildlife and people grow, and walk about unshod so his feet could breathe and feel the ground, and let the rest of the world revolve around him.

Which it did. For thirty years he presided over the hills of the Chattahoochee while governors, judges, Congressmen, preachers, professors, writers and foresters came to call on him at the little town of Suches. When he died in 1946 his funeral services at a back-country church cemetery were attended by 1500 persons from all parts of his state—the equivalent of 10,000 attending a funeral in a New York or Chicago cathedral.

This was Woody. I heard so many stories about him in the Georgia hills that for a time I almost thought somebody had invented him. Then I learned to believe them all without question. It happened this way. His great achievement, restocking deer in the mountains, has given rise to a variety of tales. The principal one is that he was inspired as a child when he saw his father kill a large buck, the last native whitetail in the state. "But how," I asked a friend of mine who had been a friend of his, "can you be sure that was the last deer of all?" "Because Woody told me so," he answered. "That's how I *know* it was the last one."

Woody was called "Ranger," even by his wife June, or sometimes "Kingfish" by his friends. At his best he was no prize winner for looks or dress, being six feet tall and 250 pounds, with a low center of gravity. He wore wide galluses to hold up his work pants but the top button, slightly south of center, was usually open for breathing space. Although he owned a pair of shoes, he would put them on only when the mountain trail was rocky or when he went to town. Dignitaries and Forest Service officials might or might not find him in his bare feet. They were welcome to take off their shoes, too, and learned that eating unshod helped in digesting the ham, chicken, biscuits, corn pone, squash, beans and such dishes which they were served at Woody's table.

As a youngster, Woody tramped, hunted and fished the ridges, coves and creeks. He and his neighbors belonged to a race of pioneers who moved into the headwaters of the Toccoa River while it was still part of the Cherokee nation. Few people outside Georgia realize the Indians were self-governing here until the 1830's, or that such beautiful mountain country extends this far south. Yet the very name of the Chattahoochee National Forest comes from the Cherokee word for "Flowering Rock," denoting the many waterfalls tumbling in the highlands, the last of appreciable size in the long Appalachian chain.

For a time Woody attended North Georgia College in Dahlonega, which his great-grandfather helped establish, but shortly gave it up to help his father run cattle in the mountains. In 1912, when he was twenty-seven and the rugged boundaries of the Chattahoochee were just being established, he went to work for the Forest Service. It was a time when a government man was a revenuer or not otherwise to be trusted, but it was the beginning of a career in which he would help to survey, purchase and protect a quarter of a million acres. His first job was measuring boundary lines, then he became a forest guard and, in 1918, district ranger.

For almost twenty-five years he never went south of Gainesville, the outpost of the mountains. Once friends suggested he go to Florida for his health. "Me go down there and drink wiggle-tail water?" And then, with a sense of home and place a man like him would feel, "What's the use to live if it can't be right here?" He loved his home country and knew every bit of it. Brook trout, which he called "specks," were his favorite fish. "I know the big trout by name," he said, "and if I'm smart I can get them on a hook."

As a ranger, Woody considered game and fish equally as important as timber; his homily on this subject to young foresters who trained under him was, "We should look at forests as a source of 'good' as well as 'wood.'" I wonder, what would Carl Alwin Schenck, the Prussian *Forstmeister*, have thought of this roughhewn mountaineer who refused to wear a dress uniform or to measure forestry in terms of lumber profits?

Yet his philosophy prevailed on one of the largest ranger districts in the Forest System. Operations were not always in strict accord with prescribed methodology. He ignored rules and regulations and

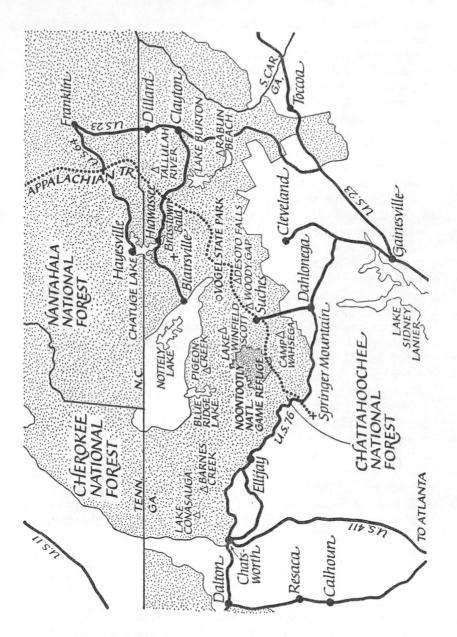

*The Blue Ridge Spilling South into Georgia*

requests for written reports. After all, Woody defined an expert as "an average boy away from home." But his district excelled in fire prevention, timber management and game protection. Once he was honored at a formal dinner for a nationally outstanding fire record (of only four acres burned in a year). Tell us, Ranger, the toast-master asked, how did you achieve this fine record? "Well, you have just got to know your people," Woody confided to his audience. "I fish with the men, buy candy for the kids and tell each and every woman if I wasn't married I'd sure like to make love to her." (He also kept a bloodhound chained under his back steps to track down firebugs and game poachers.)

Woody was the moving force in restoring deer to north Georgia and trout to many of its streams. What had happened to the wildlife? In about seventy-five years, following the forced evacuation of the Indians, the American whites, with typical disregard for natural resources, had decimated the deer herds until, as Woody said, his father killed the last one.

He started the first restocking with his own money, buying three scrawny Western mule deer left by a carnival in a nearby town, and buying whitetails soon after. He was not poor or dependent on his ranger's pay. On the side, he traded and loaned cows, farms and money. An unlikely business for a forester, perhaps, but he used it in his informal way to advance the wildlife cause and the National Forest. If one of his neighbors killed game out of season, he fore-closed the loan on his farm. He picked up more than one parcel of land within the Chattahoochee boundary for the government by fore-closing on promissory notes.

In 1927 Woody went to the Pisgah National Game Preserve in North Carolina and obtained five fawns, delicate creatures requiring as much care as human babies, to the point of being bottle-fed warm milk every six hours. When one needed a stronger formula the King-fish patiently awoke at midnight and six A.M. to mix the canned milk. He fixed bedding for them and a pen to keep the deer in and the dogs out. The five bottle-fed fawns, Nimble, Billy, Bessie, Nancy and Bunnie-Girl, became so familiar around the Woody place they learned to open the screen door and walk into the house.

Woody kept acquiring deer and placing them in the mountains surrounding Suches. In so doing, he made it fashionable for his neigh-bors to care for these beauties of the wild. Georgians thrilled at the sight of graceful deer jumping a fence or browsing in a clearing, and welcomed them to roam at will through their yards and orchards.

The herd grew in number. Under an agreement with the state, which administers wildlife protection and management, the ranger devised a system of gates and patrol for the 40,000-acre Rock Creek Refuge. Although in his day he had taken his share of turkey and deer, he now tried to postpone opening the woods to hunting. And then one year a team of wildlife specialists arrived from Atlanta. They feared the herd was growing beyond the carrying capacity of the land, a condition which would make a hunting season useful and desirable. Woody knew that one side of Rock Creek Lake had many natural deer signs, while the other side had none. Slyly, he guided them to *his* side—and they agreed to postpone the hunt.

But by 1941 about 2000 deer were sharing the forest community with the red and gray fox, woodchuck, rabbit, squirrel, possum, grouse and quail. That year the first limited deer-hunting season was held. It saddened Woody. Standing by the checking station, he watched the successful hunters bring in their bucks. "Oh, that's old Nemo," he murmured almost tearfully as one was weighed and recorded. "I've been seeing him almost every month since I put him in years ago. But never any more."

Woody had various ways of discouraging hunters. Once he found an immense bear track. The bear may have been gone, but he proceeded to enshrine its footprint. He made a cement cast of it, then affixed a metal handle; now he had a portable, imprintable bear track. He carried the cast in his pickup truck and imprinted paths, trails and roads—with a fresh sign of bear to frighten the boldest hunter. "That bear track," he allowed later, "is just about as effective as three game wardens."

He left the mark of his life's work amid the trees as well as wildlife. The prime example is at Sosebee Cove. In 1925 he negotiated the purchase of these 152 acres from Alonzo Sosebee, who had lived in the cove all his life and was then over seventy-five. A "cove," in the native lexicon, is a small valley. Likewise, what you may call a brook is a "run"; a grass meadow summit is a "bald"; a peak is a "top" or "knob," and a crown with a tangle of shrubs is a "slick." Woody had admired Sosebee Cove for years; he believed it was the best stand of yellow poplar in the state. The yellow poplar, or tulip tree, is one of the largest in the East, which reaches its greatest height in such sheltered coves of the Southern Appalachians. Sometimes it grows 150 feet high with diameter of eight to ten feet. It rises eighty to 100 feet before reaching the first branch, which makes it the prize hardwood timber of the South since the passing of the chestnut. Woody insisted on showing the cove to his superiors whenever they visited his district, asking that he be allowed to purchase it. When he did, it cost ten dollars an acre, the highest price the Forest Service paid in those days. But it was worth it, even though the cove was practically inaccessible and fire protection negligible. W. W. Ashe, a pioneer forester who knew a good tree when he saw it, visited in 1926 and judged that Woody had acquired the best stand of second-growth yellow poplar in the nation.

Today the stand averages 40,000 board feet per acre. The timber alone would be worth at least $2000 per acre, or over $300,000 for the tract. But there are no plans to cut it, for it has been set aside as a memorial to Arthur Woody. The forest floor, once trod by this barefoot ranger, is carpeted with wildflowers. The birdfoot violet, with fan-shaped leaves, rises from its short, fleshy stem to bring the touch of lilac color to forest springtime. Around it are other violets, purple-violet to lavender, occasionally white, all small and modest herbs. In early spring the low growing, aromatic wild ginger extends its solitary brown and purple flower, shaped like a large bell, between heartlike leaves. On the arching stalk of the delicate Dutchman's-breeches, finely drawn petals expand into spurs like a pair of miniature white or pinkish breeches tipped with yellow. The bloodroot, a delicate plant of the poppy family, blooms with a large flower of many white or pink petals, while its underground stem contains a juice as bright and red as blood. Late summer and autumn is the time of asters, spreading their abundant colors. Earliest is the white wood aster, its two-foot stalk trimmed with smooth, slender leaves and a cluster of little flowers at the top. Then comes the blue wave aster, thriving among the brown litter of old leaves, and a dozen others with flowers of purple, violet and pink.

Here and there in Sosebee Cove a stunted chestnut rises out of the roots of an old stump to tell a stark and mournful tale. When Ranger Woody was a hunting mountain boy, the chestnut was possibly the most loved and useful tree in America. It was everywhere in the Eastern forest, a towering giant. Its lumber was straight-grained and durable, suited for many uses, while its nuts were a delicacy to squirrels, bears, wild turkeys and the patrons of the well-known figure of his day, the vendor of roasted chestnuts. Then the mysterious chestnut blight, a fungus, arrived without warning from Asia. It was first discovered in New York in 1904, but spread rapidly, causing a forest disaster far greater than either white-pine blister rust or Dutch elm blight. In the Southern mountains the chestnut was almost totally eliminated by the early thirties. Now these gaunt and ghostly fellows strain to survive, but the blight has already claimed them.

Woody's day has ended. Though he could hardly be surpassed for sheer instinct and foresight, his successor, today's forester, has the added guidance of science and research in all their forms. Thus, far more than in Woody's time, modern forestry on private and public land is changing the face of Georgia, and of the whole South.

Now, lands denuded in the cotton era are being planted in timber; so are farms that once grew tobacco, corn and peanuts but have lain idle for years.

Now, pine fields once bled for turpentine are being managed for a continuous yield of pulpwood and a final crop of saw timber—as well as turpentine.

The beauty of modern forestry in the South is that it cares about this region, which for so long has been abused and self-abused. Many years ago when lumber companies came to harvest the virgin pine, their stockholders, who often lived in the North, insisted on quick dividends. They built the sorriest kind of towns, the sorriest kind of railroad tracks. The whole industry was based on a short life that left the land and its people in agony and impoverishment.

Modern paper and pulp corporations, in sharp contrast, have invested heavily in Southern land and mills. They employ hundreds of foresters to manage their own holdings and to encourage small landowners to grow timber as a crop. Through research, they have developed chemical by-products, new uses for wood and new processes to produce pulp from scrubby hardwoods.

Tree farms, on privately owned woodlands, have helped reshape the Southern landscape. The best of these are certified as participants in the American Tree Farm System, an industry-sponsored program which encourages landowners to protect their woods from fire, disease, insects and overgrazing, and to harvest their timber crops wisely, insuring a continual yield.

The tree-farm movement, which began twenty years ago, is administered nationally by the American Forest Products Industries. It co-ordinates the work of 1600 industry foresters who serve as inspectors to assure that standards are met. Tree farms now encompass 55,000,000 acres throughout the country, with an additional 2,000,-

115

ooo acres being added to the program every year. But tree farms have probably benefited the South more than any section. In Georgia certified tree farms total 700, covering 5,000,000 acres of timberland. Most of these (615) are small properties of less than 5000 acres each, while large corporations (the remaining eighty-five) own most of the land (over 4,900,000 acres). However, in giving credit where credit is due, let us note the health, vigor and regeneration of these holdings, and the contribution of their owners to the new face and pride of the South.

Growing conditions in the South, with its warm climate and high humidity, are near ideal. Eleven species of pine thrive in Georgia alone, with its large continuous forest areas from the northern mountains to lower coastal plains. Within fifteen to twenty years after planting, a pine will measure eight to twelve inches in diameter and be ready for a pulp thinning—or to have its neighbors thinned. Sixty years after planting, which is practically tomorrow as foresters measure time, the "crop tree" will reach saw-timber size.

But Mississippi, rather than Georgia or any other state, has shown the greatest forestry progress. And in Mississippi the Forest Service has underway the most spectacular of all its projects, although not on Forest Service land.

Poor Mississippi has had the longest road to travel. But already it leads the nation in number of tree farms (2500 with 2,800,000 acres under management) and is pressing to develop a one-billion-dollar forest industry—an effort which involves bringing 6,000,000 acres out of idleness and into timber.

The big Forest Service story is in the area with the lowest per-capita income ($600) and worst land conditions in the United States, the Yazoo River region centered around Oxford, in northern Mississippi.

One hundred and twenty-five years ago this was virgin wilderness of clear streams, pine and hardwood forest, inhabited by the Chickasaw and Choctaw. Then came the young sons of Virginia and Carolina planters to clear the wilderness. At first their clean-tilled crops of cotton and corn dotted only the valley plains. Then they cultivated the hillsides. Erosion began. But in that glory day of cotton and culture scant attention was paid to the unstable sandy loam surface, called loess, sliding into the channels of the Coldwater, Tallahatchie, Yocona and Yalobusha.

From the lush prosperous days, both the land and fortunes of the

116

people deteriorated—and not solely as a result of Civil War. Tenant farming later replaced slavery and land conditions worsened. Hills never meant for farming were cleared, burned and plowed. Railroads cut through the forests without regard for future stands.

One hundred million tons of sterile sand washed down the hillsides every year, covering bottomland fields. The philosophy and practice of landowners under these circumstances was to abandon their fields as you might a worn-out wagon or an old mule.

In 1936 the U. S. Corps of Engineers began to build the first of four dams. They controlled floodwater, but were in danger of becoming sand traps. They could have little lasting effect without treating the land, so in 1947 the broadened Yazoo-Little Tallahatchie Project was launched, with forestry and farm conservation included. That first year the Forest Service planted 200,000 young loblolly pine trees on private land, with owners' co-operation.

The second year close to 2,000,000 pine seedlings were planted. Now 50,000,000 trees are planted in a year. Imagine 50,000,000 of anything! And the goal is to step up to 80,000,000 plantings a year until 1,000,000 acres of wasteland are reclaimed.

Thousands of gullies of gaping red earth and loess that resembled miniature Grand Canyons have been plugged with fast-growing loblolly pine, which stabilizes the soil with its web of roots and mat of needles. Today these hillsides represent something of value, to be acquired rather than discarded. Not principally for cotton and corn, but for tree farms. Gully control is reducing problems of sedimentation and floods, making clean, clear water available for irrigation and industry. With improved land and water conditions, Deep Dixie can attract the new industries it needs.

Besides changing the face of the South, modern forestry is changing the size and substance of trees themselves. Through the science of genetics, hybrids, new breeds and superior strains are making their appearance, and in a generation or two will cover the managed forests. Genetic studies have proven that such factors as crookedness and size of branches are inherited, that very likely the quality of wood is, too.

The most plentiful Southern pine, for instance, is loblolly (*Pinus taeda*), the "old field pine." It often grows in moist depressions (called loblollies in the old days), developing a clean, straight trunk and reaching heights of fifty to seventy-five feet in thirty years. Within seventy years, under favorable conditions, it produces 40,000 to 50,-

117

ooo board feet of timber per acre. And because it has a thick bark and grows on low sites or in damp soils, it is relatively resistant to fire.

Its cousin, the slash pine (*Pinus caribaea*), is probably the most profitable of all Southern timber trees, producing heavy stands and high-quality resin. It is found on low grounds or moist "slashes" (not only in the South but in the Caribbean, which explains its scientific name). It is a rapid grower, too, reaching a height of forty-five feet in twenty years. But slash pine is subject to red heart disease, causing loss in young stands.

Geneticists at the Seed Tree Testing Laboratory at Macon, Georgia, operated by the state and Forest Service, are presently breeding a new tree, a slash-loblolly, combining the best features of both trees, through controlled pollination and nursery planting. It will grow higher, faster, produce better-grade timber and have qualities of disease and fire resistance. Geneticists in Mississippi are crossing loblolly and slash, both of which are affected with fusiform rust, with shortleaf pine, which is resistant to this disease.

All of which may add up to the greatest transformation in the South since the time of the fellow who presumably first said, "I believe cotton will be a profitable crop." Yet the sequence of the modern scientific revolution surely began in the time of a barefoot forest ranger.

Woody's country, the Chattahoochee National Forest and its environs, encompasses superb scenery and good people like himself. At least 125 types of trees grow in the wooded valleys and highlands. In spring the beauty of the mountains is accented by blooming dogwood, redbud, mountain laurel, azalea and rhododendron. Summers are much cooler than Georgia's coastal plains. Autumns combine southerly mildness with the color changing of hardwood trees. And waters flow swiftly and clear, tumbling into creeks, then streams and growing into mighty rivers. The direction of their flow is determined by the Blue Ridge Divide, carved through the rocks by nature millions of years ago. The Savannah flows south to the Atlantic; the Chattahoochee south to the Gulf of Mexico; the Toccoa north to the Tennessee and then on to the Mississippi.

The north Georgia scene has changed since Woody's day. No longer is it isolated. Paved roads course through the heart of the Forest. A turnpike extends most of the way from Atlanta. For that matter, more people in Atlanta, and everywhere in the Southeast,

118

have the time, money and automobiles to get around and enjoy their countryside. On a brisk weekend, 10,000 boats will take to the waters of Lake Sidney Lanier, outside Gainesville.

Starting from Gainesville, the gateway to the mountains (as well as fryer-chicken capital of the world), a choice foray into the National Forest follows Routes 11 and 75 through Cleveland. You will pass Dukes Creek Gold Mine, where Ben Parks discovered gold in 1828, starting the first big rush. In the midst of a lush, green valley, you arrive at the Nacoochee Indian Mound, 150 feet long by twenty feet high and forty feet wide, an earthen testament to an ancient Cherokee community. Here the Cherokee lived, hunted the abundant game and found safety in the high mountains from hostile tribes like the Creek.

These Indians were citizens of an enlightened nation. They had their own capital at New Echota, in northwest Georgia, their own constitution (adopted in 1827 and patterned after the Federal Constitution), and sent delegates to Washington, where they were received on the same footing as diplomats of a foreign nation.

The historic hero of the Cherokee nation was Sequoyah, the inventor of the Cherokee alphabet. He was raised in Tennessee, then moved to the area around Dalton, Georgia. He spent twelve years (1809–21) devising an eighty-five-character written alphabet. At first the Indians balked, then accepted it, and thousands learned to read and write. The Book of Genesis was printed in Cherokee, and so was a newspaper, the *Phoenix*. Sequoyah moved to Oklahoma with his people, becoming a legendary figure there as well as in the Southeast.

When gold was discovered in 1828, prospectors, adventurers and settlers flocked into north Georgia. They seized the Cherokee lands. Indians who resisted were killed or forcibly removed. In 1835 the Cherokee were offered $5,000,000 and new lands in the West for their Georgia holdings. General Winfield Scott arrived with 4000 troops, and was joined with 4000 local volunteers, to effect the ruthless removal of the Cherokees. Realizing their cause was futile, they acquiesced. The site of New Echota, just outside Calhoun, in the foothills of the western district of the Chattahoochee National Forest, is marked by a granite shaft, commemorating a dismal chapter in pioneer relations with the Indians.

From Nacoochee you can drive up through Unicoi State Park to Ruby Falls, a beautiful 300-foot cascade with new picnic tables and campsites near the base. Then, follow Route 19 to Dahlonega (Dahlon'-a-gah), once the center of the Georgia gold rush. The fields around it yielded $60,000,000's worth of gold and were so productive a Federal mint was established in 1838. But in 1849 the miners were lured west to California. The mint assayer pleaded with them not to leave. "There's gold in them thar hills," he said, pointing to the mountains around him. The Gold Museum, at the foot of Crown Mountain, displays assorted gadgets used in early mining and gold in various forms—rock, dust, nugget and coin. Gold Rush Day, held in October when mountain color reaches its peak, features a re-enactment of Dahlonega's day of glory. And everyone, visitors included, turns to panning the streams and sluice boxes.

From here drive north on Route 60 to the Cooper Creek Scenic Area, which the Forest Service has set aside for the wilderness hiker and camper. Within 1240 primitive acres you are enveloped in virgin stands of hemlock, white pine, southern pines and oaks, with flowering rhododendron heavily banked alongside the flashing waters of Cooper Creek.

Then to Vogel State Park and adjacent Lake Winfield Scott Recreation Area, operated by private management on a "special use" permit from the Forest Service. Facilities here include family cottages and campsites, swimming, fishing and hiking. And a dance pavilion, the propriety of which some people may question in a National Forest. Winfield Scott makes a good base for side trips through the mountains. The Appalachian Trail passes this way en route to its southern terminus at Springer Mountain (elevation 3820 feet), within the National Forest. Georgia's ninety-mile section of the Trail is managed by the Georgia Appalachian Trail Club, in co-operation with the Forest Service. The outstanding peak on the Trail, Blood Mountain (elevation 4463 feet) lies at Neel Gap, within walking distance of Winfield Scott. It derives its name from the Creek-Cherokee battles: they fought on Slaughter Mountain and the blood rolled down Blood Mountain.

Here you are really in the heart of Ranger Woody's home country. At Woody Gap, a memorial plaque was erected to him, but some crude individual carried it off. However, a more important memorial is the magnificent view of Black Mountain and Yahoola Valley, with Dahlonega visible in the distance below; no wonder he was content to stay close to his native hearth! The main stop at Suches, three miles beyond, is Tritt's store. But take note of the school, built of granite from Woody's quarry, lumber sawed in his mill, and on land

PLATE 1. In these Appalachian highlands American forestry was born. This is the view from the arched veranda of Biltmore Mansion, at Asheville, North Carolina, where George Washington Vanderbilt daringly engaged the youthful Gifford Pinchot to practice and prove "conservative logging." Later much of the Vanderbilt holdings became part of Pisgah National Forest.

PLATE 2. The sugar maple, a stately, versatile tree, in full autumn glory on a roadside at Ripton, Vermont, in Green Mountain National Forest, near the farm home of poet Robert Frost. Like the National Forests, the sugar maple serves many purposes. Its hard wood is prized for flooring and furniture. Its sap produces the finest maple sugar. And the spread of its branch, grace of form, and brilliant color of leaf delight the eye.

PLATE 3

PLATE 4

PLATE 5

PLATE 3. Amicalola Falls, a clear and white 250-foot cascade near the southern terminus of the Appalachian Trail in Chattahoochee National Forest, Georgia. Protection of a vital Southern watershed is one purpose of this National Forest. It was established after years of uncontrolled cutting, burning, and hunting. Its resources are managed to furnish water, timber, hunting, fishing, and enjoyment of the outdoors.

PLATE 4. Probing the Juniper River, banked with mangrove, palmetto, and myrtle, a vestige of the original Florida, in Ocala National Forest. Over 500 lakes and streams, rising from clear springs, make this National Forest a year-round fisherman's paradise.

PLATE 5. Older than the Rockies: the Selkirk Range, in Idaho's Panhandle, seen by moonlight beyond Priest Lake. The bordering lands of Kaniksu National Forest served as the pilot area for successful antibiotic control of white pine blister rust.

PLATE 6

PLATE 7

PLATE 6. A rainbow brings a welcome spray of color to the mountains of Lincoln National Forest, New Mexico. In darker days of 1950, when fire swept over and scarred 17,000 acres, a Forest Service fire-fighting crew rescued a badly burned bear cub from nearby Capitan Mountains. It was named Smokey and became the international symbol of fire prevention.

PLATE 7. In the Big Timber country of the Six Rivers National Forest, California. A private company, under Forest Service timber sale contract, logs a mixed stand of Douglas fir and redwood trees. In time this road will be used for recreation and fire prevention. With the heavy rainfall of the Klamath River drainage, regeneration will be rapid and new tree crops will grow.

which he donated. When I last visited Suches, I called on the ranger's widow, in the brick house across the road from Tritt's. It was the day her second son was retiring from the Forest Service, but she was quite proud that her grandson was already an assistant forest supervisor in Arkansas. Sosebee Cove is nearby on Route 180. The pioneer forester loved the great yellow poplars and wildflowers, which are now preserved in his memory for the enjoyment of all.

Then drive to Brasstown Bald, the highest peak in Georgia (elevation 4784 feet) via the new three-mile paved road from Jack's Gap. Climb the Forest Service lookout tower for the sweeping views of Hiawasee and Notteley Valleys, the mountain towns of Blairsville, Presley and Hiawasee, and man-made Notteley and Chatuge Lakes, spilling over the landscape into North Carolina.

Should you come this way in summer, visit the annual Georgia Mountain Fair at Hiawasee, the second week in August. The folks rally round from twenty-six counties to show their "homemade and handy" best, from canned fruit and vegetables to farm tools, homespun clothing and prize cattle.

Should you drive from here through Georgia's beautiful northeast corner on Route 23, you will be surrounded by National Forests: the Sumter in South Carolina; the Nantahala in North Carolina and the Chattahoochee. Just below the state line, visit the Dillard House, overlooking Rabun Gap and the Little Tennessee Valley, for a family-style meal of chicken, ham, beef, home-grown fruits, jellies and jams—the kind of cooking that would warm the heart and please the palate of Ranger Woody.

# CHAPTER NINE

# *The Big Scrub*

I was minding my own business, more or less, while stopping in Ocala, Florida, when I realized that something was watching me and trying to convey a message. It followed and stared at me everywhere.

The constant pursuer was a sign, naggingly persistent and inescapable. *Don't miss Silver Springs*, it suggested from the motel-room wall when I arose in the morning. *You MUST visit Silver Springs*, it insisted as I had breakfast in a restaurant. *Ocala—the home of Silver Springs*, it boasted at the corner. As I turned the corner, it directed *Silver Springs, this way, Three miles BACK to Silver Springs*, it corrected as I went the other way.

There is really nothing wrong with Silver Springs. Sight-seers have been thrilled by its jungle wonders and swamp growth ever since Hubbard L. Hart operated his small boxlike tourist steamer down the Oklawaha River from Palatka a century ago. Now you pay your money and get to see antique cars; deer species from various parts of the world; the life of Christ in diorama, and a snake expert "milking" snakes of their venom; you ride a glass-bottom boat over the springs and are shown the spot where the Indian prince and his sweetheart drowned themselves when their parents would not let them marry. (Elsewhere you may have seen where they plunged over a cliff together.)

But I wonder, is this really Florida any longer? Or is Ocala itself—spoliated and mesmerized, looking like a living television commercial, its beautiful live oaks and subtropical foliage on the verge of obliteration by the one endless billboard?

There is a saving grace. Almost adjacent to Silver Springs lies Ocala National Forest, the Big Scrub. It receives scant attention from tourist promoters in Ocala or the state, an understandable circumstance, perhaps, considering the Floridian world today is self-absorbed with newness, make-believe and high finance. Yet the Big Scrub, Everglades National Park, Myakka River State Park and a few such places

123

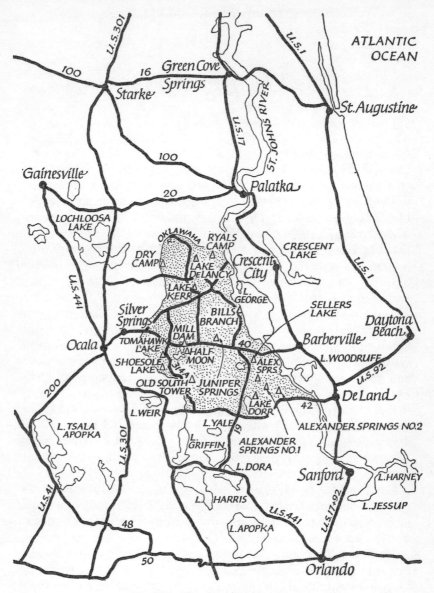

Florida's "Big Scrub," the Ocala

are welcome reminders of undiluted Florida, with its unique sub-tropical natural glories.

The National Forest is reached from Ocala on a boulevard bordered by mossy, low-spreading live oak and tall sentinels of loblolly pine, glistening with long-clustered green needles. It is our southernmost National Forest (except for the lush experimental Rain Forest on Puerto Rico) and the first one in the East. It was established in 1908 out of public domain so scrubby it had no value for homesteading, although here and there rich hammocklands were studded with wild orange groves.

The country was an exciting but impenetrable jungle, which once had been the heart of the Seminole nation. Ocala, years earlier, derived its name from an Indian village, through which DeSoto passed in 1539 on his march north and west. One of the earliest white settlements was an Indian trading post, Fort King, established in 1825, about midway between Ocala and the National Forest, and later to become central Florida headquarters in the Seminole War.

An unusual settlement was started in the Big Scrub in the 1820's by Moses E. Levy, a Portuguese Jew who had grown wealthy in Cuba, and purchased 50,000 acres here at a dollar each. His land, including Alexander Springs and the present Lake Wildlife Management Area, was cleared; his settlers built homes and planted sugar cane and tropical fruits, while Levy built his mansion at Astor, on the west bank of the St. Johns River. But this land was still unconquerable, with its swamps, 'gators and mosquitoes, and the settlement failed.

There were Indians to reckon with, too. The most notable was fiery Osceola, as hateful of whites as Geronimo would be in the West. He was a quarter-breed (his grandfather was a Scotsman) and, though not a chief, the real leader of his people. Early in the Seminole War he sent a defiant message to General Clinch: "You have guns, so have we. You have powder and lead, and so have we. Your men will fight and so will ours till the last drop of Seminole blood has moistened the dust of his hunting ground." On another occasion he warned, "I will make the white man red with blood, and then blacken him in the sun and rain, where the wolf shall smell of his bones and the buzzard live upon his flesh."

At Fort King, when the Indian chiefs were summoned from their villages and threatened with loss of annuities unless they signed the emigration treaty and moved west, Osceola speared the treaty with his dagger, shouting, "There! This is the only treaty I will ever make with the whites!" In 1835 he reappeared at Fort King. That day Major Francis L. Dade and a force of 110 men were marching overland from Fort Brooke, at Tampa, to reinforce King. But Osceola slew the Indian agent and commanding officer, while simultaneously a large band of Seminoles charged from a cover of palmetto, live oak and magnolia to massacre Dade's troops almost to the last man. It was the opening engagement of the Seminole War; the scene, at Bushnell, is now commemorated as Dade Battlefield Historic Memorial. Two years later, in 1837, Osceola was captured and taken prisoner. He died of quinsy, but first posed for the celebrated portrait by George Catlin. His last prayer was to die in the war dress of his tribe.

The greater part of the tree cover in the 360,000-acre National Forest is made up of sand pine, scrawny little fellows, neither very tall nor very wide, congregating in dense stands amid saw palmetto and scrub oak. This is the largest existing area of *Pinus clausa* in the world—and the basis of the name "Big Scrub." The tree is scrawnier than Virginia pine of the Mid-Atlantic, jack pine of the Lake States, or lodgepole pine, which rises out of the rocky soil in the high West. But the sand pine is heroic and determined. It must grow from near-sterile sand, the ground surface left eons ago when ocean-wave action removed the layer of fertile silt from the Ocala limestone. However, in "islands" of better soil are stands of longleaf and slash pine, and along stream courses and lake shores live oak, magnolia, blackjack and water oak, scrub holly and flowering subtropical plants.

The sand pine lives a short life, of about sixty years, and catches fire easily. Flames spread quickly through the crowns: in the last big blaze, the Hammock fire of 1935, fire roared through the trees at a rate of three acres per second, as fast as a missile zooming spaceward, killing every living plant and animal in its path. Since then special fire-fighting equipment, able to cross the swamps and sand, and highly organized co-operation with state agencies have kept fire damage low.

For years the light, brittle wood of the sand pine had no use except as fuel. But recently paper and pulp manufacturers have found, with their new processes, that they can use it, too. This means selective cutting and stand improvement are producing healthier trees and wildlife food plots among the scrub.

The main values of the Forest, however, are for recreation and protection of a multitude of wild animals and birds. Over 500 lakes and

126

countless streams rise from crystal-clear springs. Enough water flows from the four major springs—Alexander, Salt, Juniper and Silver Glenn—to supply a city the size of Atlanta. On the Ocala side the Forest is bordered by the Oklawaha River, which flows north, joining the St. Johns, the longest river in the state and the eastern border of the Forest, which flows north, too, until it empties into the Atlantic Ocean. Such waters make the Big Scrub a year-round fisherman's paradise—for that prize fighter, the black bass. It also yields bream, shellcracker, rock bass, red-breasted sunfish and speckled perch.

The National Forest is home of the Ocala deer, a small subspecies of the Virginia whitetail, with shoulder height under three feet. As with trees, the poor, sandy soil cannot sustain a heavy concentration of deer or nurture a particularly hardy species. But the Ocala deer is unique in that fawns are dropped during every month of the year, with the peak birth rate during May, June and July. It is not uncommon to see the fawn or fawns as young as two or three weeks, richly brown and heavily spotted, accompany their mother about the woods.

This being a National Wildlife Refuge, hunting is done on a managed basis during the two-day fall season. Hunters enter through a State Game Department checking station and are allowed out the same way with two buck deer, one grown bear or panther, or any combination of two. Shooting is also good here for squirrel, dove, quail, turkey and duck.

Deer have a better chance of survival (so do hunters, come to think of it) in the ten-day bow-and-arrow hunt. Sportsmen don't often score on deer with arrows, but they may bring in a wild hog, raccoon or fox.

The largest recreation area in the Forest is at Juniper Springs, a beautiful setting twenty-six miles east of Ocala. It is centered around the spring, from which 8,500,000 gallons of pure and sweet Florida water flow daily, at a year-round temperature of seventy-two degrees. Facilities include tent and trailer camping, rental cabins in the pinewoods, picnic tables and bathhouse from which to swim in the clear creek water. These are efficiently maintained by A. R. Marwick, a concessioner, known as the "mayor of Juniper Springs" because of his pride in the area.

Bring your canoe or rent one from Mr. Marwick for the trip on Juniper River, winding through dense jungle for an unspoiled view of natural Florida. Start early in the morning, but early, the best time

127

to see wildlife. At first, the grayness of morning twilight lingers in the fog. You glide past a clear, deep pool, a favorite water hole of game. Then sunlight comes through in patches; there is more sunlight in the morning than at noon, when the dense overstory of leaves bars the sun. You paddle through marshes of sawgrass, myrtle and pickerel weed, passing floating water hyacinth and giant ferns along the bank. A water moccasin lifts his curious head, then spins downstream. And here you find the same rich variety of birds which greeted the first European explorers and the Indians before them: A scrub jay flying ahead, crying out shrilly to warn the game. A low-flying blue heron. Fish hawks nesting in broken trees. White ibis circling the landscape. With luck, a bald eagle searching the river for food. You hear a thousand different sounds: of the mockingbird, the crane, the curious curve-billed limpkin, called the "crying bird" because of the variety of its weird wails, and many more.

This canoe trip and the Juniper Springs landscape will remind you of *The Yearling*, by Marjorie Kinnan Rawlings, the tender, feeling story about the backwoods settlers of these parts. They came from the same stock as the Appalachian mountain settler and knew as little about life beyond their own small clearings as he did. The "cracker" of the pinewoods played an elemental role in the conflict between man and nature. Thus, Mrs. Rawlings could explore the woodlore of this Big Scrub through the eyes of a sensitive lad named Jody, struggling to mature with an understanding of wild creatures.

"The bank was dense with magnolia and loblolly bay, sweet gum and gray-barked ash." Such was the scene he saw, which you are apt to see, too. "He went down to the spring in the cool darkness of their shadows. A sharp pleasure came over him. This was a secret and lovely place.

"A spring as clear as well water bubbled up from nowhere in the sand. It was as though the banks cupped green leafy hands to hold it. There was a whirlpool where the water rose from the earth. Grains of sand boiled in it. Beyond the bank, the parent spring bubbled up at a higher level, cut itself a channel through white limestone and began to run rapidly downhill to make a creek. The creek joined Lake George, Lake George was part of the St. Johns River, the great river flowed northward and into the sea. It excited Jody to watch the beginning of the ocean. There were other things, true, but this one was his own. He liked to think that no one came here but himself and the wild animals and the thirsty birds."

128

New sounds are heard along about dusk. The frogs begin their croaking. From the deep scrub you may hear hooting and hollering, as the war of survival continues unending. Birds and small furred creatures flee the predatory hawk and owl. Possums and coons scurry to cover. Bears, wolves and panthers prey on deer; and if the deer eludes him the bear might eat the cub of another bear.

Late one afternoon Jody and his father, Penny, spotted a group of whooping cranes. They crouched on all fours and crept forward slowly until they reached a clump of high saw grass and the birds were so close Jody thought he could touch them with his long fishing pole. He counted and there were sixteen. They were performing a strange, eerie dance. Father and son observed closely:

"Then the evening breeze moved across the saw grass. It bowed and fluttered. The water rippled. The setting sun lay rosy on the white bodies. Magic birds were dancing in a mystic marsh. The grass swayed with them, and the shallow waters, and the earth fluttered under them. The earth was dancing with the cranes, and the low sun, and the wind and sky. The sun was sinking into the saw grass. The marsh was golden. The whooping cranes were washed with gold. The far hammocks were black. Darkness came to the lily pads, and the water blackened. The cranes were whiter than any clouds, or any white bloom of oleander or of lily. Without warning, they took flight. They made a great circle against the sunset, whooping their strange rusty cry that sounded only in their flight. Then they flew in a long line into the west, and vanished."

The other large recreation area in the Forest is at Alexander Springs, newer and less developed but very attractive, too. Here water bubbles upward from deep caverns at the rate of 78,000,000 gallons a day, looking as clear and turquoise as the Caribbean. Filtered through limestone, the water is so clear that light rays are broken into prismatic colors. Objects sixty feet below, including clusters of blossoming coral fern, are visible from the surface. So are fishes and turtles flittering about this natural aquarium—gar, cat, eel and salt-water visitors like the mullet and flounder. A paddle boat sets forth from Alexander Springs on a pleasant, hourly voyage up winding Spring Creek.

Other new developments for visitors within the Forest include the campground along the sand shore of Mill Dam Lake, twenty miles east of Ocala; hunting and fishing camps, equipped with shelter, table and drinking water, scattered throughout; and paved roads, which make it easier to navigate through the backwood sand country. You can drive to the shore of Lake George, Florida's second largest lake, and along the way in springtime see surprising tropical vegetation like century plants and cacti in the same spectacular bloom of the Southwest desert.

There are two other National Forests in Florida, the Osceola and Appalachicola, neither of which I have seen. But there is also a fourth area, the former Choctawatchee National Forest, which the Air Force took over during World War II as a bombing and gunnery range. It rechristened the area Eglin Air Force Base and has held it to the military bosom ever since. Several years ago the Air Force escorted a plane load of conservationists, wildlife experts and writers from Washington to demonstrate it was not really land-hungry at heart, but did practice intelligent management along with use for its own purposes. On this trip I found the 350,000-acre base south of Pensacola a composition of bayous and fresh-water lakes, of land growing longleaf, slash and sand pine, with whitetail deer foraging at night alongside jet runways, and wild turkey, ducks, quail and black bear somewhere about. I mention this episode because I share the misgivings of many people about the Army, Navy, Air Force, highway department, power authority or any government agency claiming priority right to a park or forest, particularly with the suggestion it is "land lying idle that should be put to use."

But my strongest recollection is that a civilian forester, Walker Spence, was running the land end of the base. "I was here with the Forest Service when it was the Choctawatchee, and it was a great outfit," he would say. We drove around the base and he showed us 200 food plots, meadows planted with oats, wheat and rye for deer and turkey, and I think we stopped at every one of them, checking turkey tracks and never finding a turkey. "We're sure to see one at the next plot," Walker said, and off we'd go again. The wildlife experts had a great time measuring the tracks; they didn't care if they ever saw an animal, just so they could figure how long the turkey had stood around eating its lunch. Then Walker explained that a million slash pine seedlings would be planted over the base that year, and that fifteen lakes were being stocked with fish. Every so often he would start talking about the Forest Service.

In the early days, the Walker Spences faced the grim problem and abuses of turpentining, or "naval stores," on land like the Choctawatchee. Naval stores were given the name two centuries before the sawmill made its appearance in the South, that is, in early colonial days when pitch and tar produced from pine sap were used to caulk the seams of wooden ships. In that era of sail, one reason European nations sought colonies was to locate a source of naval stores. Now that wooden ships no longer sail the seas, products of pine tree sap—resin and turpentine—fill other uses (in manufacture of paint, varnish, soap, ink, plastics, linoleum), but are still called naval stores.

In the first decades of the twentieth century naval-store operations covered the pine fields of Deep Dixie. More than 50 per cent of the world's production was done in Georgia, 20 per cent in Florida. Most of the remainder was done in Louisiana, Alabama and South Carolina. Forestry was unknown. Turpentine men burned the woods so their laborers could move about unbothered by brush or rattlesnakes. Meanwhile cattlemen were also burning the woods to assure spring feed for their stock. And the farmer was setting fires, too, to prevent the fires he knew the others would set from reaching him first.

On the Choctawatchee, where the Forest Service was determined to end destructive turpentining methods, it was difficult to lease lands and enforce contracts on the basis of wise use. Frequent, deep chippings of five- and six-inch trees weakened them so severely they became easy prey to fire, insects, disease and windstorm. But the theory was, "The deeper the gash the higher the yield in gum." Throughout the South from spring to early fall, air in the woods was laden with a pungent aroma, as millions of pine trees were slashed and resin dripped into tin cans beneath the cuts, or "facings." In each camp the resin was brought to the still, an unpainted frame shed crowded with amber-colored resin, its floors gummy with resin drippings. Here the crude resin would be heated gradually until it was distilled into turpentine and resin. The dross—chips of pine wood covered with inflammable resin—was sold for kindling, and would start the fastest fire, even of green wood.

Foresters set a limit, on National Forestland, of a one-half-inch-deep cut, then they reduced it to a quarter of an inch. They showed the naval-store operators where the yield would increase far more than when the cut was one and a quarter inch, causing the tree to fade from too great a shock. Through its Naval Stores Conservation Program, the Service educated the South to conservative methods of chipping that would yield a profitable return and still spare the tree for other purposes. Today the naval-stores industry is less prominent, in light of the surge of Southern pulp and paper, although in 1960 no less than 30,000,000 trees were chipped. It is not considered practical to chip any tree under ten inches diameter. About forty to fifty trees per acre are chipped on a "front" face five years in a row, rested a year, then chipped on a "back" face for five years. Surprisingly, although chipping reduces the rate of growth, it does not lessen the value of the tree for ultimate use as lumber or pulpwood.

Turpentining is a thing of the past at Eglin Field. Timber harvest is not: 3,000,000 board feet are cut in a year and the base operates a sawmill, furnishing lumber for its own use and for other bases. Meanwhile the lakes are open to public fishing and the woods to public hunting. Walker Spence, the Forest Service alumnus, is proud of the project and the co-operation of the Air Force.

There is something to be said for the military in managing its reserve this way. The time may even come, a century or two hence, when wars are no longer fought, when bombing ranges and guided missiles are no longer needed. Then, perhaps, this place, without a billboard in sight, without "monkey jungles" or garish roadside stands, will be restored in healthy condition to the Choctawatchee National Forest.

# CHAPTER TEN

# *Wold of the Kisatchie*

"It is red hills now, not high," said Jack Burden, "with blackberry bushes along the fence rows, and blackjack clumps in the bottoms and now and then a place where the second-growth pines stand close together if they haven't burned over for sheep grass, and if they have been burned over, there are the black stubs." Jack was the sympathetic, sensitive personality drawn by Robert Penn Warren to narrate the life and times of Willie Stark, the Boss, in *All the King's Men.* Although hopelessly entangled in a harsh backwoods political machine, Jack, the ex-newspaperman and scholar of history, could not avoid viewing people and events with his moral, inner eye. The same was true when he looked at the landscape. "The cotton patches cling to hillsides," he observed, while speeding northeast on fictional Highway 58, "and the gullies cut across the cotton patches. The corn blades hang stiff and are streaked with yellow."

I felt I was following the course of Jack Burden and his entourage, across north-central Louisiana into Winnville, his "Mason City," but naturally I was not with Willie Stark, but with George Tannehill, and his boss, Ray Brandt, supervisor of the Kisatchie National Forest. We tooled down the street, as Jack would say, and hit the square. We all entered the drugstore and everyone knew George, the district ranger, who has lived here all his life, perhaps not as famously as Huey Long, the pride of Winnville, but more creditably than Earl Long, who ran his little kingdom from the ramshackle palace called "Pea Patch."

"There were pine forests here a long time ago but they are gone," Jack said. "The bastards got in here and set up the mills and laid the narrow-gauge tracks and knocked together the company commissaries and paid a dollar a day and folks swarmed out of the brush for the dollar and folks came from God knows where, riding in wagons with a chest of drawers and a bedstead canted together in the wagon bed, and five kids huddled down together and the old woman hunched

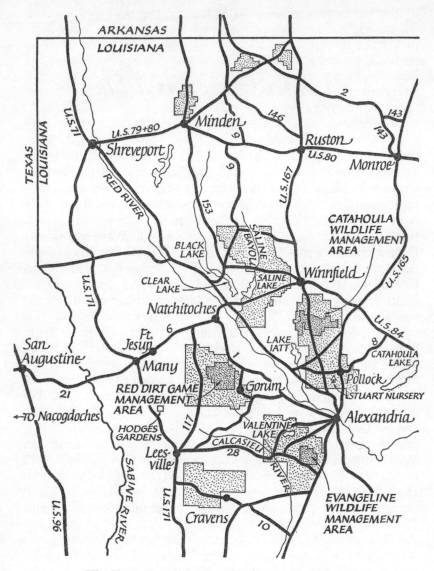

The Kisatchie, in the Heartland of Southern Pines

on the wagon seat with a poke bonnet on her head and snuff on her gums. The saws sang soprano and the clerk in the commissary passed out the blackstrap molasses and the sowbelly and wrote in his big book, and the Yankee dollar and Confederate dumbness collaborated to heal the wounds of four years of fratricidal strife, and all was merry as a marriage bell. Till, all of a sudden, there weren't any more pine trees. They stripped the mills. The narrow-gauge tracks got covered with grass. Folks tore down the commissaries for kindling wood. There wasn't any more dollar a day. The big boys were gone, with diamond rings on their fingers and broadcloth on their backs. But a good many of the folks stayed right on, watched the gullies eat deeper into the red clay. And a good handful of those folks and their heirs and assigns stayed in Mason City, four thousand of them, more or less."

It was the last time he saw Mason City, back in the summer of 1936. It was the summer George Tannehill went to work for the Forest Service and started planting trees. Jack ought to come back to see how the new order has fared.

We tooled out of Mason City—Winnville, I mean—and went to see the woods.

On an occasional sand hill we saw a stand of longleaf pine, mature trees 100 to 120 feet high, reminders of what the original forest looked like, when longleaf was comparable to the present rank of Douglas-fir in national importance. Then came the lumber boom. "In those days," said George Tannehill, the tall, soft-spoken ranger, "whistles of one town awakened the people in the next town. Sawdust from the mills was piled to the sky."

By the 1920's, as Jack said, the land was cut barren and the big mills departed. Fierce fires followed, fed by the resinous tops left on the ground. In most areas the magnificent pine forest was replaced by a jungle of scrub oak, rattan and cat briers. On this blighted land cattlegrowers and pig farmers "acquired" grazing rights by an unwritten code. They grazed year long, but every spring they burned the stubble to "green up the grass," burning tree seed and seedlings, too, while they were at it.

Hopelessly overrun by cattle, fire and trespass, the land served little civic purpose, least of all as a source of taxes. The parishes (counties) of north-central Louisiana petitioned the government to take it over. Between 1935 and 1940, when Jack Burden saw the scenery at its worst, the Forest Service was acquiring land under the Weeks Law

135

and the Emergency Relief Act of 1935 for as little as fifty cents an acre.

But the land changes. "Here in the Deep South a forester can see the fruits of his labor in his lifetime," said George Tannehill. "Or his mistakes." We saw plantations George had planted as a young forester. They were principally slash pine, the fastest-growing Southern pine, but a beautiful tree, too, with dark lustrous green needles, landscaping the roadside.

We turned into the woods. The smallest of logging operations, two young fellows, one with power saw and the other with measuring stick, was at work. But it was clearly a growing woodland. "Thirty years ago," said George, "there was absolutely nothing here. No trees and no wildlife, except for uncontrolled hogs and cattle. Now we are growing 450 board feet per acre per year. With thinning and stand improvement, we should average 800 feet an acre. In eighty years," he said, looking ahead, as foresters are forever doing, "when these trees reach their full growth, they will be at least 100 feet tall."

Shortly we would see the tiniest of trees, numbering 1,000,000 and yet so infinitesimal one might almost pick them all up and put them in his pocket. This was at the Stuart Nursery, a wide spot in the Louisiana Road. The nursery produces 40,000,000 seedlings a year, principally slash and longleaf pine, extracted from cones and planted in nursery beds. With its warm climate and humidity, the South now grows 80 per cent of all the country's seedlings. Here I saw the 1,000,000 baby trees just one day old, each of them barely a light greenish fleck breaking its way upward through soft dark earth. When they grow three and four years old they will be planted in deforested areas of the Kisatchie, as well as elsewhere in Louisiana and the South. Also at the nursery, thousands of pounds of seed were bathing in bird repellent and rodenticide to discourage friends of the field from dining on them before they take root. They will be dropped by air, a technique of seeding which is still less effective than direct planting but also quicker and less costly.

From Alexandria we entered into the heart of the Kisatchie country, the surprising "Hills of Louisiana," reaching elevations of 350 feet—veritable mountains compared with the characteristic flatland of sluggish bayous and moss-draped oaks. A sand road led upward through the wooded Red Dirt Game Management Area. Its 40,000 acres are fenced to keep the hogs out, a protection for turkey, deer, quail, squirrel and young trees. We drove through the backwoods settlements of Gorum and Flatwood, to the new Long Leaf Trail Vista, overlooking mesas of sandstone and limestone, and a swelling sea of bluish, young pines.

The name "Kisatchie" comes from the Kichai tribe of Indians, for whom this area was a hunting ground. Early settlers were drawn by the bounty of game—deer, bear, wild turkey, passenger pigeon, quail. The forest was a world of beauty, and it was called the Kisatchie Wold, a charming term brought from England or Scotland. The towering virgin longleaf pine, unlike Northern and Western conifers, allowed sufficient sunlight to filter through, in dappled light and shadow, nurturing a carpet of grass and flowers. Shallow-rooted dogwood thrived as the understory, brightening the spring with white flowers. Sweet grasses and plants covered the ground, providing food for birds and small animals.

That was in the long, long ago, when nature held its own, a balance now returning to the Kisatchie. Ray Brandt, the supervisor, was in uniform and a family group came up to him while we were standing at the Long Leaf Trail Vista. They had been using one of the new picnic tables, part of a compact little recreation area which also consisted of stone shelter, parking space and nature trails over the mesas. "We like it here very much," one of the men told Ray. "There is always a cool breeze and no mosquitoes in summer. Thank you for what you have done." These plain people found pride and quiet adventure in their own once-blighted countryside.

Ray Brandt, unlike George Tannehill, is not a Louisianian, but a Pennsylvanian. To him the Kisatchie, with all its problems, represents the opportunity to practice forestry at its finest. Under his supervision 7000 acres of bare land, or scrub-oak land, are reforested yearly (in slash, longleaf and loblolly pine). Another 25,000 acres of pinewoods are released from worthless, scrubby hardwood competition—that is, the hardwoods are cut out or girdled (cutting the cambium layer so the tree will die), allowing the pines to grow better. Thirteen thousand acres are burned to reduce hardwood brush, and 4000 acres are burned to provide seed bed for natural reproduction. Insects and disease are the constant enemy. One of the worst is Brown spot needle blight, which attacks pine seedlings; controlled fire kills the fungus but not the young tree. Then there is the newest insect to reach epidemic proportions, the redheaded pine sawfly, a small beelike creature with eight or nine pair of legs. They swarm over young pine and can strip its foliage in a few days; 1,500,000 trees

137

have been sprayed with DDT to discourage the pine sawfly. Within the game management area, 1 per cent of the land is cleared for wildlife food plots, and animals, as well as trees, are a primary consideration.

But the biggest problems are in dealing with people: people with their hogs, cattle and fire torches.

The Forest Service has 4500 hogs and 1200 head of cattle grazing the Kisatchie lands on permit. It has raised the grazing fee over the years from six cents to ten cents per head, still about the cheapest rate in the country on public or private pasture. But another 10,000 head roam the woods and fields under proprietary rights claimed by local people when this was no man's land. In the West the struggle for authority over public-domain grazing lands was fought and won early in the century, but here in the backwoods South it has been a long, difficult struggle not yet ended.

Fire is a principal reason for seemingly slow progress. Fire in the South is a tradition, a way of life, a tool of the farmer, a means of retribution, punishment, revenge, recreation, and an outlet of frustration. Eighty per cent of the nation's forest fires burn in the eleven Southern states, and half of those in Louisiana, Mississippi and Florida are deliberately set. Some recall worse days, when a pall of smoke would blanket a county, if not an entire state, blotting out the sun for days at a time.

Fires are set by a variety of people, for a variety of reasons. Moonshiners caught by revenuers may set fire to the property of the person they think gave them away. One moonshining crew may start a blaze on another crew's location to call attention to it, or to run off loggers approaching too closely to their still. Fires are set by juvenile delinquents, preferring fun with the torch to the switch-blade of Eastern cities. Sometimes they are set by unscrupulous timber buyers, in order to get damaged timber at lower prices, or by pulpwood cutters, hoping to get a job cutting pulpwood worth salvaging. Also by people turned down for employment, by hired hands who dislike their foremen and by foremen who dislike big companies. I have seen a blackened burn in the midst of a beautiful red-pine plantation caused, to add irony to injury, by a fire warden (a volunteer part-time Forest Service employee) out of spite when told his cattle would have to graze in another part of his National Forest.

The seventy-five-mile-square area of central and southwest Louisiana experiences more fires each year than any area of similar size in the United States. Two hundred separate fires have been set in the Kisatchie National Forest in a single day.

Most have been caused by stock growers fighting forestry. Tree planters, on private as well as public land, fence their land against cattle-running neighbors with the greatest trepidation. They know the hogs eat pine seedlings faster than man can plant them, but they also recognize the dangers they face.

Is woods burning a crime? Of course. It is punishable by as much as two years in jail. But first the arsonist must be caught, and then tried. Many back-country courts are reluctant to send a man to prison for burning trees, for in the old Southern code fire is still a birthright.

Much progress is being made in fire reduction. Education efforts, through country-music radio stations, fairs, school exhibits and through a friend of Smokey the Bear called "Mr. Burnit," are developing an awareness that arson is not really a credit to the South. Perhaps the most important antidote to fire, however, has been improvement in the landscape. It has too much dignity to set aflame.

The Kisatchie Wold and environs are a wonderland of nature and history. Jack Burden, who enjoyed his scholarly "enchantments of the past," should drive west from Winnfield to Natchitoches (pronounced Nak'-i-tosh), the oldest town in the Louisiana Purchase, founded in 1714, three years before New Orleans, by Louis Juchereau, Sieur de Saint-Denis. For a century the Red River brought trade and commerce; then in 1832 the channel changed course, retreating five miles east to Grand Ecore and leaving Natchitoches high and dry. Today it is a cameo of New Orleans in flavor and architecture.

The Cane River, the old Red River channel renamed for heavy stands of native cane on its banks, is really a currentless lake thirty-nine miles long. On both sides are plantation houses built in days of glory. The most eminent, Melrose Plantation, has had two famous owners. First was Marie Therese Coin-Coin, once a slave owned by Juchereau. She amassed a fortune growing indigo and built the African House, one of the South's most unusual structures, of whitewashed brick and roof of huge hand-hewn cypress slabs. In this century the plantation house (built in 1830) was the home of the late Mrs. John Hampton Henry, the celebrated "Miss Cammie," who brought literary light into the Cane River country through her collection of books and authors, including Alexander Woolcott, Rachel Field, Rose Franken, Roark Bradford and Harnett Kane, all of whom were entertained here.

The area west on Route 6 was called the "Neutral Strip," a no man's land and refuge of desperadoes following the Louisiana Purchase. In 1822 Fort Jesup was founded on the old San Antonio Trace by Colonel Zachary Taylor to clear the territory of outlaws; later Taylor returned to lead the Mexican War expedition from here. Louisiana has recently restored the fort as a state park to commemorate those early events.

Southward, at Many, lie Hodges Gardens, an outstanding 4700-acre preservation of the trees, wildlife and floral beauty that are distinctly Louisiana's. The Gardens, endowed by A. J. Hodges and his late wife, Nona Trigg Hodges, opened in 1959. There is floral bloom all year, alongside waterfalls and in pools and lakes. With co-operation of Federal and state forest services, research projects are underway at the Gardens to grow improved strains of southern pine.

Leesville, south of Natchitoches, west of Alexandria, is another town where timber was king and was ruined by it. For almost the first third of this century a generation of men arose, ate and went to bed by mill whistles. The timber they cut floated down the Sabine River to Orange, Texas, near the Gulf of Mexico. Meanwhile, that co-industry of the sawmill, the turpentine plant, flourished, too. Men worked from daylight to dark in the remote woods, chipping pine trees, collecting resin and hauling it to the stills. But turpentining died with the mills.

Leesville now is an outdoorsman's paradise, and even the worst of the timber-cutting past has been adapted for recreation. At the abandoned town of Fullerton, where the vestiges of a giant sawmill are still visible, the Forest Service has transformed the old mill pond into a sand swimming beach, with barbecue grills, bathhouse and picnic tables. Streams abound in bass, catfish, perch and bream. Leesville also is well situated as a base for hunting in the Kisatchie.

Jack Burden would be surprised at the wildlife, the squirrel, deer, fox, duck and geese, quail and dove, and bobcat. He would be surprised at the woods, too. But then, Jack's king and his order ruled over a kingdom of another day.

140

# CHAPTER ELEVEN

# Canoe Country

The bald eagle sat in his high perch, looking self-assured and imperturbable, as a great bird should. Surely, I thought, once our canoe comes abreast he will stretch his wings and soar in flight.

But if he noted our presence at all, it did not change his attitude. He remained unyielding in his black-spruce outlook.

"It takes more than us to stir him," said Larry Neff, sitting in the center of the canoe. "Now if he saw an osprey with a fish in its claws, he would swoop down, force the osprey to release the catch and then retrieve it for himself in midair.

"Or if a seaplane flew past him before landing on the water—the way they did in the old days—he might hightail out of the wilderness."

We paddled on, leaving the eagle in command of all he surveyed. A canoe with five-horsepower "kicker" passed in the opposite direction, shattering the natural stillness. But the eagle ignored it as he had ignored us.

We probed deeper into the Boundary Waters Canoe Area, the heart of Superior National Forest. Around us, on both sides of the border shared by Minnesota and the Canadian province of Ontario, were 5,000,000 acres of lakes and land and marsh known as the Quetico-Superior country, the only place of its kind in the world.

The waters were dark and cool. For a time there was not a soul in sight. We were absorbed in thought, each of his own. We were absorbed in work, as well. I was paddling in the bow; Dick Droege, a husky Californian and Forest Service veteran, in the stern. Dick was newly assigned to the Service's regional headquarters in Milwaukee and so this was his first experience in the canoe country. We paddled in unison; the longer we continued the more efficient we became. On this elemental power we fairly skimmed along, even though the canoe was loaded. From the center between us, Larry Neff, supervisor of the Superior National Forest, shopped for our supper, casting awhile, trolling awhile. That unusual bird of wilderness and open space, the

141

loon, emerged on the surface; at least he showed his long, slender neck and ducklike head. He scanned the scene, then descended for lower depths as suddenly as he had appeared.

We stopped for lunch on a rocky islet and before you could say, "Sphagnum moss up to your elbows," Dick and I were swimming, leaving our good guide to undo the bread, slightly soggy butter and other noontime accessories. The water in which we swam was darkened by a high organic content but was as pure, or almost as pure, as when the Chippewa followed this labyrinthine wilderness route.

The only human intrusion while we lunched on the rocks came from a speedboat bearing the name of a resort blazoned on its side, and carrying guests out for a sample of instant wilderness. Obligingly, the boat followed the other side of the lake. Closer at hand, we saw first a big buck whitetail deer crashing through the underbrush to cover. Then, just beyond our touch, appeared the brazen Canada jay, otherwise known as the camp robber. Why does he bear this name? David Thompson, the early explorer and geographer, described the convivial jay in this manner: "It is always close about the tents, and will alight at the very doors, to pick up what is thrown out; he lives by plunder, and on berries, and what he cannot eat he hides; it is easily taken by a snare, and, brought into the room, seems directly quite at home; when spirits is offered, it directly drinks, is soon drunk and fastens itself anywhere till sober."

We pushed off, proceeding on our way. We could not have hurried if we wanted to. More important, a wonderfully uncluttered world lay all around us, within sight, senses and fingertips. Endless lakes merged into one another. Some were merely pools or narrow natural channels, others were so large that even our knowledgeable forest supervisor occasionally would lose his bearings for the moment.

Lakes are so numerous in the Quetico-Superior they are almost beyond count: of 16,000 square miles on both sides of the border, 40 per cent is covered with lakes and connecting streams. In such a topographic situation, it was inevitable that early explorers would run short of names. On the Canadian side, one chain is composed of That Man, This Man, Other Man and No Man's Lakes. Dozens of wives, sweethearts and just plain girls are memorialized in other lake names. On the U.S. side, the Insula Lake Route, which we were traveling, begins with Lakes 1, 2, 3 and 4—but numbers understate their beauty.

The largest and best-known lakes, Basswood and La Croix, are

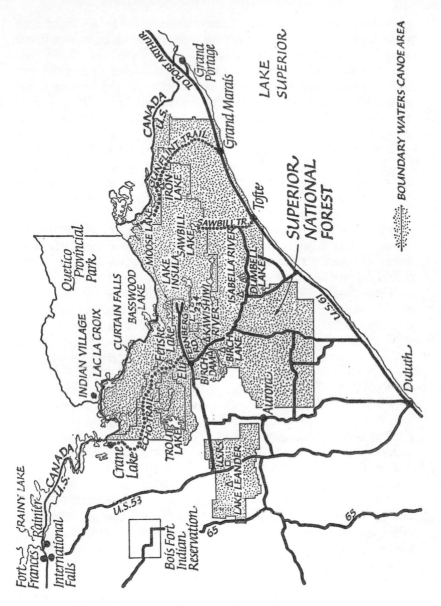

Quetico-Superior Canoe Country

more than twenty miles long. These and many others are broken by peninsulas and islands, so that each lake is almost an independent cosmos composed of subbodies of land and water. Sometimes the lakes are separated by narrow necks of land, ranging in length from a few rods to about a mile. Here the canoer portages his way overland, hiking through the woods with the canoe over his head, resting it on his shoulders, while his partner or partners carry their gear and food in back packs.

Shortly we passed a long-necked, long-legged great blue heron at his ease in a marshy inlet. It was a rare sight of one of the tallest and most beautiful water birds. Unlike that bald eagle, which refused to budge, the heron let out a deep squawk, threw back his neck and soared away.

Along the shoreline, thousands of trees were colored a deadly brown. It was a case of spruce budworm, attacking balsam fir and spruce, defoliating the trees and weakening them so they can be attacked further by borers, beetles and fungi.

"These trees will grow so weak they will blow down in a mild wind," Larry said. "They're a critical fire hazard right now. The disease is spreading faster than we can treat it. The best way to treat this area would be to cut the dead and dying. This is part of the problem of managing a wilderness area where not even salvage logging is permitted."

The Superior National Forest, as I would learn, is far from being all wilderness. Nor is the so-called roadless area a single unbroken unit. Nor is it really roadless, which accounts for its new name (applied in 1958) of Boundary Waters Canoe Area. Nor is it restricted to canoes: any size boat with any size motor is permitted.

This National Forest covers 2,873,000 acres (which makes it one of the ten largest National Forests). The Canoe Area, on the American side, consists of three sections: the Superior, in the center of the Forest, 890,000 acres; Little Indian Sioux, 103,000 acres, southwest of the city of Ely, across Echo Trail; and the Caribou, 45,000 acres, the easternmost section, reached via the Gunflint Trail from Grand Marais.

The Forest is divided in another way, too, relating to mining, timber cutting and accommodations. Zone One, the wilderness or roadless area, 362,000 acres in the heart of the Canoe Area, is closed to timber cutting, prospecting, mineral leasing and road construction. The only accommodations are primitive campgrounds; summer homes and resorts built on private land in other days are being acquired. Zone Two, 670,000 acres, fringes the no-cut area. Mineral prospecting is permitted. Timber cutting is not permitted within 400 feet of lakes and streams. Temporary logging roads and camps are permitted, but they are closed to public use and are reseeded as logging is completed. Airplanes are not allowed to fly over Zones One and Two, protecting the solitude of wildlife and the wilderness canoer. Zone Three constitutes 64 per cent of the National Forest and is outside the canoe country. It provides a border for wilderness, but includes developed campgrounds, roads, resorts and logging.

On the Canadian side, regulations in Quetico Provincial Park are generally comparable in protecting the integrity of the area for its length and width from near Rainy Lake in the west to Lake Superior, almost 175 miles to the east.

Larry warned that unless we stopped early we might not find one of the better camping spots. We pulled into a lovely islet lying in a slender waist between two large lakes. Being in the bow, I stepped for the rocky shore first, deftly, I thought, until I crashed into the water, proving to my companions then and there that I had to be a better writer than canoer.

It was about five P.M. Daylight was brilliant. We fished from shore (the best season for northern and walleyed pike is in May). The campsite was one of 200 primitive but developed sites in the canoe country. It consisted of a place to beach the canoe, a level cleared spot, rocks forming a fireplace with grate, a table and a simple, backwoods type of toilet. While dinner was cooking, a lone single-engine plane circled overhead. It was the Forest Service patrol plane, a sort of mobile fire tower flying a rectangular course, heading back to Ely, then to start all over again.

Ours was an adventure in solitude. Our nearest neighbors, two young outdoorsmen who had paddled past us to a point of land a quarter mile distant across Lake 4, were barely within sight. We watched the curling smoke of their fire and the sunlight glisten on their tent. If they had not been there, the world would have been ours alone. And they might have been thinking the same about us.

This was the kind of setting designed for bird watchers, botanists, poets, fishermen, canoers and all who believe in exercising their minds and bodies in nature's company. In our back-yard garden lowstemmed wintergreen plants waited to provide their red berries as food for game birds. Spring beauties closed their pink and white

145

flowers as shadows overtook the bright light. The hermit thrush sang a flutelike song, scurrying over the ground in search of insects and berries. Our rocky quarters were surrounded by conifers. Tall, tapering black spruce. Light-greenish northern white cedar, rising conelike, almost ornamentally so, out of the swamps. Balsam fir, the old stand-by which furnished boughs for campers' bedding in years gone by.

After dinner, Dick and I pushed off again, fishing hopefully for breakfast. The evening was still and magic. The sun spread out in a bronze sheen over the brownish-black water. We trolled and cast and drifted. We saw the work of beavers at dammed-up inlets. In the distance I spotted the bare outline of a moose drinking at the shore-line. It was the time of activity in the animal kingdom. Somewhere around us, the black bear, wolf, fox, coyote, weasel, skunk, mink, muskrat, snowshoe hare and lesser creatures were astir and on the prowl.

"Look across to that shore," Dick said. "There you can read the story of forest fires." He pointed to an area of quaking aspen, white-barked paper birch and slender pin cherry, species which reseed after fire and are dominant until they are overtaken by stronger species.

The temperature dipped, but sunlight hung over the scene until ten o'clock, bidding a long and lingering farewell. The last voice I heard was a loon, or loons, speaking in a quavering, low-pitched voice, followed by a weird reply or echo of yodeling laughter. Loon faded away abruptly into the stillness. I faded away, dreaming I was paddling backward into history, through eons and eons.

Of all who find treasures in the Quetico-Superior, I suspect the scientific historian acquires the most valuable treasures of all. Picture, for example, the delights of a paleobotanist like Dr. J. E. Potzger, of Butler University, digging into foot-deep sphagnum moss covering the rocks in shaded places, or boring deeply into the muds of bogs and lakes, and bringing forth organic material which to him reads like an exciting record of eternity, its pages fashioned out of leaves of mosses, spores of fern, legs or wings of mosquitoes, the spicular, bonylike remains of fresh-water sponges, and tiny one-celled diatoms. Occasionally, just as the forester reads of fire in a growing stand of aspen, the botanist-historian locates a charcoal "bookmark" in peat sediments caused by a lightning fire which burned the woods millions of years before the coming of man.

146

The good thing about Dr. Potzger is that slides of Quetico-Superior bog substances on his microscope are tinged with imagination. Or, as he says, "To the imaginative analyst the whole observation is an ever-changing scene of great throbbing life activities. He reads into the tiny pollen grains great forests. He hears the purring west wind in furry boughs. He pictures snow and ice, cloudy and sunny days, rushing streams of spring freshets, death crashes of great tree giants weakened by centuries of combat, germination of seeds and new forests. As he counts he wonders how many deer, wolves, bear, spruce hens and various types of scurrying animal life were associated with these changing forests."

Or witness the geologist while he examines particles of time arranged and endlessly rearranged by natural forces—glaciation, erosion, life and death—long before the short span of the human race. His record of Quetico-Superior history begins over a half a billion years ago, the Pre-Cambrian period, when the oldest rocks on the continent rose up to form mountain ranges where lakes now lie. He observes the progression of rock masses being upthrust and crushed during the growth of mountains; then the removal of the peaks by erosion, leveling the surface of the land to a rolling plain; the uplifting again of the region, followed by the mighty sweep of glaciers. Ultimately, as the geologist's story unfolds, the numerous lakes of the Quetico-Superior are shown as the gift of glaciation.

In at least four distinct glacial epochs, each lasting hundreds of thousands of years, frigid tongues of ice moved southward over the central continent. Massive icy pressures overrode the mountains, digging out the basin of Lake Superior. One glacial surge moved as far south as central Missouri; others advanced into northeast Kansas, central Iowa and the Ohio Valley. They pressed entire mountains southward, grinding them in sheets of ice more than a mile thick, scraping off soils and subsoils and planing the center of the continent.

In many places the ice gouged out basins in solid rock. In others, it produced "kettle holes," when ice blocks left behind would melt. It also dammed drainage canals with earth and stones. Finally, when the climate moderated and the icecaps shrank, these became the lakes adorning the barren landscape. Like countless gems they greeted the sun, dotted by islands—rocky crags the ice had failed to remove. Around them torrents of water cut massive channels, which became new outlets to the oceans. In the Quetico-Superior country, most lakes, major streams and rivers would flow through the Rainy Lake

147

drainage basin north into Hudson Bay waters and the Arctic. The remainder, about 35 per cent, would flow through the Pigeon River drainage to Lake Superior, the glacially formed Great Lakes and out to the Atlantic.

The geologist and botanist find that perhaps at first there was little or no animal life or vegetation in the lakes. Life began with simple diatoms and other algae invading the clear, cold waters. While glaciers still stood near, wind-borne microscopic remains of plants settled in the basins. Moss, fern and lichens moved in along the shoreline to begin the progression of plant history, leading upward to the pioneer spruce, fir and jack pine. As one generation after another died they built up the quality of the soil.

Each spring, for millions of springtimes, a rain of pollen dust fell, sifting into the water. Within an eon, lake bottoms which had been exposed solid rock, crystal-white sand or beds of gravel were covered with muds of organic origin. It took centuries to make a foot of bog, but the world was unhurried. As forests were born and died the muddy sediments deepened, continually displacing water and making its level ever shallower. The outer belt became a green carpet of sphagnum moss or a dense cover of small shrubs. In time, weed beds invaded the lake, crowding out fish life.

Where the original basin was shallow, as many basins were, all these changes may have been completed before the arrival of civilized man. But where the basin was more deeply dug by glacial action, you will see a sparkling lake which is still filling in and collecting microscopic fossils. You'll never recognize it as the same place a thousand years from now.

The arrival of man in the lakes country occurred only yesterday in time. In 1600, the period of which the historian begins to speak with some authority, the Sioux lived here. They were succeeded by the Chippewa, called the Ojibwa on the Canadian side, an essentially nomadic people who roved the wilderness in small family groups in search of plentiful food. Their staples were meat, fish, wild rice and maple sugar.

The Chippewa were as much a part of the forest as trees, water and wildlife. Their whole existence revolved around two powerful, intertwined forces: nature and religion. They believed, for one thing, they were descended from forest animals. Thus, their clan names and

148

totemic emblems represented wildlife—the bear, loon, heron, moose, eagle and catfish.

From his boyhood, the Chippewa trained to be an outdoorsman. His father taught him the rudiments of hunting, trapping, snaring, stalking. As he grew he spent countless days and weeks observing the habits and movements of animals. When he was ready to propose marriage, he had first to signify his intention, and ability to provide, by slaying a deer or other large animal and presenting it to his squaw's parents. Then, for the first year of marriage, he was required to live with his in-laws, in their wigwam, supplying them with meat before he could take his wife away to establish his own household.

The Indian traveled in a birchbark canoe, the prototype of today's canoe. When the water was free of ice, it was his only form of transportation. His canoe was light and maneuverable and he paddled it kneeling on the floor, without benefit of centerboard or seats.

In constructing his canoe, bark was cut from the living tree in spring, when the rising sap made it easy to peel from the trunk. Ribs, thwarts and gunwale framework were fashioned of cedar, with great care to insure proper balancing. To begin, the outline of the canoe was formed by stakes in the ground. Strips of bark were set in place, supported by the stakes. An inner lining of flat wooden pieces was laid, then secured together and sewn to the ribs. After the thwarts were positioned the canoe was carefully inspected to make certain every joint was properly sewn. Finally, every seam was waterproofed with hot pine pitch.

Fish were caught in all seasons. In summer he and his wife spread nets and seines. He did much fishing from his canoe using lines and hooks. At night he would paddle and drift quietly, attracting the fish with the light of a torch and then catching it with a spear. He would use the spear in winter, too, through a hole in the ice, after first attracting the fish with carved-wood artificial lures. Winter fishing had its special advantages, since he could store his fish and keep it fresh "on ice" for weeks or months.

In winter, when lakes and rivers froze, the Chippewa set aside his canoe and brought out snowshoes, toboggan and sled. Snowshoe frames were made of ash and laced with rawhide netting. Toboggans, the most popular of all winter conveyances, were made of hardwood. Cut during the winters, the wood was well soaked and heated in front of fires to curl the front ends. Cleats were placed along the sides and bottom so that loads could properly be held in place. Sides were made of ash, the runners steamed into U shapes to support the floor boards, which were held in their places by crosspieces. Both sled and toboggan were pulled by teams of two or three dogs—the only animal domesticated by the Chippewa. No, there were no horses in this country during the Indian period.

Bow and arrow was his chief means of hunting. Arrows, fashioned from the stalks of the Juneberry bush, were of several types, depending on their function. Those intended for water birds must not sink if they missed their mark; they had to float on water. For rabbits, arrows were tipped with turtle claws to deepen penetration. For deer, stone or bone heads were fastened in such a manner that the arrow shaft would pull out once the animal had been hit and began to run through the woods. In such cases, the arrow was designed not to kill outright but to bleed; the hunter would pursue the wounded animal, perhaps for hours, until it fell from loss of blood.

The main quarry were deer, moose and bear. A Chippewa would snare rabbit, muskrat and, to a lesser extent, otter and beaver. In spring and early summer, wild ducks and pigeon were his game. In winter, he pursued the red, black and silver-gray fox, the timber, prairie and bush wolves. Tirelessly, he would track one of these animals on snowshoes until it lay exhausted from continually sinking in the deep snow, completely at his mercy.

As a trapper, he caught large animals in "fall" traps, activated by a trigger; when released by an unsuspecting animal, it caused a weighted log or timber to fall, pinning the animal to the ground and very likely breaking its back at the same time. Smaller animals, otter, mink, beaver and muskrat, were caught in nets made of nettle stalk fiber.

Trapped animals were very important both for food and fur. Trap lines extended for miles across the wilderness. The Chippewa spent many hours alone studying the habits of the game he sought, then went back into the woods to check his traps and watch the trail for evidence of game.

To insure success, he invoked the spirits for luck on the trail through the use of charms. He would smoke powders, made from dried and ground herbs, at strategic points in the forest. And if this didn't work and the family was really short of food, he would turn his woman and children to fasting, painting their faces black, in penitence to the spirits.

The Chippewa were artists and one form of their art is still visible in the canoe country: the pictograph or rock painting—which canoers find on the underside of rocks hanging over the water. These were probably painted while the artist stood in his canoe, with a mixture of hematite (a ferrous iron oxide) and fish oil. They depict natural objects the Indians knew and understood—men, canoes, suns, moons, moose, loons and pelicans. The best example of pictography is found about one mile north of Lower Basswood Falls on Crooked Lake, the site called Picture Rock.

The French were the first whites to reach the Quetico-Superior. It became another link in the long water chain of exploration which they had started forging from the very headwaters of the St. Lawrence River. First, into Lake Superior, came the cross, borne by Jesuit Father Isaac Jogues. He opened the route into the farthest west of the Great Lakes in 1646, a century before the brown-robed Franciscans would begin traveling El Camino Real in California. He was followed, in 1660 by the two intrepid traders, Radisson and Groseilliers, who went on into northern Minnesota and found Indians, wilderness and beaver.

From 1731 to 1749 Sieur de la Verendrye pushed the exploration route onward. He was searching for a water passage to the Northwest, which would never materialize. However, he did establish a fur-trading route from Lake Superior to Lake of the Woods, the Voyageurs' Highway, through the heart of the Quetico-Superior country. This opened the era of beaver and adventure in wild, beautiful and serene country, and the best road in the Northwest was that great water highway, which later would form the boundary between the United States and Canada.

The thriving fur trade bound the raw frontier with the Atlantic Coast. Each year after the spring breakup, goods and supplies were started on their western course from Montreal. They were transported up the Ottawa River, across Lake Nipissing, down the French River to Georgian Bay, then into Lake Superior and to Grand Portage, the fort on the shore of Lake Superior. Meanwhile, raw furs were brought from inland trading posts by canoe to the transfer point at Grand Portage. They were loaded into the large lake canoes for the trip back to Montreal, while provisions and trading goods continued west to backwoods trading posts.

Grand Portage was alive with activity, as the meeting place of trader and trapper, of Indian and white. It was the Great Carrying Place, named for its strategic location at the outlet of the nine-mile portage to the Pigeon River, which skirted twenty miles of treacherous rapids and falls. For 100 years, from 1750 to 1850, it was one of the great markets of the empire of fur.

The history of the past hundred years is not quite so enchanting. The record is one of land abuse and controversy. Of nightmares instead of dreams until the time of the National Forest and the Provincial Park, with a few nightmares still lingering.

Below were broken little islands, roads winding among the trees and fishermen spotted on a hundred lakes. Dark waters, almost black from the air, shimmered in the sunlight, then splashed into whiteness over the rock outcroppings of Basswood Falls. The pilot, Walt Newman, pointed out the Canadian customs and ranger cabin, probably the loneliest outpost along the entire border between the Atlantic and Pacific.

"And there's Basswood Lodge," he said. "Luxury in the wilderness. Radio, telephone, hot and cold showers, electricity—all the comforts of home. It was built on private land years ago."

We flew a rectangular course aboard the high-winged De Havilland Beaver, a plane well known as the workhorse of the Canadian bush. It was the morning after returning to Ely from the canoe trip. Now we were exploring the Forest from above on a fire-patrol flight. Forest Service planes are the only ones permitted over the canoe country. I asked the pilot if this sort of run day after day ever grew monotonous. "Of course it does," he replied, "but whenever we get action, there is liable to be plenty of it. Once I spotted five lightning strikes at a time. Anyway you look at it, aerial coverage is far better in this country than the old fire towers. We can be on almost any fire within ten minutes and start to extinguish it."

Behind us in the plane were hard hats, shovels, hoseline and other fire-fighting gear. Under the belly of the plane was a specially designed 125-gallon water tank; by skimming over a lake, the pilot can scoop a tankful and then use the water to "bomb" a fire.

In Lac La Croix we saw a powerboat cut a wide-tailed swath as it passed a cluster of shiny roofs, an Indian settlement on the Canadian side. Now I could follow our course on the map, heading for home above Echo Trail, a road built through the wilderness years ago.

When we left the plane neither Dick nor I realized how soon we would see fire in the Superior. We drove from the hangar, at a lake outside Ely, to visit the Service Center, from which the Forest Service dispatches work crews and fire fighters. Walt Newman's voice was heard on the radio, reporting a fire. "I can't tell which way it's heading," he said. "It's blowing and running in all directions."

The district ranger was already directing the fire operation. Larry drove Dick and me to the fire scene on a logging road near the Kawishiwi River Campground. It had started in slash piled along the road, from a cigarette or a lighted match. Red flames leaped and spread through the woods. Fifty men or more already were fighting it with water from portable pumps they carried on their backs, and with small gasoline-driven pumps which they inserted into streams on one end and hooked on the hoselines at the other.

The woods were hot and smoky. A hissing sound roared through the trees and a wind blew up. "Now she's creating her own wind," Dick said. "When you hear that you know you've got something." The wind was created by convection of air currents, with warm air rising rapidly above the center of fire, cool air flowing to replace it. In mountain country, where convection becomes more pronounced, severe up-slope winds created by fire sometimes reach hurricane force.

Larry had gone off with the district ranger. Dick and I climbed over rocky terrain. A tractor was trying to dig a fire line to keep the blaze from spreading. "What they're probably trying to do," he explained, "is to get around to the head end. They've got it pretty well under control at the road. Now they're trying in front to keep it from spreading." The men started down both sides. Overhead the Beaver flew at about 400 feet and unloosed a spray of water. "He's bombing the head end now," Dick said. Five minutes later the Beaver was back on another bombing run.

We walked down a logging road through the heart of the fire, enveloped by flames, smoke and heat. We passed an abandoned truck and a pile of logs, peeled and neatly stacked, ready to be carted off. They never would be. The second time we passed the scene they were burning like so many matchsticks. And the third time, with wet handkerchiefs over our faces, the logs were embers and charcoal.

It took all of the afternoon and much of the night to bring the fire under control. Men would stay on into the morning and through the next day extinguishing fiery remnants in the duff and litter of the forest floor. "A Class C fire. About fifty acres," Dick estimated that night. It was a small fire, as fires go. Certainly nobody beyond fifty miles away would hear about it, and even the men involved would think of it soon enough as just another fire.

153

"Fire fighting is a damn discouraging business," Dick said as we sat at the side of the road and drank coffee and looked at the blackened, smoky, ghostly remains of a forest. He had directed hundreds of fire operations in his California days as supervisor of Angeles National Forest. "You know the final outcome will be desolation. The only question is, how much?"

Fire has visited northern Minnesota many, many times in the past century and left desolation and death. Fire began with development, when the Chippewa were settled on the reservation around Grand Portage. Homesteaders tested their mettle against rigorous winters, rocky terrain and soil too poor to produce field crops. Logging started along streams immediately tributary to Lake Superior, then probed deeper into the woods. Mining in this land of tremendous natural wealth had been a dream since the French days and with a discovery near Vermillion Lake in 1865 the Minnesota ranges became the iron-ore center of the world. Roads were cleared, sawmills and stamp mills erected and mining towns arose in the wilderness. More timber was cut for mines, houses and towns. Duluth, the forested outpost on the lake which had a population of 600 in 1869, became a grimy logging, mining and shipping center.

But with little or no protection, fire often swept through the debris left by lumberjacks. One of the worst fires in national history burned in 1894. It engulfed the town of Hinckley and surrounding villages southeast of Duluth and wiped them out. At least 400 persons were burned to death, some charred beyond identification. One body was found four years later. The year 1918 was even worse. A total of 770,000 acres burned throughout the state. High winds whipped into the woods, spurring the fire. It invaded Cloquet, one of the most important lumber towns in the Lake States, and left it in ashen ruins. At least 500 persons died in Cloquet and Moose Lake village, twenty-six miles away, which burned simultaneously.

But in the early years of the century interest arose, both in Canada and Minnesota, in saving the magnificent border-lakes country, even while it lay deserted, except for a few trappers and prospectors. On February 13, 1909, less than a month before he left office, Theodore Roosevelt established Superior National Forest—some 900,000 acres. The Canadians concurrently created Quetico (backwoods French for "quest for the coast") Provincial Park.

There was opposition, too, as there always would be in one form or another, for contention has been the destiny of the Superior National Forest. The wilderness today is no accident of natural history, though it may have started as such, but the result of unending battles, of attack, counterattack, skirmish, strategy and tactics. It is also the result of the strenuous efforts and bold ideas of individuals.

One is Arthur Carhart. He served with the Forest Service from 1919 to 1923, before going on to a career of city planning and writing (including a book on the National Forests). As a landscape architect, he first came to the Superior to devise a plan for its recreational development. He recognized the area could be "as priceless as Yellowstone, Yosemite, or the Grand Canyon—if it remained a water-trail wilderness." His was a minority viewpoint. Already there was a master plan to build roads to reach every lake and to line the shores with thousands of summer homes. Together with a handful of others, both inside and outside the Forest Service, he successfully blocked mass development and laid the basis for the statement of policy that, "No roads will be built as far as the Forest Service can control the situation, and no recreational developments will be permitted on public lands except waterways and portage improvements and such simple campground improvements as may be needed to prevent the escape of fire or to protect sanitary conditions."

Another to remember is Sigurd Olson, who led a small group in holding, as Carhart puts it, "a thin line of defense protecting this exquisite wilderness until help could rally to save it."

In 1922, Olson, a young trained biologist and scientific researcher, came to Ely from Chicago, to join the staff of Ely Junior College (of which he later became dean) and to guide summer canoe trips. One of his first battles was against the development of roads like Echo Trail. And an early major victory was the establishment, in 1926, of the Superior Primitive Area, which eliminated homesteading and prospecting permitted under archaic laws.

In the middle twenties, Olson, Ernest C. Oberholtzer, of Rainy Lake, and friends faced a powerful opponent of wilderness in E. W. Backus, lumber and power magnate, who proposed to construct a chain of power dams across the Rainy Lake watershed. This would have converted all the lakes east of Rainy into four great reservoirs, submerging islands and waterfalls, and doubtlessly leaving the shoreline a morass of stagnant water and dead trees.

Backus had influence, affluence and money to fight for his program of dams. But the harder he pressed the more support for protection of

155

the wilderness arose throughout Minnesota and the nation. The Izaak Walton League, newly organized in 1923, entered the Quetico-Superior scene and has stayed in it ever since. The Backus battle was waged until 1934, when the International Joint Commission, the U.S.-Canadian agency which adjudicates boundary disputes, set it to rest with a declaration that, "It is impossible to overstate the recreational and tourist value of this matchless playground. Its natural forests, lakes, rivers and waterfalls have a beauty and appeal beyond description and nothing should be done to destroy their charm."

After that, as Sig Olson recalled when I visited with him in Ely, "things looked safe." In 1930 Congress had enacted the Shipstead-Newton-Nolan Act, protecting the shoreline from logging and power developments. Minnesota had given similar protection to state-owned land within the roadless area. And mining was prohibited unless clearly required for the public interest.

But local people, with their own notion of how this wilderness should be run, fought on. They opposed the Forest Service at almost every turn as it tried, without adequate funds, to consolidate the wilderness through land exchanges. They opposed Franklin D. Roosevelt when he enlarged the boundaries of the National Forest and when he appointed the Quetico-Superior Committee, a national advisory body to report and recommend on the welfare of *their* area.

In 1939 and 1940, the era of the private airplane dawned over the wilderness. William Zupancich (called Billy Zup), Martin Skala, Joseph Perko and others foresaw the new day. They exercised their right, as free citizens should, to advance their fortunes. They were of Central European stock drawn to northern Minnesota by mining, but they recognized brighter prospects in land, fishing and resorts; at very low cost they acquired choice locations in the heart of the wilderness where airplanes could land.

After the war the planes arrived—in droves. Fishermen coming from the Chicago Loop poured out of the sky to Billy Zup's Curtain Falls Fishing Camp, Martin Skala's Lac La Croix Lodge and forty other such places. Eleven airplanes shuttled back and forth from Ely. It was possible to fly in, get your limit of fish and fly out before sundown. Ely became, as the chamber of commerce was proud to say, "the largest inland seaplane base in America."

As for the state of wilderness, well, that was another matter. The noise of engines shattered the age-old spell for the bear, beaver and eagle. The poor canoer would round a rocky headland and see the

156

lights of a new fishing lodge glowing from a campsite where for years canoers had built their cook fires. Sig Olson once paddled a number of days to a specially beautiful waterfall. There he encountered a group of plane arrivals. "Grand spot," said one. "Sure," agreed another, "but think of all this power going to waste." Then, turning to Olson, he said proudly, "We made it from Ely in just twenty-seven minutes. It will take you a good three days to get out."

The problem, for those who loved the woods and lakes, was dual: first, aircraft penetrating a region conceived as wilderness, and second, the development of commercial resorts on pockets of private land within the wilderness. As far as some local merchants and their chamber of commerce could arrange matters, they would stay just this way, regardless of whether in time the Superior would become a lake resort like a thousand others.

The Forest Service and Izaak Walton League felt otherwise. The Service, however, had no legal right to deny aircraft the right to land. Nor did it have authority or funds to purchase private holdings except for watershed or timber protection. The League stepped into the void. In three years it raised $100,000 and purchased 5400 acres; a drop in the bucket, considering the total of 117,500 privately owned acres, but a healthy drop.

Meanwhile aviation legislation and precedent were closely studied. In 1949, President Harry S. Truman, heeded the pleas of the Izaak Walton League and other groups (including the Quetico-Superior Committee, Wilderness Society, Minnesota Department of Commerce and Friends of the Wilderness). He established an Airspace Reservation over the roadless areas, prohibiting flying below 4000 feet above sea level, except for emergency landings.

The resort owners deliberately violated the air ban in order to test it. To deprive them of plane service, they said, deprived them of property rights without due process of law. They cited the basic National Forest Act of 1897, which provided that nothing should be "construed as prohibiting the egress or ingress of actual settlers within boundaries of national forests." Were they not actual settlers? Was not the government destroying a traditional, permissible means of entry?

No, replied the District Court in Duluth, to both questions. The President can indeed establish an airspace reservation under authority granted by the 1926 Air Commerce Act. No, emphasized the Circuit of the Eighth District, when the case was appealed; the President

157

certainly has the right, considering the legislative background of the Superior National Forest. The Supreme Court added the third and final negative decision, when it denied a petition of review. Planes do not fly over the roadless areas any more.

In 1948, on another front, Congress enacted the bipartisan Thye-Blatnik Act appropriating $500,000 to the Forest Service to purchase land on which development and exploitation "threaten to impair the unique qualities and natural features of the remaining wilderness canoe country." Since then Congress has given an additional $2,000,000, enabling the Forest Service to purchase more than 100,000 acres. It has almost made a reality of the chamber of commerce slogan, "Come to Ely, where the wilderness begins."

Now the Service has about 15,000 acres to go, perhaps less when you read this, in the massive reclamation of canoe wilderness. The principal holdouts are hard-core resort operators like Billy Zup and the Oliver Mining Company, a division of United States Steel.

Mining—it could be the next significant threat to the solitude of the eagle, the beaver, the loon and the canoer. The known supply of high-grade ore in the Minnesota Range now has an anticipated life of about twenty years. But low-grade taconite ores are limitless; planned expenditures for plants in northern Minnesota exceed $350,-000,000 over the next five years. Three new towns, Silver Bay, Hoyt Lakes and Babbitt, have already sprung up around the Forest. Besides iron, there are indications of copper, nickel and cobalt extending into the roadless areas. The present protection against mining consists of this regulation: "Mineral leases inside the Roadless Areas will not be approved unless production of minerals outside of the Roadless Areas indicates beyond doubt that it is in the public interest to permit development of minerals inside the Roadless Areas."

Is this protection adequate? At what point does commercial use become of greater public value than wilderness? Even when the Forest Service acquires every foot of private land in public ownership, the roadless areas are still not inviolate from mining.

As for powerboats, "They will be permitted until the public demands the contrary," Sig Olson said. "But the time will come when we need the wilderness even more than now, and the public will not stand for motorized intrusion in a canoe country."

There are many places in Minnesota and the Superior National Forest suited to powerboating and less-than-wilderness vacationing. Thirty-seven developed campgrounds and scores of resorts border

158

lakes and streams in restful natural settings outside the roadless areas but within the National Forest. The entire Minnesota Arrowhead Country is a great vacationland, readily accessible to 45,000,000 people within a 750-mile radius. Those who desire comfort, scenery and recreation have all the choice in the world.

But if the Boundary Waters Canoe Area is really to survive as wilderness, it should be reserved for those who are willing to travel under their own power and endure the hardships—or, as they see it, enjoy the sport—of primitive living. If you visit the Canoe Area, bring a paddle and not an outboard motor. Come not for a sampling of wilderness, but to study the drops of water in a single lake, the lichen, moss, plants and pine around its edge.

Any good camper who can pitch a tent, start a fire, clean and cook a fish can make his way in the Quetico-Superior. If you don't have your own tent, canoe or camping gear, you can rent everything you need from an outfitter. For only six dollars per person per day you can have the use of a seventeen-foot Grumman aluminum canoe, tent, complete food rations, packsacks, sleeping bag (twenty-five cents extra for air mattress), cook kit, ax and insect bomb. Or you can rent only part of the equipment. A canoe is three dollars a day.

If you have any hesitation about your own ability, you can hire a guide for twenty dollars a day, plus his food and the rental of his outfit. The guide will earn his pay. He will plan your route, paddle, keep you from getting lost, show you where the fish are biting, do the portaging, pitch camp, cook and talk back to the loons in loon language—he'll do as much or as little as you want him to do.

Plan to travel light but be sure you have a complete change of clothing from the skin out, including heavy shirt, windbreaker, slicker, strong high shoes, moccasins for slippers, compass, waterproof matchbox and flashlight. The Forest Service map is adequate, but for more detailed navigation buy a set of the maps published by W. A. Fisher Company, of Virginia, Minnesota ($2.50 for a set of fifteen), complete in detail down to the portages and their distances. It shows the twelve principal canoe routes; the longest is the Voyageurs' Highway, which takes about twenty-two days, covers 235 miles of paddling and nine miles of portaging on both sides of the border. No, there is not a chance in the world of your meeting a voyageur of the Radisson school or a Chippewa. But by the time you're through you will probably feel like one and be the better for it.

CHAPTER TWELVE

# South of Cornucopia

Whoever heard of the Moquah Sand Barrens? Hardly anyone outside Wisconsin and the Forest Service, except for the hopefuls who went broke there in the days of the beautiful land boom and have been trying to forget the place ever since.

There is really nothing wrong with the Moquah country, except for the memory of an unfortunate era in human history. It forms the interior of a remote fragment of northwest Wisconsin geography, the Bayfield Peninsula, and is air-conditioned by gentle breezes blowing in from Lake Superior. The Peninsula is rimmed by sheltered coves, villages and a shore pleasantly free of billboards and blight. The offshore scenery is enlivened by the sight of fishing boats clustered around the Apostle Islands.

This much might sound appealing to anyone, and better yet if you were told this was the most promising farmland and real estate that money could buy—especially if the word "barren" was politely omitted from the prospectus.

We should include another image: Chequamegon, which requires some effort to spell and pronounce (She-wam'-e-gun), preserves the traditional word for "soft beaver dam" by which the Chippewa called this place in the long, long ago, before the trader, trapper, logger, settler and the ultimate establishment of a 1,000,000-acre National Forest bearing the name. The Moquah, at its most barren, became the first portion of the Chequamegon. That was in 1929, after it had shared the history of forests in the Great Lakes region—and when the land boom was heading for the last burst.

Logging came to the Lake States in the middle of the last century, when the inexhaustible forests of New England began to look more than slightly exhausted. Bordering woodlands were as great as the lakes themselves, from rich hardwoods on the southern shores to valuable white pine, as well as maple, birch and aspen (called popple) on the northern shores.

161

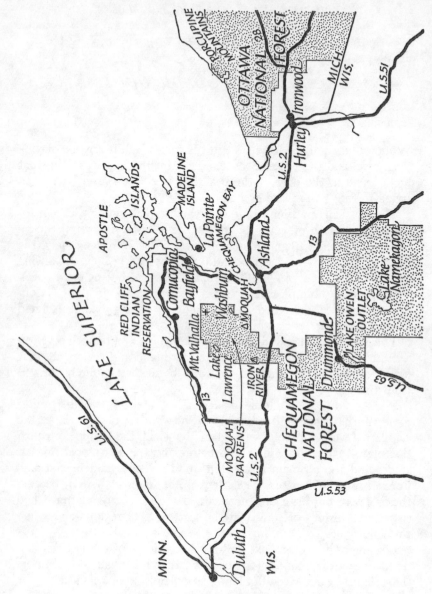

The Forest on the Great Lakes

In 1850, Ohio ranked fourth in lumber production among the states. Indiana and, to a lesser extent, Illinois, produced fine hardwoods—oak, poplar, ash, walnut, hickory, maple, basswood, cherry, elm and gum—which ranked among the most sought-after lumber in the nation.

But Michigan enjoyed the greatest wooden glory. For thirty years, from 1869 to 1899, Michigan lumber stood supreme. First, the Lower Peninsula was harvested, north to Alpena, on the Lake Huron shore, and to Manistee, which the Chippewa had called "Spirit of the Woods," along Lake Michigan. Men by the thousands were employed in logging camps and sawmills, while logs by the hundreds of millions were swept up in the famous river drives that choked the Au Sable, Pine, Saginaw, Muskegon, Tittabawassee, Manistee, Rifle and Au Gres. In 1880, the loggers moved into the wilderness of the Upper Peninsula, cutting the towering white pine along the Ontonagon, Paint, Iron and Sturgeon Rivers. The state hit its peak year in 1889, yielding five and a half billion board feet of timber.

All this would build a lot of factories, houses, towns, cities and railroads, but it did nothing for the future of the forest. The loggers began moving west into Wisconsin and Minnesota.

In northern Wisconsin they found a variety of timber: pine on light sandy soils; northern hardwood and hemlock on heavier loamy soils; mixed conifers in the swamps, upland spruce and balsam along the ridges. By 1900 the state had taken over Michigan's pre-eminent role. Wisconsin now was the champion timber producer, with an annual cut of three and a half billion board feet, largely white pine. In winter the woods were alive with the sounds of humming saws and humming lumberjacks. Logging was done by sled, the roads sprinkled with water, where need be, to assure a smooth icy coating. Spring was another time. Hurley, on the border of Michigan's Upper Peninsula, earned its dubious fame as one of the wickedest little cities in America, as loggers poured in for relaxation after a hard winter of labor and isolation. "Hurley is the word for hell," the saying went, although later it was modified to include other towns and the saying became, "Hurley, Hayward and Hibbing."

A reminder of those days of timbered grandeur, a tree the axmen overlooked, stands in the Anvil Lake Recreation Area in Nicolet National Forest, near Eagle River. This towering old fellow, called the Great White Pine, is 150 feet high with a circumference of fifty-one feet. A very young forest, only 10 per cent large enough for saw timber, and most in sapling size, looks up around it.

The timberman is not solely responsible for stripping the woods. The land was denuded by fire and by ill-planned farming on thin, stony soil, where only trees should have grown. The logger left his slash to burn. The settler burned his land to clear it. The farmer burned his pasture, believing it would result in better crops.

Fire swept across cities, fields and forests. In the first week of October, 1871, following a hot and dry summer, smoke dulled the skies of Lake Michigan from woods burning massively at a dozen places along its border. Then came the historic disaster at the foot of Lake Michigan. Chicago was aflame. It burned furiously in a tempest of wind until, twenty-seven hours after it started in the legendary O'Leary barn, the heart of the city lay in smoking ruins.

Chicago was the most dramatic fire, but others raged simultaneously and in some respects were far worse. On the Wisconsin side of the lake, on the same night as the Chicago fire, the booming lumber town of Peshtigo was engulfed. A tornado of fire roared through the city, burning every building and trapping over 600 persons. In its wider dimensions, the nightmare of history now called the Peshtigo fire covered 1,200,000 acres and caused the death of 1500 persons. Rivers and streams teemed with dead fish floating on the surface. The surface of Green Bay was covered with birds which had burned in flight and dropped. In Michigan, at the same time, other fires struck Manistee and Holland, and across the state wiped out settlements from Saginaw Bay south to Port Huron.

These and later fires were the start of the end for the great white pine. They killed any second-growth forest, just getting underway as a future crop. They opened the cones of the scrawny jack pine, the so-called "fire pine," which germinates its seed following fire.

Fire scored most triumphantly in western Wisconsin, and especially in the Moquah country, the heart of the Bayfield Peninsula. Not in a single spectacular bonfire as at Peshtigo, but in thousands of smolderings without end.

You would never know the Moquah once possessed timbered riches. That was in its storied past, the Chippewa day, when explorers like Sieur Dulhut and Pierre LeSueur came to call, and when La Pointe in the Apostle Islands was an outpost of the beaver traders. In 200 years, millions of dollars' worth of furs were transported over Moquah trails. When the beaver was depleted, loggers, settlers and fire arrived. One fire burned a million dollars' worth of lumber awaiting shipment on the west coast near Cornucopia village. The loss within the forest was greater; the pall of smoke was so heavy that as far south as La Crosse, 250 miles away, the sun was hidden for two days.

Then there were the fires of 1894. They began in July about eighty miles southeast of the Bayfield Peninsula. By September, northwest Wisconsin was aflame in a belt fifty miles wide by 150 miles long. Not a solid flame, but a spotty one. Drummond, now located within the National Forest, escaped without damage, while nearby Mason was wiped out and all its logging camps destroyed. Remarkably, only nine lives were lost, compared with 400 at Hinckley, in eastern Minnesota, which burned simultaneously.

Still, plenty of timber was produced. Of several firms operating on the Peninsula, the biggest was the Rust-Owen Lumber Company, which established the company town of Drummond in 1882. At first it logged entirely by sleigh haul. Then it built its own narrow-gauge railroad. In 1900, as white pine, the premium wood, diminished, it started cutting hemlock and hardwood. Production at the mills kept rising until it hit a peak in 1910. Other companies, meanwhile, brought their timber in immense rafts from logging camps near the lakeshore and from the Apostle Islands to mills at Ashland, Washburn, Red Cliff, Cornucopia and Port Wing.

Between 1882 and 1930 Rust-Owen cut an annual average of 25,000,000 feet of lumber, plus 6,000,000 pieces of lath, shingles and pickets. It totaled more than one billion feet of pine, plus 76,000,000 feet of hemlock and 54,000,000 feet of hardwood.

And then it was over. Henry Ford, the antediluvian antiquarian, acquired the old mill for his collection of Americana. In November, 1930, as the *American Lumberman* reported, nine days after the company closed for good, two officials were sitting in the company hotel, when they saw one of the smokestacks totter and fall. To the lumber periodical, this was "a valedictory from the old mill."

Then began another noble era, following the civilized succession since the land was wrested from the Chippewa. This was the great land boom. The companies moved west to find new sources of lumber but offered to sell their cutover Moquah holdings as "the finest agricultural lands on earth," also ideally suited for resort development or for do-it-yourself real-estate speculation. Rust-Owen engaged E. C. Hart, later municipal judge at Washburn, as its land agent. The State of Wisconsin aided with promotion efforts.

Families came by the thousands, induced to buy the cutover land at relatively high prices. Most looked at what they had purchased and never cleared a square foot. But others heeded the advice they were given. All they had to do, they were told, was burn the brush and start sowing, building and reaping a prosperous harvest.

They cleared. They burned. The land burned, reburned and kept on burning. The litter of pine needles burned. The land smoked and smoked until all layers of the soil were scraped away, until nothing remained but sand—the sandy sand you would expect to find at a beach.

A few made it farming, usually with some other job for added income. But most lasted only a few years and then gave up. When they did, the lumber company secured a quit-claim deed and regained the property.

By the late twenties, the land lay prostrate from its countless wounds and scars, unwanted. Owners became tax delinquent and let the county have their land. A few held on to dispose of their submarginal farms at marginal prices to the Resettlement Administration in 1935–36. In towns and villages from Barksdale to Cornucopia and Port Wing, businesses failed. The economic and social level of the "cutover area" was at a very low ebb.

When the Forest Service arrived on the scene in 1929 to accept the Moquah as the first National Forest in Wisconsin, it confronted a blighted scene. Degeneration of the land was complete. A forester stood somewhere in the center of the Peninsula, on a broad ridge about 1200 feet high, and looked at endless waves of barren rolling sand hills, with an occasional plateau and lake, sloping down to Lake Superior and Chequamegon Bay.

Two years later the first trees were planted. Since then 32,000,000 trees have been planted on the Moquah—22,000,000 jack pine, and the remainder the longer-lived, more useful red, or Norway, pine. About three times as many trees have been planted over the entire Chequamegon National Forest.

Today the Moquah is no longer a land of rolling barren sand hills, but a young forest of jack pine, which will never grow very tall, and of richly colored, vigorous red pine, which in time will reach eighty feet in height. Timber sales have been made, first of fuelwood, more recently of bridge timbers and telephone poles. All the timber cut in the past twenty years probably does not equal a good month's cut by Rust-Owen or Humbird Lumber Company in the old days. But come around in a hundred years or so and see the change.

Don't wait that long, after all. Drive up to the Bayfield Peninsula, the cool roof top of Wisconsin. From the east you go through Ashland, a lumber and iron-ore port, then follow the route along Chequamegon Bay, a beautiful sheltered harbor protected by the breakwater of Long Island, through Washburn into Bayfield. This town of 1200 population has an excellent boat basin shared by commercial (whitefish, lake trout and herring) and sport fishermen. From here a thousand miles of blue-water sailing and cruising lie dead ahead among the Apostle Islands. Trolling boats are available and you can try your luck for walleyed pike, northern pike, perch and lake trout.

The Apostle Islands tally to twenty-two at last count. Some are inhabited only by deer and bear. In 1954, a world's record for bow-and-arrow deer hunting was established on these islands. One, Otter Island, has a permanent Boy Scout camp. The main island, Madeline, has a long, colorful history, dating to the first French settlement and the beaver trade. John Jacob Astor's American Fur Company once had headquarters at La Pointe, the town on the island. You can reach it from Bayfield in thirty minutes aboard one of two ferries, the *Nichevo* and *Gar-How*. The island has campsites and simple overnight lodgings; also white beaches, vistas of blue waters at sunset and clean, clear lake air.

From Bayfield you can drive around the tip of the Peninsula through the Red Cliff Indian Reservation, the last of the Chippewa in these parts, to Cornucopia village, where Siskiwit River empties into the lake. And slightly south of Cornucopia you can see the Moquah Barrens—Moquah pine forest, I should say—for yourself.

# CHAPTER THIRTEEN

# Trail in the Wilderness

Jim Harrower, the local hardware dealer, mayor and Rocky Mountain historian, pointed to the cottonwood flats where the silvery threads of Horse Creek and Green River join into one.

"Benny DeVoto and I stood here and looked down at the flats," Jim said. "He was preparing *Across the Wide Missouri* at the time. Right there is the place he wrote about, where the Indians and trappers held the Green River rendezvous every spring."

We were on a treeless mesa outside of Pinedale, Wyoming. Across the valley to the east the massive mountains of the Wind River Range arose with snowy hands to touch the clear sky. In the distance to the north we could see the sheer, splendid Grand Tetons.

It was DeVoto country. As an admirer of the writer and the man, I felt a certain pride to stand in the midst of it, overlooking the scene of his classic history of the Western fur trade. From the few times I had met Bernard DeVoto, I recalled him as one who could at once be provocative and affable; a martini mixer and drinker of rare talent; a genuine authority on the West, and a staunch friend of National Forests.

Again I looked at the Wind Rivers. They were, as Alfred Jacob Miller, the artist, described them well over a century ago, "as fresh and beautiful as if just from the hands of the creator." Jim Harrower looked up at the mountains, too. They were his back yard. He had worked for the Forest Service for fifteen years, had hunted lion above 13,000 feet. Yet after a lifetime of riding those lonely, snowy crevices, he was no less captivated than I.

Wilderness is that way. The next two weeks I followed the trail through a barely touched natural domain of tall timbers and a thousand clear lakes, of massive rock formations almost as large as those in Yosemite Valley, of living glaciers and flowery alpine meadows, and of snowy starkness high above timberline. Yet for all its rugged grandeur and importance in Western history, this region is incredibly little

169

known, like an undiscovered marvel of the Rocky Mountain chain.

The Range, to properly set the scene, extends about 100 miles north and south astride the Continental Divide, and is almost entirely within the Bridger National Forest, named for Jim Bridger, the legendary scout and trapper. The Bridger Wilderness, on the western slope of the Divide, covers 383,000 acres, an area larger than Grand Teton National Park. It contains a concentration of great peaks just under 14,000-foot elevation, including Gannett, the highest in Wyoming; Frémont, which General Frémont climbed on his vaunted expedition of 1842; and Sacajawea (Sak-a-jee'-wah), named for the Shoshone girl who was guide and heroine of the Lewis and Clark expedition. She is buried at the Shoshone Reservation on the eastern slope of the Divide.

This is water country, where snow, rain and glaciers flow down from the heights into creeks and streams. On the western slope they form the Green River, which heads south into Utah to join the Colorado. On the eastern flanks, the Wind River and other streams flow into the Big Horn, the Yellowstone and ultimately the Missouri. The northern waters are tributaries of the Snake River, moving northwest to join the Columbia.

I was with a group called the Trail Riders of the Wilderness, sponsored by the American Forestry Association. Each summer about twelve such groups set forth on pack trips of eight to fourteen days into National Park and National Forest wilderness areas. Similar trips are conducted also by the Wilderness Society and Sierra Club. The wilderness system was started in the Forest Service about thirty-five years ago, when it recognized the American outdoors would not last forever. All types of recreation are found in the Forests, but wilderness is unique in providing these hardy experiences that exercise the muscles of body, mind and spirit. The Service now protects 14,000,000 wilderness acres from road building, timber cutting or other mechanical intrusions.

Our group numbered twenty-two, roughly half men and half women, of varying riding ability. There were three doctors, a banker, a young woman biologist, schoolteachers and assorted others who would share equal rank and privilege.

The twelve-day ride started at the Box R Ranch, in a green-meadowed valley at 7600 feet on the slope of the Wind River Range. The bossman of the Box R, Walt Lozier, furnished food, horses, tents, wranglers, and led the way. Strapping Lozier, almost as tall as was

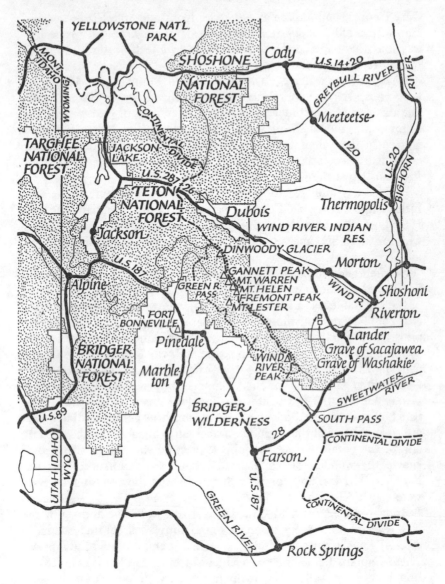

*Jim Bridger's Country*

Gary Cooper, and almost as talkative, looks and rides like a cattle-man of the old school. As we would learn shortly, he can weave his way smoothly between the rockiest peaks, and feels as much at home in the woods as under his own roof.

Having drawn a brave black horse named Midnight, I fell in line heading up the open sagebrush hillside. Ahead lay an aspen forest, like a gateway to the timeless wilderness. Hundreds of years of human history, and thousands of years of natural history before it, were written in these mountains, one of the most rugged sections of the entire Rocky chain. For centuries it was a favorite hunting ground of Indians. It was the heart of Jim Bridger's empire.

Bridger was probably the greatest of the mountain men. He had little learning, but spoke French, Spanish and a dozen Indian tongues. He talked straight with the Indians and knew them as well as any white man of his time. Of three women he married in his lifetime, all were Indians.

Opinion and estimates of Jim Bridger vary, but generals for whom he scouted said he knew every mountain peak, deep gorge and stream of the West. He was a born topographer, who with a stick or piece of coal could scratch on the ground a map more accurate than any in print. As a youngster of seventeen, he first came to this corner of Wyoming with General William Ashley's Rocky Mountain Fur Company in 1823. In the next twenty years, rawboned, gray-eyed "Old Gabe" discovered many of the landmarks between the Rockies and Sierras. He was the first white man known to have visited the Great Salt Lake; he tasted the water, spat a mouthful and said, "Hell, we are on the shores of the Pacific," and actually thought the lake was an arm of the ocean. Except for John Colter, he was the first to make known the wonders of Yellowstone, about 100 miles northwest of the Wind Rivers, and for years his stories of the spouting geysers were called "Jim Bridger's lies."

Bridger ranged north to Canada, west to the Pacific and south to New Mexico, but every summer found him back in this country, especially in the cottonwood flats, which lay behind us and the Box R. There Captain Benjamin Bonneville had built his log fort in 1832; from then on the valley became the nerve center of Western mountain fur trade. From 1833 to 1837 (except for '34), the annual rendezvous was held here on the Green River. The pack train would arrive from the East in time to meet groups of trappers who had spent the year in the mountains; they would turn over their beaver pelts for transport back to the states and be outfitted anew. It was not merely the season for trade and supply, but for roistering. Hundreds of Indians, of nearly every tribe in the Rockies, would set up lodges, bartering skins, robes, horses and women, replenishing their outfits and filling themselves with whisky.

Dr. Marcus Whitman, while pioneering the Oregon Trail, came to the rendezvous of 1835, and in a very delicate operation removed an Indian arrowhead which had been imbedded in Jim Bridger's back for three years. Alfred Jacob Miller painted, in his softly toned water colors, the rendezvous and the mountains from almost every angle. His famous lake pictures, which illustrated *Across the Wide Missouri,* were of New Fork Lake, almost on the course of our trail ride.

We soon saw some beautiful lakes on our own. So numerous the lake namers of the past had run dry of inspiration and simply called one group the "No Name Lakes," they were crystal-clear, unpolluted waters, the kind in which you could drink, swim (when the temperature was warm enough) and fish. We caught rainbow, cutthroat and, at the higher altitudes, even the choice California golden, a fighting trout which bends a rod about as far as a two-pound fish can bend it.

Wildlife presented itself early, a moose minding its own business on the other side of Section Corner Lake, our first night's camp; he agreed to keep his distance if we would keep ours. Later, we caught fleeting glimpses of antelope and deer, although there were too many horses and people for anything more than binocular viewing. "If you want to get any closer," Walt said once while I was trying to stare a deer in the eye, "you'd better come back in the fall and we'll hunt that rascal. Unless you want to go higher for bighorn sheep or bear. This is one of the best spots you'll find anywhere for rare big game."

Of twelve days in the wilderness, eight were spent on the trail, four in layovers. The daily mileage ranged from nine to sixteen—uphill, downhill, alongside sheer rocky crests, across streams and green meadows. In such an exercise, a horse is clearly man's best friend. A rider may doubt his ability to manage a steep grade, but as long as he trusts his mount, they will usually make it.

Time in the Bridger refused to blend into monotony. "There are no two days alike here," said Ernie Rosenau, a New York photographic salesman back for his fourth year on this same ride. "I don't think I've ever seen the same sight twice. You know, we could probably drive this whole route of ours in three hours, if a road ran through here, and would see practically nothing of it." The variety of scenery and geology in this compact area was tremendous. The third day, for instance, we rode through blue-green stands of spruce and pine along the shores of Trapper and Little Trapper Lakes, favorites of the early trappers and reminders of their role in opening the West. They blazed trails, located water and grass, named the lakes and rivers. (On the less romantic side, the wealth they produced, as De-Voto said, went east into other hands and stayed there. By 1840 they had cleaned out the West of beaver, which has not yet come back.)

Trapper Lake was one of the few places where we encountered company, a handful of canoers and fishermen who had hiked in. They were doing it the hard way, but in the more advanced school of wilderness travel. We met a couple who had been in the wilderness a month; they were pleased to meet us, but certainly were not suffering for their lack of radio or other forms of human chatter. This same day we ascended to Crow's Nest Lookout and signed our names in the register placed by the first group of Trail Riders to explore the Wind River Mountains in 1935. Almost 2000 feet below lay Pine Creek Canyon, extending eastward to Fremont Lake, the largest natural lake in Wyoming except for Yellowstone.

We were now in the country explored by General John C. Frémont in 1842, camping at nearly 11,000 feet at Frémont Crossing, the base of the mountain he climbed and named for himself. His expedition had been directed by the government to study "the rivers and country between the frontiers of Missouri and the base of the Rocky Mountains; and especially to examine the character, and ascertain the latitude and longitude of the South Pass, the great crossing-place to these mountains on the way to Oregon." With Kit Carson as his guide, Frémont reached South Pass, below the tip of the Wind River Range and continued to the headwaters of the Green River. He was drawn to the higher peaks by their icy caps glittering in the bright August light and determined to scale the highest. He was mistaken in his choice, as it developed, although *his* peak, a jagged, truncated mesa of stone, was the most spectacular. He and five companions set out from camp. They rode beneath a perpendicular wall of granite working their way to the summit, then dismounted and climbed afoot in thin moccasins of buffalo skin. It was a magnificent instant in the history of American exploration: Frémont, ever dramatic, drove a ramrod in the rock and "unfurled the national flag to wave where never the flag waved before."

We were less than 2000 feet from that site. Around us, great peaks flanked the Continental Divide: Gannett, Lester, Sacajawea, Warren. From Indian Pass, we could see the Dinwoody Glaciers; the snowy peaks of the Three Tetons, far northwestward, bright in the haze, and the forested trough of the Wind River Valley calling from across the Divide.

Here Frémont was overcome by the power of natural stillness. It was "a concourse of lakes and rushing waters, mountains of rock, dells and ravines of the most exquisite beauty, all kept green and fresh by the great moisture in the air and sown with brilliant flowers—everywhere the glory of magnificent scenes." This was to be the setting of Albert Bierstadt's massive, exciting "Rocky Mountains," painted in 1859. It hangs in the Metropolitan Museum of Art in New York.

From Frémont Crossing, we rode through a snowbanked pass at 11,000 feet. Icebergs floated over the Titcomb Lakes. Rainbow trout in those clear waters swam much too happily for the fishermen among us. Dozens of granite boulders, upthrust by glacial action, blocked the stark horizon above us, a scene of fierce beauty almost beyond reality.

We descended below timberline, a welcome relief from barren rock and tundra. Our campground in Trail Creek Valley was surrounded: spruce, alpine fir and a wall of mountains with an occasional lodgepole pine, brave but weak, growing out of the rocky cliffside. Around the campfire, Walt delivered a considerable speech. It took some prodding from his audience and assistance from his partner and wife, Nancy. She looks and rides like a Wyoming girl, although she came west from Rhode Island in 1940 as a "dudeen" and stayed to marry Walt.

"My parents homesteaded the Box R in 1900, when they came from Colorado in a covered wagon," he said. "My father built the house I was born in, and where we live today. He was one of the first outfitters around Pinedale. He would take a wagonload sight-seeing up through Yellowstone and they would hunt big game on the way back.

"Carl Rungius, the artist, came out and stayed at our house. Sometimes he rode with my father, but often alone, into the mountains to paint the animals of the Rockies."

While down below I had viewed the scene of the Green River

rendezvous which DeVoto described; now here was the arena of the venerable Rungius, whose paintings of big game hang in the Museum of Natural History and like places.

"Well, I helped my father," Walt continued. "I didn't have much schooling, which explains why I don't blather at the mouth. When I was fourteen I started renting horses for a dollar a day, sort of outfitting on a small scale. Later, I went in for bronc riding and bulldogging in the rodeos, and once I owned sixty head of bucking horses.

"This *was* great cattle country. But there's not enough grazing left to compare it with the Deep South, where the grass grows fast and high. Sure, wc'll always grow some cattle. I've got about 125 head of Herefords. But the future of this country, as far as I'm concerned, is in dude ranching and in wilderness pack trips like this one."

Nancy told about the logistics involved in planning a movement such as the Trail Riders. We realized there were lots of animals involved but it was still surprising to learn the total was sixty-four horses and eighteen mules. They carried the twenty-two Trail Riders, eight wranglers, plus Walt and Nancy. The baggage was toted in panniers (pan'-yers), cowhide covered boxes (adapted from the French word meaning "breadbasket") strapped to the pack animals—eighteen panniers with duffel and gear, twenty-two loaded with food.

There was no letup in beauty or discovery. Woods and valleys were abloom with wildflowers. The lupine, as indigenous to the West as the cowboy, was everywhere. Many delicate pea-type flowers, violet-blue, pink, yellow or white, adorned the full length of its stem rising above the leaf of five to seven spoon-shaped leaflets. The prettiest, I thought, was the lupine of alpine elevations; it was the smallest, with leaflets not more than a half inch long and erect stems bearing deep blue flowers. On moist meadows and slopes the small white and golden flowers of the saxifrage grew from a slender stalk above its wavy round leaves. On the hillsides was the Indian paintbrush, Wyoming's state flower, a tall herb, almost two feet high, with vivid red bloom. Small wintergreen, with shiny, lustrous leaves, white flowers and red berries, claimed the shady dells. Masses of colorful bluebells, buttercups and tall sunflowers swept across the open meadows, and even above timberline the phlox spread mats of white and violet color across the rocks and tundra.

At one point we came to the confluence of plunging streams forming the headwaters of the Green River, and found the color really is

176

green, caused by milky glacial particles suspended in the water. At another, we passed Old Squaretop, a towering 3500-foot rock in a field of deep bluish-green Englemann spruce; something like the valley of Yosemite without all the usual company. From our camp at Clear Creek we climbed White Rock Mountain and came down with fossils of imbedded seashells and crustaceans left by the inland seas of prehistory.

I could go on with the wonders of natural history, scenery and wildlife until the time we headed back for the Lozier Ranch and civilization. But better yet would be to suggest that you experience the Bridger, or another of the wilderness areas, yourself. A pack trip is not the most arduous expedition in the world, particularly if you bring along your sense of humor and do not expect too much convenience. Age, as Walt Lozier noted, is neither an asset nor a barrier; a sixty-five-year-old conditioned to outdoor living is better equipped for the trail than a twenty-five-year-old who is not in shape.

Stopping at a dude ranch like Lozier's Box R, primarily an old-time cattle outfit, you have the National Forest wilderness at your back door and can arrange a pack trip of any length. There also are campgrounds you can drive to within the Forest and use as a starting point for back-country hiking.

Wilderness is friendly, not forbidding. Now that experts have so many plans for its disposition, enlightened use, enthusiasm and appreciation will help place it in proper perspective. Best of all, perhaps, is that a wilderness like the Bridger is endowed with the absence of artificial noises, the absence of artificiality and a tremendous store of basic, nourishing reality.

# CHAPTER FOURTEEN

# *Wilderness Sentiment and Science*

That chronic bookworm and bird watcher, Henry David Thoreau, was, as you might imagine, the originator of the wilderness scheme. At least he appears to be the first of record to propose saving some of it. The very sort of thing you could expect from a man who spends his time dreaming in the woods, instead of applying his ingenuity to converting natural wealth into material wealth.

"The kings of England," Thoreau wrote, "formerly had their forests to hold the king's game for sport and food, sometimes destroying villages to create or extend them; and I think they were impelled by a true spirit.

"Why should not we, who have renounced the king's authority, have our national preserves, where no villages need be destroyed, in which the bear and panther may still exist, and not be 'civilized off the face of the earth'—our own forests, not to hold the king's game merely, but for inspiration and our own true recreation?"

His suggestion was little heeded. It was considered unnecessary, impractical. And, after all, he was an Easterner. George Catlin, the artist, had ideas along the same line but then he had gone forth to experience and paint the West, which entitled him to slightly more credence.

One century after Thoreau, areas of wilderness are preserved as he suggested. Not all the species of animals and birds of his day have survived to enjoy it. Gone or almost gone are the passenger pigeon, manatee, trumpeter swan, heath hen, ivory-billed woodpecker, Audubon bighorn of the Black Hills, golden bear and condor. But we are endowed with vast areas—vast, though sometimes they seem to be shrinking—for "inspiration and true recreation."

The Federal Government owns 85,000 square miles of wilderness, a larger body of land than Indiana and Kentucky combined. This is the sum total of 167 separate tracts: eighty-four within National Forests; forty-eight in National Parks; twenty in National Wildlife

Refuges and Ranges, and the remaining fifteen on Indian reservations.

For the traveler in search of solitude and rugged outdoor adventure, these afford tremendous variety of climate and scenery, even though most are in the West. For example, I have sampled a cross section of National Forest wilderness in the desert country of the Superstition Mountains, Arizona; the high Rocky Mountain divides and jagged granite peaks of the Wind River Range, Wyoming; the big game country of the Anaconda-Pintlar, Montana; the San Gorgonio Range, with the highest peaks in southern California; the rain-drenched Douglas-fir forests and glaciers of the Northern Cascades, Washington. And east of the Rockies, the Quetico-Superior canoe country, Minnesota, and the small wilderness gems of north Georgia.

Between Thoreau and the present, enthusiasts of the natural and the wild arose to assert their viewpoint before a nation bent on civilized advancement with its accompanying good and evil. In 1871, Yellowstone National Park was established to protect a 1,000,000-acre wilderness. In 1885, New York created the Adirondack Forest Preserve, and in 1894 adopted a constitutional amendment to prevent timber cutting. The Forest Preserve, the amendment declared, "shall be forever kept as wild forest lands. They shall not be leased, sold or exchanged, or be taken by any corporation, public or private, nor shall the timber thereon be sold, removed or destroyed."

The position adopted in New York was contradictory to the principle of preservation through use, advocated by Gifford Pinchot. The amendment resulted as a reaction to a horrible New York scandal of fraud, bribery and illegal cutting on state forests, but Pinchot felt the voters were following the wrong course. "I have always regarded the sentimental horror of some good citizens at the idea of utilizing the timber of the Forest Preserve under Forestry," he wrote later, "as unintelligent, misdirected and shortsighted."

Nevertheless the modern concept of wilderness was born and reached fruition in the Forest Service. Thus we now meet Aldo Leopold, as first of the two singular individuals most responsible for translating the dream and sentiment of Thoreau into a twentieth-century science.

Leopold, a native of Burlington, Iowa, was graduated from the Yale Forestry School in 1908. The following year he arrived in the Southwest and became absorbed in wildlife management, which led logically into the study of wilderness. He found that game conservation early in the century had given birth to two major ideas. The first was the reservation or park idea, by which threatened species were withdrawn into an outdoor museum for safekeeping. The second was the refuge idea, by which hunters' kill was limited to the natural increase of the game—and this was a National Forest role.

"The administration of the National Forests of America has for its real purposes the perpetuation of life," wrote Leopold, "human, plant and animal life. Of first importance is human life, and so closely related is this to tree and plant life, so vital are the influences of the forest, that their problems have been fashioned into major problems of forest management and administration.

"Of next importance, and ever increasing, is the problem of animal and bird life. Driven from their once great range by civilization the wildlife that was at one time America's most picturesque heritage has found refuge in the National Forests."

In looking across the Southwest in 1909, Leopold saw six immense roadless areas, each larger than half a million acres, providing refuge for wild creatures and wilderness sportsmen. These were the Jemez and Datil-Gila, in New Mexico, and the White Mountains, Blue Range, Tonto Rim and Kaibab, in Arizona. But would these remain inviolate without some special protection? Leopold considered the timber famine, of which Pinchot had warned, a matter of quality rather than quantity. He suggested the emphasis on logging under intensive forestry be limited to richer, accessible forest regions, capable of producing high-quality timber, while dedicating remaining regions to various forms of recreation, game management and wilderness. As he watched the roadless areas cut by roads, he warned that, "The existence of a wilderness-recreation famine has emerged as an incontrovertible fact."

Leopold proposed a system of wild areas for the Southwest. He had four goals in mind. First, to prevent the annihilation of particular rare plants and animals, like the grizzly. Second, to guard against disruption of areas still wild. "Disruption," he warned, "may come from unexpected quarters. A deer herd deprived of wolves and lions is more dangerous to wilderness areas than the most piratical senator or the go-gettingest chamber of commerce." Third, to secure recognition, as wilderness, of low-altitude desert generally regarded as valueless for recreation because it offered no pines, lakes or other conventional scenery. And fourth, to induce Mexico to co-operate in wilderness protection. "We have no faunas or floras which have not been abused, modified or 'improved,'" he wrote, "but in the Mexican mountains the whole biota is still intact with the single exception of the Apache Indian, who is, I fear, extinct."

Leopold served as secretary of the Albuquerque and New Mexico Game Protective Associations, both of which endorsed establishment of a wilderness area embracing the hazy blue Mogollan Mountains above the Mexican border at the head of the Gila River in Gila National Forest. It came to pass that in 1924 the regional forester approved establishment of the first wilderness area, protected against timber cutting and road building. The boundaries of the Gila Wilderness were drawn by Leopold. The development in forest management was less than earth-shaking, but he kept writing such articles as "Last Stand of the Wilderness" in *American Forests* and "Conserving the Covered Wagon" in *Sunset*. He warned that the new Federal Highway Act would doom the few remaining wild areas. This has happened: of all the wilderness he first saw in the Southwest in 1909, only the Gila remains of any great size, and it has been split down the middle and pared at the edges.

From 1933 to 1948, Leopold was professor of wildlife management at the University of Wisconsin, and a distinguished authority in his field. In books and articles, he stressed the interdependence of all living things, from arrow-weed thickets and cottonwoods on up to coons, skunks, avocets, heron and deer. "The outstanding scientific discovery of the twentieth century," he wrote in 1947, one year before his death, "is not television or radio, but rather the complexity of the land organism. The last word in ignorance is the man who says of a plant or animal, 'what good is it?' If the land mechanism as a whole is good, then every part of it is good, whether we understand it or not."

While Leopold introduced the wilderness idea and was responsible for establishing the first area in New Mexico, Robert Marshall brought the concept to maturity during his career as chief of recreation in the Forest Service and as a founder and president of the Wilderness Society.

In 1935, Marshall, together with Benton MacKaye, Aldo Leopold, Bernard Frank, Harvey Broome, Ernest C. Oberholtzer and Robert Sterling Yard, organized this Society, which ever since has pursued the goals they defined: "to secure the preservation of wilderness, conduct educational programs concerning the value of wilderness, encourage scientific studies, and mobilize co-operation in resisting the invasion of wilderness."

Robert Marshall was then thirty-three, with only six years of his creative life still ahead. He was born in New York City and, as he said, "spent many hours dreaming of Lewis and Clark and their glorious exploration into an unbroken wilderness." He climbed his first mountain, Ampersand in the Adirondacks, when he was fifteen, beginning a career of voracious hiking and mountaineering. He climbed all forty-six Adirondack peaks above 4000 feet. Then he headed for Western mountains, and on to the Alaskan ranges. On at least 200 occasions he walked thirty miles in a single day, and once walked more than seventy miles.

The achievements and endurance of Marshall and people like him belie the idea that wildlife and wilderness enthusiasts are theorists only. "There is nothing comparable to mountaineering in its demands for physical competence and deftness and stamina and courage," he once wrote. "The glory of conquering a summit which has baffled humanity by its ruggedness throughout all the passage of world history up to the present moment affords elation which nothing could equal. This reward of standing on an unscaled summit culminates hours of thrilling adventure involving perfect co-ordination of all parts of the body, perfect equilibrium while calmly holding on by toes and fingers to the cracks of a rock wall overhanging several thousand feet of sheer drop, perfect judgment concerning which route is possible and which unconquerable, and perfect co-operation with a climbing partner on the other end of a rope, which, without warning, may need to be skillfully used to save one's falling partner from death or may be the means of jerking both partners to extinction."

His toughest climbs were in Alaska, where he scored first ascents of great peaks. Once he hiked through deep limestone gorges surrounded by precipices and jagged pinnacles, but was still fresh and going at the rate of four miles an hour when he returned to camp after thirty miles.

Marshall studied forestry at Syracuse and Harvard Universities, then obtained a doctorate in plant physiology at Johns Hopkins. His entire working career was spent in the Forest Service, except for a four-year interlude with the Indian Service, during which he helped establish twelve roadless areas on Western reservations.

In 1930, he defined wilderness as, "A region which contains no permanent inhabitants, possesses no possibility of conveyance by any mechanical means, and is sufficiently spacious that a person in crossing it must have the experience of sleeping out. The dominant attributes of such an area are: first, that it requires anyone who exists in it to depend exclusively on his own efforts for survival; and second, that it preserves as nearly as possible the primitive environment. This means that all roads, power transportation and settlements are barred. But trails and temporary shelters, which were common long before the advent of the white race, are entirely permissible."

Marshall, although charged with development of National Forest recreation, insisted that scenic highways not be allowed "to run wild." To him, the National Forest System was uniquely fit to provide two distinct vacation environments. One, the comfortable and modern. Two, "the peaceful timelessness where vast forests germinate and flourish and die and rot and grow again without any relationship to the ambitions and interferences of man."

With his philosophy and forcefulness, he contributed to the establishment of regulations adopted in 1939, the year of his death, under which 14,000,000 acres of National Forest are still protected.

These administrative regulations provide that the Secretary of Agriculture, on recommendation of the Forest Service, may designate unbroken tracts of 100,000 acres or more as "wilderness areas" and others of 5000 to 100,000 acres as "wild areas." Within their boundaries, commercial timber cutting, roads, hotels, stores, resorts, summer homes, camps, hunting and fishing lodges, motorboats, airplane landings are all prohibited. Under the regulations, wilderness areas are not modified or eliminated except by order of the Secretary, with provisions for public hearings before any wilderness is established, modified or eliminated.

The Bob Marshall Wilderness, created in 1940, is a living memorial to this young New Yorker, who died long before his time yet gave more than a lifetime's leadership to the interest of natural resources. Located in the Lewis and Clark and Flathead National Forests, and bordered by the Lolo National Forest, the Bob Marshall Wilderness covers nearly 1,000,000 acres of rugged Montana mountain country. The serpentine backbone of the Continental Divide runs through it. At the Chinese Wall, the Divide breaks away eastward in thousand-foot sheer cliffs for a distance of fifteen miles. The Flathead Alps, an offshoot of the Divide, challenge the best rock climbers. The Marshall Wilderness is home of the nation's second largest elk herd, as well as

184

moose, grizzly bear, black bear, deer, mountain sheep and mountain goats. Outfitters in the Kalispell and Great Falls areas specialize in summer pack trips and late-fall big-game hunting into the wilderness.

Now we are in a new era. The wilderness areas are not really remote any more. Our social order, with its penchant for progress without plan, has advanced upon them from all directions and would sweep across and civilize these vestigial traces of untamed America if there were no barriers. With this pressure building, new questions await answer. The first one is, should the wilderness be rededicated to serve a "higher" purpose?

Yes, say lumbermen, cattlemen, loggers, miners, power developers, oilmen and some resort operators. Their mission in life is to provide for material wants; therefore, wilderness to them represents "single purpose forestry, providing special privileges to a few." Or, as the Western Pine Association puts it, by "locking up" timber within wilderness areas, we deprive dependent communities of their "very life-blood."

This timber consciousness, in which lumber companies would suggest that they are generous to a fault, placing the welfare of local communities before their own corporate interest, has grown into a creed and a battle cry in the Pacific Northwest. By cutting more timber, the saying goes, we improve the lumber industry and therefore insure prosperity for all. Also cited is the decisive advantage of managed forestry; I recall reading an article by an industry forester warning that to preserve *any* Douglas-fir wilderness is not only wasteful but criminal. Of course, reforestation and sustained yield are highly desirable in most of America—and there still are vast areas which require development in this direction—but we also need areas of substantial size, for learning, if for no other reason, where trees go their own way without thinning, planting or breeding, and where wildlife goes its way without management or manipulation of cover. Ideally, there ought to be some place where natural fire, predators and disease are not inhibited, and if the nation really made proper use of its space, in cities and in the country, we would be able to afford the "luxury" of true natural evolution.

But if economic prosperity is really the objective, one must wonder how much would be gained by logging the wilderness, or whether the lumber people would not do better for themselves to campaign for access roads into nonwilderness areas, which have not yet been open to cutting or brought under management. But they are determined to fight on a line of principle of land use. Accordingly, wilderness is shown as a wasteful luxury. At best, it should be limited to areas above treeline—in the interest of dependent communities. And let us not forget the 25 per cent money earned on timber sales which the Forest Service contributes to our local county. Or, as someone politely suggested to me in the heart of the Northern Cascades, "You Easterners want to tell us what to do with our land. You want to take it off the tax rolls and lock it up. You don't want to cut timber, but Forest Service revenues from timber sales help to build roads for a great many more people than use the wilderness."

Somehow, I wonder if "you Easterners" are really as bad as that. Gifford Pinchot was an Easterner roundly denounced, although he surely saved the West. As Bernard DeVoto presumed to say, the public-lands function of some Easterners is to prevent the West, every little while, from committing suicide.

Robert Marshall was an Easterner who recognized wilderness as a modern treasure of all the nation. As a forester, he defended the so-called "locking up" of large areas.

"The most important factor that tends to break down the wilderness," he argued, "is the mistaken application of the good old utilitarian doctrine of the greatest good for the greatest number in the long run.

"It might be said, for instance, that the total amount of pleasure which could be derived from a highway along the Sierra skyline would exceed that which could be gotten from a trail. When one considers, however, that there are millions of miles of highway in the country, many of them exceptionally scenic, and not another area left in which one can travel for several weeks along the crest of a mountain range without encountering the disturbances of civilization, it at once becomes apparent that, from a national land standpoint, this area would be more valuable as a wilderness."

He convinced many of his contemporaries in the Forest Service. The Wilderness Society and other conservation groups rallied to support this point of view, and have supported it ever since. But timbermen and those who deprecate wilderness persist in drawing a picture in which only 1 per cent of all National Forest visitors explores the wilderness, although it covers 8 per cent of National Forestland; on this simple mathematical formula, they claim the other 99 per

186

cent of visitors is being deprived of its rightful share of recreation opportunity.

Happily, we have more than timber groups to speak for us, and to furnish testimony on whether wilderness serves a single use, dual use or many uses. Biologists, ecologists and other scientists measure wilderness in more than immediate human terms. They appreciate the wilderness as the home of a million game animals. They need the wilderness as a laboratory for the study of biology, as a means of understanding the impact of man on his environment. And in support of the scientists are scholars, outdoorsmen and just people who may never see a real wilderness in all their lives but feel proud and enriched to know it exists in their country.

Add these people together and you have a force which the Seattle *Times* called a "powerful lobby of extreme conservationists." This lobby, recognizing the absence of wilderness legislation, has been asking Congress to define a national policy and establish a Wilderness Preservation System of Federally owned areas. The lands involved would be managed by their separate agencies, but gain added protection by legislation, instead of only by administrative regulation. The Wilderness System, which may already be an accomplished fact, would be devoted to recreational, scenic, scientific, educational, conservation and historic uses.

It will come to pass. Support has strengthened for the wilderness bill since it first appeared on the Congressional scene in 1956. But from now until the end of time wilderness will demand even more sympathetic understanding, for the problem is not the preservation of pure unadulterated wilderness, which no longer really exists, but of maintaining a delicate balance between fragile nature and human use and human surroundings.

For example, Isle Royale National Park is the only public land not contiguous to a nonwilderness, being totally bordered by the waters of Lake Superior. All others interact with outside conditions and influences. They are subject to a considerable degree of management— and should be recognized as such. The peaceful forest timelessness without "any relationship to interferences of man," of which Robert Marshall spoke, will never again exist in totality. Fire, disease and insects are controlled in order to protect the wilderness and the lands beyond it, yet this alters the natural pattern of plant growth and animal populations.

Add the impact of people. First there was only the Indian, following the narrowest trail. Then came the white man and a wider trail, and more white men and more trails. Now our horses overgraze the meadows. Campsites are beaten down to resemble a well-trod city park. Saddest of all is to ride deep into the back country, look down into a clear lake and see beer cans shining from the bottom. Yet this is only the beginning. Wilderness travel is on the increase, to the point of doubling, at least, within ten years. Before long, natural solitude will be hard-pressed to survive. The key to its survival is enthusiasm for wilderness, and recognition of the need of minimal man-made improvements to preserve it wild.

It should not be necessary for you to visit wilderness now, before it vanishes. But lend your interest to protecting it, that is, if you believe it should be protected, and expect no easier trails when you come for "inspiration and true recreation."

# CHAPTER FIFTEEN

# Earthquake on the Forest

Twenty miles below Dr. Irving Witkind's field trailer, not south but straight down, the growing earth shuddered.

The aspen trees around his camp high in Red Canyon swayed, though no wind stirred them. His Weimaraner blinked and arose on its haunches. Horses at ranches in the valley below grew suddenly unnerved and sang out.

When the trailer started rocking, Dr. Witkind awoke from what may have been a dream about a beautiful earthquake. Then he realized the dream was real. He was the most fortunate geologist in the world, sitting on a major earthquake at the instant it began.

As earthquakes go, this was a big one, the kind to compare with the great San Francisco quake of 1906, and to tell nearby Yellowstone to move over and share attention as a marvel of nature's behavior. The initial shock equaled the force of 200 atomic bombs. It was felt from the Dakotas westward to the Pacific Coast. In Seattle it broke loose the floating amphitheater from its moorings in Lake Washington. And halfway across the Pacific it caused the water level to fluctuate around the Hawaiian Islands. But the earthquake was large in tragic proportions, too, striking without warning and claiming innocent campers for burial in the earth's bosom.

This could have been Dr. Witkind's fate that fearsome, moonlit night of August 17, 1959, in Madison River Canyon, Montana. But to him, in his search of the pattern of the earth's structure and its resources, the earthquake was a magnificent geological picture. "We already had a story," he told me on the scene one year later. "The night of the earthquake that story was repeated." But how long has it been told? I asked. "Repeatedly," he said, "over the last 40,000,000 years."

Dr. Witkind, who works for the United States Geological Survey, was in Gallatin National Forest for his second summer of field research, performing his part in a vast project to map the basic sub-

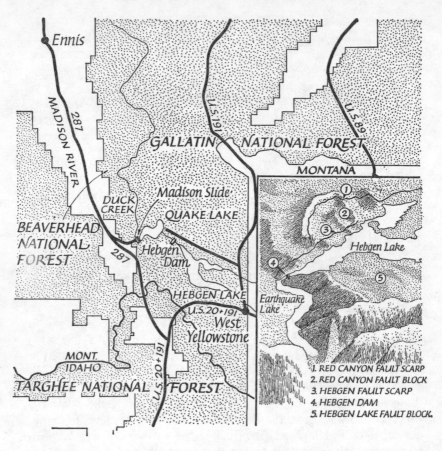

Where the Growing Earth Trembled

surface of America, which few of us realize still remains largely uncharted. I found this handsome Brooklynite (Brooklyn College, Columbia University and Colorado University for his doctorate in 1956) was probably the most popular man in Madison County, the West Yellowstone vicinity. "Why, he could run for office here," one of the foresters told me, admiringly. "He's in such demand to explain the earthquake I doubt he has bought a dinner all summer. I could listen to him night after night myself, because he renders geology so understandable, and his field covers the earth, its land, sea, air, clouds —the planet in entirety."

"The truth is this state really gets a hold on you," Witkind said the morning after I had heard the tribute. We were sitting in his trailer at six A.M. and even that early he was packing his gear, preparing to saddle his horse to ride into the hills. He was right: anyone who loves the outdoors is enchanted with Montana. The geologist finds an added lure. "I grabbed at the chance to come," he said, "because this is really geology at its most exciting—and I don't mean only because of earthquakes."

The rest of us may enjoy the Montana landscape, with its mountain vastness, but Witkind probes this outdoor laboratory to understand fully how it came to look this way and what it will look like in the future. In sandstone, shale and limestone outcroppings he perceives the Cryptozoic Eon, more than 1500 million years back in time, yet spanning three-fourths of the total history of the earth. In Madison limestone, the best-known formation in Montana, responsible for the bold scenery of the Gallatin, Madison and Beaverhead Valleys, he interprets the Paleozoic Era, which began 300,000,000 years ago when amphibians began crawling out of the sea and the earth's first forests began to grow.

Montana's geology is a history of earthquakes. The first recorded quake of recent times occurred at Helena during the mining days of the eighties, splashing placer dishes in the streams. Helena had sixty-four shocks between 1903 and 1935; during the last one, 1200 separate reverberations were felt during an eighty-day period. The most recent quake in Madison County, until 1959, occurred in 1947. It was intense, too, spreading tremors over an area of 150,000 square miles.

None of these was a volcanic earthquake, in which molten lava or hot rocks are heaved upward from boiling depths twenty-five to a hundred miles below the surface. The Montana quakes are the result

191

of stresses building up over long periods between huge masses of subterranean rocks.

For example, the mountainous area north of Hebgen Lake in Madison County has undergone two great episodes of mountain building through earthquake action. The first began at least 40,000,000 years ago and lasted millions of years. Rocks were bent and broken, flexed and pushed over one another. Some rocks that had been nearly horizontal were tilted on end. Others were completely turned over. The second episode began 20,000,000 years ago and has continued intermittently to the present. In this period, blocks of the earth's crust settled unevenly, forming irregular depressed areas, which are the beginnings of the Madison, Three Forks and West Yellowstone Valleys. Some patches did not subside, but were elevated and became mountain ranges surrounding the basins.

Evidence of these rock actions were clearly seen in many places, even before the 1959 earthquake. Remnants of overturned rock folds form the ridges along Route 287. Elsewhere are signs of "faults," the schism in the rocks; of "thrust faulting," thrusting of one rock mass atop another, and of "fault scarps," fresh clifflike breaks in the earth.

In 1959, Irving Witkind was sitting on top of it. "You see, fundamentally what a geologist does is to map the attitude of rocks," he explained. "By so doing he tries to understand the sequence of how the rocks got in this shape." He was in the process of charting old existing faults. Two of the great subsided blocks were beneath him: the Red Canyon block, twenty square miles in size, and the more massive Hebgen Lake block, 150 square miles. Each had dropped repeatedly and unevenly over millions of years, causing earthquakes and fault scarps, warping, tilting, then quietly eroding to conceal the evidence of stresses building between these two blocks far below the surface.

"The intriguing thing," said Dr. Witkind, "was that stresses were released along old existing breaks. It confirmed the picture we had discerned. In fact, I had drawn lines on a map of a series of old fault scarps." On my note paper he sketched several blue lines to show their location, then added a parallel red line for the new break. "When the earthquake hit, it repeated the pattern of history."

It was the height of the summer season. The bars in West Yellowstone were busy (full or not, they *are* busy). Eight miles north, at the

Duck Creek-Y, many travelers paused that day to read the road signs. They could travel due north on Route 191. Or they could follow the Y on Route 287, west through Madison River Canyon and then north. A number decided that instead of going on they would stop here at Hebgen Lake, just west of the intersection. There were several resorts, a motel and three Forest Service campgrounds. They could swim or go boating in Hebgen Lake, an artificial body of water behind a 720-foot power dam across Madison Canyon, or they could fish in Madison River, below the dam.

It was a pleasant vacation area. There were 250 campers in Rock Creek Canyon, six miles below the dam, where Route 287 and the Madison River wind between canyon walls. They slept in tents, trailers or outdoors to enjoy that clear moonlit night. If a geologist among them observed the mountain flank, rising 1300 feet above the canyon floor, he might have noted it was composed mainly of deeply weathered, very soft metamorphic rock on the upper slope, held in place by stronger white crystalline dolomite, like a natural retaining wall at the base.

The pattern of geology chose the instant of 11:37 P.M. to announce boldly that it was following its historic course. Grating one against the other far below the surface, the two blocks dropped—unevenly, with their north sides down, as they had dropped in the past. They released an explosive violence, ripping and tearing the earth and shaking it for almost two minutes during the first shock.

When the Red Canyon block dropped, a fresh scarp rose up from the depths. It cut a winding path through the canyon westerly and then curving toward the lake, breaking the road in four places. Trees were uprooted. Dislodged rocks and boulders tumbled down the slopes in avalanches, digging craters at the bottom. The clear night became gloomy with clouds and rain fell.

Around the Duck Creek-Y, sleepers were driven from their beds. One rancher said he was glad to get up because he felt a continuing sensation of his bed dropping beneath him. Austin "Pete" Bailey decided he would drive diagonally across the Y to see how his friend Roland Whitman was faring, but plunged into a fresh scarp nine feet deep before he could leave his driveway. Ernest Culligan, a Californian, who had built the Blarneystone Ranch as a quiet refuge, suddenly learned that he had chosen the old Red Canyon Fault as a homesite: his house dropped ten feet just after he and his family escaped.

Route 287, along the lake, buckled, curved and cracked. A quarter mile of it slid into the lake. Directly after the main shock, sand spouts, or blowholes, of compressed water and sand burst into the air. For three hours they resembled the thermal wonders of Yellowstone.

The damage, however, caused by the Red Canyon drop was relatively slight. The effect of the Hebgen Lake block was far more severe.

The vibration it created rocketed upward to the lake. Water began to slosh back and forth, like a tidal wave, washing onto one shore and then across to the other. This action would last almost twelve hours, spilling high over the dam three times. Cars and trailers along the shore were submerged. One family, asleep in a house trailer fifty feet above the lake, awoke with the first tremor to find water swirling around them. Parents and children scrambled for high ground while their trailer floated downstream. Summer homes and resorts close to the water, particularly on the north shore, were flooded. Cabins were tilted and wrenched askew on their foundations.

Mrs. Grace Miller, seventy years old, was alone in her cottage, Hilgard Lodge, at the water's edge. Realizing the ground was splitting around her and slipping into the lake, she rallied her dog and departed, shoeless, with only a blanket around her, crawling uphill through sage and brush. Her house floated away until it was stopped by the dam. But Mrs. Miller was more concerned for her life; in the darkness she kept falling into crevices five feet deep, climbing out and struggling ahead until she reached the safety of Kirkwood Ranch. Howard Wells, owner of that resort, found himself with an overflow house of stranded and injured tourists. His water supply was ruptured by the earthquake and almost became a serious problem, but he succeeded in repairing one line.

Later, when the Hebgen waters settled, it would become evident that the lake had tilted. On the south shore, boats and docks were left high and dry on ten feet of exposed lake bottom, while on the north shore, jetties and beaches were submerged. To geologists the tilt of the lake would be the best evidence of the attitude of crustal block below the surface, which they could not see, let alone photograph.

As the earthquake moved toward its fearful climax downstream, the dam and the ground on which it rests dropped about ten feet. The core cracked in four places. The spillway cracked, tilted and twisted out of line. One of the principal questions of the night and the next day was the status of the dam. Had it burst, disaster would have swept into communities downstream on the Madison River. But if concrete ever proved its strength and value it did so when the Hebgen Lake dam held.

Six miles below the dam the earthquake struck Rock Creek Campground. Tents and trailers lurched. Now the major tremor produced a secondary phenomenon of immense human consequence. Within half a minute the dolomite mountain base cracked open. It released the upper slope and the entire mass, almost a mile long, slid across the canyon floor. Eighty million tons of rock raced at a speed of 100 miles an hour through the heart of the camping area, its leading edge climbing 400 feet up the north wall.

Tragedy was everywhere. At the first reverberation, a mother and father stepped outside their tent to look after their children, in sleeping bags on the ground. They were struck by a violent blast, generated by the landslide displacing air in its path. The husband was swept up, grasped a tree and was "strung out like a flag" until his hold was broken. As the mother lost consciousness she saw one child blown away and a car tumbling past her. Her husband and three of four children would be found dead the next morning.

As the ground rocked again and again in aftershocks that seemed to foretell the end of the earth, pajama-clad campers dodged tumbling boulders and rocks. Tents were gone and forgotten as those who survived tried to escape the engulfing mud and water and reach high ground.

The whole plumbing of the earth went haywire. Big springs became bigger, discharging large amounts of fine sediment and turning the water in every stream and river a blotchy, cloudy brown. New springs spouted, rising from very ancient crystalline rocks, doubling the flow into Hebgen Lake and the Madison River. Other springs and wells, dependable water providers for years, were shut off. But the greatest change was born of the slide. It blocked the valley and barred the Madison River from its outlet through the Missouri flats and the Gravelly Range. A huge dam was formed. Many campers were picked up by the backwashing waters and found they were floating atop a new lake. An elderly couple, two miles back of the slide, were submerged in their trailer. They climbed on the roof and crawled into a treetop, where they spent five hours until they were rescued.

Within a few hours the growing lake stretched five miles upstream,

195

almost reaching the Hebgen Lake dam, and was 180 feet deep in the gorge.

The world knew that tragedy had struck Rock Creek Canyon and Hebgen Lake, but no one could tell the number of dead or whether new havoc and flood lay ahead. The surviving campers huddled high up the north side of the canyon, prayed and waited. Forty-two miles downstream, at Ennis, the first reports were that the Hebgen Lake dam was demolished; the town was evacuated at three A.M.

At dawn a reconnaissance plane flew over the scene. It was followed by other planes carrying Forest Service smokejumpers from Missoula, who parachuted to the ground with first-aid equipment, food and communications equipment. By evening the score of injured and most others were evacuated by Air Force and Forest Service helicopters. Nine were counted dead. How many others were buried beneath the 38,000,000 cubic yards of rock? No one would ever really know, although the official calculation was set at nineteen.

A new problem arose. The huge, unstable newly formed dam might wash out and send a flash flood downstream; or, the waters of the new lake might back up to Hebgen dam, weaken it and cause a flood from that direction. Within a week the Army Corps of Engineers started to cut a temporary spillway across the crest of the slide to ease the pressure of dammed-up waters. Then, with bulldozers and heavy equipment, the engineers cut the spillway an additional fifty feet deep.

This scene is probably the most awesome sight in America: the immense scar in the midst of a forested mountainside; the boulders of light, pinkish dolomite and crystalline gneiss and schist splattered across the canyon floor to form a sepulchral cover over nineteen campers who never knew what hit them; fading treetops poking above the surface of the waters, now called Earthquake Lake, to remind us of the time before August 17, 1959.

The Forest Service has designated the entire site, covering 38,000 acres, as the Madison River Canyon Earthquake Area. Interpretive displays at key locations explain the geologic story. At the Cabin Creek Campground, you can see where the Hebgen Fault Scarp at one point split through the ground beneath a fireplace, and at another where it not only cleft the earth but dropped one side ten feet. At the slide, the Forest Service has established three observation points, which overlook the entire scene.

As for Irving Witkind, he sat through 270 aftershocks, or secondary reverberations, in the twenty-four-hour period following the earthquake. At long last he made his way to Bozeman, seventy miles north. He entered the office of the Gallatin National Forest in the Post Office Building. Supervisor George Duvendack and Earl M. Welton, who knew him, asked Witkind for details. "No, no," he exclaimed, "I've got to phone in!" He placed a long-distance call, but when his chief replied on the phone, Witkind gasped, stammered and was utterly speechless a full minute.

For the remainder of the summer he and colleagues of the Geological Survey studied the cause and effects of the earthquake. They learned much from the tilted position of Hebgen Lake. They located the focal point, or epicenter, of the quake at a point ten miles north of the Duck Creek-Y. Geologists in nearby Yellowstone National Park found that geysers had exploded violently in reacting to the quake. Subsurface workings of the Park had been rearranged so that some geysers suddenly erupted after years of quiet, while other spouters ran dry.

But the next year, when I met him, Dr. Witkind had resumed his basic work, charting the geology of the old faults, and enjoying outdoors Montana at the same time. "This state has absolutely everything," he said, "deer, buffalo, horseflies, some of the oldest rock formations on earth. Who could want anything more?"

He was right. The state has absolutely everything. It may be quake country, but so is California, and the chance of a repetition of the freak accident of August 17, 1959, within the next century is about as remote as the return of the late road agent, Henry Plummer. More important, the entire region surrounding the Earthquake Area and Yellowstone National Park, including portions of Wyoming and Idaho as well as Montana, encompasses natural grandeur of the Rocky Mountains. And here at least a half dozen National Forests furnish some of the Rockies' finest fishing, riding, camping, hunting and vacation scenery.

To outline some high points of this wider area, let us say you are approaching from the east on Route 312, southwest of Billings, Montana. At Red Lodge you start the seventy-mile Beartooth Highway, a spectacular drive through the heart of the mountains in Custer, Gallatin and Shoshone National Forest, reaching an elevation just under 11,000 feet.

The road, built to modern standards and engineered for safety, follows three major switchbacks and delightful turns like Mae West Curve and Big Thrill on the way up. Seven campgrounds along swift-flowing Rock Creek are close by, should you decide to stay a while. From parking turnoffs you can look into purple canyons dotted with lakes and toward distant glaciers cradled in snowy peaks. At Bennett Creek Divide, or Beartooth Pass (elevation 10,942 feet), sweeping vistas encompass an area as large as all the New England states combined. The Nez Perce Indians crossed this way centuries before the first white man and called the route "path above the eagles" for the panorama of mountain ranges they observed here.

Descending on the Wyoming side, at 9000 feet you arrive at Beartooth Lake, a favored spot with trout fishermen. Beartooth Lake Lodge, consisting of a main building and twenty rustic cabins, overlooks the lake and faces Beartooth Butte, a 1500-foot-high mass of granite. The Lodge is moderately priced, has horses and boats for hire, and an outdoor setting hard to beat. Continuing down below timberline, the highway leads through a forest of Englemann spruce in Sunlight Basin into Cooke, Silver City and Yellowstone, on the route of John Colter, the early explorer, in 1807.

South of West Yellowstone lies Island Park village, Idaho, an outstanding resort area entirely within Targhee National Forest. The village, lining U.S. 191, a thirty-three-mile-long "main street," is distinguished, if for no other reason, by the pleasant absence of tawdry honky-tonks which characterize so many tourist towns.

Island Park is year-round vacation country, with stream and lake fishing in summer, big-game hunting in the fall and skiing at Bear Gulch Basin in winter. Twenty resorts, lodges and dude ranches are reasonably priced. The Forest Service has added new campgrounds, trailer and boating facilities at Buttermilk and McRae Bridge Campgrounds, and has modernized older areas.

Two large lakes, Henry's and Island Park Reservoir, plus seventy-five miles of river and stream, offer the fishermen the chance to catch almost every variety of trout, as well as whitefish and blueback salmon. But the most unusual body of water is Big Springs, the largest fresh-water spring in Western America, where the North, or Henry's, Fork of the Snake River wells up in its headwaters to start its long voyage to the Pacific. Children, especially, will enjoy walking on the bridge above the springs and feeding the trout. These fish are called tame, but I suspect they are just too smart to go elsewhere!

Along with summer recreation, the Targhee serves other uses. It is summer rangeland for cattle and sheep. Timber is harvested. In autumn it becomes choice hunting ground for deer, elk and bear, and is one of the few places where sage hens are sufficiently plentiful to permit an occasional open season.

If you want to see—but not shoot—truly unusual waterfowl, drive across Red Rock Pass into the Centennial Valley of southwestern Montana. Here the 40,000-acre Red Rock Lakes Migratory Waterfowl Refuge has become the principal nesting ground of the rare trumpeter swan, that magnificent snowy-white bird capable of flying eighty miles an hour. The refuge was established in 1935, when a count showed only seventy-three of these birds in the United States; now to these shallow lakes and marshes, cushioned from human intrusion on the north by the Beaverhead National Forest and on the south by the Targhee, the flocks arrive in late February and March and sing forth in trumpetlike mating calls. In summer you may see blue herons and other stilt-legged birds who find sanctuary in this primitive frontier.

North of West Yellowstone, National Forestland extends upward into Montana. Driving in this direction from the Earthquake Area, Route 287 follows the Madison River through a broad valley bounded by the 11,000-foot peaks of the Madison Range in Gallatin National Forest on the east and the Gravelly Range in Beaverhead National Forest on the west. The Madison River in the vicinity of Ennis is considered among the best trout streams in the United States. This entire region, for that matter, has great appeal with its dude ranches, camping, hunting, and Western history. Fourteen miles from Ennis, little Virginia City, once the territorial capital, is probably the best restored ghost town in the West. It was founded in 1863 when lucky Bill Fairweather washed a pan of gravel from a stream bed and found gold; presently he was joined by 10,000 eager prospectors, plus an assortment of cutthroats and killers. Among these was Henry Plummer, the California road agent, who came here as sheriff. He and his gang terrorized the town until a vigilante committee arose to smite them down, hanging twenty-four.

Let us conclude this tour in Helena, the small state capital, where Last Chance is the main stem, named for the four miners who struck

199

pay dirt on their "last chance." Anyone who wants to fathom the Montana story should visit the State Historical Museum, across the street from the capitol. Among a series of dramatic dioramas is one showing the fierce winter of 1886–87, when thousands of head of cattle perished in snow and ice, a tragedy which led to fencing and winter feeding. But the best part of the Museum is the gallery of paintings and sculpture by Charles M. Russell, the self-taught cowboy artist, a combination Mark Twain and Will Rogers, who through his great work expressed humor, pathos and tender feeling for his land and people. Some of his letters are on display, too, with lovable passages like this one written from Los Angeles in 1921, five years before his death: "Friend Jonnie, You know all artists should know the human form so a few days ago I went to Long Beach to study anatamy. Theirs all kinds of it out there all sises and shapes both hes and shes."

CHAPTER SIXTEEN

# Fire in the West: 1910

Beer sales ran unusually high all summer in the virile mining towns of the Northern Rockies.

The increase in consumption was due not simply to exaggerated thirst, but to intense, unending heat accompanied by the driest dryness anyone could remember. From the first of April on, the usual spring rains did not fall. The hills barely greened at all. May and June broke heat records. July followed with a fierce hot spell together with drying southwest winds from the Columbia plains. Crops burned up in the fields long before harvest.

Miners, loggers and the habitués of saloons found weather trends a favorite topic of discussion, between boilermakers, but by midsummer they had a much livelier subject—fire. The West in 1910 lived in a climate of fire. It was an intimate, personal companion to many of these men, who had taken work as Forest Service fire fighters, and before autumn's moisture finally dampened and cooled the countryside it would involve thousands more.

Fires broke out in June from the Great Lakes to the Pacific Coast, mostly caused by "dry lightning" strikes from severe electric storms, with little or no rainfall. The Forest Service was at best ill equipped. It lacked trails, lookout towers, man power or fire-fighting matériel. The year before, Gifford Pinchot had asked Congress to authorize increased fire protection and control, but his traditional Western opponents in the Senate blocked the necessary appropriation.

A form of fire control had been established under the General Land Office, before transfer of Forest administration from the Interior Department to the Agriculture Department in 1905, but it was primitive. Trails, where they did exist, were rough. There were scarcely any technically trained men. Fire fighting was fashioned of sheer heartbreak and futility. As one ranger in Colorado recorded: "About ten o'clock one hot windy day a man came in and called to my attention the fact that the Forest was burning. When I stepped to the door of our little one-room office and saw the smoke rolling up to heaven twelve miles away on the side of the Sangre de Cristo Range and in front of a Colorado gale, I felt more incompetent for what was ahead of me than I have ever felt about any other job before or since. We had no lookouts and no understanding with anyone about reporting or suppressing fires. We had no tools or equipment of any kind. The ranger of the next district was forty miles away with no telephone connections. He was not traveling by auto. There was, in fact, none in use in the region. I had never been close to a fire, much less had any instruction as to how to go about fighting one."

Fire protection was a critical need, as it has been ever since, for without it there can be no grazing, lumbering, watershed or wilderness to enjoy. Fires are written in the history of the West, started by natural causes long before the first slash burned in the wake of logging or the first lighted match was carelessly discarded. The California big trees show the record of a great fire in 245 A.D., of others in 1441, 1580 and 1797. Englemann spruce show signs of fires in Colorado dated about 1676, 1707, 1753 and 1781. The limitless, expansive West has witnessed natural fiery disasters far worse than Europe's historic "dark days," "red rains" and "black snows."

Thus, the Forest Service began at once in 1905 to organize itself as a fire-protection force. In 1910, when the fires struck, it may have lacked equipment but not ideas or training. It needed them all, particularly in the white-pine belt of northern Montana and northern Idaho. Only a few trails were open in the Forests; they followed natural routes formed by main divides and ridges in the vast wildernesses of the St. Joe, Clearwater, Coeur d'Alene, Salmon and Flathead Rivers. Many of the steepest river canyons of the St. Joe and Clearwater were completely inaccessible.

In Missoula, Montana, Regional Forester William B. Greeley and his assistant, Ferdinand A. Silcox (both of whom would later serve as Chief of the Forest Service), mobilized their forces. They were charged with safeguarding 64,000 square miles of timber- and water-producing mountain wilderness, but at the outset of the season one man was regularly guarding an average of 250,000 to 400,000 acres. Additional men were hired to fight the first big fires in June. As no rain fell and dry lightning swept the mountains, others were taken on. By mid-July 3000 were employed.

Who were these men? They were lumberjacks, miners, home-steaders, loyal local people fighting to protect their homes. They were also "pickups," the traditional source of fire-fighting man power, who came from everywhere, recruited and shipped in from the skid rows of Missoula and Spokane; drifters and floating labor, sometimes more hindrance than help; members of the IWW, Industrial Workers of the World, the "Wobblies," blacklisted perhaps in mining towns and West Coast waterfronts, but able and willing to work. Few credentials were required of pickup fire fighters, and few were presented.

As new crews were organized, equipment and provisions—axes, mattocks, shovels, crosscut saws, wash boilers, tubs, coffeepots, frying pans—were bought from local stores until supplies were exhausted. They were transported to primitive fire-fighting camps in the mountains, where men lived their lonely lives in the womb of wilderness aflame. They worked in soot and sweat, their eyes grew red-rimmed and swollen, their lungs parched. Their objective was to clear a line beyond which the flames would not pass. With ax and mattock they cut away brush and trees, then shoveled off moss, leaves and humus until barren, mineral soil lay exposed in a lane two or three feet wide. Sometimes they cut their line close to the advancing fire, at other times well ahead of it in order to start a protective backfire to meet the oncoming blaze. Such fire lines had to be patrolled constantly, so that any wind-whipped embers dropping beyond them could be immediately extinguished, or to reshape the lines if new fires started. When he turned in for the night, the fire fighter slept on the ground with only a shoddy blanket or one cheap soogan (a type of Indian bedroll) to keep him warm.

It was disheartening, desperate work. The big question in every fire camp, in every mining town, in every Forest Supervisor's office, in the Regional Office in Missoula and throughout the West was, "When will the weather break?" When would it rain? Or would the humidity, at least, rise to dampen the dry woods? It didn't rain, but the fire lines held. By early August over 3000 small fires and ninety large ones had been brought under control, demonstrating for the first time, on a large scale, that fire could be controlled.

Then on August 10, a day of low humidity and high wind, fires picked up. Flames arose in the back-country districts of the Clearwater, Flathead and Selway Rivers, where fires beyond reach had burned for weeks. They danced back and forth across the Bitterroot Range, the natural mountain barrier between Idaho and Montana, from Clark Fork in the Panhandle to Lolo Pass, west of Missoula.

Fire lines had to be extended greatly. They were thinly scattered and strained, with five- or ten-man crews serving in critical locations which demanded 100-man crews. The few mines and logging camps still operating were shut down to furnish additional man power. President Taft ordered ten U. S. Army companies dispatched to the area; they did little fire fighting on arrival, but provided police protection. By the third week of August the Forest Service commanded a force of 10,000 in the Northern Rockies.

But men armed with axes, mattocks and shovels were inadequate defense against the immense blowup of fire and hurricane that started on Saturday, August 20. In two terrible days it roared all the way from Canada south to the Salmon River. It engulfed almost completely 3,000,000 acres in a vast semicircle 160 miles long, from Clark Fork to the Selway River, and thirty to fifty miles wide, across the Montana-Idaho border. The whole region became a raging torrent of flame, jumping rivers a quarter mile wide. The heat of the fire and the great masses of flaming gas created great whirlwinds which mowed down swaths of trees and uprooted whole hillsides of timber in advance of the flames. The hurricane winds blew at 100 miles an hour. Forest rangers were almost torn loose from their saddles; later they said the roar sounded like a thousand freight trains passing over a thousand trestles.

The sky turned ghastly yellow; then, by four o'clock, black dark. The Bitterroot Valley, east of the main blaze, was covered in a choking pall of smoke. The *Western News* in Hamilton reported the valley was wrapped in semidarkness. A rain of ashes fell; the air was so charged with fine incinerated particles that vision was almost impossible. A baseball game was underway at Hamilton. The Butte team, losing 7–3, asked that it be called at the end of the fifth inning because of darkness. (On replay the next day, Butte lost anyway, 17–3.) "Under the peculiar atmospheric conditions," the *Western News* recorded, "objects appeared in an unnatural yellow glare. At night the sky glowed red with the reflection of the flame surging through the forest fastnesses."

In a wider arc, critical fires were burning now in the Cascades of Oregon and Washington, Montana, Idaho and eastward in Minnesota (where forty-two persons died). Smoke rode cloudy trails to Denver, a thousand miles from the Idaho-Montana line. The British ship *Dumferline* reported the smell of smoke 500 miles west of San Francisco and a haze interfered with navigation on the Pacific for days.

But the heart of the fire lay astride the St. Joe and Coeur d'Alene Mountains, a fabulous mining belt, where gold had been discovered in 1882, lead and silver soon after. The fire swept through lumber and mining camps at the base of steep, forested canyons, virtually destroying Taft, Haugan and De Borgia on the Montana side.

The fire centered its attack on the larger towns of Wallace and Mullan, across the mountains in Idaho. Life became quite grim in both. On August 15, burning bark, which had ridden the winds for miles, landed in the streets like mortar shells and set awnings afire. In Wallace, the people moved their furniture into the ball park for safekeeping. The busiest men in town, outside of the fire fighters, were insurance men writing fire policies. Wallace resembled a military outpost at the brink of war, occupied by 1800 fire fighters, two companies of soldiers and 3400 fearful civilians. It was headquarters of the Coeur d'Alene National Forest, where Supervisor William G. Weigle had been working night and day for weeks trying to save the town, of mostly wooden buildings, and the forest around it. Mullan, seven miles east, was also briskly preparing for the worst. This town of 1700 population had eleven saloons, or one for every 155 inhabitants, and undoubtedly all were booming, what with members of the crack volunteer fire department thoroughly parched after setting protective backfires, and homeowners after wetting down their roofs daily. Mullan, unlike Wallace, however, was not hemmed in critically by canyons, but faced an open valley on the South Fork of the Coeur d'Alene River.

As fire advanced toward its fateful climax of August 20, crews of the Northern Pacific responded heroically by organizing rescue trains for runs to Spokane and Missoula. Women, children and hospital patients were the first evacuated. Troops rode flat cars to fight spot fires and remove burning windfalls from the tracks while the relief trains ran through a sea of flames. Heading eastward on the twentieth, the last train made its dash to safety just before trestles and bridges burned behind it. Its whistle moaning through the smoke, the train picked up more refugees at Mullan, Saltese, Taft, De Borgia, Haugan and Tuscor.

It was Saturday. A high wind rose over Wallace about noon, great thunderheads of flame were spotted to the south and west, and Supervisor Weigle, in one of many harrowing, hair-raising, heroic performances by Forest Service personnel and civilians on this day, rode out to reconnoiter. Before long he was caught in a rush of flame and was hopelessly trapped. He abandoned his horse and rushed through a burning mine mill to seek refuge in the mine tunnel. But the tunnel began to cave in, threatening to bury him alive. Covering his head with his coat, Weigle plunged through the flaming wreckage into a tiny creek. In a few hours he worked his way back to Wallace, his eyebrows singed and his clothes scorched. He found the town aflame and turned to assisting in caring for the dead and injured.

In the evening, when the fire was at its worst, townspeople gathered in the ball park. Prisoners were released from Shoshone County jail. "I think everyone that night was praying for his own salvation and for the town's," recalls venerable Fred R. Levering, manager of the Chamber of Commerce museum, who was present at that frightful scene of fifty years ago. "At first the flames were heading straight for King Street, the heart of town, from the west side of Placer Creek. Almost miraculously the wind changed, diverting it to enter from the east. It burned a hundred buildings, or one third of the town, but three brick buildings in its course slowed it down and gave the fire department a chance to save the rest of Wallace."

Two lives were lost in town. Hundreds were left homeless. Hundreds more, homesteaders, ranchers and fire fighters, injured and burned, straggled in from the hills.

In a lesser tragedy, beer drinkers eyed with helpless dismay a river of their favored brew flowing from the burning Sunset Brewery down King Street, froth sometimes reaching knee high. Fortunately, all surviving saloons were well stocked. "The flumes which brought our water into town," as Mr. Levering recollects vividly, "were burned completely. Most people drank beer. There was so much lye in the water after it had been running through burnt wood it made your mouth sore." Saloonkeepers were doubly popular because they also helped forestall typhoid, caused by dead animals contaminating creeks and rivers. One woman in Mullan did succumb to typhoid but almost all teetotalers forgot their pledge of abstinence.

Meanwhile the greater drama of the two-day disaster was being enacted in the hills.

Seven fire-fighting crews were trapped by the terrific uprush of fire. They were cut off and doomed unless they could find safe hiding places.

Nature was rampantly unnatural. Bear, deer, elk and mountain lions stalked the camps, fear of man overcome by a greater terror. Birds hopped about in the thickets, choked by stifling heat and smoke. The fragrance of summer flowers yielded to a malodor of smoke. Withered

206

ferns and grasses were covered with gray ash, a hot hoarfrost. Dead animals, horses, elk, deer and bear, were evident everywhere. A pitiful grouse hopped about with his feet and feathers burned off.

Men suffered similar fates. It was almost fatal to drink from ashen, alkaline streams, polluted by dead fish. Those who quenched their thirst became deathly sick.

In one crew on Big Creek, thirty men lost their lives, while others lay prone for hours in the chilling waters of a tiny stream, almost suffocating from smoke, hair crisping on the back of their heads, burning skin peeling from their necks. Of those who perished, seven had sought shelter in a small cave and were burned beyond recognition. Three were crushed by a falling tree. One man was pinned only by a foot. Comrades only a few feet away heard his cries and prayers, but were powerless to help. He dug and fought to tear himself loose until overcome by unconsciousness before death.

In a crew on Setzer Creek, one man, fear stricken, shot himself to death. Nearby, twenty-eight men were burned beyond recognition. On the West Fork of Big Creek, eighteen men died.

Tragedy, violence, heroism and prayer are the components of fire fighting, an historic lore of the woods as worthy of remembrance as the make-believe of Paul Bunyan and the lumberjacks. In this lore lies the story of Ranger Joe Halm. Halm was a rugged ex-football and baseball star at Washington State College, dispatched to the St. Joe Wilderness, with crew and pack string, sixty-five miles across the Bitterroot Range. It had taken them days to slash the way to their position on the fire. They went to work building lines and it seemed they had the fire corralled. Then came the big blowup, when the whole countryside burst into flame. Halm and sixteen men were cut off, but found refuge at a small gravel bar in the midst of a stream. The wind rose to hurricane force and the fiery heat became intolerable. All the horses in the pack string burned to death. Halm exhorted his men to dash back and forth in the shallow stream heaving bucketfuls of water as high as they could to drench burning trees above them. A few yards away a great log jam, deposited by an old cloudburst, which long ago had washed limbs, leaves and debris to this rocky trap, became a roaring furnace. Their drenched clothing steamed and smoked. A giant tree crashed into their little gravel sanctuary, blinding and showering the men with sparks and spray. After hours, the screaming, hissing and snapping of millions of doomed trees and the shower of sparks and burning brands diminished. They knew they would live, although during the chilly night the red glare still lit their little world. The next day Halm led his crew picking its way back toward civilization. It took them a week, during which some of his favorite newspapers, including the Spokane *Chronicle* and the Portland *Oregonian*, eulogized the dead athlete. But they had a better story to report when he arrived in safety.

However, the principal individual hero of the fire was the ranger of the Wallace district, Edward C. Pulaski. Among Western foresters his name has become legend, both for his actions in 1910 and for the fire-fighting implement he later devised. Pulaski was born in Ohio in 1868, a descendant of General Casimir Pulaski, the Polish patriot who served with Washington in the Revolutionary War. He came to Idaho alone during the gold rush when he was only fifteen. He prospected, worked as a smelterman and foreman of a cattle ranch, where he did all the blacksmithing, until he entered the Forest Service. Although not a college-trained forester, he knew every crag and corner of his own district. It was said there was nothing his men could do that he couldn't do better. He was as well respected as the toughest logging camp bull-of-the-woods, but was popular along with it. During the fire Supervisor Weigle had placed him in charge of 150 men along a ten-mile stretch on Placer Creek. At the instant of the blowup, he and forty-two men were cut off and surrounded by fire. "It was his knowledge of the hills that enabled him to save their lives," relates Fred Levering, Pulaski's old friend. The men panicked, but Pulaski assured them he would get them out or to a place of safety. He knew the location of the nearby War Eagle mine tunnel and led his men and two horses to it, then, after they all entered, he held wet blankets over the entrance. Flames swirled about, clamoring for entry. Heat, smoke and gas seeped through. Timbers supporting the tunnel caught fire. His men were gripped with fear and one started to bolt for the outside. Pulaski ordered him to halt, drew his revolver and threatened to shoot the first man who tried to leave. He commanded them to lie on their faces, and while they did he dipped water from a little stream with his hat and dashed it on the burning timbers. Pulaski stood guard at the mine entrance until he was burned, overcome by gas and heat and fell unconscious from exhaustion. Many others fell unconscious, too.

After a two-hour rendezvous with death, the flames passed on and the men crawled out of the smoking tunnel. "The boss is dead," said one. "Like hell he is," retorted Pulaski, although flame and smoke had seared his eyes and he had to be led out. The two horses were in bad shape and were shot. Five men had suffocated, but without Pulaski's leadership all forty-two would have perished.

About one A.M. on Monday, August 22, the wind shifted. For the first time in weeks humidity rose to slow the fire. On Tuesday a precious, prayed-for drizzle was gratefully received. Snow was reported on higher ranges. One week later the heavens shed rains in earnest on the West and the remaining fires in the Northern Rockies settled down to burn slowly, steam and finally to die.

Now it was time to measure the full extent of the fire's destruction. Little by little the whereabouts of fire crews, mine crews, prospectors and homesteaders became known. Seventy-eight fire fighters had died: seventy-two in the Coeur d'Alene National Forest, four in the Cabinet, two in the Pend Oreille. Seven civilians had died, bringing the total to eighty-five. But years later old-timers insisted many more had perished, the bodies unfound amid the charred timber.

Most dead fire fighters were buried where they lay. Those burned so badly they could not be identified were wrapped in blankets and sewn in heavy canvas. In 1912, fifty-three corpses were exhumed under contract with a local undertaker and reburied at the cemetery at nearby St. Maries, south of Coeur d'Alene Lake; it has since become the unique final resting place provided by the government for fire fighters who perish in action.

Second to the deaths, the burning of 3,000,000 acres was a staggering loss. Forest Service cruisers entered the area as soon as the fire had cooled to prepare the way for salvage logging of damaged timber, but this was a minor recoup in the face of utter destruction of six to seven billion board feet of virgin Idaho white pine. It was estimated the timber lost would have kept a large sawmill in operation for a hundred years.

The character of the forest changed. Erosion by fall rains scoured gullies to bedrock and in place of woodland bare granite rock appeared. Many areas were invaded by inferior lodgepole pine and brush in place of white pine. Scorched trees were inviting hosts to bark beetles, which in 1914 spread to healthy trees in epidemic proportions. With snags and dead timber lying over the ground, fire bred fire and at least 30 to 40 per cent of forests burned in 1910 reburned over the years and have constituted a continual hazard.

Fortunately, under protection and fire control many other areas have reseeded naturally, and the Forest Service has replanted nearly

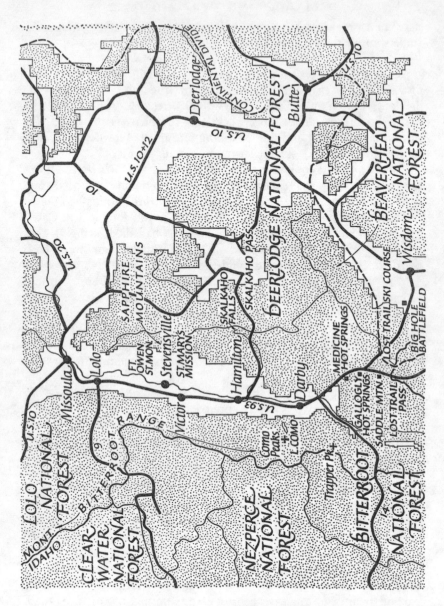

*Bitterroot Valley, Missoula to Lost Trail, and the High Country*

150,000 acres. On better growing sites, trees are approaching saw-timber size and in a few years the cropping cycle can get underway. But it will be more than a century before prefire conditions are fully restored.

The 1910 fire was epochal. It was the first great fire to be fought and not accepted supinely. It encouraged timber owners and logging operators to form private fire-fighting groups. That was more than ever came out of a forest fire before.

Private citizen Gifford Pinchot, who had been dismissed from his post as Chief of the Forest Service in January, spoke out before the ashes were cool, charging that Congress was responsible for loss of life and property, and particularly those members who had opposed appropriations for fire-fighting equipment. His old antagonist, Senator W. B. Heyburn, of Idaho, was asked to comment on the accusation, but said it was not worthy of serious consideration because of Pinchot's lack of experience in fire protection. Nevertheless the public was shocked and awakened. Three national magazines, *Collier's*, *Harper's* and *Everybody's*, told the story of the fire and its consequences in detail. The next year, when Congress enacted the Weeks Law it provided Federal aid to state and private forest owners to develop fire protection.

Ranger Pulaski, the hero of the fire, was hard at work in 1911, too. His vision was impaired as a result of his siege in the War Eagle tunnel, but he labored to devise a new type of fire-fighting tool, combining the features of a grub hoe and ax. The first model was made by cutting one blade off a double-bitted ax, then welding it at right angles to its former position. For a while a detachable shovel was a part of the implement. But in 1913 Pulaski omitted the shovel and completed a product much like the one in use today, but with a shorter shank. By 1920 the pulaski was the most sought-after fire-fighting tool in the Northern Rockies, and commercial manufacturers were asked to produce it. The shank was lengthened, the mattock bit narrowed, and the whole made from tooled steel. This did not enrich Pulaski personally, but until his death in 1931 he could enjoy the satisfaction of knowing the instrument he designed was a basic part of the fire-protection arsenal. Today a fire fighter would no more set forth without his pulaski than would a baseball player step to the plate without his best bat.

CHAPTER SEVENTEEN

# A Fiery Western Weekend: 1960

The morning began cool and bright and seemed at first as clear as any other summer morning west of the Continental Divide, where the green Mission Mountains and the Flatheads smile up at the snowy Bitterroot Range.

Then I looked north of the airport. Beyond the hills, scuddy haze and smoke clouded the horizon. A commercial-airline pilot preparing for an early take-off mentioned that on the previous afternoon he had seen traces of smoke level with his wing tip at 16,000 feet and as far east as Wichita.

The hour was five A.M. on Saturday, the most peaceful time of the week to anyone who has completed his forty hours of labor and rests in warm dreamy contemplation of a weekend at ease. But there were no such prospects at the Missoula County Airport, the focal point of the fire-torn, fire-weary Northern Rockies, where the day's aerial warfare against violent natural forces had already begun.

It was the third weekend of July, 1960. Fires throughout the West reached an awesome peak. They had struck early in a tinder-dry springtime and were now burning in California, Oregon, Washington, Idaho and Montana. Summer heat combined with an absolute lack of moisture to create the most critical fire season in thirty years.

Six thousand fires burned in the West that summer. At least twenty-five covered more than 3000 acres, each the size of the Gettysburg Battlefield. The largest swept over 35,000 acres of southern California; the Angeles National Forest alone had to fight three fires of 15,000 acres each within its boundaries.

The last two weeks of July proved the worst period, a time to compare in terms of intensity, if not disaster, with the well-remembered fiery fury of 1910. The area burned in these fourteen days totaled a quarter million acres. During this fortnight the Forest Service, together with co-operating states, cities and private landowners, spent $1,000,000 a day in fire fighting. A force of 25,000 men was mobilized

213

like an army of infantry, artillery and air force. For the toughest jobs on the ground in California the Forest Service dispatched its "hot shot" crews, the commandos of fire fighting, and called up its southwest Indian shock troops of the Navajo, Apache, Hopi and Pueblo tribes, who are said to bear up under extreme heat and smoke better than anyone. For its artillery the Service organized a formidable brigade of 400 tractors and bulldozers, plus 600 tanker and pumper truck trailers. So much equipment was required that all sources in the West were heavily strained and sometimes completely cleaned out. It was the same way in rallying an air force of 300 planes and helicopters. As the Seattle helicopter service told its would-be clients through a sign above its booth at the airport, "Closed. Sorry, but we're off fighting forest fires."

They were fighting the same old grim war of the Western states, but with modern means. Airplanes and helicopters were now their platforms in the sky, from which they could spot and inspect remote mountain areas, supplementing the older lookout towers. The air had become a whole new avenue of attack against forest fires.

The Northern Region of the Forest Service was hard hit. On the worst day in July, 205 separate lightning-caused fires were burning in the mountains of Idaho and Montana, including six "project fires" of more than 1000 acres each. Planes and helicopters "bombing" with retardant chemicals from five bases, crack airborne smokejumpers and 5000 men on the ground with modern equipment had brought fire fighting a long way from the tedious times of foot and horse travel in the wilderness, but they were still insufficient against nature and the weather.

Thus, as the third July weekend began at Missoula County Airport, five A.M. was a livid hour. The fire dispatcher poked his head out the front door of the Aerial Fire Depot, looking rumpled and red-eyed after a night on the telephone and radio, receiving calls for help from local National Forest officers. Four smokejumpers, wearing their football helmets and heavily padded jumpsuits, climbed aboard a twin-engine Beechcraft waiting for them like a taxi at the front door.

"Early morning like this is the best time to get away," said tall, sandy-haired Earl Cooley, "while the air is still calm and stable. Our plane will be next. We'll get the cargo aboard and be off in a half hour."

The Missoula Aerial Fire Depot, the largest of eight such bases in the West, lay cradled in the center of mushrooming fires. Two of the worst burned thirty miles north of the city, one on the Blackfoot Indian Reservation, where I would soon be heading, and the other at Gold Creek on private land, while a third burned on Saddle Mountain, in the Bitterroot National Forest, 100 miles south. These were, on that weekend, the major concern, although any of 200 others might have erupted to disastrous proportions.

Along the flight line, the hangar of the Johnson Flying Service, the contract mountain-hopping air force of the Forest Service in this region, was alive with pilots and mechanics preparing its generally antiquated fleet for action. Most planes were curios: a Ford tri-motor, several World War II bombardier trainers, B-25 medium-range bombers, TBM Navy torpedo bombers, long outmoded everywhere except when pressed into service in modern fire fighting. A gleaming helicopter rose almost vertically as if to say to its older brothers, "This is the way it should be done."

Across the field a TBM was receiving a tankful of borate pumped through a hoseline from the "slurry," a huge vat in which two men mixed sodium calcium borate with water to form a thick, pinkish sludge. I learned that this substance when sprayed from the air coats trees and other vegetation as a protective cover against fire and remains effective even after the moisture evaporates. Years ago the Forest Service started aerial spraying of water from crop-dusting-type planes. Later it tried B-17 and B-29 bombers, but found them too unwieldy for low-level, slow-speed maneuvering. Besides borate, the Service has been using bentonite, a newer chemical, which is proving more effective, and has also been increasing its force of contract-operated helicopters; they are more expensive than surplus war planes, but are adaptable for many uses.

In front of the Depot, fork lift buggies were loading the plane in which we would fly. They streamed across the concrete apron from the fire warehouse, a long low building storing enough equipment for 5000 fire fighters. "Right now the warehouse is the busiest place, and maybe the most important in this whole show," Earl told me. "They'll probably move thirty tons in and out today, both by parachute drop and by truck to fire camps easy to reach."

Our plane was a DC-2, an ancient pre-World War II transport, loaded with 3600 pounds of cargo to drop to the fire camp in the isolated Jocko River Canyon on the Blackfoot Indian Reservation. For the most part, the thirty crates to be dropped had in them cans of gasoline for bulldozer and power saws, and cartons of hot rations,

215

which felt warm against my legs in the plane cabin. The Jocko Canyon fire already covered 3500 acres, with daily afternoon "blowups" skipping along the treetops and hopping across fire lines.

Flying north, a wall of haze and smoke rolled outward from the flames below. Fires erupted like miniature Vesuviuses off the mountain peaks. Burnt timbers looked like so many charred, used matchsticks. The pilot descended into steep, box canyons, while Earl and his helper opened the door in the rear of the plane (there were only the three of us in the cabin) to look for the fire camp. They spotted it at the edge of a lake; we flew at 300 feet, then down to 100 feet, barely over the treetops, while I shut my eyes, hung on, and just about bid the world good-by.

The pilot flew a roughly rectangular course, honking a horn in the cabin as a signal to drop a load. Earl and his helper shoved it out, the static line opening the parachute almost immediately. The pilot gunned the motor, banked and turned sharply at the same time almost as though he were climbing the mountainside.

We went round and round. I peeped through one eye, then both, and decided the best course of action was to help by pushing the crates to the rear, as a diversion from terror. Only fifteen more to go, I thought. Then only ten. On the ground below we could see the Indian fire fighters unpackaging the crates, although three or four had landed in treetops. Finally we were done and the pilot climbed out of the canyon. Earl's helper, an older man, sat down in the corner bucket seat in the rear; he closed his eyes in relief, his face turned ashen pale and I knew I was not the only fearful passenger aboard.

"Thanks for the help," Earl said when he came and sat with me. "It was a very tough spot. Didn't have much time between drops, did we?"

While we talked, it developed he was a veteran of thirteen years with the smokejumpers; he had been in charge of training new recruits but was now working principally for the new Equipment Development Center in devising new fire-fighting clothing.

On the way back to the airport, we flew over the Gold Creek fire. "There goes the bird dog," Earl pointed out. It was a light single engine plane flying 300 feet below us. Its job was to guide by radio the borate bomber which followed seconds behind it: a TBM hedge-hopping through a smoke-filled canyon to unload its borate cargo.

When we returned, half a dozen smokejumpers were loading their gear into another twin Beechcraft. It was one of twenty such flights

216

made this day from Missoula. Each man's fire pack weighed about forty-five pounds. It consisted of his pulaski and shovel; first-aid kit; two-day rations, canteen, flashlight, and paper sleeping bag.

The first Forest Service experiment of record in the use of a parachutist as fire fighter was made as far back as 1934 by Tom V. Pearson at Ogden, Utah. Pearson hired a stunt jumper at a county fair for $25 to fly over the forest and test the practicality of landing in the trees. Not only was Pearson's report rejected, but his $25 voucher was disallowed—and he had to pay it out of his own pocket. Five years later, the scene shifted to Missoula, where David A. Godwin, a forester, and Frank M. Derry, a professional jumper, conducted a series of dummy tests and live jumps, and taught Forest Service employees how to jump in the open and then in timbered areas. The following year jumping began in earnest both in the Northern Rockies and the Pacific Northwest.

Smokejumping proved so successful the Army studied it closely and adapted many Missoula ideas and techniques for training paratroopers. During World War II the Forest Service instructed paratroops in timber jumping and fire fighting as a precaution against the threat of Japanese balloon fires in Oregon. Paradoctors and medical corpsmen were also trained at Missoula for airborne search and rescue missions.

"We have about 150 men here," Earl said as we walked through the parachute loft. "Every spring we recruit new men. There are plenty of applicants but the requirements are strict. A man has to have at least one season of fire-fighting experience on the ground and weigh under 180 pounds. He must be over eighteen and under twenty-seven when he applies.

"That's why you'll observe most of the fellows are of college age. They'll work two or three summers while they're going through school —many of them are in forestry school. The pay is $2.33 an hour. Of course, some of us like the work and stay with it. Al Cramer, who is busy packing his chute, has been here eighteen years and made 125 jumps."

After smokejumpers are accepted, they undergo a four-week course of fire fighting, physical training, first aid, stretcher bearing and seven practice jumps. Then they are ready for action and average about ten jumps a season.

We walked into the equipment room, where Earl showed me the smokejumper's uniform. The helmet was like a regular football helmet, but with a complete face mask. He donned a suit of nylon with styrofoam padding in the shoulders, back, elbows, knees, hips and rump. "I doubt that I'd feel anything," he said, "even if a mule kicked me."

The smokejumper wears two parachutes, a large one on his back, and a small chest pack should the other fail. The large chute is slotted, that is, it has three openings which enable the smokejumper to steer, turn and slow down his descent while he picks a safe place to land.

Why are smokejumpers so valuable in fire fighting? They reach remote points in forty-five minutes, compared with a possible two days afoot. They arrive fresh and untired and have already observed the fire from aloft. Smokejumpers have proven they can put out small fires and prevent them from developing into large ones.

The emphasis is on safety first. The men always jump in teams of two or more and from a minimum of one thousand feet. The Forest Service is proud of its record of more than 20,000 jumps without a fatality on the actual jump operation. However, like fire fighting in general, smokejumping is dangerous business. There have been injuries and deaths. The worst disaster, the 1949 Mann's Gulch Fire, in the steep, jagged Gates of the Mountains near Helena, claimed the lives of thirteen smokejumpers. Three hours after they had landed they were trapped in a blowup on the ground and could not outrun it.

Now the Equipment Development Center, where Earl works, is devising new and better fire-fighting gear, such as aluminized, fire-resistant lightweight clothing; larger, lighter sleeping bags, and an easy-to-handle combination power brush cutter and trench digger—the new pulaski of the space age.

Sunday morning was chosen, without asking heavenly sanction, as the time of crisis on the Saddle Mountain fire. "We have 1600 men," Homer "Skip" Stratton, the fire boss, told his chief, Harry Anderson, supervisor of the Bitterroot National Forest. "We can form a fire line and hold it." Both men knew that if they could not turn the tide the fire might spread up and down Bitterroot Valley and last for weeks. Already it covered 3000 acres. The day before it had leaped Route 93 and started a new blaze of 350 acres. They looked out the windows of the ranger station and saw smoke rolling over the mountains and canyons. It mushroomed skyward like the cloud of a small atomic bomb. They would order their men to hit the fire hard in the morning, when the weather was still cool and the day's moisture—such as it might be—was at its highest. By afternoon low humidity would combine with 100-degree temperatures to create blowups on the mountainsides, as they had the last four days.

This fire had started with a lightning strike on the steep flank of Saddle Mountain, the 8800-foot sentinel at Lost Trail Pass, astride the Idaho-Montana border. There were similar strikes all over the West the same day, fingers of electricity sent forth from towering, flat-topped clouds. This one hit home in a stand of dry, dead lodgepole pine killed by beetles thirty years ago. It picked up speed when it reached a ground cover of brome grass, or cheat grass, a "flash fuel" which grows where cattle have been overgrazed.

When the fire was reported, most of the regular personnel of the Sula Ranger District were already involved in putting out other fires. John Hall, the district ranger, took two men and drove a pickup, loaded with fire packs, power saw and radio, in the direction of Saddle Mountain. They were able to reach the Lost Trail Ski Area, within two miles of the fire, but from there confronted tough going down a rock slide. At this point, when he saw the fire covered two acres and was spreading fast, the ranger radioed to order aerial borate spraying. Had it arrived, the combination of air attack and the men on the ground might have extinguished the fire, but the TBM and B-25 borate bombers, like the smokejumpers, were preoccupied with more flagrant and demanding fires elsewhere.

By evening, highway maintenance men, old hands in the woods, and ranchers had joined John Hall on the fire. It now covered forty acres and was still spreading. The ranger radioed a message to the Forest headquarters at Hamilton asking for a force of 100 men.

Harry Anderson, a young supervisor but a veteran forester and a World War II PT-boat commander, received reports of new fires on all five ranger districts of the 1,000,000-acre Bitterroot. Based on the weather picture, more fires were forecast. He assigned Skip Stratton, a fire-fighting expert who had entered the Forest Service as a smokejumper while studying forestry, to take charge of the Saddle Mountain operation, and called the regional headquarters at Missoula for reinforcements. Half the supervisors of the twenty-two forests in the region were doing the same.

The fire swept over Saddle Mountain. The girls' camp at Gallogoly Springs retreated to lower ground. The second day the fire covered an area equivalent to 320 football fields; the third day it had multiplied fourfold and spread over 1200 acres. Fire fighters faced a difficult struggle to establish a defense line; though the fire was only a mile and a half from the main road, it burned across an inaccessible, vertical grade. Against the normal rules of fire behavior, downdrafts and eddies of air sucked it erratically downhill, spotting flames along the mountain flanks 2000 feet below Saddle Mountain peak. The fury of the fire created its own cumulo-nimbus stormcloud, whipping hot blasts across the terrain.

Meanwhile the fire-fighting force grew with the fire. At first there were fifty men, their power saws humming on the hillside as they opened a fire line of one and a half miles long. By the end of the second day the fire fighters totaled 220 and more were called. From Wyoming came Crow and Cheyenne Indian fire fighters. The United States Employment Service, having exhausted its man-power supply in Montana, recruited in Idaho, Washington and Oregon. Tractors and bulldozers were brought in from Missoula, 100 miles north, and from Salmon, Idaho, fifty miles south.

A fire-fighting organization was set up with headquarters at the ranger station. At the top was the fire boss; under him were safety officer, service chief, line boss, plans chief, communications officer, timekeeper, registrar, air-operations officer and others. The basic fire-fighting structure results from fifty years of Forest Service experience, geared to speedy mobilization and equally quick demobilization once the emergency passes. Feeding the men was a large-scale operation. Cafés in nearby Hamilton and Darby prepared 1300 sack lunches before field kitchens were established. Twelve women cooks, ranch wives in the area, were hired to run the kitchen at the ranger station. As field kitchens were established on the mountain, each was provided with four cases of eggs, 1000 pounds of potatoes, 1000 loaves of bread, 200 pounds of luncheon meat, plus several quarters of beef, quantities of bacon and ham and kitchen equipment.

The fire was fought not only with man power and logistics, but with knowledge. The control office planned strategy and tactics based on reports from helicopter reconnaissance, weather forecasts and radio communications from the fire lines.

On Sunday morning, the fifth day of the fire, 3000 acres were aflame. Four camps had been established, one at the ranger station and three in the hills. The personnel of the Sula District had risen from thirty men to 1600. Of these, seventy-five were "overhead," supervisory Forest Service officers from the regional office and others flown in as reinforcements from the Lake States and the East.

But most of the 1600 men were "pickups," the traditional fire-fighting personnel, receiving a minimum of $1.77 per hour as unskilled labor and camp flunkies with various grades upward such as cooks and power-saw operators on up to $2.21 an hour for bulldozer operators. What manner of men were they? The loggers and ranchers of Sula Basin came to protect their own countryside. Some of the others came from distant parts because they wanted to work. Many came because they wanted not to work, feeble and tired—the lost, lower depths. One or two mixed milk and gasoline for drinking whisky, some of those on kitchen detail prepared food with unclean hands, and some simply vanished down the highway without doing any work or collecting any pay.

But now the time had come to control the fire. Bombers from Missoula sprayed it with borate. Thirty bulldozers ground their way over the mountainside building fire lines. Claude Blodgett, a modest, small local timber operator, stated his firm position on preservation of natural resources by driving his caterpillar almost vertically to the peak of Saddle Mountain. Behind the dozers came the fire-fighting infantry, scraping the fire line down to mineral soil. Hundreds of men advanced to cut lines with power saws. Hundreds of others crawled up rocky slopes, spraying with back pumps which they had filled in mountain streams. And still other battalions advanced with pulaskis and shovels, relying on dirt to cool and smother the fire. The men moved along snakelike, one stripping the underbrush with his pulaski, his partner behind him shoveling down to mineral soil. Occasionally an expert brawny fire fighter would heave a shovel load of smothering dirt twenty feet into a flaming tree.

By midafternoon the army of 1600 men had completed a twenty-one-mile fire line. The flames were corralled within its periphery. They fell back to their camps, where they used their hard hats, without liners, as washbasins to clean the smoke stains from their arms and faces; the acrid odor and breath of smoke, however, would linger for weeks in their lungs and nostrils. Even as night cooled the fire, flames were seen advancing through the treetops. With Ranger John Hall, I stood alongside a creek in Camp One watching spot fires on distant cliffs looking like the lights of tall apartment houses in the night. We saw burning logs roll loose and downhill to start new fires.

"This fire will keep burning for a week," he said, "but we've got it

221

under control. Tomorrow we'll start mop-up operations and hope for a break in the weather."

Monday morning the fire still burned, but the worst was over. Moisture rose. Then rain fell lightly. One fire camp was closed and the finance officer started paying off 500 men. Within a week the complement would be reduced to only 125, kept on as insurance until the end of the fire season. The total cost of fighting the Saddle Mountain fire of 1960 was substantially over half a million dollars, but the area burned during those fiery days was 3000 acres—instead of, possibly, 3,000,000.

# CHAPTER EIGHTEEN

# The Ranger

"Listen to him! Another member of the Sula Ranger District demands to be heard!" I obeyed the ranger and opened my ears to the vibrant, resonant bugling of the tawny-colored elk bull. At first he had eyed us curiously, then with this explosive song seemed to invite us to share the beauties of Hidden Lake and its precipitous rocky border rising upward to the crest of the Sapphire Range. "I wonder why he's alone," the ranger said. "With those antlers and his call, he should be surrounded by a huge harem of cows." We dismounted, tied our horses to slender trees in the meadow and watched the elk across the lake. He drank his fill, casting a rippling reflection between two white masses projected on the water from snowy crevices high above. Then satisfied, he turned to make his way toward a forest of Alpine fir and Englemann spruce, flickering his light-colored tail as a last farewell.

"He and a thousand more elk are the pride of the district, and our greatest problem—that is, if we could single out one problem as the most important," said Ranger John Hall. "They're no real concern during summer when they're grazing here, on the upper range, but as soon as the first snow falls, the elk and deer move down and browse on the same bunchgrass slopes the ranchers will need for their cattle in the spring. In some places they cause more damage to the soil than cattle, besides harm to tree growth. Then, when the food is all gone, they starve to death.

"Sure, we can reduce the number of cattle grazing on the district, as we have been doing. But we need to determine the proper balance between our big game, cattle and other uses of the forest. That's why we have studies underway to learn the complete picture of wildlife and cattle, what they eat, and what their carrying capacity should be. Once we have the facts, then the job will be to show stockmen and sportsmen what must be done, whether it means reduced cattle allotments or an increased kill during the hunting season. These are some of the complications that keep a ranger's life from ever turning dull."

We ate our lunch of sandwiches and fruit while looking up to Pintlar Peak, on the Continental Divide. The air was clear and cool and we were now a wilderness world away from Sula Basin and the ranger station, where we had started out the day before. There, the front yard was still worn bare from the bivouac of 500 men two weeks earlier and from the trampings of 1000 more who had come to be hired, set forth to fight fire on Saddle Mountain, and then returned to be discharged. But, here, barely 300 persons, wilderness campers and hunters, would make an appearance all year.

Both places, and diverse others, were the direct responsibility of John Lawrence Hall, ranger of the Sula District, which covers a quarter million acres of the Bitterroot National Forest. He is one of 800 district rangers, the basic core of our National Forest System. John is a young ranger, age thirty-two, on an old district, established at the turn of the century, but a modern ranger, strikingly unlike the traditional concept, or misconcept, of a very woodsy fellow.

The contemporary ranger is an outdoorsman, a scientist, an administrator and a planner. He must like and understand people, for he is a collaborator of skiers, campers, cattlemen, loggers, Boy Scouts, Girl Scouts, Campfire Girls, the Izaak Walton League, garden-club, state and county officials and other Americans who depend upon his district for their livelihood, recreation or inspiration.

Why is a ranger? "Because I am doing what every forester wants to do," I once was told by a man who has administered the same district in the Lake States for twenty years, "that is, to make the land healthy and productive, and to increase the growth of desirable trees. I don't see this district only as it stands today, but as I think it will be 100 years from now, the time of my children's children. My son is a new forester. I hope someday he will come here and that when he does he will find it a wonderful district."

But why is John Hall, specifically, a ranger? To try to understand, I spent a week with John, followed him in the course of his day, almost from the time he awoke until he went to bed; ate with his family; rode and camped out with him on the wilderness trails, and talked with his neighbors.

I found the people respect their ranger, but they have their distinct and forceful points of view, sometimes conflicting—as between ranchers and sportsmen on the wildlife question. The ranger does

224

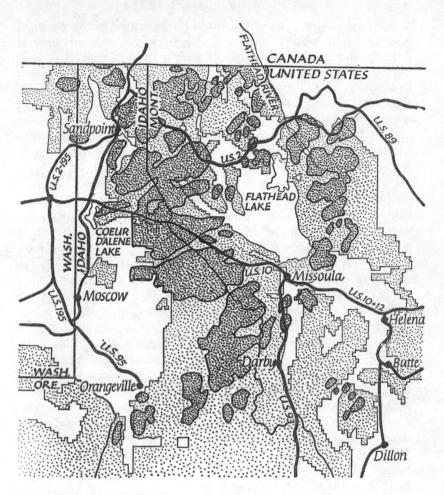

*The Fiery Devastation of 1910 (in black)*

not have the easiest job in the world in convincing either group of what he might consider the best course to follow, and certainly not the sportsmen. Stockmen have seen their grazing allotments steadily reduced, and see more reductions coming. "The rancher is in more of a squeeze all the time," Paul Wetzsteon, Jr., told me. This handsome, husky young man had his hands full of grease, looking up from a tractor he was repairing, but he spoke from knowledge as well as experience. He was graduated at the head of his class in animal husbandry at Montana State College in 1953, then returned to Sula Basin to build a house next to his father's, which is next to *his* father's. "We need the National Forest summer range to survive," he said, "but, as far as game is concerned, remember the stockmen furnish a large part of their winter feed, not on government land but on our own property. I'm interested in protecting wildlife just as much as any sportsman. I *am* a sportsman. But when you get overpopulation to the point of being a menace, I think the time has come to get realistic and see what can be done to increase the harvest during hunting season."

But Miles Romney, the long-time, outspoken editor of the weekly *Western News* at Hamilton, expressed a contrary viewpoint. "I, for one, resist the encroachment of some stockmen on the wildlife range, and the support they receive from some officials of the Forest Service and the State Fish and Game Department," he told me. "Why is there a feed problem? I'm not an expert, but I'm dubious about there being any real experts. Anywhere I go I find lots of browse for elk and deer. We had an exceedingly heavy kill the last two years, when we had open hunting on doe. Now we have a limit of one buck and one doe, the way it should be. The reduction was made because of pressure of sportsmen, pressure against the Forest Service and the State Game Department."

Sandy-haired, stocky John Hall, follows in a long line of rangers who have had to deal with such problems. He and most of his contemporaries are college graduates, and often hold masters' degrees in forestry. It was not that way in the beginning. Before Gifford Pinchot gained administrative control of the National Forests in 1905, the ranger was appointed, directed and paid by a state superintendent, a patronage dispenser. As an old-time ranger recalled, "One of the first constructive steps was to send me a rake, with instructions to clean up the floor of my district—which was only 250,000 acres.

"When I asked for instructions, my superior said, 'Go and range.'

When I asked where, he said, 'You know better than I do. You claim to be a woodsman and I don't.'" In the early days, more than one saloonkeeper was appointed a ranger. Others were waiters, doctors, blacksmiths, who were political appointees and did as little ranging as possible.

But there were plenty of good men attracted to the work. They were impatient of convention and survived by meeting emergencies alone and unaided. They were the spirit of the Old West, typifying adventure, hardihood and love of a wild land. Forest Service officers around the turn of the century hadn't been to school, didn't know silviculture and didn't wear uniforms. And some were incompetent. But most worked hard to protect the forests from fire and misuse. The ranger had no automobile, no telephone, few trails and few boundaries. He received sixty dollars a month and was obliged to provide his own horse and feed. But as a rule he had community respect, which meant more than official prestige.

Among those early rangers was Jesse W. Nicholson, crack rider with Buffalo Bill's Wild West Show. He appeared with Annie Oakley and Johnnie Baker, the champion marksmen, before he joined the Forest Service. In time he became an important official in the grazing division. Another was Frank Hammatt, educated as a priest before he took up cowboy life and became Buffalo Bill's chief wrangler; he was best known as a "two bottle" man. Then there was Ed Hunter, who worked on the district south of Yellowstone Park. He had unlimited courage and endurance, but his aggressive disposition once caused a question to arise regarding the ownership of some cattle. The sheriff of Teton County took Ed into custody. One evening he talked the sheriff into attending a dance at a ranch on the Snake River—and while the sheriff enjoyed himself Ed swam the river and proceeded to distant parts, ending forever his career in forestry.

Young Easterners had hard going in a world of Westerners. One ranger who came to New Mexico from the sophisticated East (he had political influence and a desire to see the great open spaces) committed the grave antisocial indiscretion of telling one cow outfit he had seen another branding its calves. This caused his boot heels to be shot off in a saloon; to vary his step, he was roped and jerked up and down a high post. The next day he was told he must kill somebody to restore his authority in the community. But he refused: that would, he said, be just another Western crudity, while the subtler Eastern revenge would be to cheat his enemies in a poker game. His relationship with the community seemed to worsen with time and an investigator was sent from headquarters to probe his behavior. But by then his intrepidity had won many friends, and even his enemies resented outside bureaucratic interest in a local official's public life!

Few rangers traveled with arms, although they often came in contact with poachers on government land who were not inclined to parley with anything but rifle or revolver. They found themselves in the middle of the sheep wars, striving to preserve law and order over contested grazing lands of the public domain. Bill Kreutzer, appointed a ranger in 1898, although unarmed, once turned back a score of gunslinging cowmen. Fortified with courage after a long bout at the local saloon, they arrived at the border of the Gunnison National Forest determined to raid a sheep camp and drive it out. But Kreutzer, armed only with sober courage and legal right, sent them off. He was one of the few professional men of those days; his father had been a German forester before him.

Perhaps the first official ranger station, certainly one of the country's earliest, was built on the district adjoining John Hall's. H. C. (Hank) Tuttle and Than Wilkerson met at Alta, Montana, on the west fork of the Bitterroot River, in 1899, with dual responsibility of patrolling 300,000 acres of newly created Bitterroot Forest Reserve. Their only shelter was an old wagon sheet, their only equipment axes they had furnished themselves. With materials at hand they erected a one-room cabin of peeled lodgepole-pine walls, split-puncheon floor, a roof of poles with layers of lodgepole bark topped with a foot of dirt. They had to buy hinges, nails and the one glass window from their own funds, since the government had made no appropriations for anything like a ranger station. But when they erected a flagpole and hoisted a flag aloft, this *was* a ranger station. From then on, they proceeded as they pleased, since there were no instructions to guide them. In recent years their cabin has been restored by the Lions Club and is an historic landmark of Bitterroot Valley.

Unlike almost all the early rangers, John Hall began his life in the East, in Muncy, Pennsylvania. He fished, hunted, followed the lore of animals and trees and, like many youngsters attracted to forestry, always wanted a "good outside job." His boyish urge was to find adventure in the outdoors. But listening to his story of growing up and entering the practice of a profession was like following the evolution or development of a character in a novel. After military service, he attended the forestry school at Pennsylvania State University and almost failed to make the grade the first year. That summer he went to California to work on a blister-rust-control crew in Sierra National Forest. The second summer, he drove to Alaska and became a truck driver and grease monkey on the Alaska Highway project. On the way home he and an equally adventurous partner fished, boated and slept on the shores of Lake Nipigon, in the Canadian wilds, then spent two weeks picking tomatoes; both raised beards, of course. The third year, he grew more serious. His class camped in Allegheny National Forest and absorbed practical forestry problems, including an unscheduled 500-acre fire. By the time of his graduation in 1951, he was president of the Forestry Council and a member of Alpha Zeta, the honorary agriculture society. "I had also learned to ignore the jibes of the business students," he recalled, "who thought we foresters were a bunch of clods."

After Penn State, John studied for his master's degree at the Yale University School of Forestry, one of the first forestry schools in the country, established by a grant of $300,000 from the Pinchot family in 1900. He sat in the same classrooms where every Chief of the Forest Service from 1905 to 1940 had been either student or teacher, and where Gifford Pinchot himself had been a lecturing professor. Thus armed with book learning, he joined the Forest Service, on the immense South Tongass National Forest of Alaska, beginning as all young foresters do, tramping the woods and blazing timber, for cutting, with spray gun and paint. Then he worked on a research project, designed to learn the effect of logging on salmon streams, which constitute a primary consideration in Alaskan economy and recreation. In 1954 he became one of the youngest district rangers, on one of the largest districts, in the Forest Service. He celebrated by marrying Carol Peterson, a nurse and Ketchikan native. (Foresters seem to have a penchant for marrying nurses or schoolteachers; or perhaps I should say nurses and teachers are drawn, usually with tolerance, to foresters and their outdoor ways.) The Chatham District of the North Tongass National Forest, which he administered, covers more than 4,500,000 acres, much of it water. Often he traveled by boat, spending weeks on end probing glaciers and fjords, disembarking with rifle as protection in event of meeting an inhospitable brown bear. He enjoyed the tremendous variety of his district: administering the ski development at Mendenhall Glacier, outside Juneau; logging 20,000,000 board feet of Sitka spruce, western hemlock, western red cedar and Alaska cedar; protecting the wealth of salmon for sport and commercial fishing; managing wildlife, including the Dahl sheep, the only white mountain sheep in the world, and studying wildlife problems, such as the effect of logging on the habitat of the brown bear. After two years he was promoted to the supervisor's staff, working on timber management, recreation and wildlife for the entire North Tongass Forest. His pride was an integrated recreation plan for Mendenhall Glacier, complete with campground, trailer park, swimming pools and a hotel like Timberline Lodge at Mount Hood, which is now being developed.

John and Carol loved Alaska, but came to the Sula Ranger District so that he could broaden his experience and knowledge of forestry, particularly in dealing with range management and fire control. Developing this varied background is part of the process of advancement in the Forest Service, perhaps to a position as forest supervisor or to a staff assignment in a regional office.

Here they live, 200 yards from the ranger office, in a five-room white frame house, for which they pay the government sixty dollars monthly rental. They now have four little Halls (with a five-year difference between the oldest and youngest) and one large dog. From their front door an unfettered lawn of ponderosa pine carpets the slopes south toward Lost Trail Pass. To the west the Bitterroot Range thrusts its saw-toothed peaks and ridges skyward, while directly behind their house to the east are the rugged Sapphires. The vast country around them is composed of National Forests—the Bitterroot, Lolo, Nez Perce, Clearwater, Deerlodge, Beaverhead and Salmon—with high mountain lakes bordered by sheer cliffs and snow and pine. Easterners will understand on viewing these magnificent distances why many Idahoans and Montanans are not anxious to attract industrial wealth or new population; they figure they have ample wealth. On the other hand, old-line officials of stockmen's associations and other chronic advocates of "giving the land back to the states" will understand why the rest of America can never permit them to dismember these national treasures.

Tiny Sula, three miles north of the ranger station, is the only town, really a settlement, in the district. The center of community life is the Sula post office and store. Before the coming of the white man this was a favored camping area of the Flathead Indians, and here Lewis and Clark met the Flathead in 1805. Alexander Ross, the Hudson Bay trapper, wintered here in 1824 and from his visit the site has been called Ross' Hole. After Chief Charlot and his tribe were moved, settlement began in 1895, and most of the ranches are now run by second and third generations.

To Ranger Hall and his wife social life is limited principally to pot-luck dinners every other month, and the stockmen's poker parties. About once every two weeks, or every three weeks in summer, the family drives forty-five miles to Hamilton for "dinner out" at a café with red-checkered tablecloths, then for a visit to Forest Service friends. But John is one of those people who combine their work, social activity and recreation.

"Here I am riding with you in the wilderness heart of the Rockies," he explained. "This is my work, to inspect the construction job of our trail crew and study the wilderness environment. But as an outdoorsman I want to be here. This same principle applies after working hours. Working hours? A ranger's day is supposed to start at eight A.M. and end at five P.M., but very few rangers get to work after seven-thirty or quit before six in the evening. Well, let us say there's a meeting one evening of the Ravalli County Sportsman's Club at Hamilton. As a ranger I should be listening to sportsmen's gripes, but as a sportsman I would be there anyway, enjoying the meeting and, who knows, perhaps griping a little on my own. Or there might be meetings of the stockmen's association, the loggers or some other group in Hamilton, but I enjoy them, too.

"The same is true of the ski patrol—part work and part recreation."

Little wonder that every weekend during the winter John is on hand at the Lost Trail Pass Ski Area, where, under a "special use" permit, a ski operator runs four gas-powered rope tows on National Forestland. But he doesn't come alone. Being a firm family man, he brings the children, and skis downhill with one at a time seated snugly in a "kiddy carrier" strapped to his back.

Winter is John's busiest season. His working force is down to the five year-round employees. This is the time when he is supposed to catch up with reports and planning but, like most rangers, never quite makes it. He takes grazing applications and talks with ranchers about their problems. He travels on snowshoes and skis to observe the key winter game range, on which elk, moose and deer, down from their heights, are browsing the grassland. In some quarters they have already chewed up and stifled reproduction of ponderosa pine and Douglas-fir. Winter is a time of death to elk through disease and malnutrition, but the losses are largely of one-year-olds. Yet winter feeding of hay, when it has been tried, only concentrates large numbers of elk on poor range.

In spring, orange-yellow masses of flowering balsamroot sweep across the slopes of the Bitterroot Valley. The working force at the ranger station begins to expand from five, including two other professional foresters, to a summer force of thirty. As soon as snows melt, work crews start on timber-stand improvement, pruning, disposing of brush and slash to remove fire hazards and planting young ponderosa pines. Later they will go on fire and lookout duty, trail construction and campground cleanup. Then John checks his summer grazing range for readiness, to be sure plants and grasses are blooming well. He rides with the ranchers discussing new methods of grazing, and encouraging them to move their herds about to avoid overgrazing. At the same time, he signs up the ranchers, later the loggers, to be on call for fire duty; they are the backbone of his fire crews.

In summer, 1600 head of cattle turn out to pasture on the Sula District. These are almost entirely purebred Herefords, which have long replaced the Longhorn on the Montana range; they belong to sixteen permittees, who pay around sixty cents per head a month to graze on the National Forest. At the same time, loggers are cutting timber under the ranger's supervision; his wildlife is in the upper reaches of the district; campers are in the three campgrounds, and fishermen are casting for trout in the streams that flow into the Bitterroot. And from this drainage the East Fork of the Bitterroot flows north into the Clark's Fork of the Columbia at Missoula, then joining the main Columbia and the Snake in eastern Washington; thus part of John Hall's mission is to protect the stability of the soil and the continued flow of water from these mountains to ranches, towns and cities clear to the Pacific Coast. Then there is always the threat of fire in summer, which takes precedence over all else.

We had long departed the higher reaches and started down, our trail following the East Fork from its headwaters at Hidden Lake. At one point the trail swung a wide arc through a sloping alpine meadow at the peak of summer bloom. John identified golden poppies, showy blue-and-white columbines, creamy white globeflowers, Rocky Mountain kalmia, the dwarfed white dryad, asters and blazing Indian paintbrush, a community abloom. Then we picked up the rocky trail between steep canyon walls, passing Star Creek Falls close enough to feel the spray as it plunged downward more than a hundred feet.

In the morning the skies had been clear, but now they clouded. The wind blew and a million bare lodgepole pine trees shivered. Off in the distance we saw lightning.

"John, if you don't mind," I said, "I prefer not to die of a lightning strike on the trail."

"I don't think you have to worry too much about lightning in here as you do these falling trees. The trail crew just finished opening the trail and look at it now. Keep your eyes and ears open, and duck when you see one fall."

The horses picked their way around and over downed timbers. Now and then we would hear a tree crack apart as it yielded to the wind, then thud deeply as it fell to the forest floor. Rain began lightly, gladder tidings to the ranger than dry lightning. It was a long way to the corral, where we finally unsaddled the horses and turned them loose. A long day of riding, about twenty-five miles by the ranger's estimate.

Later, under a bright midnight moon, we sat on the steps of the ranger station.

"You know, we were talking about the things a ranger has to do," John said. "But all those—timber management, issuing 'special use' permits, handling road maintenance, grazing, fighting fire and the rest —they're day-to-day routine. They go on year after year, just like the weather. But the important thing, or perhaps the enjoyable thing, to a ranger is not what he does, but what he plans.

"For example, I submitted a report on revising the boundaries of the Pintlar Wilderness. It was not a question of making it smaller or larger, but a better wilderness, sealed off from outside influence and more compact within its natural, topographic barriers. When the wilderness areas were first established the boundaries were not well defined.

"The district needs a management plan to insure the best use of all our quarter million acres. We should have more wild areas, scenic areas and recreation units. One ideal place is Fish Lake, although we still have the problem of deciding whether it should be left in its natural state or developed with roads and recreation facilities. On the other hand, where we have a good ponderosa stand with no outstanding scenic values, it should be primarily a timber area. We need an over-all transportation plan, to show where new roads should go to tap for timber, or for recreation. We should have research and interpretive services on the geology and history of our district.

"The big thing is to determine the proper balance between game and cattle. The timber areas should be managed to increase our capacity of game and range. I showed you Douglas-fir and lodgepole-pine logging, where the skid roads open access for cattle and the clearcutting opens patches of added forage for late spring, summer and early fall. But the important point now is that if the ranger sees that land is being abused, he must do something about it. He has to make decisions acceptable—more important, understandable—to the stockmen and sportsmen. After all, how could we really practice land management without public support and encouragement?"

The odds are against John ever getting rich, regardless of how effective a plan he develops for the Sula District, or how high he may advance in the Forest Service. As a district ranger, his base salary is $8000 a year. During the summer fire season he receives an additional "unscheduled differential" of twenty dollars weekly, although he may be on fire duty without letup for days on end. In the same period, his fire dispatcher will receive hourly rate overtime pay and earn more than he does.

"Oh, I guess I could quit the Forest Service and earn more in private industry or in some other line, but I doubt I would be any more content," he said. "My family may never have everything in life, but I can provide for them on a ranger's pay. I develop a campground, build a trail or conduct a timber sale and feel I've done something for my country and the coming generation. Money can't buy that feeling. After all, there is a psychic income in knowing you will leave the land in better condition than you found it."

Driving north on Route 93, you will have no trouble noting the boundary of the Sula Ranger District and Bitterroot Valley. They begin at Lost Trail Pass, the Idaho-Montana state line. Evidence of the 1960 fire on Saddle Mountain will be plainly visible in bare hillsides and charred timbers, although salvage logging, grass seeding to prevent erosion, and timber planting (Douglas-fir and Englemann spruce) were begun almost before the smoke had settled.

Twenty-three miles east lies the site of Big Hole Battlefield, which Chief Joseph and 400 Nez Perce Indians reached in the summer of 1877 after traveling from Idaho south through Bitterroot Valley. They were in flight from the U. S. Army but were endeavoring peaceably

234

to reach Canada and freedom from reservation life. An Army unit overtook them here in a surprise attack, a needless tragedy in which Indian women and children, as well as warriors, were killed. The Nez Perce fought off the whites, continuing south and east, then north toward Canada, but were captured a few miles from the border.

In traveling north you are following the route of Lewis and Clark in 1805. Try to picture the valley as they found it. It was then the main center of the Flathead Indians, who had moved westward from the Bozeman Valley and Three Forks area. Half their sustenance was derived from small animals and plants like the bitterroot, but once or twice a year they returned to their old domain to obtain buffalo. Members of the Lewis and Clark expedition reported the Bitterroot country was carpeted with ponderosa pine, with scaly cinnamon brown bark and resinous aroma, reaching heights of 150 to 225 feet. In 1855 Chief Victor and others signed their basic treaty with the United States, hoping their home, the Bitterroot Valley, would be their reservation. But they were uprooted and moved to the rugged Jocko Canyon Reservation north of Missoula. It was another of those unhappy, undistinguished chapters in the white man's relationship with the Indians. Chief Charlot, protesting against the forced move, remained with a handful of his people on the old ground through years of desultory harassment and destitution until 1891; at last, in utter impoverishment and defeat, they rode north.

If you visit the Sula District in summer, you will have the choice of three campgrounds; several guest ranches and working ranches; 115 miles of stream and fifteen mountain lakes loaded with cutthroat, rainbow, Eastern brook trout and whitefish, plus the Anaconda-Pintlar Wilderness with elevations up to 9000 feet on the crest of the Continental Divide. One of the campgrounds is located next to Medicine Hot Springs, a natural spa, on private land, of the most refreshing and relaxing mineral waters west of White Sulphur Springs; I offer this testimonial on the basis of a bath taken at the end of twenty-five miles on the trail.

If you're a hunter, remember the wilderness is yours in autumn, for elk, deer, upland grouse, black bear and mountain goat, and for cougar in winter. This is sportsman's country with rough going and plenty of cover for game. Local outfitters charge thirty-five to fifty dollars per day per person for a party of four, including guide, cook, horses and food. The usual length of time for a party of four to fill out with game is about five days to a week.

Hamilton, the heart of the Bitterroot Valley, lies at the foot of the snowy Bitterroot Range, with wide streets, clear, clean air, an adequate number of saddleries, barbershops and saloons. Into this valley first came the traders and trappers. Then, in 1841, the Jesuit missionary of the Rocky Mountains, Father Pierre-Jean DeSmet, established St. Mary's Mission near Stevensville, fifteen miles north. In 1850, it became a trading post presided over by Major John Owen, and thus was named Fort Owen. It was Montana's first white settlement, which shows the youth and newness of this country; the Fort has recently been restored as a state monument. In visiting Stevensville, be sure also to see the tiny squared-log mission church which Father Anthony Ravalli built in 1866 and decorated with statues he carved by hand.

In the 1880's, Marcus Daly chose the Bitterroot Valley for his private empire. He had already made his fortune, fairly and otherwise, in Butte and Anaconda and crossed the Sapphire Range to claim thousands of acres of virgin timber, lush grass in the bottom lands and rolling hills of seemingly unlimited pasture. His Anaconda Copper Mining Company became Hamilton's first business and was in continuous operation for forty years, but along with his company store, timber, mining and farming, he enlarged his interests to the collection and breeding of thoroughbred horses. Later, settlers were attracted to the environs by irrigated farming of sugar beets and fruits, some of which is still carried on.

A very worthwhile (and free) point of interest is the Historical Museum in the Chamber of Commerce Building at Hamilton. It tells the story of the Valley from Indian days and early white settlement by means of invaluable and well presented handcrafts, furnishings, rifles and revolvers.

A final story, about dudes, told by Robert H. Fletcher. A bard of the range and author of the good-humored historical markers along Montana's highways, he concedes that city people intent on a Western vacation are pretty good folks, after all; sometimes they do get on a Westerner's nerves but other times can be right amusing. A terribly British lady, his case in point, once elected to ride on roundup. She and Sage Collings of the U Cross spread were coming in from circle and crossed a badly damaged ranch bridge. Said the fine lady to Sage in her richest accent: "Mr. Collings, your breeges are veddy much in need of repair." To which Sage meekly replied: "Yessum. I aim to get a new pair if I ever get to town."

# CHAPTER NINETEEN

# *Pasteur of the White Pine*

Everyone should choose a favorite tree, an individual species to understand well and recognize wherever he may find it. Only a landscape architect or a forester can be expected to know them all, but there is nothing to prevent the rest of us from selecting our personal, special friends among the giants of the plant world.

Thomas Jefferson expressed the enrichment derived from his affinity with a particular tree, the sycamore, or plane tree, the most massively proportioned American hardwood. "I never knew before the full value of trees," he wrote his daughter, Martha Randolph, from Philadelphia in 1793. "My house is embosomed in high plane trees, with good grass below, and under them I breakfast, dine, write, read and receive my company."

But if you were to choose the western white pine you would share the favorite of Virgil Moss, a very modest man who speaks glowingly of the tree but barely of his great personal accomplishment to rescue it from the threat of decimation.

Mr. Moss has known and loved this tree for the fifty years of his life in Idaho and eastern Washington. To him the silver pine of the Northwest mountains is "the most beautiful tree of all." As a forester, as well as a practical, determined research scientist in plant pathology, he sees his favorite, *Pinus monticola*, in terms of more than beauty. "Why, it's a wonderful tree in every respect," he told me in his soft-spoken way when I met him at the shore of Priest Lake, in upper Idaho a few miles below the British Columbia border. We were sitting in the headquarters of the Forest Service blister-rust-control project, on the west shore of the lake. I could see it was a large, beautiful body of water bordered by green mountains. It was almost a distracting influence but Virgil Moss was far too engrossing. His tall body was relaxed, but his gray eyes disclosed depth and spark behind them. "The white pine grows fast and reproduces generously," he said. "With its attractive color—silvery gray bark and bluish

green leaves—and its stately form, it is highly desirable for park ornamental purposes. But more important, it means a lot to the economy
of this state. As a timber tree, it has hardly an equal in the variety
of its uses."

Just as Virgil Moss feels toward the tree, so should the western
white pine feel toward him. So, too, should the other five-needle
pines, the sugar, limber, whitebark, bristlecone and foxtail; and perhaps other trees, as well. For his pioneering contribution to forestry
and the world of trees is comparable in its quiet way to the contributions of Dr. Jonas Salk or Dr. Alexander Fleming or Louis Pasteur
to the world of people.

The epochal achievement of Virgil Moss, still little known beyond
the circles of plant pathology, was to find a way to protect the white
pine from its most dangerous enemy, the fungus disease called blister
rust. This he did through painstaking, trial-and-error research which
finally reached success with an antibiotic formula, called Acti-dione.
Acti-dione and more recently a new preparation, Phytoactin, have also
proven effective in treating the other five-needle pines. And they may
now open the way toward antibiotic treatment of other tree diseases,
including oak wilt, Dutch elm blight and chestnut blight.

The efforts of Mr. Moss in white-pine blister-rust control are part
of a massive Forest Service program aimed at many tree diseases and
deadly insects. Diseases claim a greater toll than does fire. They kill
more of our nation's trees than are cut by loggers. New diseases
emerge while old ones fade. Some attack only trunks of trees; some
only branches, or seeds, or leaves, or seasoned woods.

Blister rust is among the most widespread forest diseases. Another
in the Northern Rockies, dwarf mistletoe, deforms and kills larch and
lodgepole pine and impairs the quality of Douglas-fir. In the South,
fusiform gall rust attacks slash and loblolly pine. In the East and
Middlewest, oak wilt has threatened to destroy forests of red and
black oak.

But the most tragic disease of all undoubtedly has been chestnut
blight, which came to this country on Asiatic chestnuts and quickly
spawned and swarmed through millions of American trees. The fungi
formed yellow-brown cankers, or infested sores, on stems and
branches, multiplying until they finally killed individual chestnut
trees by "girdling" the trunk; that is, cutting the cambium layer
needed for growth. Chestnut blight has proved a major forest catas-
trophe, for it eliminated a great tree of the East, prized for both its

238

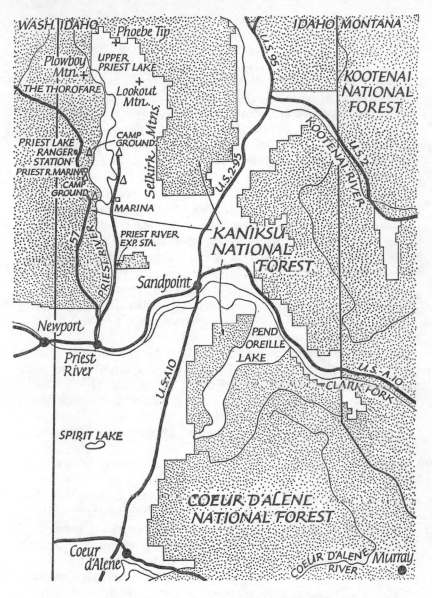

White-Pine Country of Idaho's Panhandle

appearance and its timber. Here and there you may see chestnut trees still standing, gaunt, defoliated, forever in the winter of their days. Oaks, yellow poplar and other hardwoods have been substituted for the chestnut, but they can never really replace it.

Then there are insects—moths, weevils, caterpillars, worms, beetles, sawflys, termites, borers. They march, dig, fly, bore, crawl, reproduce within trees and nourish themselves and their young. Some, like the bark beetles, are the mortal foe of conifers. Others, like the spruce budworm, are foliage eaters, disrupting the process of photosynthesis by which the tree absorbs the sun's energy for its own growth.

Insects are the worst of all enemies of trees. They cause twice as much damage as disease, and seven times more damage than fire.

Normally, insects and fungi are controlled by parasites, predators and diseases which make *them* sick, and by freezing weather. But sometimes the biotic balance is disturbed and the forest becomes a fertile field for epidemic. (This is the reason foresters say the best way to prevent epidemic and preserve a healthy forest is to harvest aging and weak trees, safeguarding the young, sturdy and resistant.) Sometimes insects or disease are accidentally introduced from abroad. These foreign visitors find conditions ideal in their new environment, free of their old predators and parasites.

Such was the case with the fungus of the white-pine blister rust. It started in Russia, or at least the *Cronartium ribicola* was first reported there in 1854. It spread across Europe and arrived in the United States around the turn of the century, on cultivated currants. Again, in 1921, it appeared in British Columbia and northern Washington, apparently having entered on white-pine nursery stock shipped from France.

Over the years blister rust has spread relentlessly. It has swept across eastern white pine from Maine to North Carolina to Minnesota. In the West it now extends halfway down the length of California and as far inland as Wyoming, attacking all the five-needle pines. In Montana, where white pine is a highly valued commercial species, it is feared that a few years may see it completely succumb to rust, despite efforts to control it during the past quarter century.

Blister rust first shows its presence in small discolored spots of a single bundle of needles. Then the bark around the needles swells and discolors. Inside the bark, fungi are growing and spreading. The following spring powdery white blisters push through the outer layer, a sign that living tissues are dying. Needles on dead branches turn

240

PLATE 8

PLATE 8. The perpetual snow of Mount Hood, in Mount Hood National Forest, Oregon, rises above green giants of the forest and the foreground of squaw grass and rhododendron. The summit of this queen of the Cascades is reached by more climbers than any snow-capped peak in the world, except Mount Fujiyama, Japan.

PLATE 9

PLATE 9. The Pacific Coast Rain Forest—a family on the nature trail near Quinault, in Olympic National Forest, Washington. In the famous "Big Acre," growing conditions are so favorable that centuries-old giants are still healthy and adding growth.

PLATE 10. White-face Herefords graze a mountain meadow bordered with lodgepole pine in Roosevelt National Forest, Colorado. The Forest Service now has underway a twenty-year program of revegetation designed to permit a substantial increase in grazing use, without harming the soil cover.

PLATE 11. A band of sheep grazing in Muddy Meadows, high country summer range at the base of glacial-carved Mount Adams in Gifford Pinchot National Forest, Washington. In winter, the meadows, trees and all, will be under deep snow.

PLATE 10

PLATE 11

PLATE 12

PLATE 12. Around the campfire, after a day's ride in San Juan National Forest, Colorado. Forest Ranger John Mattoon sits amid this group of outdoor enthusiasts and explains with pride the activities on his Ranger District.

a copper color, appearing like reddish "flags" in the crown of the tree. Unchecked, the fungi ultimately girdles the trunk and kills the entire tree.

The fungi, however, do not spread directly from pine to pine. They are drawn also to currant and gooseberry bushes—called ribes—which transmit them as an intermediary. Blister rust may spread hundreds of miles from tree to ribes, but the spread from ribes to pine is usually only a few hundred feet, or a mile at the most. Blister rust lives happily on the ribes leaf, infecting it, intensifying, maturing in great hairlike columns, producing new cells, or sporidia, which become so heavy the leaf may fall from their weight—then sending forth young, eager spores to ride fall winds to the white pine. The cycle is endless, although blister rust does relatively little harm to the ribes.

In 1923, efforts began to control blister rust. That was five years before Virgil Moss entered the University of Idaho. The point of attack was not the pine, but the ribes. It was a matter of hand pulling and grubbing, of digging out the gooseberry and currant bushes. And until the Moss antibiotic breakthrough, it continued, with special tools like a cast chrome steel pick, as the principal means of ribes eradication.

Refinements and other methods were tried. In some places fire was employed, in the hope of burning out ribes bushes and the seed stores. Logging practices were planned with light to moderate cuttings, leaving a half-canopy of shade in the hope ribes would perish without sunlight. Experiments were conducted to see how far from the pine the ribes actually would have to be dug out.

In time, 23,000,000 acres were brought into the white-pine blister-control area. One billion, three hundred million ribes bushes were removed.

But it became clear that destruction of every single living ribes bush would not end the problem. Seedlings burrowed in the humus emerged after disturbances such as logging or fire, for seed can be stored before germination for a hundred years or more. And from a timber viewpoint, the rate of ribes destruction could assure only one-half of the current annual cut (200,000,000 to 300,000,000 board feet) in the years ahead.

So the problem was defined in new terms: not only eliminating the ribes, but continuing to grow white pine despite the disease. Could this be done? Virgil Moss, among others, was asked to find the answer. Born and raised in the western white-pine country, he had already devoted his entire working career to the study of blister rust, starting with the Department of Agriculture's Bureau of Entomology, which later became part of the Forest Service.

Everywhere he had looked in 1941 and 1942, pinelands were turning reddish brown. Ribes had a thriving summer in 1941, when moisture and temperature were favorable. In the fall, blister-rust spores swept across the mountains to the Cascades.

"By 1949," he recalled to me, "it was very clear there would be no white pine left if we didn't get to the host, rather than just the transmitter. The best white-pine lands in the world were critically affected. You could look at any stand and see the signs and see them dying."

Other entomologists were working on the same problem. In one project it was shown the disease could be slowed if cankers were removed in the same way a surgeon removes a tumor—that is, by cutting out all the diseased tissues of trunk cankers and pruning infected branches. The cost was high and skill was required in this laborious operation.

Mr. Moss recounts the course he followed:

"I started by experimenting with antibacterial chemicals used in agricultural crops," he told me at Priest Lake. "I tried several hundred formulae in the laboratory, seeing how they would react to fungicide which I had cultured on the dead and dying bark of many trees.

"At first I wasn't particularly interested in antibiotics, and especially not in Acti-dione, but it kept asking to be tried. The Upjohn Company suggested it to me as a possibility. It was a fairly new product made from streptomycin cultures. It had been tested on Dutch elm and slash-pine fungus diseases, without success. On the other hand, it had shown promise in treating a fungus disease of turf.

"When I decided to try it, I had first to develop a number of emulsifiers, trying to find the right one to penetrate tissue and spread upward through the tree. I sprayed about 500 diseased trees on the Coeur d'Alene National Forest, using five different formulas. For two years I kept examining these trees microscopically down to their needles, bark and tissue. Acti-dione did show a positive reaction on the branch cankers, but it wasn't moving upward into the tree. I reported the disease could be slowed down, but I doubt that anyone paid much attention.

"In 1951 and 1952 I worked with other chemicals, as well as Acti-dione. And by 1953 I knew I could kill an individual canker. At that time I used the 'excise method,' cutting away dead and dying bark and then spraying the wound with Acti-dione. It was hardly practical because it meant treating each canker individually. I changed the formula and tried different concentrations. At one point, I even tried using a veterinary syringe, inoculating a tree as if it were a horse.

"I was working all alone. Nobody believed antibiotics would ever prove effective, perhaps because they had never been successful on trees before. Even today, pathologists say it just doesn't make sense and some don't believe it is working. But I knew that it had to be tried all the way.

"In 1954 and 1955 I worked on the 'slit method,' cutting hatchet slits one to three inches long through the canker. I also tested a number of carriers. One of the cheapest, stove oil, was most effective, although people with whom I discussed it insisted it would kill the trees!

"The year 1956 was a major turning point. Henry Viche, the timber-management officer of the Kaniksu National Forest, was very interested and established blister-rust control through Acti-dione on a project basis. This took it out of the laboratory and really set it in operation. We treated 20,000 trees with the excise method. The next year we switched to the slit method and treated 100,000 trees.

"This was encouraging, but still not the answer. Even the slit method was laborious and costly, requiring individual inspection and treatment of the cankers. We needed something simpler and quicker. This proved to be the 'basal-stem method,' whereby *all* trees, infected or not, are sprayed around the base and the Acti-dione absorbed through the bark. In 1958, a total of 295,000 trees were treated by slit or basal-stem methods."

That was the major breakthrough. The following summer Mr. Moss walked through stands of white pine which had been sprayed with the basal-stem formula. The trees were alive and well, the blister-rust cankers very dead. It was the signal to the Forest Service to move into high gear. In 1959, some 4,000,000 trees were sprayed; the project was expanded to other National Forests and to Glacier National Park. In 1960, the total was more than doubled, to 10,000,000 trees on the Kaniksu, St. Joe, Coeur d'Alene, Clearwater and Kootenai—Idaho's five great white-pine forests.

Now, within ten years, it is planned to treat the entire white-pine forest of the Northwest, starting with areas that need it most. The

Forest Service estimates that in so doing it will save at least 20,000,-000 trees.

At this point, 80 per cent of effort and expense is directed toward antibiotic control, the remaining 20 per cent toward ribes eradication. "So far," Mr. Moss explained, "antibiotics can only save white pine already infected. In the future we may have aerial spray and nursery-grown seedlings with blister-rust immunity, but until then ribes destruction must still be carried on, although to a much lesser extent."

Mr. Moss offered to show me blister-rust control in action and we left for the forested hills above Priest Lake. With us was his associate, strapping Quentin W. "Cap" Larson, who has spent thirty years on the project at Priest Lake, which he now supervises. He began in the 1930's in the Civilian Conservation Corps; his office is located where once he was quartered. Cap has roamed the mountains, hunted big game with bow and arrow and fished the choice spots of Priest River and Priest Lake.

We went to see two of the ten forest camps, in which college boys were based to work on the blister-rust project and on fires when they are needed. From the Kalispell Creek Camp, we followed thirty young men as they loaded on a truck and set forth to their area of the day. Behind them came a tanker truck loaded with the liquid spray.

We followed into the woods, where the boys worked, armed with back pumps from which they sprayed all trees.

"Each man should cover about two acres a day and treat 450 trees," Cap Larson explained. "The whole operation is simple because they spray all the trees without consultation, or wondering whether it has blister rust. On trees less than twelve feet tall they spray the lower third, otherwise they drench it to a height of five feet. They can't go too high because Acti-dione is toxic to the needles."

Mr. Moss pointed to the area around the diseased canker. In four to six weeks after spraying it would begin to turn light brown, then darkening, the result of the antibiotic overcoming the fungus within the tree. In time new growth would develop and cover the canker. It is known thus far that Acti-dione remains effective at least two years, and possibly much longer.

How expensive was it to spray a single tree with Acti-dione?

"Let's figure it this way," Mr. Moss replied. "The Acti-dione costs $200 a gallon, but it takes only one-half fluid ounce per gallon of mixture with stove oil. All right, now you want the cost of the stove

244

oil—seventeen to twenty cents a gallon. The answer is that we figure it costs three to five cents to spray one tree."

That sounded like a fair taxpayer's investment. Virgil Moss may have experienced inner feelings of grandeur and glory, but he didn't express them. He answered all my questions, but was far from effulgent. We had parked on a loggers' road about a thousand feet above Priest Lake. I could see the reddish "flags" of blister rust flying in the green seas of white pines. One question I wanted him to answer was, How did he feel personally about his achievement?

Being a researcher and not a promoter, he smiled rather defensively and answered in his own way.

"It's true that it didn't come easily," he replied. "I think we've discussed most of the highlights, not the interminable details and the heartbreaks. But success, if that's what you call it, makes you work all the harder, and there is still so much to be done before blister rust is really licked."

He outlined five projects, which begin where Acti-dione leaves off.

First, experimental aerial and helicopter spraying of white pine was begun in 1960, with the antibiotic Phytoactin (made from yeast at the Pabst brewery). First results showed it nontoxic to needles and harmless to fish and wildlife. Should aerial spray prove effective there would be no limit to the possibilities of disease control.

Second, since 1959 Mr. Moss has directed blister projects at Yellowstone, Glacier (where the disease has been rampant), Grand Teton and Rocky Mountain National Parks, as well as in the National Forests.

Third, he has established test plots of whitebark and limber pine in order to measure the full effectiveness of antibiotics on those species.

Fourth, since 1958 he has worked in the Forest Service nursery at Coeur d'Alene trying to develop an immune breed of white pine through the artificial inoculation of ribes infection in young trees.

Fifth, the new Northern Idaho Forest Genetics Center at Moscow is also conducting a project to breed disease-resistant trees. At the Experimental Seed Orchard in Sandpoint it is planting and grafting young pines from parents which stood originally, in healthy condition, amid fungus-infected trees. Thirty per cent of seedlings produced in the first generation offspring of Sandpoint trees are expected to be disease-free, the second generation about 50 per cent disease-free, and by 1980 it should produce annually 20,000,000 seeds of totally disease-free trees.

Many trees other than the white pine may soon be receiving antibiotic treatments. Other Forest Service research men are benefiting from the work of Virgil Moss, and have been following their own lines of investigation. Three of the worst and most difficult to fathom diseases—oak wilt, Dutch elm blight and chestnut blight—have shown signs of giving way under the touch of antibiotics.

Speaking of the chestnut, there are other heartening developments in forest genetics. Over 1000 large trees, which somehow survived the blight and achieved full growth, have been assembled at Bent Creek plantation in the Pisgah National Forest, North Carolina. Research foresters have been grafting and breeding a new generation from these healthy trees. Will their progeny prove to be resistant to fungus? It is still too soon to know, but after five years the young breed has shown the will to live and grow and to surmount the deadly threat of blight.

I asked Virgil Moss to recall the singular moment of his research. A laboratory instant, perhaps, when the one-thousandth formula reacted surprisingly? No, there was no such single incident. Perhaps, then, one great time?

"Yes, I think there was one greatest thrill to remember," he replied. "It was not in research because, as I said, learning is a never-ending story. But one day I was working in the Clearwater National Forest. A gyppo logger, a small-scale operator, came up to me and said, 'Thanks for what you have done for the white pine.' It was bread and butter to him. And I believe he loved the tree as I do. To think that he would know of my work and would appreciate it to the point of coming up and thanking me—well, that's the reward I'm proud of."

Priest Lake, quite apart from the battle over blister rust, deserves wide attention in another sense. It is one of the most beautiful, gracefully formed lakes in the United States, bordered with those green slopes and rocky landmarks, and with a delightfully primitive air. It lies north of Lake Coeur d'Alene, north of Lake Pend Oreille, in the upper tip of the Idaho Panhandle, cool summer country, reached by driving through forests of white pine and spruce, passing logging trucks and sawmills.

This is not all virgin forest, but second growth following severe fires. There were large ones in 1925, 1926 and 1931. The last was the worst: it started one August morning and by nightfall had destroyed 26,000 acres of timber and ranchland. Although 1500 men fought the fire, it was six weeks before the ninety miles of fire line were completely under control.

The best way to enjoy Priest Lake and Upper Priest Lake is to travel by boat. If you don't have your own, you can rent one at Linger Longer Lodge, Jim Low's or the Granite Creek Marina. But many of the best spots for picnicking and camping, as well as sight-seeing and fishing, can be reached only by boat. For a shoreline base, you can choose from state campgrounds on the east side, three Forest Service campgrounds and several resorts with sand beaches on the west side.

The lakes, carved by glacial action, measure twenty-six miles in length. The lower lake is eighteen miles long and an average four miles wide, dotted with islands. Fishing, as Cap Larson would say, is almost too good to believe. If you find the right spot between Kalispell and Papoose Islands, you may bring in a mackinaw of thirty pounds or more. The biggest caught here to date weighed over fifty pounds. Also very popular here are the kokanee, the little landlocked salmon, and the Dolly Varden, with cutthroat found in the bays and creeks.

Priest Lake is bordered by the Selkirk Mountains, which are not part of the Rocky Mountains, but an older, and therefore less abrupt and more rounded, formation. But you will see distinctive peaks and landmarks on the rugged eastern shore: Chimney Rock, a virtually vertical granite slab; Gunsight Peak, Lion's Head and Smith Peak, the highest point in view (elevation 7650 feet); also Bottle Peak, Kootch Mountain and Distillery Bay. These mountains are tremendous wildlife and autumn hunting country, the home of black bear and grizzly, deer, elk, moose, mountain goat (sometimes visible with binoculars or even the naked eye), and caribou, which have vanished almost everywhere but here. White pine, ponderosa pine, Douglas-fir and cedar slope down to the water's edge. Wildflowers, shrubs and berries bloom among the trees and in open fields.

The two lakes are linked by a languid, two-mile-long natural serpentine canal called the Thorofare, in which everyone slows down to appreciate the beaver and heron. The Thorofare would be a fitting, perfect gateway to the wilderness of Upper Priest Lake, except for the horribly misplaced hamburger stand. The same unfortunate story of a

247

parcel of private land in a strategic location being put to commercial use.

Upper Priest is the more primitive lake, still accessible only by boat (although an access road is planned). Here you may see an osprey diving for his dinner. Or gulls and kingfishers, perhaps a brood of hooded mergansers, certainly native ducks, and flocks of geese in late summer and fall. Stop at the beach at Trapper Point for a picnic and fish for cutthroat in the evening. In the mountains due north, barely fifteen miles away, lies Canada and the source of the Priest River.

# CHAPTER TWENTY

# *Los Rancheros y Rancheritos*

We were driving on the gravel byroad in Chimayo Valley, beneath the towering Sangre de Cristo Range. Along the road and in the *corrales* were horses, sheep, cows, goats and burros, livestock in more than usual variety, if not quantity. My friend Fred Thompson, the Indian trader, who operates the trading post at Santo Domingo pueblo, remarked, "You have cattlemen in here, too, you know."

We rode through the village of Truchas, named in the long ago as Nuestra Señora del Rosario de las Truchas. Beyond the mission school and the squat adobe houses clinging to the hillside, Fred stopped the car at the edge of a crude picket-fenced corral. "I didn't stop because of the view," he said, "but it is one of the greatest and half of what you see—even into Colorado—lies in the National Forests." We were on a high plateau, overlooking the Rio Grande Valley, with the Rio Chama and other tributaries merging into the Rio Grande, and the Jemez Mountains beyond it. Directly above us was snowy Truchas Peak, 13,000 feet high, in the Pecos Wilderness.

"These people here obviously are not very large ranchers," Fred said. "You can see their little farms behind us. Each one is like a narrow strip of land ending at the stream, which they call '*acequia madre*,' or main ditch. The farms are small because when they're handed down from one generation to the next they're divided among all the sons. Now they're so tiny one brother usually buys the inheritance of all the others.

"But how much can they make raising their beans, corn, pepper and squash? They have no industry, except for the weavers at Chimayo. Survival is marginal. They need the National Forest for whatever fence posts, firewood and house logs they can cut and sell —and whatever grazing privileges they can get for their cattle. They've had their grazing permits reduced along with the big ranchers, though I doubt any of them owns more than six, eight or ten head. Maybe they should be reduced even more, if you think of getting this hillside in shape and protecting the Rio Grande, but remember, the Spanish-Americans in these *placitas* have lived in New Mexico longer than any of the rest of us, except for the Indians."

Listening to Fred, the transplanted Easterner, reminded me that we were not talking about cattle barons but probably the smallest grazing permittees in the whole National Forest System. They may have been damaging the physical resources of the land, but, as my friend had said, they constitute a human resource.

Complex is the word for grazing—a crucial, critical use of the National Forests. The large and small livestock operators need the summer range of the mountains, but their herds are extremely damaging to the soil unless they are limited and controlled. To some stockmen use of the range of the National Forests and other public lands should be theirs by right, since grazing began in the days of wide-open public domain—the unfenced range. Consequently, from these quarters we hear the most chronic demand, far more than from the logging industry, to turn Federal lands over to the states, or to release them to private ownership.

Cattle were introduced into the United States by the forefathers of the Southwestern Spanish-Americans. They were numerous in Mexico by the middle of the sixteenth century. An Englishman, Robert Tomson, reported in a letter to his friends at home: "There is a marvelous increase of cattell which dayly do increase and they are of greater growth than ours. You may have a great steer that hath a hundred weight of tallow for 16 shillings and some one man hath 20,000 head of cattell on his own. They have a great increase of sheep in like manner. They have much woole and as goode as the woole in Spain."

When Coronado and his troops advanced north from Mexico in 1540 into New Mexico toward the grassy prairies of Colorado and Kansas, they brought with them 1000 horses, 500 cows, more than 5000 rams and ewes. These were driven along to slaughter for food when needed, and to stock the ranges around settlements the Spaniards established.

Later, cattle ranching began on a large scale in the Southeast, too, especially in Georgia. There were annual roundups and branding of calves, long drives to tidewater markets and conflict over the use of open range. Rustlers followed their trade and were dealt with summarily when caught. Cattlemen of the Eastern colonies, as others would be a century later on the Great Plains, were fearless, resourceful and armed, providing effective protection against Indians. The Battle of Cowpens, South Carolina, in 1781, was fought on a well-known roundup and branding ground, and some of the best revolutionary troops were the hardy cowboys of Georgia and Carolina.

However, as the open range came under the farmer's plow, ranching was forced westward, first over the Alleghenies and in time to the fringe of the Missouri River. It was destined from the beginning for greater success in the Southwest. The country was ideal for stock growing, with its vast open lands, mild climate, lush grasses for cows and horses and broadleaf herbs for sheep.

The face of the early Southwest has been painted in many ways and probably overpainted. Undoubtedly, vegetation was far more luxuriant and water more abundant than in our time. Grass was frequently reported "as high as a cow's back," if not as high as the head of a man on horseback. Tucson was established on the Santa Cruz River because of the available wealth of wood, water and meadowland. Water was sometimes too plentiful; in the eighteenth century travelers sometimes had to wait for weeks to move their horses across the swampy expanse of the Santa Cruz.

River bottoms, forested with giant mesquite, were the homes of beaver. Great herds of antelope and elk roamed the grassy plateaus, feeding on nutritious grama grasses. The woods and plains were filled with wildlife, including deer, turkey, buffalo, quail and dove.

With settlement and diminishing rainfall the character of the landscape changed. After 1800, the beaver were trapped and their dams destroyed. The valleys were stripped of their mesquite and the ironwood was cut from the hills to furnish fence posts and feed lime kilns. With disappearance of vegetation and water, the wildlife dependent on these essentials retreated either to higher ground or to extinction.

Nevertheless, all of the earlier changes in the West, both natural and man-made, were reduced to sheer insignificance by the post-Civil War grazing upheaval, otherwise known as the "beef bonanza." The exploitation was so intense that scars and damages left in a single generation of time may never be erased, regardless of all the care, science and conservation practices bestowed now and hereafter.

"I believe," reported General Luther P. Bradley to the War Department in 1868, "that all the flocks and herds in the world could find ample pasturage on these unoccupied plains and the mountain slopes beyond." The officer added a prophecy, "The time is not far distant when the largest flocks and herds in the world will be found here, where the grass grows and ripens from year to year."

The conditions were ripe for the tide of cattle and sheep to sweep cross the Western territories from the Mexican border to the Canadian. The Indian wars were substantially over. The rail links were extended from East to West. Federal land policies favored free, unrestricted grazing. In a way, they compelled it, since any grass left standing by one herd would surely be eaten by the next. The growing country needed beef. And fortunes were waiting to be made, perhaps even greater than in the California gold rush.

Beginning in the 1870's, promoters and speculators went into Texas and bought thousands of long-horned cattle and moved them north. Big cattle outfits were formed; they were not Western owned, but had their financial roots instead in the East and in Europe. The seventies and eighties were the era of the cattle barons and the cattle drives from the ranges and ranches in southwest Texas and along the Rio Grande in New Mexico to northern railheads, then into the new open ranges to the north.

Charles Goodnight had blazed a trail from Texas along the Pecos River to Fort Sumner, New Mexico. Then, together with Oliver Loving, he extended the trail northward into Colorado and Wyoming. Over this route more than 250,000 head of cattle trailed to market.

The rich grazing lands and the ready market for beef at Fort Stanton and Fort Sumner brought in many enterprising ranchers who ran great herds on the open range of New Mexico. In the twenty years after the Civil War an estimated 300,000 cattle roamed the plains, with almost 90,000 calves born each year. By 1875, John Chisum was credited with having the largest holdings of cattle in the world, possibly 100,000 head. His headquarters were near Roswell, but the annual roundup of the Cattle King of the Pecos reached from the Texas Panhandle west to the Rio Grande and down into Old Mexico. His petition to President Grant for a patent to a vast part of this area was denied, but for years no one dared challenge his rule and he enforced the edict, "Settlers are unwelcome."

Hundreds of thousands of cattle were disgorged from the Southwest, pouring over the backbone of the Rockies into virgin unstocked lands. With herds advancing beyond the Missouri River from the East, the frontier ended not with people but when the longhorns met the better Eastern breeds and started chewing the same grass.

They met all the way from the Rio Grande in northern New Mex-

LOS RANCHEROS Y RANCHERITOS

ico and Colorado to the Cascades of Oregon and Washington. In western Kansas, the Red Desert of Wyoming and Utah, across Montana and the Dakotas they pressed ahead in a search for grass. Ranges that would have been fully stocked with one cow per forty acres carried one to every ten acres. As fast as a blade of grass showed above ground some hungry animal gnawed it off.

A more devastating, planless period would be difficult to match in history. Because grass was abundant no winter feeding was done, many owners preferring to risk the loss of their stock. But in the severe winter of 1886–87 thousands of cattle perished on the northern plains with losses ranging up to 50 and 60 per cent. In 1893, the Southwest underwent much the same experience. Even worse was the lasting effect on the land and on wildlife of massive, unending overgrazing. Valuable grasses and forage plants thinned and disappeared. In some places they were replaced by cheat grass, the fiery flash fuel, in others by weeds like Russian thistle. Juniper and mesquite invaded the open grasslands of the Southwest. The face of the land changed. Trampling hoofs stripped the protecting layer of decaying plant materials from the soil, which then dried up and arose in the windy, swirling dust bowl or washed in unchecked floodwaters, leaving the bare gravel and sand now called "desert pavement." Cacti and like vegetation multiplied and predominated as they had not before.

The mountains as well as the lower elevations were affected. For instance, before the Civil War, grass in the canyons of the Wasatch Mountains of Utah was said to stand from six to twelve feet high, so dense the explorers could barely penetrate the thickets, and certainly was "belly deep to a horse." By the turn of the century, vegetation was reduced to stubble six to twelve inches high, and the original forage was largely replaced by unpalatable weeds and shrubs. Likewise, Mountain Meadows in southwestern Utah during the years of exploration before the war was a beautiful valley of green grass extending for miles, bounded by piñon- and juniper-covered hills. By the turn of the century the grass was gone, replaced by desert shrubs, juniper and great gullies draining away the water. Erosion was so bad that even if the meadows were ungrazed the grass would still not come back.

As for wildlife, it was either exterminated through loss of its food source or, as in the case of antelope and elk, was driven from lower hills and valleys, where once it flourished, to its final refuge in the mountains.

Livestock grazing was not solely responsible for this immense damage to the West. Other factors were present, including: drought and diminishing rainfall; fires after logging; erosion caused by mining and by farming on land ill-suited for cultivation. But as the nation entered the 1890's, although the day of the big trail herds was over, conditions worsened as a result of unchecked grazing conflicts.

Sheepmen began to get a foothold on the range. The sheepman was better able to cope with the elements than the cowman. He had his herd under his eye at all times and could move it to better feed whenever the supply ran out. Sheep rose higher and found edible weeds on steep cliffsides. In sheer self-defense many cowmen joined the ranks of the woolgrowers. Every spring bands of sheep numbering 2500 to 3000 would follow the melting snow into the mountains. They were far too many to graze without injury to the range. And by night, fires were built to keep away predatory animals and show the advance of rival herds. But fires were seldom extinguished and added one more devastation.

In the same period, homesteaders, or "nesters," added a new conflict to the open range. When settlement under the land laws overflowed the prairies, homesteaders located along the streams of Western valleys. They blocked cattlemen from reaching water, except at their sufferance. In some cases, such locations were chosen to force stockmen to pay a toll. The operator of a large livestock company might buy out the homesteader, but this didn't end the problem, for the next newcomer would claim the land and the trouble started anew. When the cattleman placed one of his hired men on the land he was apt to find his confidence misplaced, for the man would either sell out to someone else or repeat the "holdup" process against his old employer.

By 1895 not an acre of open grazing land was left in the West. Sheep- and cattlemen trailed their herds from one part of the range to another in search of feed. Armed men fought for the control of ranges they had learned to call their own. In the anarchy that ruled the West they fought the nesters in Johnson County, Wyoming; they fought each other in the Blue Mountains of Oregon; and in the Tonto Basin, Arizona, forty lives were taken inside a few years. The first and probably the greatest battle was fought on New Mexico ground, in the Lincoln County War of the late 1870's. It began over competition for government beef contracts, grazing rights and water, reaching a climax of five months of bitter violence and bloodshed, including a three-day gun battle in the town of Lincoln. Billy the Kid, who had worked on John Chisum's ranch, was a leading participant.

The greatest paradox, however, was that of all the land the cattle kingdom grazed and fought over, it actually owned less than 1 per cent. The remainder was national domain. The stockman determined that because he had used the land it was his to control as a "right." Many others did not agree. Among these, Major John Wesley Powell, the famous geographer and director of the United States Geological Survey, defined the Western livestock grower as "a trespasser on the public domain, an obstacle to settlement, and at best a crude forerunner of civilization," a sticky characterization which has plagued its bearer in national thinking ever since.

Recognition of the abuses to the range and the watershed contributed to establishment of the Forest Reserves, which at first were closed to grazing, as to all uses. Cowmen knew their first ranger of the 1897 period as "one of our old boys of the range," who had turned traitor and sold himself, as Judas did.

"We were peeved," recalled one old cattleman, even after their grazing privileges had been restored, "when he asked everyone using the mountain ranges to fill out a lot of blanks as to when we first began to use the range, the number of cows we owned, how many calves branded each year, where were our ranches, how much hay did we raise for winter feeding, and a lot more. We didn't tell such things to the county assessor, much less this reformed cow person."

But when they were told they must take out permits to graze in the Reserves, they did so, willingly at first, often lying freely and fluently about the numbers of stock and brandings. Why worry? After all, they concluded, Washington was 3000 miles away and the permit cost them nothing. When the first ten-year permits were offered, one old Montana stockman sent his back with a penciled reply, "Dear Mr. Supervisor. Don't want no permit for so long, because I'm 72 years old and I calculate can't live ten years more. Send one for a year and see what happens."

The big difference came with the Forest Service and Gifford Pinchot, who fought and won one of the toughest battles in Western history. Their victory achieved stability for a large, key portion of the

255

Western range. It asserted lawful authority, management and improvement over lands abused for generations.

Let's pick up the thread in 1900, when grazing was, as Pinchot said, the "bloody angle" and center of the most bitter land controversy. That spring Pinchot was in Arizona, with Frederick V. Coville, botanist of the Department of Agriculture, to investigate the effect of grazing at higher elevations on the water supply of the Salt River Valley near Phoenix.

His personal experiences, as always, were delightful. At one point, while he and his companions were riding sixty miles across the desert from Winslow to the Mogollan Rim, their canteens and water keg gave out. The only water they came across was a stagnant, green pool, adorned by the horns of rotting carcasses of cattle. Representatives of the Woolgrowers Association, who had arranged the trip, shrugged their shoulders rather hopelessly. It was drink or go dry. Pinchot drank, suspecting the whole affair had been rigged to test the toughness of Eastern tenderfeet. By night, however, his hosts feasted him royally, on young mutton cooked on an iron plate on top of the campfire.

"This trip established what I was sure of already," he reported, "that overgrazing by sheep does destroy the forest. Not only do sheep eat young seedlings, as I proved to my full satisfaction by finding plenty of them bitten off, contrary to the sheepmen's contention, but their innumerable hoofs also break and trample seedlings into the ground. John Muir called them hoofed locusts and he was right."

In those days forestry, as a young profession, centered around the harvesting and growing of trees, was prejudiced against grazing because of its destruction of tree reproduction. Nevertheless, as a practical consideration, Pinchot believed that if grazing was completely prohibited the Western ranchers would not quit fighting until they killed off the Forest Reserves.

"Every sheep owner should have the sole right to his range for a reasonable time and for a reasonable charge," he proposed, "but for overgrazing he should forfeit his permit and the money he paid for it. And the same if he or his herders are guilty of forest fires." Pinchot was admittedly biased against sheep, which he thought ten times worse than cattle, but also felt that when strictly limited and controlled even sheep grazing could proceed without harming the forest or plains. And so it was decided.

There were still other questions to resolve, including the means of bringing to an end the chaotic conditions of the Western range, of determining who really had the right, or privilege, to graze his livestock on the public domain. Part of the answer was suggested by the Public Lands Commission (of which Pinchot was a member) when it recommended to President Theodore Roosevelt in 1905 that grazing districts be established in the Department of Agriculture and that moderate fees be charged. "At present the vacant public lands are theoretically open commons, free to all citizens," the Commission reported, "but, as a matter of fact, a large proportion has been parceled out by more or less definite compacts or agreements among the various interests. These tacit agreements are continually being violated. The sheepmen and cattlemen are in frequent collision because of incursions upon each other's domain. Land which for years has been regarded as exclusively cattle range may be infringed upon by large bands of sheep, forced by drought to migrate. The general lack of control in the use of public grazing lands has resulted, naturally and inevitably, in overgrazing and the ruin of millions of acres of otherwise valuable grazing territory. Lands useful for grazing are losing their only capacity for productiveness, as of course they must when no legal control is exercised."

The real answer came on the heels of the report when the Forest Service was granted administrative jurisdiction over the Forest Reserves and proceeded to institute regulations over grazing. For the first time peace and order—though not exactly tranquillity—settled on the range.

"Never before in the history of any nation," wrote Will C. Barnes, who later became Chief of Grazing in the Forest Service, "had this subject been taken up by a government force in a constructive manner and methods of control put into effect that had for their purpose the protection of the forage cover on lands in public ownership. Indeed, very little had ever been done along these lines on private lands. It was a new science and a new field of adventure. It called for a complete overturning of venerable and long-established ideas and methods. There were neither precedents nor guides to follow; the men in charge built up their system of regulated grazing from the very foundation stones."

The more irascible stockmen fought the new governmental regulation in 1905, as they have fought it ever since. They fought to keep the National Forests to a minimum in size. Consequently, foothill areas were withheld from the Forests, on grounds that they were not

257

needed for watershed protection, and remained under administration of the General Land Office. Very early in the game Pinchot realized the best way to meet their prejudice against government officials was to employ Western men, who could talk their language, understood their problems and knew their ways. Among those who joined him were Will Barnes, who had won the Congressional Medal of Honor in 1881 for bravery against the Apache Indians; Albert Potter, representative of the Arizona Woolgrowers Association, who had served Pinchot that potion of terrible green water en route to the Mogollan Rim; and Jesse Nelson, one of Buffalo Bill's best trick riders and a cowman of the old school.

The new regulations were clear and constructive, but hard for some of the stockmen to take. The Forest Service announced permits for grazing would be issued on a priority basis, first going to small owners who lived in or close to the Forest and whose stock had regularly grazed on the range; then to others of the surrounding area who had used the range, and finally, to owners who had no prior use. It required permittees to own a certain amount of cultivated land and water, eliminating at once nomads who had used the public domain for many years without supervision. But perhaps the hardest pill of all to swallow was the requirement to pay a grazing fee. It was not much, only six cents per head in New Mexico for a whole season, and less than it cost for grazing rights on private land, but the stockman was irked by the very idea of paying *anything* for what he thought was his by right of conquest and use.

For the Forest Service the first years were the toughest. Theodore Roosevelt said in 1907 the principal opposition to regulation came from owners of wandering bands of sheep and others who had gained control of great areas of public land by owning water at strategic points; whatever the source it was reflected in strong political pressures, which have really never relented. Despite them, the Forest Service spelled out rules and regulations, including the following in effect in 1911:

> To drive stock across a Forest it is necessary to get a permit from the nearest Ranger or the Supervisor, except along a public road.
> A permit is also necessary to drive stock across a Forest to reach private lands within it, if the stock grazes along the way.
> Get a permit from the Supervisor before constructing drift and pasture fences and corral.
> On new National Forests existing conditions will not be changed

suddenly. Owners of stock will be given ample notice if it is necessary to make a cut, so that they may adjust themselves to the new conditions without financial loss.

Do not graze any stock on a National Forest without a permit or drive stock across National Forestlands without a permit or construct fences without a permit. The law forbids it. And to guard the best interests of all the people the law will be vigorously enforced.

The law *was* enforced. The Forest Service won its fight to assert national ownership over the lands in its jurisdiction. In so doing, it helped to end the range wars, at least on its range.

But the public-domain grazing lands which remained under the Interior Department were not as fortunate. In 1933, the public domain remained a pitiful no man's land. That year Congressman Edward T. Taylor, of Colorado, in striving to bring a form of legislative order out of grazing chaos, said, "There are large areas where it [the public grazing land] is a free-for-all and general grab-and-hold-if-you-can policy with roving herds using the range." Representative Taylor bemoaned the "guerilla warfare between and among sheepmen and cattlemen," and the rule of taking all the grass there was for taking. But, he conceded, "if you do not, somebody else will take it, and you have only invited the intrusion of other stock."

Thus, in 1934, the Taylor Grazing Act was adopted "to stop injury to the public grazing lands by preventing overgrazing and soil deterioration, to provide for their orderly use, improvement and development, to stabilize the livestock industry dependent upon the public range."

But it hasn't worked out that way. Even today the Bureau of Land Management (BLM), which administers the 161,000,000 acres of Interior Department grazing lands, is embroiled in trying to determine "priority periods" showing who properly is entitled to first use. Instead of encouraging physical improvement of the range, groups representing the larger stockmen have campaigned for low budget and low staff for the BLM, and low permittee fees.

Some members of the powerful lobbying groups tried for years with all their might, to wield the same influence on the Forest Service. Their stated goal was to terminate public ownership and protection of grazing lands. Even at the first meeting of the American National Livestock Association, held in Denver in 1898, one serious proposal was to transfer Federal lands to the states. The stockmen took heart in the twenties from Herbert Hoover, who broadly declared, "Our Western states have long since passed from their swaddling clothes. Moreover, we must seek every opportunity to retard the expansion of Federal bureaucracy and to place our communities in control of their own destinies."

The real drive began after World War II. A group of stockmen of the Livestock and National Woolgrowers Associations formed a "joint committee," which proposed that permittees be given the opportunity to buy the land on which they grazed substantially at their own price. It was not a particularly popular campaign among stockmen—for it gave nothing to those without permits and very little to the small operators—but it generated loud noises in Congress. Senator Pat Mc-Carran, of Nevada, roundly denounced swivel-chair cowboys and Eastern bureaucrats; Congressman Frank Barrett, of Wyoming, singled out the Forest Service as his special target and conducted a series of vituperative public hearings in the West. "The Forest Service is a child of Congress," he said, "grown up without parental discipline or instruction, an arrogant, bigoted, tyrannical offspring, the same as any offspring reared in the same manner, void of respect of law or the rights or feelings of other people."

This sort of thing went on at high pitch for about eight years, with a variety of unsuccessful legislation and proposed budget reductions. The peak was reached with introduction of the Stockmen's Bill, also known as the Uniform Land Tenancy Act, in 1953. It was designed simply and directly to grant stockmen holding grazing permits a monopoly control over public lands. For example, among its provisions, it would have given permittees the legal right to transfer or sell their permits. It would have given them the exclusive benefit of any increase in grazing capacity, due to improvements such as reseeding. It would have prohibited the government from changing the boundaries of their grazing areas, or from changing the kind of livestock allowed—whether cattle or sheep. It would have given any permittee the right of legal appeal before a court any time he chose to dispute an administrative decision.

The Stockmen's Bill failed badly, as other bills like it have failed before and since. For every pressure applied by the livestock associations, the American Forestry Association, Izaak Walton League and many other groups responded with a vigorous counterbalance. Then there were the "uninformed Eastern writers," who insisted on analyzing and reporting the stockmen's design in the public prints. Lester Velie, then of *Collier's*, achieved a measure of unpopularity among lobbying stockmen for his articles, but Bernard DeVoto and *Harper's* were thoroughly despised. "Simple, clear and stinking" was how he summarized the efforts to gain exclusive control of public resources. Besides these outsiders who kept talking about the national interest, many Western writers and newspapers, including the Denver *Post*, Salt Lake *Tribune*, Arizona *Times* and Silver City (New Mexico) *Daily Press*, were just as opposed for local and regional reasons.

In the final analysis, the bill was probably defeated on the stockman's own ground. More livestock associations and outfits like the Dude Ranchers Association registered opposition than support. The concept of singling one commercial use as the primary one above all others could hardly strike a popular responsive chord.

"Cattle growing," editorialized the spunky Silver City *Daily Press*, "is probably the second industry (to mining) in this part of New Mexico and the prosperity of the cattlemen contributes largely to the prosperity of the area. However, there are other interests to be considered. Among these are the worth of the mountains as a source of water for farms, industries, settlements, minerals, woodland products, and recreation. As watersheds the forested heights are critical indeed. Continued overuse causes erosion, flash floods and finally a crippled economy.

"The Forests and everything in them belong to the people. The people of New Mexico own the wildlife of the forests, but they permit private interests to dictate the terms under which they may enjoy their heritage. The stockmen will never be satisfied until they have their claims to a vested right in the public lands confirmed in law. For the people to supinely surrender their rights in the remaining public lands just doesn't make any sense."

Or, as the Erie (Pennsylvania) *Times* observed from a farther corner, "Frankly, the thing smells about as bad as a goat farm."

The Western cattleman does have his problems and reasons for concern about his future and the future of his industry. On his own land he manages to grow and provide winter feed for his stock, but the size of his herd depends on the amount of range available during spring, summer and fall. Over the years he has seen the public range constantly shrinking. He can remember when it was possible to travel for days and see only a few sheepherders or a few range riders or an occasional prospector. Now he encounters campgrounds and fishermen. Wildlife, which he helped to feed and perhaps save from ex-

261

tinction, is competing with his stock for forage. Because of fire protection, timber has grown up and reduced the grazing possibilities by just that much. He is denied entry into other areas because of watershed protection. The Forest Service, which once furnished 25 per cent of all grazing in the Western states, has been cutting back steadily on the length of the season and in number of cattle allowed on the summer range. (There now are about 15,500 permit holders grazing 3,750,000 cows, horses and sheep in National Forests, about one-fourth less than twenty years ago.) Our cattleman thinks these reductions may sometimes have been made needlessly and summarily. "In the old days," as one large New Mexico rancher told me, "the Forest Service had fewer men but they built more trails and worked on range improvement. Now they have more men and less range." On the other hand, on this particular ranger district the ranchers pay a total of $2500 a year in grazing fees—and feel they are paying too much—while the income from timber sales amounts to almost $150,000.

Well, we are not going to settle an argument here. In fact, I'm not really trying to start one. Let's put it this way. Through range management and revegetation the potential of the range can be increased 150 to 300 per cent. Toward that end, the Forest Service has underway a tremendous twenty-year program during which it will spend $300,000,000 in reorganizing the landscape to the stockman's advantage. In many places ranchers are co-operating with their effort and money. Ultimately the program will cover seeding of 5,000,000 acres with grasses and legumes; fencing 50,000 miles; developing 30,-000 watering places; spraying weeds and uprooting millions of juniper and mesquite. This may not be as fast or widespread a program as some cattlemen would like, but they will have more use of 60,000,000 acres of National Forest suitable for rangeland. And so will all the rest of us, for our diverse needs.

It was the best crop of piñon nuts in at least seven years, said Fred Thompson, speaking of products of the National Forests. We had stopped in Las Huertas Canyon and were shaking the nuts loose from their open cones.

In the hills around us, nut hunters—principally Spanish-Americans and Indians gathering nuts to sell—had camped all night. Now in the early morning they would look for breakfasting blue jays to lead them to the most plentiful areas among the woods.

"Pick up a pound and you can make forty cents," Fred told me. "Last year, when the crop wasn't as good, I would have paid you a dollar a pound."

The piñon nut is really a large wingless seed, a delicacy with birds, wildlife, Indians and Easterners who call it the Indian nut. It reaches us via traders like Fred who buy it from the pickers by the bushel and ship it east by the ton.

We had started from Albuquerque and entered the Cibola National Forest on the Sandia Loop or "Turquoise Trail." We drove through Tijeras Canyon, parting company with the plush new motels and high-speed traffic of Route 66 for the piñon-covered hillsides. Route 44, not quite the most modern highway in New Mexico, follows a winding, climbing course through several vegetation zones—juniper and piñon, pine, spruce-fir—to timberline. The reward for "making the grade" to Sandia Crest (elevation 10,678 feet) is the tremendous vista, more than a hundred miles. From the Forest Service observation point we saw the Rocky Mountains to the North; the Rio Grande flowing its southward course through sprawling Albuquerque, 5000 feet below, and fading into the haze; traces of ancient volcanoes, mesas, Indian pueblos, and the peaks of the Colorado plateau, seventy miles west. Then we started downward toward Las Huertas Canyon, where we stopped in the picnic area to gather nuts for a while. The Sandias are a playground of Albuquerque, with picnic areas, campgrounds, hiking and riding trails and La Madera Ski Area at 9000 feet.

Touring northern New Mexico can be a many-sided experience, as in traveling from modern Albuquerque to the high wooded Sandias, then descending to Bernalillo and still another environment at the Santo Domingo Indian pueblo and its trading post, presided over by Fred Thompson. The 1800 Domingo Indians, though they now have electricity (and a few television sets) and pickup trucks in place of horses, still adhere to their ancient beliefs and adobe-hut living, wrapping themselves in blankets and robes. One of the earliest missions was established here by the Spanish conquistadores in 1605, but the first priests were massacred during the Indian uprisings soon after. The present mission church remains seatless and the floor consists of trampled dirt. The ceremonial dances at Easter and on August 4 (Green Corn Dance) are considered among the finest performed by any of the pueblo Indians. Fred Thompson, who used to be an insurance salesman and scoutmaster in Rochester, New York, trades

263

and barters with the Indians, and deals with vacationers shopping for Indian crafts (rugs, blankets, turquoise and silver jewelry, pottery) with integrity.

Santa Fe, thirty miles north of Santo Domingo, is a favorite with everyone who visits the Southwest. The state capital is rich in atmosphere and history, flavored with the traditions of Indians, Spanish-Americans, Westerners and assorted Easterners-gone-native. The signs of antiquity are visible everywhere, for Santa Fe was first settled in 1610 and thus is the oldest seat of government in the United States. Actually, it did not become part of our country until it fell in the Mexican War of 1846. Around the city are mountains, the Jemez and Sangre de Cristo. Only sixteen miles from the city, snow lies on peaks of the Santa Fe National Forest until late June and there is usually skiing at Santa Fe Ski Basin from Thanksgiving until Easter. The double chairlift provides a fast ride to 11,200-foot Promontory Peak, while the new pomalift in Snowbunny Bowl serves several new trails plus the practice slope.

We had traveled north beyond Santa Fe when I complained about the unhappy roadside blight along the main road, Route 64, to Taos, and Fred said, "Let's take the byroad through Chimayo and Truchas." The distance proved to be about fifty-five miles via State Road 76, only ten more than the direct route, but the Spanish-American farming communities en route were like a world apart, a completely rural old Spanish world of log and adobe, of sheep and goats, and the classic mountain scenery of the Sangre de Cristo Range. The mountains derive their name, "Blood of Christ," from the reddish tint on snowy peaks at sunset. The most up-and-coming of the *placitas* is Chimayo, where for generations the colorful "Chimayo" blankets have been skillfully woven on handmade looms; at the Ortega family establishment the shopper can watch his blanket woven, if he is patient. The winding road through the village is lined with lilac hedges and patio walls covered in June with yellow roses. Six miles beyond, over a steep winding road, lies Truchas, perhaps the strangest of the villages, clinging to the hillside, with the sweeping view of the Rio Grande Valley below and the Truchas Peaks above it.

Beyond Truchas the paved road ran out and we were driving on gravel surface, still climbing. It was not a spot I would have chosen to run out of gas. In each community we had seen the typical Spanish pueblo church gracing the plaza. The one at Las Trampas, the Church of the Twelve Apostles, begun in 1580 and built with four-foot-thick adobe walls, is unique. Once there were two bells, of gold and silver, each bearing a distinctive name—María del Refugio and María de la Gracia. Several years ago María del Refugio and its tower were stolen, leaving María de la Gracia to toll alone. Recently "la Gracia's" tower was torn down and she now tolls above the church door. The last of the villages on Route 76, Penasco, is one of the more prosperous. There are no lodgings along the route, but there are campgrounds and trailer sites along the country road to the east. At the headquarters of the Penasco Ranger District, directions are provided in English or Spanish.

Taos, like Santa Fe, is rich in history, art and artists. Taos pueblo, two miles from the "modern" town is the premier of all Indian pueblos, the most painted, the most photographed (for a fee), yet preserving the ancient independence and mystery. Taos is headquarters of Carson National Forest, named for Kit Carson, a Kentuckian by birth, who chose to live here during his great career of hunting, scouting and trapping in the West. He is buried in a memorial state park facing the Kit Carson Home and Museum.

Within three to twelve miles from Taos are fifteen campgrounds in the National Forest, located near streams and lakes and hiking trails. In a wider range there are many more. One of the most attractive areas, the Red River country, lies directly northeast of Taos. In addition to campgrounds, a number of guest ranches, offering varying degrees of informality, are located on private land adjoining the Forest.

Whether you are staying any length of time or touring through northern New Mexico, one place of compelling interest you should visit is the new Ghost Ranch Museum near Abiquiu, built on a sweeping plain above the Rio Chama. Children, above all, will love it as they learn the why and wherefore of nature in New Mexico, for Ghost Ranch has been developed with the most genuine, knowing care. Its guiding spirits are Arthur N. Pack, a man of means and a true conservationist who prefers spending his money in useful, though often nonremunerative, channels, and his associate, William H. Carr, an educator-scientist with a light touch. (Instead of signs saying, "Do Not Feed the Animals," there is one requesting, "Do Not Feed Your Fingers to the Animals, Their Diet Is Carefully Supervised.")

Mr. Pack and Mr. Carr are also responsible for the older Arizona-

Sonora Desert Museum at Tucson, Arizona, which we will visit later. Here at Abiquiu, 20,000-acre Ghost Ranch was presented in 1955 by Mr. and Mrs. Pack to the United Presbyterian Church as a conference center and the museum built more recently on land leased from the Church. It is an indoor and outdoor living display of animals, birds, reptiles, insects and plants. Even such seemingly complicated sciences as geology and ecology become understandable through clear explanations at the very sites involved. Dinosaur enthusiasts will be delighted with the display of local dinosaurs unearthed by an exploring party headed by Dr. Edwin H. Colbert, the famous paleontologist of the American Museum of Natural History in New York.

Ghost Ranch is almost surrounded by the Santa Fe and Carson National Forests, so it is appropriate that one of its display areas should be the "Beaver National Forest." Within these several acres, the uses, products and the conservation role of the Forests are clearly depicted, and explained by the talking beaver (a friend of Smokey the bear).

Smokey: on another occasion I visited his birthplace, or at least the place where this famous bear was rescued during a forest fire in 1950 and started on his way toward becoming the symbol of fire prevention. It was in the Capitan Mountains of the Lincoln National Forest, about 160 miles south of Albuquerque. If you are nearby, or driving south to El Paso, youngsters will appreciate stopping at the log museum dedicated to Smokey in the village of Capitan. In a pass above the mountains Smokey, a badly burned, fear-stricken cub, was found by a fire-fighting crew in the midst of a blaze that swept across 17,000 acres. He was first flown to Santa Fe for hospital treatment, then on to the National Zoo in Washington, D.C., where he makes his home and poses for his poster portraits which carry fire prevention messages throughout the world. But around Capitan the blackened scars of the fire, in which Smokey's mother and thousands of other animals perished, have still not faded from sight or memory.

In this area, Sierra Blanca, the White Mountain, is the most southerly peak of 12,000 feet in the United States. The stone Monjeau Lookout Tower, across a valley from the mountain, provides an excellent viewpoint of its tall slopes and the southeastern New Mexico desert. Most of Sierra Blanca lies within White Mountain Wild Area (the summit is in the adjoining Mescalero Apache Indian Reservation). You may be disheartened to learn the boundary of the

266

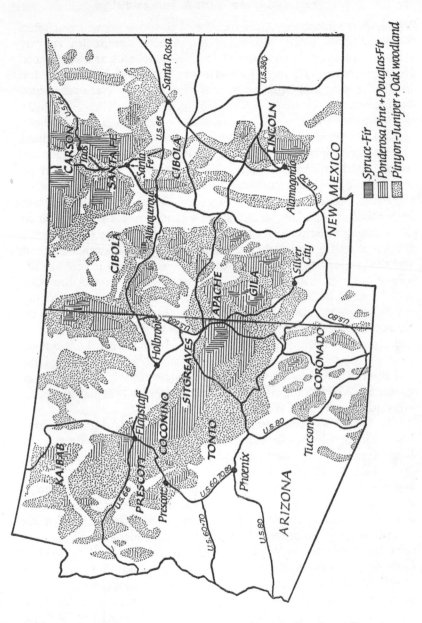

Vegetation Zones, 3500 to over 10,000 Feet, in Southwest Forests

Wild Area required redrawing because of the advancement upon it of Ruidoso, a commercial amusement and resort center. Such is the pattern of private ownership that if you weary of trees and nature and the like, you can repair to the race track at Ruidoso Downs, next to Hollywood, and still be within the Lincoln National Forest boundaries.

Race tracks are fine where race tracks belong, but in the National Forests pack trips are more fitting. Among those I hope to take one day is the trip through the half-million-acre Gila Wilderness near Silver City. Four centuries of settlement around it have lightly touched the rough, precipitous Spider Range, or Sierra del Gila, as the Spaniards called it. The Gila country was a sanctuary for the Apache Indians during three centuries of warfare. They were first penetrated in the late seventies and eighties, when silver, gold and other minerals and the grazing boom attracted settlers to southwestern New Mexico. I have only set foot inside the wilderness once, following the "Catwalk," a rocky hiking trail alongside Little Whitewater Creek, a plunging flume gorge, near Glenwood Ranger Station, reminiscent of the flumes in New Hampshire 2500 miles away. Of course, vegetation and climate are considerably different. In New Mexico at the lower elevation (4500 feet) I was in a piñon-juniper woodland; had I ridden toward the mountains, however, I would have entered pine and spruce thickets, aspen glades and high meadows, where elk, deer, bear and turkey find their refuge.

The Gila is a special, sentimental wilderness. Anyone who loves the outdoors, whether he can ride, hike, look or simply dream, will think it so stopping along Route 260 near the Arizona line north of Silver City at the Aldo Leopold Memorial, dedicated in 1954, beneath the bluish Mogollan Mountains. "Heavy clouds and strong winds blew out of the west during the ceremonies," reported the Silver City *Daily Press*, but a healthy crowd insisted on hearing the several addresses eulogizing Aldo Leopold and his efforts toward establishment of the first National Forest wilderness. To his own lasting credit, Clinton P. Anderson, who perhaps should have been more swayed by demands of his grazing constituents, spoke proudly of his personal relationship with Leopold. "Thirty years ago he enlisted me in the cause of wilderness areas in general," the Senator said. "It was the true wilderness that attracted him—the places where he could go and be alone, the spots in the White Mountains of Arizona or in the forests of New Mexico where a man could lose himself in his surroundings and be dropped into complete comradeship with nature. I talked to Aldo Leopold many times about the development of a wilderness area. There it would be possible to preserve scenic beauty and the natural accompaniments of the restricted country, the fish and wildlife which had once owned these areas for themselves and now had become the hunted as man moved into these protected areas. We now become trustees of his inheritance. Those of us who may visit within the wilderness have an obligation to see that the work of one generation shall not be sacrificed by those that come after. We have an obligation to make sure that this area may remain untouched for generations and perhaps centuries to come."

CHAPTER TWENTY-ONE

# *Watering the Desert Garden*

With all proper regard for the water needs of booming Arizona, let us enter a kind word for the unwanted, unwelcome and unloved phreatophyte, the scourge of the Southwest.

It may always be evil, but is never unholy. There is something to be admired in one natural creature that declares defiantly to another of superior force, "I have as much right here as you." As John Muir said to Gifford Pinchot when they came upon a tarantula at the Grand Canyon . . .

But I have gone ahead without properly introducing our phreatophyte (pronounced free-at'-oh-fight) and his brothers and cousins. They are plants that cluster like an overgreedy, thirsty gang along the stream beds. They sink their roots deeply and claim priority on the available water supply.

The most unpopular phreatophyte is the tamarisk, or salt cedar (*Tamarix pentandra pall*), a shrub that grows twenty feet tall and stands lush green in contrast to most gray semidesert vegetation. It also appears to be the most resistant to uprooting. There are others, too, shrubs like mesquite, greasewood, willow and baccharis, and trees of the streamside and valley bottom like the cottonwood, mountain ash, alder and the mottled, light green sycamore.

Equally unpopular are the scrubby oak called chaparral, and piñon and juniper trees, which made their way across the arid landscape as a result of overgrazing of grassland in the last century. However, they do not absorb nearly as much water as the phreatophytes.

Arizona, where water is the most important and critical of all resources, has its reasons for concern about these shrubs and trees. On the theory that a drop saved is a drop earned for human uses, it was seriously proposed several years ago that part of Arizona's mountain slopes be completely stripped of trees and sown with grass. This sounded promising to cattlemen, who would have gained new fields for grazing. But there were others who said, "Why waste the hillsides on grass when we can pave them and bring all the water into the valley?" In the quest for water the threat of erosion inherent in this plan became a purely secondary consideration.

Fortunately, more studied thinking has prevailed. In 1956, the University of Arizona, State Land Department and Salt River Valley Users Association (which administers the water supply in the Phoenix area) rallied diverse interests all in need of water: timber, industry, farming, livestock, mining, fish and wildlife, and of Federal and state agencies managing lands through which water flows. They agreed that research and experimentation could point the way to recovering more rainfall and delivering it to the consumer. Out of the meeting the Arizona Water Resources Committee, a citizens' group headed by Lewis Douglas, former United States ambassador to Great Britain, was founded. The Watershed Management Program was established as a part of the state government.

The National Forests play a key role in this program, for they occupy most of the high reaches which first receive the snow and rain destined for Phoenix and the Salt River Valley. More than ten major research projects involving water production are being conducted by the Forest Service in Arizona. Like projects are also underway at other Forest Service research and experiment stations throughout the country. Water and the National Forests are in a sense synonymous. The Congressional Act of 1897 declared one of their principal functions would be "securing favorable conditions of water flows." In the eleven Western states today, National Forests comprise 21 per cent of the land but furnish 53 per cent of the total water runoff.

Why is water so important? And especially so in Arizona?

Whether in the form of rain, snow, ice, dew or fog, water serves in many ways to maintain life and vigor. The nutritive value of food crops may be affected by the amount of water, or moisture, which they receive while growing. Other foods, such as fish, lobster, crabs and duck are found in oceans, lakes and streams. Wildlife must have water. So must the skier, swimmer and modern sight-seer who enjoys the sight of waterfalls, lakes and snowfields.

In ancient times the maximum total daily water requirement for all purposes may have been three to five gallons a person. Even today primitive people of Asia and Africa scoop up water from shallow pools or streams and carry it home in jars. In some places they store it in the trunks of hollow trees and seal the openings with wet clay to keep it uncontaminated.

But we, in our civilized way, with running water, flush toilet, lawn sprinkler and swimming pool, use sixty gallons or more a person each day.

Little wonder Los Angeles must look far beyond its environs for its water supply: to the Owens River, on the east side of the Sierra Nevada, 240 miles away, and to the Colorado River, 450 miles away.

During a six-year legal battle in which Arizona fought for its water rights on the Colorado River, some 25,000 pages of testimony were bound in forty-three volumes (each two inches thick) and some 4000 exhibits were introduced. Even within the state competition over water is spirited. In Williams, during a 1960 dispute, the editor of the *Daily News* vigorously denounced the Salt River Valley Users Association as a ring of ruthless dictators. "The greedy hogs," he wrote, "are not going to let one drop of water go to anyone else."

The picture was considerably different sixty years ago. In the marvel of the universe called Arizona, scenic wonders almost outnumbered people: the Great American Desert, sparkling with its landscape of cactus, yucca, cottonwood and phreatophytes; the contrasting forest, particularly ponderosa pine, covering one-fourth the state, rising from desert and mesa to snowy peaks; and stunning examples of geology like the Grand Canyon, Monument Valley, Superstition Mountain and Oak Creek Canyon. At the turn of the century the Apaches had only lately been subdued. Almost everyone in Phoenix, all 3000, could remember the 1891 flood, when the Salt River swept away one-third of the town.

Then the Reclamation Act of 1902 was adopted by Congress, launching the Salt River irrigation project (as well as many others to follow elsewhere). Centuries earlier, aboriginal Indians in the same area had tapped nearby rivers to irrigate their dry lands; so had the first Spanish and white settlers. They built long ditches for food, forage crops and homesites. Finally, at the start of the twentieth century, there came a realization that natural, seasonal flow of rivers was inadequate; Theodore Roosevelt recognized that only the storage of spring floodwater by large dams and reservoirs could solve the water supply problems of the growing West. We accept such things more readily today, but they were daring in Roosevelt's time. The highest dam in 1902, in Furens, France, was 170 feet. When Roosevelt Dam, 280 feet high, was completed on the Salt River in 1911 it impounded as much water as the world's previous three largest reservoirs combined.

At the beginning of the century Arizona had slightly less than 200,000 acres under irrigation. By the 1930's, with new water available from storage reservoirs on the Salt River, the acreage under irrigation rose to more than 1,000,000. The first field crops required only two to three acre feet of water per growing season. Later, cotton, garden crops and fruits required year-round water and some four acre feet of irrigation.

As the Arizona garden-in-the-desert grew in popularity, population and farm production, wells were sunk to tap underground water. In the ten years following World War II the volume pumped from the ground doubled. Pumps were pushed twice as far downward, to 250 feet. And during this time the trend in precipitation was waving like a danger signal at half-mast, and falling.

Now Arizona has a population of almost a million and a half (compared with 200,000 when it became a state in 1912). Phoenix, the nation's fastest-growing city, is inhabited by a quarter million persons who delight in winter warmth and tolerate summer. Apart from other needs, they must have water to fill their 4000-plus swimming pools.

Arthur Carhart speaks of "local boomers" in Arizona, who seek only immediate results and profits. There is also the case of the state political personality who arose at a meeting of the Water Resources Committee, urging action but asking everyone to keep the problem a secret. "Water is the all-important subject of misinformation," he said, "and the general attitude among many people in other areas of the country is that Arizona has run out of water or that in two or three years we will be dried up. We must present an accurate and true picture of this condition as well as talk about the many wonderful assets our state has to offer, such as our Right-to-Work law and the fact that we do not have a manufacturers' inventory tax."

The charm of the Right-to-Work law, however, may have to suffice for a while. The Arizona Watershed Program is not geared to the short range but to the long-range welfare of water users and the state, as it should be, based on research and learning.

What is a "watershed"? Once it was defined as the drainage divide separating the waters flowing into different rivers or oceans, like the Continental Divide. Now the larger drainages are commonly called river basins by the experts. The term "watershed," or "watershed area," applies to the drainage basin of a river or stream which comprises a social and economic unit. A very small watershed—a few hundred to a few thousand acres in which water flows into a single channel—is a subwatershed.

The watershed of the Salt River, and of its tributary, the Verde River, encompasses 10,000,000 acres of land. It varies in vegetation from semidesert to grassland to forest, and rises in elevation from 1325 feet to 11,000 feet. Summer temperatures at the low elevations are often higher than 100 degrees, while winter is never really cooler than springtime. But at the higher elevations, above 4000 feet, temperatures are mild in summer and cold enough for sustained snow in winter. Most water for the Salt River Valley is produced in the form of snow in the mountains; the very summit, covered with spruce, fir and aspen, is the most productive, with more than thirty inches of precipitation. From these heights water must move through many miles of stream channels to the large reservoirs formed behind Roosevelt, Mormon Flat, Horseshoe and other reclamation dams, where it is stored awaiting use.

But only a fraction, possibly as little as 10 per cent, of the rain and snow that falls in the mountains reaches the reservoirs. What happens to the rest? Part is evaporated in the atmosphere. Part is absorbed by trees for their nourishment and growth, and by shrubs like chaparral and salt cedar.

This was the reason for the proposal to strip the mountainsides of timber and for the dire unpopularity of the salt cedar and other phreatophytes. The timber has had its friends. Arizona's ponderosa-pine belt, the most productive in the country, is important economically and in stabilizing the soil of the watershed. But the phreatophytes have no such evident values.

How much water really can be saved? Some key answers will be learned in time from the Beaver Creek watershed project, which I visited on the Coconino National Forest. It covers a quarter million acres on a tributary of the Verde River. When the project began in 1957, soil scientists first surveyed the area. They found fifty soil types, some deep, some rocky, some shallow; some would absorb water slowly and erode easily, while other soils would absorb water like a sponge. A large part of the study involved the ponderosa pine, a hardy, prolific tree; it grows in amazing density, sometimes with 6000 to 10,000 stunted trees congested in a single acre, competing for water, light and soil nutrients. Watershed specialists feel that intensive thinning of the pine forest may increase the water yield considerably; consequently, in the fourteen subwatersheds the Forest Service is trying to learn the answers to such questions as, If pine production is reduced by 30, 40 or 50 per cent and the remainder converted to grass, what will be the effect on water yield? On soil stability? On the quality of timber? What will be the cost?

What do trees and lesser plants really do with the water they ab-

275

sorb? Botanical processes are far from completely understood. But water is even more essential to the development of a tree than of a human being. Three-fourths of a living tree is either water or manufactured from it. Roots absorb moisture in the soil and pass it upward with nitrates and minerals through the trunk into the leaves, through which the moisture returns to the atmosphere in the process known as transpiration. There is a saying, "Horses sweat, men perspire, women glow," to which the botanist adds, "and leaves transpire."

Conversely, carbon dioxide, which the tree extracts from the air, moves into a water solution as soon as it enters the cell of a leaf where it combines with the sun's energy in the growth process called photosynthesis.

Inside the tree, all movements of materials and chemical reactions take place in water solutions. As much as 1000 pounds of water may be transpired for every pound of dry wood produced. But whenever water content declines, growth is curtailed. If it drops too low, irreversible changes take place and the tree dies.

Through centuries of evolution various plants have adapted themselves to particular conditions of moisture on earth. Deciduous trees like the oak and maple require moisture year-round. Conifers like the pine can survive where it is concentrated in winter. Chaparral occupies the driest forest environment. Cacti have devised tissues which enable them to retain water through prolonged drought; they have long surrendered their leaves in order to reduce transpiration, and shifted their function to the green outer cover of the stem.

Then there is that rascal, salt cedar, and the other phreatophytes that have adapted themselves, alas too well, to water-rich sites where they can sink their roots deep and luxuriate. Salt cedar produces seeds in great numbers through a long blooming period from April through September. Seeds germinate on wet soil or on watery surfaces, floating to the streambank and sowing large areas as the water recedes. The Salt River, with its high flows and sand bars, produces ideal conditions for the establishment and growth of salt-cedar shrubs; they line the banks for many miles above Roosevelt Dam, standing unshamefully as though to say, "Here we are, first in line at the water trough."

Remove salt cedar? Stamp it out? Pull it up by the roots? It refuses to die and stay dead. Scrub oak, the most common chaparral species, is tough to kill, defying fire and herbicides. But it can be treated by repeated burning followed by repeated grass seeding. Salt cedar is tougher, virtually immune to the best control measures devised so far. Burn or cut it near the ground level and the root crown will produce new sprouts. Cut it below the surface with a root plow, when the soil is dry, and the plant may be dead or may resprout when river waters overflow. Chemicals demand repeated treatments, at best. And if salt cedar is uprooted in one place, it may take over at a point where mesquite, or some other plant, has been eliminated.

Is there, perhaps, a moral message inherent in the stubborn behavior of this natural creature, as determined to stay in its place as we are determined to remove it? Possibly the design of the salt cedar, before it meets its fate, is to plead for all living resources in the future of the Southwest.

Speedway Boulevard it was called in the old days, when soldiers raced out from Tucson to Fort Lowell in buckboard or on horseback. Their main purpose in Arizona was to war against the Apaches. But when they were not actively engaged or riding in high gear back and forth to town, they would climb the Santa Catalina Mountains and explore the pinewoods and snowbanks.

The military era ended in 1891, five years after the surrender of Geronimo. The fort was abandoned, but Speedway Boulevard has remained the name of the main road and the Santa Catalinas have become the Mount Lemmon Recreation Area, where in less than an hour it is possible to travel from semidesert spring or summer almost into winter. This mountain is Tucson's playground, visited by nearly 1,000,000 people in all seasons of the year.

The climb spans 6800 feet, measured vertically, from an elevation of 2300 feet above sea level to 9100 feet at the Mount Lemmon Snow Bowl. It leads through a progression of four of the seven "life zones," the divisions of plant life between Mexico and the Arctic Circle which are determined principally by climate and rainfall. The only three not represented are the Dry-tropical, with less than six inches of rain, and the Hudsonian and Arctic-alpine, with more than thirty inches. But the summit of Mount Lemmon is a veritable Canadian island surrounded by the ocean of Southwest desert below it.

The foot of the mountain, beyond Speedway Boulevard and the ruins of Fort Lowell, is the gateway to Coronado National Forest, a large, versatile domain scattered in several sections across southern Arizona to the border of Mexico. Here, at 2300 feet in the Lower Sonoran life zone, with only ten inches of rainfall, the landscape is semidesert—mesquite, creosote bush, yucca, palo verde, ocotillo, cottonwood in the stream channels, and twenty-five types of cactus, from tiny pincushions to the gigantic, towering saguaros.

Spring is the magic time for these strange, unusual plants. There is nothing to compare with the vivid scene they create during April and May, the principal blooming months. Across the desert floor are short-lived wildflowers of many colors, including the pink and purple sand verbena; the sundrop, which opens its delicate yellow petals at night and closes soon after sunrise; the violet-purple curling scorpionweed; the lavish poppy, covering wide sections of desert with a cloth of gold. Above them, the misty green-branched palo verde, the state tree blooms in pale yellow. The ocotillo, formed of slender, wandlike stems, bursts into scarlet clusters at its tips. Penstemon, usually on the rocky hillsides, flames in various colors from violet to deep red.

Giants of all are the saguaro (suh-wa'-roh) cactus, standing like gnarled, primitive pillars, grotesquely beautiful, particularly with its creamy white spring flowers. Except for one or two spots in California, the saguaro is limited to northwestern Mexico and southern Arizona, reaching its greatest size and concentration in the Tucson area. The saguaro, the largest tree of the American desert, grows to forty or fifty feet in height, lives about 200 years and weighs from six to ten tons. Following soaking rains, the saguaro's widespread root system draws in immense quantities of water—possibly as much as a ton, storing it for extended dry spells. In excessive rainfalls some greedy saguaros may drink so much they split open at the seams.

The saguaro, striking though it appears today, plays a fading role in the desert community. Hungry, thirsty rodents, avoiding the spiny armor, chew into the succulent tissue unmolested. Well, not quite unmolested; there are snakes, hawks and owls. These predators have kept the rodent population within bounds; but now the hunters are the hunted, vanishing themselves under human pressures. In addition, the old saguaros now stand on practically bare soil, as a result of overgrazing of livestock years ago. Consequently, seedlings are deprived of moisture-holding duff and the protective shade of low-growing brush, so that only an occasional seed produces a plant. The new generation of saguaro is sparse. The effect of its decline will be felt on birds like the flicker, wren and woodpecker which depend upon it for nest and food. Reverberations are unending when the biotic balance suffers such disturbances.

The highway climbs through semidesert grassland in the plateaus and foothills. Constructing the road was a tortuous project, begun in 1933 and completed in 1950, but it reduced driving time to the

278

summit from three and a half hours to one hour. The road is named
the Hitchcock Highway for Colonel Frank Hitchcock, publisher of the
Tucson *Citizen*, who campaigned for it. The Molino Basin camping
and picnic area at 5000 feet lies in the Upper Sonoran life zone, with
vegetation of piñon, juniper, oak chaparral, sustained by sixteen to
twenty inches of rainfall.

Weird rock formations, erosion formed, lie along the ascending
highway. Windy Point Vista faces south, high over Tucson and the
Santa Cruz Valley, the Rincon Range and the Santa Ritas, near the
Mexican border. At 8000 feet in the Transition zone, ponderosa pine
grows on south and west exposures with Douglas-fir on north and
east slopes; the annual precipitation is almost twenty-five inches,
much of it in the form of winter snow. Bear Wallow Campground in
this vicinity was the first Forest Service recreational unit in the Catalinas, started in 1918 with a $100 appropriation for three picnic tables,
one toilet, one fireplace and a hitching rack. All supplies were moved
by burro.

San Pedro Vista faces the vastness of southeastern Arizona and the
high ranges protected in the Coronado National Forest. As on Mount
Lemmon, grazing long ago was drastically reduced in order to protect
the watershed. In the distance, at the foot of the Chiricahua Mountains, lies Camp Grant, scene of a tragic massacre in 1871, when a
band of Americans slaughtered 128 Apache Indians in a matter of
minutes. The Federal Government had just begun to activate a peace
policy in dealing with the Apaches, which this rash, thoughtless act
completely upset. The Dragoon Mountains, lying midway from the
Chiricahuas, was the stronghold of Cochise, the Apache leader, and
his burial place.

Mount Lemmon Snow Bowl, at 9100 feet, lies in the Canadian
zone of pine, Douglas-fir, white fir and quaking aspen, with thirty
inches of precipitation. Skiers who use these slopes in winter may not
realize it, but the snow underfoot, or under ski, seeping into the
ground, will recharge Tucson's falling water table. However, anyone
who visits here in summer and has the hiking instinct can follow
Sabino Canyon and fish in the creek on the way. Water, after all, is a
friendly sort of resource which tolerates people in their pursuit of fun.

Tucson has many attractions, but the one place to see in order to
understand and appreciate the natural treasures of the Southwest is
the Arizona-Sonora Desert Museum. It ranks among the truly great
points of interest available to American travelers, educational but
never dull, entertaining but never tawdry. Plants and animals are

279

shown as personable, understandable neighbors of people through ingenious treatments devised by Arthur Pack, William H. Carr and their
associates. For instance, one exhibit interprets the desert underground
through a tunnel, in which visitors view plant roots, prairie dogs bur-
rowing about, bats, rattlesnake dens. The watershed exhibit explains
graphically the water problems of Arizona and the nation.

The new luxury hotel at Apache Junction should do wonders for
the place. Undoubtedly, it will be run well, being part of the chain
that operates such high-quality resorts as Westward Ho in Phoenix
and La Concha on the beach at San Juan, Puerto Rico.

Theodore Roosevelt passed through Apache Junction in 1911,
heading for the confluence of Tonto Creek and the Salt River to
dedicate the dam named for him. He said the vast, wild country presented the most sublimely beautiful panorama nature ever created.
There were not many people in the neighborhood to see it at the
time. It was known as the land of the Lost Dutchman, an elusive,
illusionary mine somewhere in the Superstition Mountains, and of
the Apache people who had fought hard for it and lost.

Now Phoenix, heading toward a population of 1,000,000 by the
turn of the century, is spreading out toward the Junction. The big
hotel may be thirty miles from downtown, but in a few years it should
be right in the heart of things.

Beyond Apache Junction, that is to the east, away from Phoenix,
lies the Superstition Wilderness Area, an unconquered vestige of natural history, part of the Tonto National Forest. Like a reddish, bold
landmark of the desert, the Superstition Mountains rise abruptly from
the desert floor of some 2000 feet elevation to 6000 feet.

The topography on the north flank, which I visited one day on
foot, is extremely rugged, with sheer canyons and stark rocky formations, the most striking of which are Weaver's Needle and Black
Cross Butte. Yet even this seemingly forbidding country turns into a
flower garden of desert plants and shrubs. For instance, there is the
slender-stemmed night-blooming cactus (*La Reina de la Nocha*) with
large white flowers that open but once a year—from sunset until early
morning. Or the barrel cactus, a stocky, five-foot-high water tank of
the desert, which blooms yellow, pink and orange flowers. It serves a
useful purpose to rats, mice and rabbits, who gnaw into its tissue for
moisture, and to knowing, thirsty humans, who slice off the top and
squeeze liquid from the pulp. The fuzzy-spined cholla (cho′-ya) cac-

tus comes in several varieties: tree, cane, Christmas (which ripens in December) and jumping.

Why is it called the "jumping cholla"? I learned the reason sharply and unforgettably when I stepped on one. Two or three cactus sections detached from the plant, their spines plunging through the canvas shoe I was wearing. I jumped. Then I tried to extract the cactus but ended with it sticking to both hands. My companion pulled out the cactus with a pair of pliers!

The Weaver's Needle vicinity supposedly is the location of the Lost Dutchman mine. It receives its name from Jacob Waltz, the "Dutchman," who arrived in Florence and Phoenix several times with sackfuls of gold nuggets and mysterious murmurings about his hidden mine. On his deathbed in 1891, he gave vague directions to it. Prospectors have been hunting for it ever since. Several have died in the process, particularly those who tried in summer when temperatures reach 115 or 120 degrees and water is so scarce that even the cacti grow thirsty.

In contrast with the lonely magnificence of the Superstitions, the Apache Trail, Route 88, skirting the wilderness on the north, leads to the chain of Salt River dams and lakes, the Phoenix seashore. Of all the marvels in Arizona, the spectacle of people enjoying water in these immense desert canyons is far from the least. At Canyon Lake, the first of three reservoirs accessible on the Apache Trail, anyone can rent a powerboat and join the scores skimming over the water passing the mighty buttes and mesas along the shore, yielding a wide berth to water skiers and fishermen.

The Apache Trail was built early in the century in order to move equipment to Roosevelt Dam, the first major project of the Bureau of Reclamation. Freight wagons behind twelve- and sixteen-mule teams traveled back and forth for five years before the mighty dam was complete. Much of the Trail is still on the original roadbed laid out during the construction period, and feels like it. On reaching precipitous Fish Creek Canyon, the average traveler will wonder whether the trip is really worth it. It is. Anyone who starts this way should continue to Roosevelt Dam, in the narrow gorge below the meeting place of Tonto Creek and Salt River. The clear blue lake stretches over twenty-five miles, surrounded by mountainsides lush (if "lush" is the word) with saguaros, while far off in the northern distance, above the desert, lie the green mountains of the Mogollan Plateau. Almost everything within the compass of the eye lies within

281

the Tonto National Forest, the largest in the Southwest, established in 1905 but subsequently enlarged to nearly 3,000,000 acres to protect the Phoenix watershed. Together with adjacent National Forests and Indian lands, it *is* the Phoenix watershed.

Two thousand feet above Oak Creek Canyon, near Flagstaff, Lookout Point commands a fragment of geology and scenery which writers have been describing for years in the most glowing terms. Now it is time to add a few words of requiem. The natural gem of cool waters and green forest bordered by sandstone cliffs has acquired defects: commercial-amusement crannies and "rustic" resorts of varying design and appeal, generally adding only planless dissonance to the landscape.

Half the land in Oak Creek Canyon is privately owned, the other half publicly owned as part of Coconino National Forest. The private portions were carved out of the National Forest during the homestead era. But thirty years ago, when Oak Creek Canyon was a wilderness retreat enjoyed principally by hardy Flagstaff residents, the land could have been purchased at low cost and protected in a manner to justify its description. Funds to purchase land to fill in erratic Forest boundaries in the West were not available then, and are still not available.

The Forest Service portion of the Canyon has been developed with streamside campgrounds among the pines. One place youngsters love is Slide Rock, a natural shoot-the-chute, where they slip Levi's over their bathing suits and slither through a rocky channel into a shady pool—another use of Arizona water.

The Red Rocks area south of Sedona has been the background for countless motion pictures. The Hollywood cameramen will now have to adjust their shooting to avoid "Cathedral Vista" homesites and the trailer-park village, occupying choice parcels of private land, in their pictures of the Old West. The Chapel of the Holy Cross, a beautiful contemporary Catholic church, deserving of the scenery, confronts Cathedral Rock, the most massive and impressive formation in the entire Oak Creek Canyon. In driving to Schnebley Hill, a lofty vantage point, the Canyon and its surroundings are seen at their natural best, as beautiful as the Grand Canyon, if in miniature, filled with a thousand sandstone spires, minarets and domes, glistening scarlet in the sunlight, with changing hues of purple, orange-yellow and russet.

CHAPTER TWENTY-TWO

# *Loggers of the Olympic Peninsula*

The guthammer sang out sweetly. It had been a hoot owl day and the loggers were long cleaned up and ready for supper. The bullbuck and I headed for the cookhouse on a wooden walk pocked and fuzzy from the tramping of calked boots.

Thinking about the strange new language I had acquired, I stopped along the lawn where the camp superintendent was weighing the slender, eighteen-inch-long fuel moisture stick. It was so delicate a procedure that he picked up the ends with wires in order to avoid adding the moisture of his fingers to the scale.

"I doubt there'll be logging anywhere on the Peninsula tomorrow, let alone a hoot owl," he said. "The stick shows hardly any moisture at all."

Around the camp, steep-faced mountains, shaggy green with a million Douglas-fir trees, bespoke the wild grandeur of the Pacific Northwest. But the slopes were spotted with intermittent light patches, created by "clear-cut," or block, logging. Each patch stood forth boldly, as though to demonstrate that wildness and grandeur lie completely within our control.

The scene was Camp Grisdale, from which crews of the Simpson Timber Company are logging some of the roughest, steepest wooded slopes in America. Earlier I had watched them in their conquest of the lonely, defiant terrain of the Wynoochee watershed, lying within the Olympic National Forest.

Bulldozers, Diesel-powered yarders (powerfully cabled winches) and whining gasoline-driven chain saws are the tools of the modern logger. Soon after dawn I had followed two men, the "fallers," watching them climb a sheer embankment at a forty-five-degree angle and cut down a 200-foot tree within thirty minutes—and most of that time was spent in clearing the brush as a safety precaution and calculating the best angle at which to drop the tree. After it hit the ground, thudded and settled, they "bucked" it into log lengths of thirty-two

283

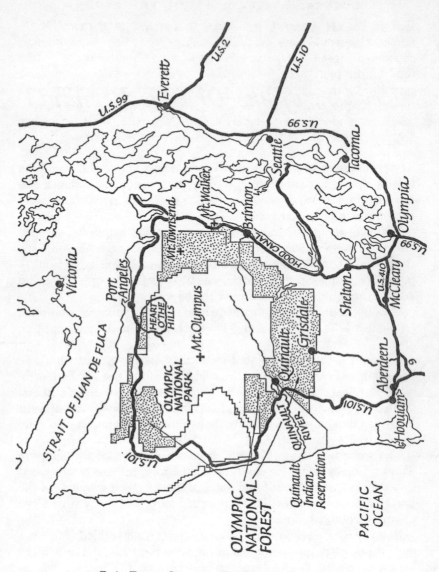

Rain Forest Country—the Olympic Peninsula

feet. In the old days, when buckers used a crosscut saw, or "Swede fiddle," this would have taken hours. As soon as they were through, chokermen rigged and pinned the logs into a "necktie party." Then the "whistle punk" (an honorable workman, despite the lowly title) gave the tooting signal to the yarding engineer and the logs were carried on the aerial cable, swinging through the air a quarter of a mile over underbrush, gullies and streams to the landing, or "hot deck," to be loaded on a truck and make their way down the steep mountainside.

The terrain may have been difficult, but the Simpson men were logging one of the most luxuriant forests of the Pacific slope, if not the entire world. On the Olympic Peninsula, superhumid growing conditions are ideal. The massive Olympic Mountains block and intercept the moisture-filled Pacific winds, wringing rain, snow and mist. For six or seven months the western side of the Peninsula is almost completely enshrouded. (Curiously, the northeast portion, deprived of moisture by the mountain wall, is almost as arid as a desert.) The heavy rainfall and moderate temperature combine to make the Peninsula a magnificent evergreen domain. It reaches its highest development in the rain forests along the Pacific, serene botanical gardens comprising the entire sweep of plant progression from fungi, mosses and lichens to immense trees 300 feet high and a thousand years old.

The Olympic Peninsula is a marvel of the original America. It lies in semi-isolation, bordered by waters of the Pacific, the Strait of Juan de Fuca and the clustered cosmos of Puget Sound. In time past its rugged mountains and dense forests resisted the intrusions of modern civilization more stoutly than the rest of the Pacific Coast and it is still quite possible to observe the course of nature largely undisturbed. In a way, the Olympic Mountains remind me of the Great Smokies in the East: their isolation, the lush development of their forests, the preservation of a portion of each within a National Park and the use of other portions as National Forestland. Additionally, the Olympic Peninsula presents a stark geological story, with more than a hundred living glaciers in the high country, six major glaciers on Mount Olympus alone. These are vestiges of massive sheets of ice, which plowed, scraped and scoured the earth in at least four surges spread over millions of years. The last mighty glacial movement retreated northward only 11,000 years ago.

In the intervening years, growing conditions have been so favorable

285

that the Olympic Peninsula has bloomed into a forest of giants. One speaks of the predominant trees as the "big four" of the Olympics. In the progression of plants from the smallest to the greatest, the climax tree generally is either western red cedar or western hemlock. That is, where the forest is left to its own devices, undisturbed by the violent touch of man or nature, these species become dominant, crowding out the others and depriving them of sun and soil. Western red cedar, growing largely in moist valley bottoms, reaches heights of 175 feet. It has a cinnamon-red, fibrous bark and flat, lacy sprays of almost fernlike leaves. The western hemlock, a little smaller than the red cedar, grows at elevations up to 3000 feet, a tree of dignity, of dark russet-brown bark, showing abundant and long cones at the ends of its branches. The top shoot of the tree, with glossy green leaves, bends over in an arc. Then, in the rain forest, there is the energetic Sitka spruce, which achieves heights of 200 feet in 100 years—and is apt to live 700 more. It towers over all other spruces and can be easily recognized by testing its bright bluish-green needles—they're sharp.

The last and mightiest of the big four is the Douglas-fir, second only to the Giant Sequoia in size of all trees on the continent. This stately, wonderfully proportioned tree grows to heights of 250 feet, and sometimes of 300 feet, with a clean shaft, clear of limbs for 100 feet. In age, the larger trees may be from 400 to 1000 years old. The Douglas-fir was discovered by Dr. Archibald Menzies, in 1791, on the west coast of Vancouver Island, but was named for David Douglas, the roving Scottish botanist, who brought a specimen back to England for the Royal Horticultural Society. Douglas-fir is a singular tree. It is a botanical puzzler, bearing resemblance to spruce and fir, as well as hemlock and yew; its Latin botanical name, *Pseudotsuga taxifolia*, means "false hemlock with a yewlike leaf." As a timber source, it is the most important tree of the Northwest, prized for its strength and immense size free of knots and other defects. But Douglas-fir is not a climax tree. In the course of uninterrupted competition, it yields in time to hemlock and red cedar. It demands full sunlight to grow, which is one reason it is logged in clear-cut patches. In the past, forest fires, caused by lightning, have exposed the forest floor to sunlight, providing an inviting condition for Douglas-fir seed sown by "mother" trees in nearby woods or even miles off.

Camp Grisdale, forty miles from the town of Shelton, is almost as unique as this great tree. Virgin stands of Douglas-fir are being logged in the wild, jagged depths of the Peninsula once considered beyond

286

reach. The working area, partly private land of the Simpson Company and partly National Forest, is being managed as a single unit to insure continual growth of healthy timber for centuries to come. The company has yielded to the Forest Service the regulation of cutting on its land, which borders on the revolutionary as far as many traditional commercial timber operators are concerned.

Loggers themselves are singular people. At Grisdale they live at one of the last logging camps. In these days of highway mobility, most men who work in the woods prefer town living, traveling back and forth in crew trucks called "crummies" (a word which persists from the old days). But Grisdale survives in a forest setting near the Wynoochee River, a village of fifty frame family units, four bunkhouses for single men, a two-room school, store and recreation hall. Here men speak the universal language of loggers, handed down from the first woodsmen who felled the white pine of New England and refined as the timber harvest moved westward across the Lake States to the last frontier on the Pacific Coast. In this colorful lingo, a "misery whip" is the crosscut saw once pulled back and forth through logs, hours at a time; a "bunkhouse lawyer" is the logger who orates to his mates, asserting knowledge on all subjects, including sin; "bullbuck," the supervisor over the cutting crew; and "hoot owl," the early work shift, from predawn to noon, operated during low humidity periods of midsummer to reduce fire hazard.

• We responded to the "guthammer," the dinner bell. I had always heard that loggers ate well. Early cooks were Chinese, attracted to the woods from the Mother Lode mining country of California. They specialized in fresh meat and fresh vegetables, kept the floors, tables and dishes spotless. Tradition was that loggers ate fast, well and were seldom well mannered. Robert Marshall, the champion of wilderness (and an eminent forester), once studied eating habits in a logging camp. Of 100 diners under observation, he noted that twelve were "two-tool men," using both knife and fork to feed their faces, while thirty-three commonly depended on their forks for "harpooning," or bread spearing. After meals, he listened closely to ten conversations for fifteen minutes each, and counted an average of 136 unprintable words per conversation.

But loggers, like logging, have changed. The men I ate with ate well, and their table manners were worthy of the best restaurant in Seattle. I was almost ashamed to reach out at arm's length for the butter. The cookhouse, laid out like a cafeteria with long benches,

287

was immaculate. Why should this be so? I asked the "gut robber" (the head cook). "Well, in a logging camp," said the old gentleman, "cooks are proud because they know their customers."

After supper, as we stood on the steps of the cookhouse, the camp superintendent, a captious but likable citizen named Clarence Lockwood, discussed with me the relationship between the Olympic National Park and Olympic National Forest.

Theodore Roosevelt set aside a large portion of this last great virgin forest by establishing Mount Olympus National Monument in 1909. Today the National Park, created by Congress in 1946, occupies 890,000 acres in the heart of the Peninsula, while the National Forest borders it with 628,000 acres. For years the ratio has been disturbing to timbermen, chambers of commerce and a few foresters, who follow the instincts of their profession to log and grow trees, and spread the benefits of scientific management and crop rotation.

"The trouble with that Park," as my friend Lockwood said, "is that there is no access except by pack horse. Now if they would only log all that downed and dead timber, they would get enough money to build a road so that everybody could enjoy it." It was much like the reasoning I had heard from timbermen elsewhere concerning National Forest wilderness areas. Nevertheless, the Olympic National Park represents our last glorious opportunity to preserve an estate of giants—trees, elk and bear, and all wild things, free to follow their natural course with a minimum of manipulation or interference. Sustained-yield timber cutting should apply to most of our forestland. But here on the Olympic Peninsula, Americans are proving they can afford to reserve 890,000 acres for the natural sciences and the national soul.

Lockwood, a bull-o'-the-woods of the old school, advised me that he disliked Easterners in general and forestry graduates in particular. Like all the men I met in the logging camp, he was free of guile, proud of his work and of growing a new generation of great trees. We crossed the landscaped plaza between the bunkhouses. One would hardly expect a well-trimmed grass lawn, flowering rhododendron, English spruce and weeping-cedar trees, but they were thriving in this setting. In the center of the area was the historic showpiece of the camp, Simpson Locomotive No. 1, a relic of early railroad logging.

Then he and several others invited me into the frame building housing the camp office. They recalled the old days of logging. Conditions were rough. Talking was not allowed at meals. There were shacks for bunkhouses. You packed your own bedroll and blankets. You worked as long as it was light enough to work. Logging was a hazardous affair and it was not considered unusual when a man was killed in the rigging.

But how, I asked, did conditions change? Enlightened corporate interest? Intervention by the Federal Government, such as in the New Deal?

"Politicians, hell!" one man replied, the first and only "hell" or "damn" I had heard. "It was the union. The union changed conditions in the thirties." There was no expression of disagreement.

It was still light outdoors. Three of the men suggested we ride again over the countryside they were logging. We boarded a crummy and climbed sheer cliffs on a very bumpy road. Construction of logging roads through this rugged country costs an average of $21,000 a mile, which shows how resistant the landscape can be to change by man. We passed stands of towering Douglas-fir almost 300 feet tall and so close together they were almost rubbing elbows. Many logged hillsides, which had looked bare from a distance, were actually green with new vegetation.

"Clear-cutting does look at first as though we're scarring the land forever," said my friend, the bullbuck, "but in this country Douglas-fir comes back quickly. Once we're through logging on a setting, the slash is burned and the mineral soil is exposed. Then four- and five-year-old trees are planted. Natural seeding will come in, too, from the surrounding forest. Five years after we've cut an area the second growth is ten feet high. In twenty-five years the new trees are thirty-five feet high.

"You can't cut Douglas-fir like ponderosa pine with selective logging, where you take only the mature trees and leave the young. These trees are so tall and thick they depend on each other for protection. They're shallow-rooted because there's so much moisture available they don't have to go deep for it. They guard each other from the wind and if we took some, those we left would probably be blown over.

"But cutting on staggered settings of sixty to 100 acres is one form of selective logging. Compare it with the old days, when they started at the upper end of a valley and sheared everything in sight to the other end. With the kind of sustained yield we have now, it should be possible to keep cutting in a continual cycle forever."

We were driving down the knife edge of a sheer cliff about a thousand feet above the Wynoochee. Dusk had caught up with us. The hillside was ablaze with vivid magenta fireweed, standing erect like a miniature forest of color. Abruptly, the driver slammed on the brakes. A deer was trapped in our headlights, a shocked, frightened creature with absolutely no place to hide. To his left he faced a plunge to the canyon floor far below, to his right the cliff bank too steep to climb. He turned and ran ahead of us, fleeing downhill in terror until he could bound into brushy refuge. "Head for home!" someone shouted after him.

Back at the bunkhouse, there were four beds to a room. A tall young logger and I shared one room. It was not quite as elaborate as the Olympic Hotel in Seattle, but on a par with YMCA's.

"I think it would be hard to get much closer to nature than we are here," my bunkmate said. "Every logger is an outdoorsman or else he would be working at something else under a roof. I love all growing things. I love the freedom of the woods. We have machines. But we push the machines. They don't push us.

"But I'll say this much. You were talking about the National Park earlier. They should leave those beautiful sections people pack into on horse just as they are, without gutting them."

Loggers, I concluded, are solid outdoorsmen, motivated by the same instinct as the hiker, horseman and wilderness enthusiast, with the good fortune to live and work in the natural environment the rest of us are privileged to touch only briefly.

Large timber companies own a considerable portion of the Olympic Peninsula. Weyerhaeuser, Crown-Zellerbach, Simpson and other substantial outfits practice much the same type of scientific forestry on their private lands as does the Forest Service on public land. They plan their logging with full concern for the safety of their men and the ever-present danger of fire. When they log one generation of trees they plant a new generation. Smaller outfits may not have the same long-range concept of logging, but they are encouraged to do the right thing by statutes like the seed-tree law and the carefully spelled-out state safety code.

The constructive approach of loggers toward land of the Olympic Peninsula matured in the early 1940's, when the first unit of the "Keep Washington Green" program was organized here. Instead of learning that fire and forest destruction were inevitable, school children have since been taught to respect the trees of their community as the next generation's way of life. In 1941, the American Tree Farm System was born in Grays Harbor County and has spread from this Northwest Pacific corner across the nation to stimulate the continuous growing of trees by thousands of private landowners, large and small.

The most recent advance of the large companies has been to open their lands to public recreation. Outdoor enthusiasts are welcome to fish their streams and lakes, hunt their woods, pick berries in their fields, picnic and camp at attractive and often well-developed sites. This may come under the heading of public relations as far as the companies are concerned, but even the most critical public must feel a sense of appreciation—particularly in this era of shrinking outdoor spaces.

The Simpson Company, a progressive logging and manufacturing outfit with holdings in Washington, Oregon and California, operates under an unusual relationship with the National Forest in the Grisdale area. Many years ago, the early presidents of the company, Sol Simpson and his son-in-law, Mark Reed, adopted what was then a unique philosophy. Contrary to the prevailing view that land once logged was worthless and was best disposed to the local county for tax delinquency, they held on to their cutover holdings, protected them from fire and started to grow new trees. After the company town of Shelton was practically burned to the ground in 1910, Mark Reed began it anew by building his own home there. But the cycle of harvesting Douglas-fir is somewhere between eighty and 150 years, depending on local conditions. The Simpson seedlings of the turn of the century have grown to 100 feet and before long—say, forty or fifty years—will be young adults ready to be cut. In the early 1940's Simpson foresaw only a few years of logging left on the quarter million acres it owns on the Olympic Peninsula. Towns like Shelton and Mc-Cleary, dependent on the timber economy, faced a bleak tomorrow. However, behind the Simpson property the rugged Wynoochee watershed, within the National Forest, held out the promise of furnishing sufficient Douglas-fir to sustain the mills. Consequently, the Forest Service and Simpson entered into a co-operative arrangement, pooling public and private forests of 300,000 acres for the next 100 years. Their agreement provides that cutting must be based on sound standards, prescribed by the Forest Service, and that the timber must be manufactured locally. The Shelton Co-operative Sustained Yield Unit was devised very carefully to assure protection of the public interest. It took an act of Congress in 1944. The sale price of the timber is subject to review, based on current market values, among other stipulations. Shelton, all but given up as a ghost town, has had a new lease on life.

The old timber tycoons of the Olympic Peninsula, who logged first with bull teams, then with horses, then with railroad locomotives, were less deserving of kind words. They gained ownership of their land with cunning and connivance. As Gifford Pinchot recorded, some of America's heaviest timberland was eliminated from the Olympic National Forest on the utterly imaginary ground that it was most valuable for agriculture—and nearly every acre passed promptly and fraudulently into the hands of the lumbermen. They logged without restraint, without any concept or interest in regeneration or fire protection.

The favorite historians of the lumber industry either overlook completely or condone the past. "Nobody denies the timber barons were greedy," according to one popular scholar of the Northwest, "though probably no more so than other men." This may be true. It may be a rational justification for turpitude. But it would be a sad moral foundation upon which to build an enduring social order.

Fortunately the lumber industry is more concerned with writing a constructive record of the present rather than with rewriting the past. Perhaps they will also let up in their effort to reshape the Olympic National Park.

The National Park is dedicated to the preservation of a unique wilderness, a national treasure. The Olympic National Forest is dedicated to conservation through multiple use—and one of its uses is to screen the inner wilderness from external influence. Both areas have their proper purposes, with their fates intertwined like the tall Douglas-fir trees supporting each other in the forest.

Anyone who works up an appetite while traveling along the Hood Canal can take time out at the Seal Rock Campground to dig a few clams and oysters out of the sand. Or you can stop anyway to enjoy the cool setting where the forest dips down to the water's edge. If you have a boat along you can launch it from the dock and look up toward the glistening Olympics from the middle of the canal, a crooked watery finger of Puget Sound.

Seal Rock lies on Route 101, the Olympic Highway, which encircles the Peninsula. Along the way are many National Forest campgrounds and scenic areas where visitors perceive the remote beauty and extraordinary fertility of this corner of Washington State. On the east side, Mount Walker Summit (elevation 2769 feet), near Quilcene, looks deep into the ridges and valleys, as well as off to Juan de Fuca Strait and the distant Cascades. Then there are drives into the green recesses along the Dosewallips, Duckabush, and Hamma Hamma Rivers, which derive their names from the Indian tongues —and may they never be renamed.

But the most beautiful area, within access from the highway, lies in the southwest corner of the National Forest, bordering Lake Quinault. Fishing, boating and swimming are enhanced by the scenery of dark forests rising upward from the water. Along the lakeshore are two campgrounds, summer homes and a hotel, Lake Quinault Lodge, and nearby is the reservation of Quinault Indians, who have lived for centuries here on the Pacific Coast. The Quinault River, which runs through the lake, is a short one on its journey from the mountains to the sea. Indian canoemen take passengers down the fast, white waters, often shooting the rapids, for the last portion of that journey from the lake to the ocean beach.

Within walking distance is the rain forest of the Quinault Natural Area, including the "Big Acre," the greatest known stand of Douglas-fir in the United States.

Similar forests parallel the Pacific Coast from Alaska to California, but none is more lush than in the western valleys of the Olympic Mountains. The abundant waters from the Pacific mist combine with waters from the snowfields, glaciers and streams. The climate is mild, yet wet, with more than 130 inches of precipitation a year. The trees are among the largest and most majestic in the world. They are not as large and perhaps not as majestic as the redwoods, but here one feels the presence of more color and the activity of more living things than in the somber redwood forest. In the morning, as dawn arrives, the trees drip with moisture in the warm sunlight. The forest is filled with soft green light and shadows. Light filters downward between towering giants, through the translucent leaves of vine maple, bounding from one green surface to another.

Trees, shrubs, flowering plants, giant ferns, mosses, lichen, fungi and animals express themselves as members of the rain-forest community. Plants and animals we can see and many we cannot. The forest litter contains a large population of mice, shrews, salamanders and worms. Insects and microscopic creatures live in dead snags and live trees. There are signs of elk, who have come down from the

293

mountaintops during the previous fall and winter, to leave their foot-prints in the hardened mud, teeth bites on browsed trees and shrubs, and those telltale elk pellets scattered in clusters over the ground. These are the Olympic elk, the largest member of the wapiti family except for the moose, growing as heavy as 900 or 1000 pounds. The elk is the greatest citizen of the forest, but each creature plays his part in the unending, interrelated process of life, growth and death.

Walking along Willaby Gorge, one can see a vertical distribution of plant life extending like the floors in a building, upward from the subbasement of Willaby Creek, sixty feet below, to the overstory, the skyscraper penthouse of Sitka spruce, 225 feet above. In the bottom, crooked vine maple sprawls over the water with curtains of moss. It mingles with red alder, a tree covered with a lovely grayish bark, which is in reality a mass of lichens feeding on the bark. Lichens per-form important forest functions, attracting minerals from the air, disintegrating rocks into soil and forming soil themselves. On the banks sharp pointed swordferns grow as tall as young trees, furnish-ing a green background to blooming shrubs, berries and wildflowers. The small, delicate oxalis, a pale white, bears leaves like a three-leaf clover. The shrubby salmonberry, a favorite elk browse, grows at least three feet tall in dense thickets, with red flowers and salmon-red fruit. Trillium is the most beautiful and common plant of the moist woods with its triad of petals at first pure white, then turning dark rose with age. They serve the forest by protecting soil from washing and by conserving moisture during dry periods.

The rain forest is enriched with mosses at all elevations. At least seventy kinds are present. Most are known only to specialists and do not have common names. Some, bright green, cover rocks, which in time they will crush into inorganic soil. Others grow like airplants from the limbs of trees, draped in fragile beauty like mysterious poetry of the forest. They ascend to the tops of the highest trees and they cover dead trees on the forest floor.

Fallen trees fill an important function. They feed fungi, bacteria and mushrooms. They are nurseries for spruce and hemlock, whose seedlings prefer rotting wood. Seeds take root on broken stumps, reaching the soil after creeping down the full length of the stump, or growing over a rock outcropping, baring the root structure to the eye as though it were looking through a tunnel in the soil.

Farther along the walk, within the Big Acre, there is a typical "nurse tree," on which a botanist can identify six different lichens,

294

moss, liverwort, huckleberry and a hemlock tree. The nurse tree, a fallen Douglas-fir, has probably been lying here for 300 years and was at least that old when it fell.

This single-acre plot was laid out in 1948 within the densest part of the grove in a way to encompass the maximum possible number and the tallest of trees. It has since become a famous acre in forestry; a replica is shown in diorama in the Hall of North American Forests in the American Museum of Natural History in New York. I will not tell you how many board feet there are within the acre; how many high-grade-veneer logs it would yield, or how many six-room houses the trees would build. I will say they are 285 feet high and that after 375 years of life on our world these trees are growing, in the ideal conditions of the rain forest, more vigorously than youngsters half their age are growing elsewhere.

I should not call attention to the largest parts of the scene, but to the smallest. Without them there would be no process of change, and really no scene at all. Here are the hemlocks, 100 to 175 feet tall, young and growing. They may in time become the climax tree in this setting. But look far below them, too. Observe the tips of fleshy mushrooms, the fruit of fungi, the whortleberry and oxalis. Listen to the muted warbling of a thrush singing from the streamside in a late afternoon or the downy woodpecker poking about for his supper among the insect larvae burrowed in the dead snags. This is the life community of the forest, whispering a soft and subtle message in behalf of all its creatures.

# CHAPTER TWENTY-THREE

# *Timberline on Mount Hood*

I was riding the chairlift to Silcox Hut, listening to the merry clickety-clack of the cable rolling over the pulleys and wishing it would snow about twenty-one feet so I could watch skiers sail across the top of Timberline Lodge almost one mile below. It was not very likely, considering that it was midsummer. But high above the lift the volcanic summit of Mount Hood glistened with its perpetual cover of snow and glacier, reminding that winter here was never far behind.

South lay a vista of the Cascades, rising from their green glory to whiten the horizon with a series of distinctive 10,000-foot peaks. Mount Hood lies roughly midway in the mighty Cascade Range, which extends in a wide belt from Mount Baker, Washington, just below the Canadian border, to Mount Shasta in California. But also, I thought, this mountain represents the quintessence of Oregon, the highest meeting place of people and their vigorous natural environment.

To view the scene without people, or to look at Mount Hood from a distance, as hundreds of thousands do every day, it would still be a marvel. It was born of volcanic eruptions and remains semiactive—one of the few such in the United States. On certain days vapor and gas are visible issuing from the crater. After its volcanic formation, the mountain was cleft by glaciers, leaving rivers, canyons and alpine streams in their wake, and eleven living glaciers as vestiges of the last great ice sheet.

Considering only the physical circumstance, Mount Hood, as the 11,245-foot queen of the Oregon Cascades, serves as the barrier between two astonishingly different climate zones and forests. On the western slope, moisture and rain are abundant. The pattern of plant life is dominated by the massive Douglas-fir. But almost immediately after crossing the Cascade crest, the moisture diminishes sharply. Douglas-fir yields to ponderosa pine. Then moisture all but disappears, the landscape becomes a treeless, arid plateau, better suited to cattle than timber. The transition effected by high mountains blocking the Pacific winds is so sharp and sudden that it becomes visible in the course of a thirty-minute drive.

Vegetation changes are apparent on the mountain itself. Approaching timberline, Douglas-fir yields to trim alpine fir and grassy highland meadows colored with wildflowers. Above timberline, alpine flowers and shrubs arise from volcanic soil during the brief summer to creep to the very edges of glacial ice and snow-crowned summits.

Mount Hood is a complete entity, but not in its own right. It benefits from the human touch, as we benefit from touching it, from experiencing the inner precincts of a great mountain. When I visited the Mount Hood National Forest in summer I followed berrypickers and young campers on trails through the woods. They sang and the mountain sang with them. I followed older people traveling on roads to Timberline Lodge and walking off on quiet trails to places of wonderment and worship. I conjured the winter scene of skiers by the thousands traveling and tumbling downhill, all feeling that the clash and turmoil of civilization lay far behind and that sheer joy in facing elemental forces lay ahead.

Timberline Lodge is a masterpiece of human contribution to the mountain. The architecture, the craftsmanship in its construction and the magnificent views it commands are matchless in America. It commemorates the best creative performances of those depression-born agencies, the Works Projects Administration and Civilian Conservation Corps. And it has lived an intriguing history of ups and downs, or possibly I should say of ins and outs, during its quarter century.

The idea of the lodge was conceived in 1935 by a group of civic-minded Portland businessmen, who organized as the Mount Hood Recreational Association. The highest peak of their state was only sixty-five miles from Portland, but was a landmark beyond reach. The closest point to the summit within access was Government Camp, a settlement less than halfway up. It derived its name from a shortening of the term "Government Encampment," dating back to the early settlement days when a government wagon train was stranded by an early snowfall and encamped for the winter. They envisioned and promoted a make-work project that would transform the vast snowfields into a magnificent skiing area.

Federal agencies welcomed the opportunity to realize the Portland dream. The Forest Service, for example, felt Timberline could be a

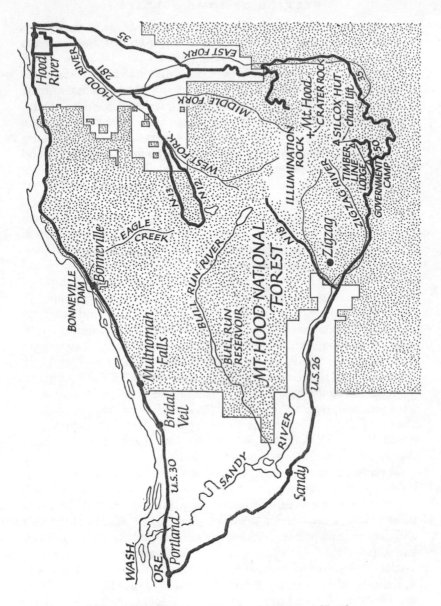

*The Circle Trip from Portland to Mount Hood*

pilot project for similar lodgings and chalets elsewhere in the Forest, providing facilities unequaled anywhere in the United States for the enjoyment of winter sports.

CCC workers hacked and blasted a road to the area. From there on it became a fine-arts project, based completely on native Oregon materials and spirit. The architecture was called "Cascadian." Whether it has ever been used again as such I do not know. It combines a massive stone base supporting a four-storied, 360-foot-long chalet with a tremendous shingled roof, surmounted by a 750-pound brass and bronze weathervane. Time and talent were on the side of the builders. Massive glacial-scarred rocks were quarried, cut and set in place. The stone fireplace, ninety-six feet high, weighs 400 tons. Massive ponderosa-pine pillars, forty feet high and three and a half feet thick, support the main lobby. The lobby and mezzanine floors are made of oak with pegged settings.

The quality and detail of handcraft in leather, metal, wood and stone have hardly been duplicated since—and certainly are not found in any current construction, public or private. The main entrance to the Lodge, a door of metal and wood ten feet high and weighing 1000 pounds, is precisely balanced to yield lightly to the touch. Everywhere are woodcarvings, metalcrafts and paintings, hand-wrought iron, handmade furniture, hand-carved railings and newel posts. In the lobby over the main entrance there is a woodcut of an Oregon mountain lion, life-size. Three panels in the main stairway, carved from redwood, depict the pioneers' trek west. Woodcarving in relief above the fireplace represents the animals of the Mount Hood National Forest, black-tailed deer, mule deer, Roosevelt elk, Rocky Mountain elk, black bear, antelope.

Government sewing projects sent hand-woven draperies and upholstery in original designs to decorate its rooms and windows. WPA artists, who were among the outstanding talent of the thirties, contributed over 130 oil and water-color paintings of Mount Hood flora and fauna. Perhaps the best known of these artists is C. E. Price, whose paintings now form a gallery on the mezzanine.

After two years and $1,000,000's worth of construction, the Lodge was dedicated in 1937 by Franklin Delano Roosevelt. Five million dollars could not duplicate it now. And of course, just about no one today would build an uneconomical hand-carved beauteous accommodation for only 230 guests.

In the first fourteen years Timberline was leased by the Forest

Service to the quasi-public organization of Portland businessmen and bankers. They paid a small annual rental and a percentage of the profits. Some years there were no profits, but they usually recouped in succeeding good years. By 1952 the businessmen had grown mildly disenchanted with their noble experiment. It was a time-consuming, unremunerative enterprise. They decided that individual investment would serve the resort better and transferred the lease to a three-man operation. That was when Timberline's troubles began. But at least, at the outset, they were honest troubles. The partners put a lot of money into improvements and ran out of working capital. Within eighteen months they were in debt to the tune of $80,000, with no profits foreseeable.

The magazine *Sports Illustrated* in 1956 published a finely drawn report on these and subsequent developments. The three partners transferred their lease to one man of dubious qualifications. Undoubtedly the Forest Service erred in approving this transfer and in not acting more promptly to prevent the debacle that followed. The new operator made his small quarterly payments under terms of the lease, but this was about all. The deterioration of the great resort began at once and proceeded swiftly.

In 1954 the chairlift was out of order. The rope tow was buried under snow. Dirt was piled in kitchens, lobbies and rooms. Timberline became known as a place of strange, lurid goings-on. Skiers went elsewhere, promising they would never again go to the Lodge on Mount Hood.

Ultimately the Sandy Electric Cooperative, one of many creditors of the ski operator, grew tired of promises instead of payment and shut off electric power to the Lodge. "The darkness fell on Timberline," recorded *Sports Illustrated*, "and it seemed like the darkness of death."

From January to March, 1955, the great Lodge lay empty, dark and forlorn. Its only guests were small rodents in quest of winter shelter, invading at will along with piles of snow through shattered windows. The Forest Service, reacting to the full gravity of Timberline's deterioration, searched everywhere for a new operator. They found him in Richard L. Kohnstamm, one of the skiers who loved Timberline. Kohnstamm was not a professional businessman nor even a Westerner. Nor did he heed the Portland banker who warned him to steer clear. A New Yorker, then in his late twenties, Kohnstamm had come to Portland from Columbia University. By pro-

301

fession he was a social worker at the Neighborhood House, but a well-financed social worker, a member of the Kohnstamm & Co. chemicals family.

When he acquired the lease, Dick Kohnstamm, an intense fellow (who had lost none of his zest or enthusiasm when I met him five years later) hired industrial cleaners to clear the cobwebs out of Timberline Lodge. In the kitchen they found grease inches thick. In the bedrooms hand-woven draperies had been used for rags and shoved into shattered windows to keep out the snow. Initials were carved in the railings and the woodwork generally was pretty well scarred.

Timberline Lodge has come a long way since Dick Kohnstamm took over the operation. Besides renovating the interior of the building, he installed a $100,000 double chairlift below the lodge and a heated swimming pool. The Forest Service has made a number of improvements, too, though perhaps not as many as Kohnstamm would like. However, attendance is what it should be—close to the best of any ski resort in the country. In winter as many as 4000 skiers in a single day swarm beautiful, snow-hung trails across the wide slopes. Timberline is not considered an advanced or extremely difficult ski course, but it does have the longest run of all, starting from 10,000 feet down to Government Camp, eight miles below. It also has one of the longest seasons, aided by the use of Sno-cats, which carry skiers to the high reaches of perpetual snow, trampling a few early flowering anemones on the way up. Lodgings at Timberline consist of dormitory beds at low cost for youngsters and luxurious rooms and suites, which are not outlandishly priced.

Summer is an active season, too. Although Timberline Lodge originally was conceived as a ski resort, it lies at the start of thirty-five-mile Timberline Trail, winding upward and around Mount Hood. A three- or four-day trip, afoot or on horseback, the Trail dips into Zigzag Canyon, ascends to flowering mountain meadows in view of glaciers, tumbling waterfalls, with Hood River Valley far below and Cascade Range to the horizon. For those who cannot quite make the hike upward into the precincts of the Mount Hood Wild Area, there are shorter trips around the Lodge, as well as the ride on the Magic Mile Chairlift, the first mile-long lift in the United States, rising to the 7000-foot elevation at Silcox Hut (named for Ferdinand Silcox, former chief of the Forest Service).

There is also the view from the picture window. As one who en-

302

joys and appreciates travel in the wilderness the hard way, I concede willingly there is pleasure, too, in luxuriating in the comfort of a deep chair with a long drink while identifying rugged mountains in the distance. In the National Forest there is room for many outdoor uses, each in its proper place.

Mount Hood National Forest is a major timber-producing forest of Oregon, which for some years has ranked as *the* leading timber-producing state. The million-plus-acre National Forest, spilling over both sides of the Cascades, encompasses several valuable species of trees. On the western flanks are Douglas-fir, clear-cut in blocks up to forty acres in size, plus stands of hemlock and silver fir. Across the divide, ponderosa is harvested selectively. Ideally, several generations of trees grow under the same forest canopy. The mature or overmature pine trees are cut first, enabling the youngsters to rise straight and strong, and assuring a perpetual yield.

The network of roads through the National Forest, however, is not yet sufficiently vast. Only fire and disease—and not logging trucks—can reach too many areas. These areas have not been designed for wilderness travel, biological study or recreation. Once brought under intensive forestry management, they will help the nation grow as much new timber as it harvests.

With such stands of timber yet to be tapped, Oregon will likely continue to hold the lead in timber production, which has shifted about in the past century from Maine to Michigan to Minnesota to Louisiana to Washington. There is another reason. By the time the flag of timber leadership was unfurled aloft in Oregon twenty years ago the facts of forestry were fairly well revealed. The state had already set up its own forestry department and was practicing fire protection. In 1941 it enacted a Forest Conservation Act, the first of its kind in the nation, with state-supervised harvesting and reforestation.

There are four major timber-tree nurseries in Oregon. The largest, operated at Corvallis by the State Board of Forestry, produces about 6,000,000 trees a year. A large part of this production is for planting on the "Tillamook burn," where one of the saddest chapters in forest history was written. In 1933 fire swept over 270,000 acres of the Tillamook forest in northwest Oregon (largely state and private lands), and returned again in 1935 and 1945 to extend the area of the burn by almost 100,000 acres. The remainder of new trees grown at Corvallis is for sale at cost to farmers and other forest owners. At Bend the Forest Service operates a nursery producing about 4,000,000 trees a year for National Forest planting. A commercial nursery near Salem is growing trees primarily for private owners, and a new state-owned nursery is getting underway at Elkton.

Besides leading in timber, Oregon has become the number-one deer state. Hunters bring home more than 125,000 animals a year. Yet the herds are growing larger, making even higher record-sized harvests possible without depleting the stock. Annually about 22,000 hunters seek big game animals in Mount Hood National Forest alone. But within a few years it should be able to accommodate many more, for as timber management is extended, deer will multiply; they prefer cutover lands where browsing is plentiful. The danger then will be to prevent deer population from becoming so great that they starve from lack of food, to say nothing of chomping an entire generation of small trees in the process. In the wilderness, nature achieves its own balance in the struggle for survival through disease, predators, fire, unending forces of violence and subtlety. Addition of the human element disturbs the balance. Wildlife management, a modern science far from fully appreciated by hunters or those who love wild animals as natural creatures, becomes highly essential. It weds nature and man.

In the two Northwest states, Oregon and Washington, 22 per cent of the land area lies within National Forest boundaries, mostly at high elevation where the snow falls early and lingers long. As a result, 90 per cent of winter sports, skiing, tobogganing, skating and a little snowball fighting, is enjoyed in the National Forests. Besides Timberline Lodge, Government Camp, Sno-Bunny and Cooper Spur, which draw 300,000 skiers to Mount Hood National Forest, some of the other noted Northwest National Forest ski areas are Mount Baker, Stevens Pass, Snoqualmie Pass in Washington, and Hoodoo Bowl, Willamette Pass and Warner Canyon in Oregon.

Skiing is a real phenomenon of modern times. Like golf, it was never intended to be a mass sport, or an inexpensive one. No one has ever tried to make it out to be one. Yet skiing has zoomed to the point where some 5,000,000 enthusiasts turn out during the season. It is not uncommon these days to observe a small child, not fully able to walk, learning to ski. Or to find his grandfather, or someone's grandfather, learning next to him.

The surge in skiing began in the East, but has found its fullest glory in the West, where snows are deeper and last longer. The sport first captured public imagination at the Lake Placid Winter Olympics in 1932. The first rope tow was installed at Woodstock, Vermont, in 1934, the first chairlift at Sun Valley, Idaho, in 1937. The skilift and its various improvements have revolutionized the sport; instead of suffering through the uphill climb, skiers can be towed by cable, or ride a chair or an enclosed gondola, with more time for the thrills and spills of the descent.

In some places of the West, skiing begins in November and lasts until April or May. Some of the larger, well-established ski clubs own their own lodges, built and maintained by summer work parties of members. Federated groups like the Far West Ski Association and Pacific Northwest Ski Association collaborate closely with the Forest Service. Not only do they encourage the sport of skiing and improvement in facilities, but ski schools on National Forest land are required to have instructors certified by them.

At Steamboat Springs, Colorado, a mountain community of 2000 astride the Continental Divide, surrounded by the towering peaks of Routt and Arapaho National Forests, skiing is part of the school curriculum. Through the combined efforts of the public schools and Winter Sports Club, youngsters "study" a variety of ski subjects right up to jumping, cross-country and slalom. Ninety per cent of all students participate in the grade-school meet, when races are held through the heart of town. This explains why tiny Steamboat Springs has produced far more than its share of nationally ranked skiers.

In some places there is skiing in sight of the desert. One is Charleston Peak, in Nevada National Forest, overlooking Las Vegas, Nevada, and Death Valley, California. Another is Mount Lemmon, in Coronado National Forest, high above Tucson, Arizona, probably the country's southernmost ski center.

Californians now have seventy-five ski areas on National Forestland. From one end of the state to the other, they are always within a few hours' driving distance of skiing. In the south the heaviest concentration is the vicinity around Lake Arrowhead and Big Bear Lake. In the north, most areas are clustered along U.S. 50 near Echo Summit and along U.S. 40 near Donner Summit on the Nevada state line. In the latter section skiing began at the time of the California gold rush, when racers used elongated skis which they called "snowshoes." On these fourteen-inch boards, steering and braking with a single pole, they plummeted down the mountainsides at speeds reported up to eighty miles per hour.

The entire Sierra Nevada mountain chain, unbroken for 250 miles, has emerged as a domain of winter sports. With snows up to three and four feet starting in late October, the snowpack builds up to firm depths of twenty-five feet or more. One of the largest areas developed in the Sierras since World War II is the Sugar Bowl, reached by a mile-long aerial tramway which starts upward from Route 40. The most celebrated and probably the most glamorous spot is Squaw Valley, scene of the 1960 Winter Olympics. It overlooks Lake Tahoe, a beautiful body of water too deep to freeze, ringed with pine forests and mountain peaks. The newest large scale area, Mount Shasta Ski Bowl, spreads across the south side of mighty Mount Shasta, which Joaquin Miller once described as, "Lonely as God, and white as a winter's moon." This bowl is so wide it can accommodate 5000 skiers without collision—when they are all watching where they're going.

New areas continue to open, and often with something new or different to offer. Alpine Meadows, in Bear Valley, just south of Squaw Valley, features European-type "cross-country" skiing, in which skiers shift from one slope to another, rather than remain in the same vicinity all day. Paradise Inn, at the south end of Tahoe, has an "escalator," or moving walkway, to carry skiers aloft. Mammoth Mountain, near Bishop, complete with 200-room hotel, is located in a portion of Sierra National Forest where snow is likely to fall in early October and remain fit for skiing until July 4.

Many lesser-known places are appearing on the map of Western skiing. No longer is glamorous Sun Valley the only name in winter sports associated with Idaho. Bogus Basin, eighteen miles north of Boise, is despite its name a good place, boasting a new double chairlift 4000 feet in length with a 900-foot vertical rise. Skyline Ski Area, near Pocatello, has a long new Pomalift of 3400 feet with a vertical rise of 1300 feet. New Mexico, little thought of as a ski state, has nine areas in altitudes from 7000 to 11,000 feet, best known of which are the Santa Fe Ski Basin and Taos Ski Valley.

How ski centers have altered the look of their communities! Aspen, Colorado, and a hundred places like it years ago were cleaned out of their mineral treasures and abandoned as ghost towns. Then the natural features in surrounding National Forestland were recognized. Aspen now has the longest chairlift in the world, to the mountain summit at 11,300-foot elevation, and a bright, year-round outdoor sports mission to fulfill. The mission at Aspen, at rejuvenated Timberline Lodge and at other places like them is one that makes their mountains smile, for it involves people, lots of people, perhaps even a few who are potbellied. Skiers may grumble somewhat at the end of a cold weekend lift line, like touring symphony musicians waiting to register at a second-rate hotel. But once they start downhill their voices, like the symphony orchestra before an audience, ring forth in resounding joy.

CHAPTER TWENTY-FOUR

# Southern California

We were cruising down the Freeway from Hollywood to the Los Angeles airport, keeping pace with traffic at fifty miles per hour, or perhaps it was sixty, when I thought I heard a hub cap fall to the concrete and roll away irresponsibly. Shouldn't we stop and try to recover it? "Don't be silly," my friend laughed. "Anybody who stepped out in this scramble would be killed in a split second. It will be much simpler to buy a new hub cap."

Happily, this sort of Freeway free-wheeling does not quite exemplify all of modern living in Southern California, although it often appears so on the surface. As in the case of my friend, many people arrive at the end of their working day at pleasant hillside homes within view of the ocean or the mountains. They raise flowers throughout the year in their patio gardens. Few are affected or especially influenced by the little world of celluloid and celebrities. They may have to tolerate smog and traffic tie-ups during the week, but on the weekend they have a great and genuine natural domain around them to explore.

The contemporary marvel of Southern California, of the entire state, really, lies not in its industrial expansion or dizzying population spiral, but in the survival of that natural domain. In many other states the beauty of the outdoors has not fared well against economic pressures. However, the best of California has never lost the edge to the worst of it. There may be more people in the city and the city may have spread into a "city complex," 250 miles long and seventy-five miles wide, from the Mexican border north to Santa Barbara, but one always feels the ardent, enduring presence of the land; there is always some place close by where values are not quite measured in the number of new homes, new depositors, new shopping centers, new industries.

The National Forests are very much a part of the fabric. Only fifteen miles from the Freeway to the airport the San Gabriel Moun-

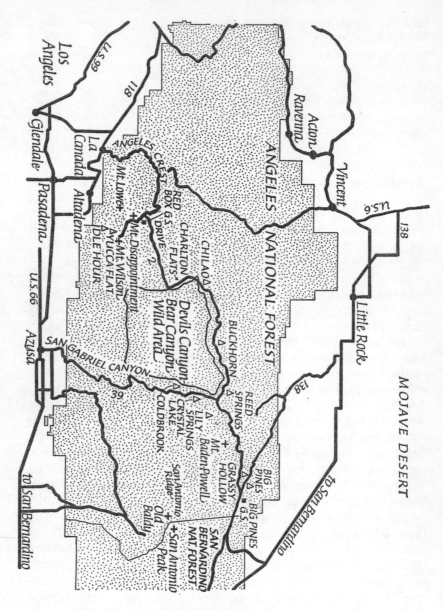

The National Forest, Useful Neighbor to a Great City

tains rise sharply within the Angeles National Forest. The three other National Forests of Southern California—the Los Padres, San Bernardino and Cleveland—lie within the sprawling megalopolis, too, touching Mexico and spilling eastward over the mountains to face the desert. These four National Forests do not produce the greatest volume of timber, do not support the largest herds of livestock, but they *are* closest to the most people. They are the breathing space of cities, dotted with summer camps for children, campgrounds for families, ski slopes, riding trails, picnic sites, scenic motor drives. And beyond the roads are wild lands screened from the influence of our time and protected as sanctuaries of wild creatures and the primitive traveler. The four Forests comprise the watershed of Southern California, in which protection of eroding brush-covered mountains is complicated by a constant threat of fire. If the National Forests did not exist as a natural frontier, neither would the cities, suburbs, citrus groves or much else of modern Southern California.

Californians realized early the need of reserving land as public forests. As Pinchot said, sentiment in the West varied according to the occupations of the people, but California, in particular, was the staunch friend of forestry. John Muir played a major part in cultivating the sensibility of his state, as well as giving voice through his magazine articles to a growing national movement. In Southern California, Abbott Kinney led the way toward establishment of the Angeles National Forest.

Kinney is most remembered, whenever he is remembered, as the developer of Venice, the Southern California beach town. He launched it nobly, with canals for streets, with gondolas and gondoliers, and an aura of culture. Later the town changed into a massive amusement park known as Coney Island of the West. However, Kinney was also a botanist of distinction, an officer of the American Forestry Association and chairman of California's first Board of Forestry, established in 1885. Those were the days before his Venice promotion.

In 1880, Kinney built a ranch in the San Gabriel Valley. The route from Los Angeles passed through what is now Pasadena, a crossroad of one store and one schoolhouse bordered by orchards and by ranches beyond. When he looked aloft at the San Gabriel Range, above the valley and foothills, he saw brush-covered mountains, the source of the San Gabriel, Los Angeles, Big Tujunga and Santa Clara Rivers which flowed to the communities below. Kinney recognized the need of protecting the mountainsides, and was alarmed to see the covering being removed by clearing or fire, leaving barren mesas.

"Trees and bushes, and in fact nearly all vegetable growth have a great power of holding rainwater and retarding its flow until it has time to sink into the earth," he wrote, explaining a belief which later would be universally accepted. Yet he expressed it with clarity a decade before even Pinchot appeared on the scene. "The leaves, twigs and branches intercept the raindrops and diminish their force. The roots and fallen leaves and sticks hold back the water and divide its currents. Besides this, these impediments protect the soil so that it does not cut, thus the water does not get into the well-defined channels where it can concentrate its force. The humus or soil of the forest and brush land has remarkable powers of absorbing moisture. It is like a sponge, in this respect, a quality of the greatest importance to perennial springs. Thus the destruction of the bushes has caused another change. The rains that were formerly absorbed on these lands are no longer taken in. Torrents have been born; orchards, vineyards, roads, fields and fences, formerly safe, and which no one ever thought open to floods, have been damaged, partially destroyed, or altogether washed away.

"The necessity of the hour is an intelligent supervision of the forest land and brush lands of California, with a view to their preservation in such proportion to the other lands of the state as scientific forestry may demonstrate to be necessary to the welfare of the commonwealth."

What was the state of things in San Gabriel Valley before Kinney's time? During the Spanish and Mexican periods cattle raising was the chief use of the land. The social and trading center of Southern California was the Pueblo of Los Angeles, founded in 1781 as a village of adobe homes and shops. By the 1830's and '40's, many *rancheros* either had homes in the Pueblo or would ride in to attend bullfights, church, fiestas or to business affairs.

The *rancheros* were said to be the best horsemen in the world. But with the 1849 gold rush, much of California's best grazing land was taken up for farming and they began to overgraze the valley and foothill ranges. Then they took their cattle and sheep to the higher mountains—one sure sign of spring was the sight of bands of sheep and herds of cattle climbing to the summer range.

The Spanish Californians, however, made little use of the San

Gabriel Mountains except as their source of water. The *rancheros* did not like the chaparral covering, which made poor pasture for their cattle and was difficult for their riders to penetrate. To protect their legs, the *vaqueros* had to wear chaps, a word derived, like chaparral, from the Spanish *chaparra,* or evergreen oak.

Chaparral? It really is a catchall term of the Southwest. The plant species included in the chaparral forest vary with location, amount of rainfall, rate of evaporation induced by warmth and wind, and the expert who happens to be expounding at the moment. The chaparral of Southern California's hills is composed mostly of evergreen shrubs, mixed together in a fantastic, sprawling tangle, growing eight to twelve feet high. Among these are the pointleaf manzanita, with grotesquely crooked, red-barked limbs and glossy leaves, and an attractive urn-shaped blossom in early spring; rabbit brush, a coarse pale sprawler; Ceanothus, or "wild lilacs"; creosote bush, easy to identify by its musty-smelling leaves, resinous twigs, and small yellow flowers; holly-leafed cherry, and California white oak, or gambel-oak, which varies in size from a spreading shrub to a tree.

Although the early Californians avoided the chaparral-covered slopes, they did enter the mountains on a rather savage, inhuman mission: to hunt and capture grizzly bears for the Sunday bull-bear fights in Los Angeles. In the lower part of Millard Canyon, the Arroyo Seco and the area now under water behind Devil's Gate Dam a band of *vaqueros* would swing their lassos over the giant beast until they had reduced him to harmless submission. Then they dragged him to the ring on El Toro Street. The grizzly sometimes dispatched one bull adversary after another. Finally he met his own doom. The spectators, thirsty for blood, shrieked in delight at the sight of noble animals ripping each other apart.

Squatters, homesteaders and bandits were the pioneer settlers of the Angeles National Forest. Even before 1850, when California became a state, they found their way into hidden canyons and fertile valleys which the *rancheros* scorned. One of the earliest settlers was Henry Dalton, the Englishman, who paid Luis Arenas $7000 in 1844 for a 4400-acre ranch—the Azusa de Dalton. He built a thick-walled adobe ranch house near the mouth of San Gabriel Canyon. Dalton Canyon bears his name. In the early seventies the beautifully timbered Chilao Flat was used to change brands and pasture cattle stolen by the black mustachioed bandit Tiburcio Vasquez of Monterrey. This fellow had an inglorious twenty-year career, which began at the age of fifteen when he stabbed a constable and joined a band of horse thieves. Thereafter he led his own company in a daring series of robberies and murders, always one step ahead of the sheriff's posse and the vigilantes. Finally he was captured in Hollywood in 1874 and hanged a year later. Vasquez Rocks, the huge upthrust between Soledad and Mint Canyons, supposedly was the scene of many a merry chase led by the bandit chief with lawmen bringing up the rear.

John Muir visited the San Gabriel Mountains, too. In 1877, he went prowling about and found that even the bears made their way through the chaparral only with difficulty. He was compelled to creep for miles on all fours, through thickets which had become wood-rat villages. His sole companionship came from bears, wolves, foxes and wildcats. For all the solitary travels of his lifetime, Muir probably never experienced loneliness or fear. "Oh, I am not afraid of anyone robbing me," he once told a muscular, brawny youth who barred his way through the woods, "for I don't carry anything worth stealing." This didn't satisfy the wilderness holdup man, who asked Muir if he carried shooting irons. He had none, but threw his hand back to his pistol pocket, marched up close and said daringly, "I allow people to find out if I am armed or not." Then he was allowed to proceed in peace.

What was he looking for in the San Gabriels? Undoubtedly he was fascinated by the botany of chaparral. Perhaps at times he was pursuing the pattern of geology, of the massive fault, or rupture in the earth far below the surface, which extends two-thirds the length of California, then northwest under the Pacific and south across Mexico into the Caribbean. Finally, in hiking through the San Gabriels he arrived at a high summit, a part of the vast, jagged mass upthrust by a mighty underground movement long ago. He saw not the slightest sign of human presence. As far as the eye could reach, the landscape was one vast bee pasture, a rolling wilderness of honey-bloom.

The 1870's were the last years of Southern California's isolation. Until then, large California land holdings were held by a few. Edward F. Beale, for example, owned a 200,000-acre domain in Tejon Valley, composed of four original Mexican grants, which he purchased at bargain prices after he had been appointed Surveyor General of California and Nevada in 1861. Why was he not reappointed four years later? Lincoln is quoted as explaining with a quip: "He became monarch of all he surveyed." Beale, when he was commander of Fort Tejon, once conceived the use of camel trains in the California desert, as in the Sahara, and sold the idea to Congress. Two shiploads arrived in Los Angeles and were dispatched across the mountains. The animals really did not feel much at home. They frightened mules and horses and foundered on rocky soil. Almost everyone gave up, but not Beale; he rode behind his camels in a sulky 160 miles to Los Angeles, to prove their worth.

But the fact clearly remained that practical overland connections were lacking with the East. Then the generous Federal land-grant policy brought the transcontinental railroad into northern California in 1869. It also carved the public domain into a grotesque checkerboard, presenting the railroad with alternate sections along its route to do with as it wished. The Southern Pacific pushed south through the San Joaquin Valley, reaching Los Angeles in 1876. The Santa Fe arrived in 1885.

The railroads now had millions of acres to sell and many transcontinental passenger seats to fill. The boom of land and people began. Round-trip tickets from the Missouri River to California were sold for as low as fifteen dollars and for a few days at one dollar. The Santa Fe organized the California Excursion Association to turn attention to the land of sunshine and, eventually, subdivisions. Special cars, with cooking and sleeping facilities, were placed in service so the California-bound settler could transport his family, his possessions and his livestock all under his own hand and eye.

Land prices leaped skyward. Land was sold everywhere—at the curb, at saloon bars, in restaurants, on the site, at all hours of day and night. Elephants, freaks, free lunches and bands were employed to draw crowds in a monstrous show that was larger and more spectacular than Disneyland. The mountains, deserts and beaches all were on the auction block. Between January 1, 1887, and July 1, 1889, sixty new towns and cities were laid out in Los Angeles County alone.

Somehow the hand of restraint had to be felt. Elsewhere I have spoken of fire as the cruel handmaiden of development in New England, the South and the Lake States. In California, fire swept the state in no lesser proportion. It began in the sheep period and carried over into the new surge of agriculture and settlement. "A great portion of the woody plants that escape the feet and teeth of the sheep," wrote John Muir in his book *The Mountains of California*, "are destroyed by the shepherd by means of running fires which are set everywhere during the dry season for the purpose of burning off the old fallen trunks and underbrush, with a view to improving the pastures, and making more open way for the flocks. These destructive sheep fires sweep through the entire forest belt of the range, from one extremity to the other, consuming not only the underbrush, but the young trees and seedlings on which the permanence of the forest depends; thus setting in motion a long train of evils."

Most burning was done as the sheep were taken down from the mountains in the fall. Smoke was so thick that at times it was hard to see at midday. Fires burned thousands of acres almost everywhere, destroying the mountain cover of timber and brush. Lush, green lands became rolling granite ridges. Yet no attempt was made to stop fires unless someone's place was threatened; then back fires were set and usually the fire headed in some other direction.

But sheepherders were not solely culpable. They were the prime scapegoats, and continue so in history, because of their known practice of burning. But in the 1880's, with the great boom, land was cleared for agriculture—citrus, olive, grape and walnut—in Southern California. An official state report of 1885, referring specifically to the counties of Los Angeles, San Bernardino and San Diego, and the wanton carelessness of the planters and settlers warned: "Every year disastrous fires sweep off vast areas of the mountain covering. These owners set no watch and take no heed of their property, and the fires run into and destroy the timber as well as the brush. This careless and wasteful destruction of the forests is injuring the climate, the agriculture and the future prospects of Southern California."

This statement resembles the writings of Abbott Kinney, or at least the reports he began signing the following year as chairman of the State Board of Forestry. In its first report, the Board declared, "The present fires which desolate the forests of California are a violation of the law and are exceedingly destructive to public property. After continued earnest effort, in many cases with legal advice at our own expense, we are obliged to report that we cannot arrest or convict these fire-setters without the assistance of special officers who can be sent into the mountains to secure evidence and find the depredators." Worst of all were the southern counties. There was perhaps no part of the forest in Ventura which had not been ravaged by fires. "The destruction of the forests in the southern counties," warned the report in its conclusion, "means the destruction of the streams, and that means the destruction of the country."

Forestry in California was not far behind. On March 3, 1891, Congress enacted the Forest Reserve Act, authorizing the President to set apart and reserve in any state or territory the public-land forests "wholly or in part covered with timber or undergrowth, whether of commercial value or not." Almost immediately after the act was passed, Southern Californians were knocking at the White House for Forest Reserves. Their principal reasons revolved around watershed protection and fire. There were little timber values at stake. But year after year uncontrolled fire had burned the brush cover from the hills, producing disaster in the valley areas through alternating erosion, flood and drought. Nevertheless, much to its credit, the Los Angeles Chamber of Commerce cited the role in public recreation which a Reserve might fulfill. On December 20, 1892, President Harrison proclaimed creation of the San Gabriel Forest Reserve. This was followed within two months by the creation of a Reserve in the San Bernardino Mountains and of the Trabuco Reserve, farther to the south, the beginning of the present Cleveland National Forest.

Farther north, in the pine-timbered Central Sierra Nevadas, President Harrison set aside another large area in 1893, the Sierra Forest Reserve, consisting of 4,000,000 acres. In this general area, Yosemite and the Mariposa grove of giant sequoias already were under National Park protection. Thus, with creation of a Forest Reserve, a large part of one of the greatest mountain areas in the world was saved to the public.

Some of the large landowners were disturbed at the permanent protection accorded to a domain of this size. They had acquired millions of acres under liberal land laws and subsidies, and had indulged in various land rackets and frauds. For example, during the tenure of the Timber and Stone Act, almost 3,000,000 acres of California land passed into private hands but only the smallest percentage was ever used for settlement by the applicant himself. The practice of "dummy entrymen" was about as widespread as in Oregon. In addition, about 10 per cent of public lands in California had been granted by the Federal Government to the state—much of which the state proceeded to give away for a mere $1.25 per acre. Thus, the extension of Forest Reserves faced a degree of opposition in California, as elsewhere, but public revulsion against timberland frauds and chronic sheep overgrazing, along with awareness of watershed protection, was far more decisive. By 1905 a total of 15,000,000 acres was included within the Reserves in California.

317

Forestry followed some curious routes in those days. In 1906, Inman F. Eldredge, one of the handful of trained foresters on duty in California, was assigned to locate boundaries on the desert side. It was a serious, important project aimed at keeping sheep out of the National Forests. They were already forbidden but herders persisted in entering, claiming they couldn't identify the boundary lines. "Cap" Eldredge traveled with a group of four boundary locators, plus cook and horse wrangler. They covered a distance of 140 miles up and down rugged, volcanic-formed obsidian ranges without once seeing a tree. Only when they crossed the wagon route of the twenty-mule teams hauling borax from Death Valley were they within reach of desert outposts selling water and provisions. They went about their dry, dusty and unsung mission, establishing markers every quarter of a mile, at the top of every ridge and bottom of every gulch. On both sides of the markers they painted the words, "This Is a National Forest." But they had to write in two languages, Spanish as well as English, for many California sheepmen were Basques, the great flockmasters of history, who felt completely at ease in the rugged Western mountains. On flat plains, Eldredge and his crew were obliged to build their markers out of sagebrush, tying flags of muslin.

In such ways did the Forest Service enter into California's history, tradition and way of life. Now there are nineteen National Forests in California. They cover 23,000,000 acres, although this figure is deceptive—4,000,000 acres within the boundaries are privately owned. The Forests extend from the Cascades through the heart of the Sierras, where snowfalls sometimes pile in wintry depths of 500 inches, south to the desert and the Mexican border. As a source of timber, they yield a billion and a half board feet yearly. The principal trees harvested are ponderosa pine, sugar pine, and white and shasta-red fir in the Sierras; Douglas-fir and the towering redwood along the northern coast; Jeffrey and Coulter pine further south. The Forests are open to regulated grazing by about 100,000 cattle and 80,000 sheep. But they also include four major wilderness areas totaling 1,000,000 acres, plus fourteen smaller wild areas. These places are the refuge of the coyote, wildcat and mountain lion; they provide running room for the fleet antelope.

The National Forests have long been loved and enjoyed for their scenery and the opportunities they afford for outdoor recreation. Even in pre-automobile days, Southern Californians would turn out by the hundreds at Eastertime to pick poppies, the cloth of gold cov-

318

ering the desert hillsides after a rainy winter. In the late 1880's, visitors liked to take the "Grand Round," a carriage drive from Los Angeles to Pasadena and the mountains. First stop was the famous new Raymond Hotel, commanding a magnificent view of orange groves, growing Pasadena, and of the San Gabriels to the north. Then the carriage drive continued to Pasadena and the foothills, on to San Gabriel Mission and back to Los Angeles. Shortly the Mount Lowe Railway was built to the 3300-foot elevation; it was the creation of Professor Thaddeus S. C. Lowe, the famous Civil War balloonist. The first passengers ascended this spectacular incline on the Fourth of July, 1893, from Mountain Junction, Altadena, and for the next forty-five years a visit to Los Angeles was hardly complete without taking this ride above the city. Atop Mount Lowe stood the Echo Mountain House, which advertised itself as the best hotel in Southern California. Among its attributes it included the purest of water, most equable climate, ferny glens, babbling brooks and shady forests. Bravely and immodestly stated, but visitors found all these and more. For a time the energetic Professor Lowe planned to fly passengers to the mountain summit in an airship. He organized a corporation, printed a handsome prospectus, sold subscriptions and gained the endorsement of the Pasadena Board of Trade, but his dream never reached reality.

Then came a hiking era. Sunday and weekend hikers thronged canyon trails in a mass display of sport and vigor. For example, Sturtevant Trail led up through beautiful Big Santa Anita Canyon alongside a tumbling stream and through spruce groves, connecting with another trail to the top of Mount Wilson. Pack trains of burros, mules and horses plied their way up and down these trails in great numbers. By 1919, congestion was so heavy that 5000 hikers were tallied in a single weekend. As for pack animals, the Forest Service had to issue regulations to ease the traffic jam. Pack trains were given the right-of-way over all horsemen and pedestrians. A bell was required on at least one animal in every train. Those in charge must be above eighteen years of age. No bicycles allowed, and definitely no motorcycles.

The day of the donkey ended twenty years ago. Now paved highways lead upward through deep, tortuous canyons into a realm of swiftly changing vistas. At one point, sharp peaks wear a cover of chaparral. But soon they give way to somber, pine-studded slopes and rolling timberlands, then to a mountainside shimmering in Western sunlight, or to a misty forest at twilight.

The most famous route is the Angeles Crest Drive, which starts from La Cañada (Can-ya'-da), a neighboring community to Pasadena, and takes about two hours to drive, or three hours including the new link with the San Gabriel Canyon Road. The Drive winds upward through groves of spruce, oak and bay trees, and rocky gorges strewn with fern, to Red Box Divide, marking the crest of the ridge between drainage areas of the San Gabriel and Arroyo Seco (dry creek) Rivers. The Divide was named for a large red box, a landmark for years, in which rangers kept fire-fighting gear. On the West Fork of the San Gabriel possibly the first ranger station was built with funds provided by the Federal Government. That was in 1900, a few months after two rangers in the Bitterroot Valley of Montana had erected a station with their own money. Here in the Angeles National Forest all of seventy dollars was allocated for a log-cabin headquarters. The rangers of those days paid all their expenses, including horse maintenance, out of their salaries of fifty dollars monthly. They were lucky if they got to the nearest town or store three or four times during the summer season. They fought fires in dense brush with crude tools, built trails and camped out as often as they slept under roof. In 1901, Supervisor Everett B. Thomas announced in a letter to Washington that rangers in his Forest were wearing uniforms. They were the first to do so in the United States. The design possibly was his own choice: the style of the Cavalry with light-colored sombrero hat. The jacket had brass buttons engraved with eagles, while on each side of the coat collars the letters "S.G.F.R." (San Gabriel Forest Reserve) were embroidered in gold wire. "The uniform is very neat and handsome," Supervisor Thomas reported proudly, "and the rangers have all been happily in favor of wearing them."

A spur road from Red Box leads on to Mount Wilson (elevation 5710 feet), a great landmark and magnificent viewpoint of Southern California. It is not without blemish. The road was blazed to the summit in 1864 by Benjamin Davis Wilson, a pioneer trapper and settler. In 1889, the mountaintop was homesteaded, although no home was ever built; the government simply gave away 1000 of the most valuable acres in Southern California for use as a resort. That year Professor W. H. Pickering of Harvard University arrived and began to erect Mount Wilson's first telescope and dome, which he later moved to Peru, either to flee the rattlesnakes or to get a better view of the southern sky. In 1904, the owner of the mountain granted a long-term lease to the Carnegie Institution of Washington to erect an observatory, which has since extended the frontiers of knowledge into the depths of outer space. The Mount Wilson Hotel Company, which operates an ancient wooden lodging house, now charges an admission of fifty cents to the mountain, declaring in a folder that it is "fundamentally responsible for the astronomy privileges afforded the public." Be that as it may, the views from Mount Wilson are superb. On a clear day you can see Catalina Island sixty-seven miles away, well beyond the ships in Los Angeles Harbor, and at night the sparkling lights of sixty cities, a sight unequaled in the world (and probably undreamed of by Carnegie astronomers when they chose the site sixty years ago). Eight telescopes, white buildings, towers and domes, operated by the Carnegie Institution, are scattered among the trees. The observatory with a 100-inch telescope and an adjacent museum, displaying spectacular astronomical photography, are open during certain hours. There is no admission fee.

There are signs of heavy and varied recreational use at many points along the Angeles Crest Drive. Or, to put it another way, here is the evidence of people's kinship with and affinity toward their mountains. At Charlton Flats, one hour's drive from downtown Los Angeles, there is a large picnic area in a beautiful grove of ponderosa pine and incense cedar. At Chilao, three miles north, there are camping facilities as well as picnic tables. Chilao is an entry station into Devil Canyon-Bear Canyon Wild Area, 36,000 acres of rough, rugged country with elevations up to 8200 feet. Twin Peaks, its most prominent feature, is a challenge to explorer groups and mountain climbers. This is winter country, too, with chairlift and ski slopes operating from December to March at nearby Waterman Mountain. Newcomb's Ranch Inn, at Chilao, if my calculations are correct, is the closest place to Los Angeles where skiers can order hot buttered rum.

The Drive winds around Waterman Mountain and now links with the San Gabriel Canyon Road into Crystal Lake, one of the few natural lakes in the mountains, with facilities for swimming, boating and fishing, as well as camping. Eastward toward the desert, another new road leads to Big Pines Camp, a cool retreat in summer, with swimming and fishing, and a ski center in winter. Those of us who are out for the drive can return along the San Gabriel River (which may or may not have any water in it). A fair degree of gold mining was done in this region in the 1850's, and again in the 1930's when

321

throngs of depression victims panned prayerfully, but without much success. Between times, it was the refuge of gentlemen and scholars like John Knox, known as the "Bad Man of San Gabriel," Twitchlip Kelly, One-Eyed Mountain Charlie, Two-Gun Doc Rosenkrantz, Peg Leg Bill Coynes.

Now a series of dams lies astride the San Gabriel, designed to stabilize the stream channels and to reduce watershed erosion. Elsewhere in the Forest no less than seventy concrete structures are being erected to control flash floods and prevent silt and rock from rolling into the Santa Anita Reservoir. These dams are a sort of stitching at the seams, holding the eroding, fragile land in place until the time when pine roots and fallen leaves and sticks, of which Abbott Kinney spoke, spread a protective web across fire-scarred and chaparral-covered hillsides.

The Angeles National Forest does not really have the superlative kind of scenery to be found in the Sierras or the Cascades. Some people would even consider it depressing, with its scrawny brush on the western flanks and barren sandstone knobs and pinnacles facing the Mojave Desert on the east. But I think of it as a beautiful specimen of America and I wish that when foreign dignitaries are brought to the West Coast to see our regular folks at work and play in the Brown Derby and Disneyland someone would say for once, "Let's show them the Angeles Crest." The Angeles Crest may lack glamour in the usual sense, but here is a living place at the back door of a great city, where trees grow, mountains erode, fires are fought, water is stored for orchards and gardens and a million people escape to natural reality.

Fifty miles north of Hollywood, as the condor flies, Carl B. Koford camped inside a cave in Los Padres National Forest. By day he would traverse jumbled granite cliffs and brush fields where there were no trails, and by night he would keep vigil on an eerie moonlit world outside his cavern door.

He lived this way, on and off, a total of 500 days, back-packing, cave dwelling, climbing and observing. When he departed from the Sespe Wildlife Area in the Topatopa Mountains he carried with him the story of a vanishing American, the California condor, struggling for survival in its very last, shrunken stronghold.

Dr. Koford watched a magnificent bird, unsurpassed by any on this continent for the breadth of its wingspread, often extending ten feet from tip to tip. He saw it take off from clifftops and ledges, circling into rising air currents, occasionally flapping heavily until borne aloft, then setting on a long glide toward a ridge or knoll miles away.

Less than 100 of the condors (*Gymnogyps californianus*) now remain, although once they ranged all over California, into the Pacific Northwest, Mexico and as far off as Florida. Lewis and Clark reported sighting condors feeding on fish and whales when they neared the mouth of the Columbia River in 1805, but within forty years the shy wilderness bird disappeared from that region. In California, before man came, the condor fed on carcasses of antelope and dwarf elk. With the advent of stock raising, it found new sources of food in the carcasses of sheep, cattle and horses. But the odds of settlement, invasion of nesting areas and unrestricted hunting were against it. By 1900 the birds were rare, yet even then many were shot and many eggs taken by curiosity collectors.

Now the bird, in the remnant of its forces, has protection of Federal and state law. The Forest Service has given it special recognition in the Sespe Wildlife Area for twenty-five years. It is one of the rarest living species, delicately balanced on the brink of extinction. Dr. Koford's study, aimed to learn more about the condor and how to save it, was conducted in behalf of the National Audubon Society and the University of California.

He watched the bird by day and night, with endurance and patience, through mating, incubation of the single egg, childhood, first unsteady flight from brush, rocks or trees, and finally adulthood and its spectacle of soaring through space.

The condor perches on clifftops, potholes and bare branches, a bird larger than the turkey vulture, with orange head and neck, a triangular patch of pure white on the undersurface of the wing. It often doesn't leave the perch until several hours after sunrise, apparently awaiting favorable air currents. On windy days it sets forth early, on calm days late, but always first stretching one wing and then the other as though testing the breeze. In taking off from level ground in calm air, the condor runs with great strides, neck outstretched and wings beating for twenty yards or more.

Circling in air currents, the condor rises. Now and then it flexes its tremendous wings or gives a single wide flap to increase speed. Just as a large transport plane takes more time to turn than small aircraft, the condor requires about fifteen seconds to turn a full circle in soaring, while turkey vultures, golden eagles and large hawks circle in about half that time. Condors flap their wings at a rate of about twice per second, while the other birds flap more rapidly.

Unlike the South American condor, the California condor does not kill. It is not a predator, but feeds on carcasses, principally of livestock. Once, where roads were favorably located, Dr. Koford followed nine condors for forty miles from their roost to find them feeding on a dog. Sometimes as many as thirty condors dine together, consuming within ten minutes a calf or deer, eating almost all the skin and innards, leaving the skeleton and hide. Then, after their meals, they frequently visit the clear pools atop waterfalls near their roosts. They drink, bathe and stand in the sun with wings outstretched. Young birds often spend hours at the pools nibbling grass, sticks and pebbles, nipping each other playfully and sunning.

By night, as Dr. Koford observed from his cave within a half mile of the roosting area, the condor crouches down on clifftop or tree branch, resting his breast on the perch, with head and neck thrust out of sight under one wing. Thirty of his friends and playmates are settled in the roost in the same eerie manner.

The remaining 100 condors live a precarious existence. Stock raising, which furnishes most condor food, has dwindled. Anyway, the modern stockman prevents the death of cattle on the open range and quickly disposes of his dead cattle. However, stockmen within reach of the condor country are encouraged to leave carcasses for the birds to feed upon, and many do. The condor is wary of humans, fleeing from their nests, or even their nestlings, when they are disturbed. And outside the Sespe Wildlife Area an increasing number of roads has furnished hunters, campers and photographers access into back country.

In 1937 the Forest Service took steps to close the game refuge in the Topatopa Mountains, east of Ojai and Fillmore, to public entry. This was not simple. The Service lacked the authority to prevent oil leasing and, when oil was discovered in nearby Cuyama Valley, the condor sanctuary faced a serious threat. Since then, an area sixteen miles square has been set aside (efforts were made to protect a larger realm), with oil and gas operations prohibited except by directional or slant drilling, which does not disturb the surface of the area.

Occasionally a few condors are seen as far north as Fresno, as far south as San Diego and Baha California. When I was traveling about the Los Padres National Forest, I kept both eyes peeled in the hope of spotting one but all I ever saw was a raven or a hawk. The usual luck. However, I'm willing to leave the condors to their own country (oil and all) and settle for Dr. Koford's account.

"The California condor," he wrote, "is a majestic bird in its natural rugged environment as it sweeps in superbly controlled flight over crests of ridges and great slopes of tangled chaparral. The air passing through its wing tips sets up a steady whine as it is pressed into service to keep the great glider aloft. The condor passes overhead, the sound recedes, and the bird now circles and scans with keen eyes the ground below and the activities of its fellow condors."

A year doesn't go by without critical fires in the National Forests of Southern California. They occur all over the state but especially in the four southern Forests. Summers are dry—so are springs and autumns. Fires are caused accidentally by children playing with fire, by fireworks, car exhausts, flue sparks. Many times they are set deliberately and maliciously. Once begun, by whatever cause, flames of burning chaparral sweep up the slopes with all the speed of a prairie fire, and with heat far more intense. Consequently, fire becomes so grave a hazard that some areas are closed during the dry summer, just when people most need and want to retreat to the cool mountains.

But a year doesn't go by without somebody trying to do something to reduce the danger and damage of fire. "In spite of tremendous advances in fire fighting," an official of the National Lumber Manufacturers Association remarked in discussing Southern California, "the only difference that I notice in thirty years is better news coverage." He is entitled to his opinion, but I think many people would disagree. For example, members of women's clubs, the Sierra Club, Boy Scouts, teachers and school children are trying to protect the National Forests through their Penny Pines Plantations.

Penny Pines are grove plantings of green pines, which are far less flammable than chaparral and slow down fires in their course. The idea was born in 1941 in the Sportswomen's Club of San Francisco. "We would like to plant seedlings in burned-over areas," the Club proposed to the Forest Service, "and use this program to acquaint people with conservation and forest use."

The idea spread. Penny Pines has since become a byword in the schoolroom, and a household word through the work of the California Federation of Women's Clubs. In Southern California, San

325

Diego clubwomen established the first Penny Pines Plantation in Cleveland National Forest. It requires sixty-eight dollars to purchase one acre's stand of trees, but Californians contributed their pennies, dimes and dollars to the cause. One teacher grew African violets for her class to sell to raise money for its own grove. Four young women presented a plantation as a memorial to their uncle. A women's club in San Gabriel Valley made and sold litterbags.

Over $30,000 has been raised to purchase three and a half million seedlings from state nurseries at Mount Shasta and Placerville. They are now growing in ten National Forests and some of the first planted are now forty feet high. Forest Service fire crews do most of the planting during the winter months, the one season when fire danger is at a safe minimum. But they are helped by volunteers, Boy Scouts, Sierra Club members and other outdoor groups. In the southern forests they often use the "Spanish method," placing three rocks around the seedling to conserve moisture and to discourage small, hungry animals from nibbling. Scouts during their Conservation Week not only plant trees, but prune and thin.

Penny Pine planters have a long way to go. Over 1700 fires burn yearly in California's National Forests. The damage and dangers are almost beyond belief. For example, destruction caused by the fires of 1960 would have equaled a half-mile-wide belt from one end of the state to the other. In 1955, the Haystack fire in the Klamath National Forest burned 87,000 acres and caused $25,000,000's worth of damage. In 1953, fifteen men were burned to death in the Rattlesnake fire in Mendocino National Forest. In 1959, over 2500 men fought for nine days to control the Refugio Canyon fire, which burned 85,000 acres of valuable watershed in the Los Padres National Forest near Santa Barbara. These fire fighters included Marines, state police, Los Angeles firemen, along with the Forest Service. There are no jurisdictional barriers when it comes to fire in California.

In these circumstances, fire fighting becomes a specialized skill. The Forest Service has trained hot-shot crews for commando duty in the toughest spots. "Pre-attack" plans include the location of base camps, helicopter sites, estimates of number of men and equipment needed, answers to questions of slope and soil, all designed to win a head start—or at least to win an even break once the fire begins.

All very grim and often heartbreaking, but possibly one day the brush-covered and blackened hills will be green with Penny Pines.

Farewell, condor and company. Farewell, tawny desert and purple mountains. Farewell, I thought, while racing through the metropolis of the Pacific Littoral to the airport. We arrived barely in time. I wished my friend the last farewell, grabbed my bag and hurried to the airline gate.

As sometimes happens in these cases, the plane was late. And at this point, I believe, this narrative through our National Forests had its beginning. Shortly, the hour was dusk.

# CHAPTER TWENTY-FIVE

## *Whose Woods These Are*

The woods, as we have seen, are lovely, dark and deep. Through them we have traveled a considerable journey, pursuing a thread of science and history and poetry and politics as it winds and unwinds. But have we come to the end? Or to the beginning? Or found the threads of the thread?

There is no end, no beginning, no neatest of packages. Ahead lie many miles to go, unanswered mysteries of life. I wonder why the tree does really grow. I wonder about the little worm, which Charles Darwin revealed as one of the great architects of the earth and its history. I wonder about all the uses and conflicts for our shrinking land, and which view is absolutely right and which is absolutely wrong.

I wish I could be as sure as some of those with positive and precise outlooks regarding our National Forests.

I wish I could be as sure as the National Lumber Manufacturers Association, which believes it is basically wrong for the government to own productive forest land.

I wish I could be as sure as the Sierra Club, which believes that grazers on National Forests are "rough riders" who are bound and determined to "continue the depredations of soil on the nation's steep rangelands." And that "saw-log foresters are gouging the steep slopes, silting streams and reservoirs, adding to floods, destroying fisheries, in country where they need not and should not be operating."

I wish I could be as sure as some of the people in Nevada, Idaho and other states who want to change certain National Forests into National Parks because they are convinced a tourist bonanza is sure to follow.

I think the reasons behind such proposals are unworthy of the National Parks and cheapen their concept as museums of America. But everyone has a right to his conviction and the more people who take an interest in parks, forests and forestry, the better our land will be. Possibly in these pages I have expressed opinions with which you disagree. By all means, feel free. The main point is that more of us ought to be aware of the background, problems and prospects of our National Forests in order to insure a future course, whatever it may be, based on the fullest democratic expression.

Forests are no more static than people. The National Forests have been undergoing change, and a changing relationship with the national fabric, since the first day of their establishment. So have their uses. Timber, water, mining, recreation, grazing, scientific study, protection of wildlife and wilderness.

For example, I am leafing through a little forty-two-page book, *The Use of the National Forests,* the well-known "Use Book," which bears the hand of Gifford Pinchot. Here, in the 1907 edition, Pinchot explained that the main objectives in creating National Forests were to prevent their destruction by fire and reckless cutting, ". . . to save the timber for the use of the people and to hold the mountain forests as great sponges to give out steady flows of water for use in the fertile valleys below." Land was still plentiful in America. Pinchot could afford to talk of National Forests as encompassing both public and private holdings within their boundaries and of their role in opening the West. He was also mindful of the political realities of the day. "The main thing is that the land, as well as what grows on it, must be used for the purpose for which it is most valuable," the early Use Book declares. "On it may be built stores, hotels, residences, power plants, mills and many other things. All these are advantages to National Forests, because they help to get the fullest use out of land and its resources. Railroads, wagon roads, trails, canals, flumes, reservoirs, and telephone and power lines may be constructed whenever and wherever they are needed, as long as they do no unnecessary damage to the Forest. Improvements of this kind help to open up the country, and that is what is wanted."

Recreation? A lone paragraph sums it up: "Quite incidentally, also, the National Forests serve a good purpose as playgrounds for the people. They are used more or less every year by campers, hunters, fishermen, and thousands of pleasure seekers from nearby towns. They are great recreation grounds for a large part of the people of the West, and their value in this respect is well worth considering."

Now, recreation is a major use and not an incidental one. The

330

West *has* been opened and the National Forests are more like a barrier to prevent it from splitting wide open, from seam to seam.

With all the multifarious pressures, are we getting the most we can out of our National Forests? In certain ways, we are not.

One is the matter of summer homes. The Forest Service has learned, sometimes painfully, a lot about recreation and the kind of facilities it should provide. Thirty years ago the Chief of Recreation decried the invasion of "the noisy, inconsiderate barbarian, purposely scornful of the tenets of neatness, sanitation and fire protection." He expressed comfort in finding proportionately fewer of this type, "the novice, the amateur in woodcraft and nature study, the person whose liberty and means are still so new that he has not learned to use them." His joy was in the increase of visitors who "realize the beauties of the forest cannot be plumbed by swift and noisy movement from point to point, or by hasty and superficial sampling of only the most obvious and inescapable elements, and desire means whereby they can tarry and seek out the true spirit of the forest."

For these people who ostensibly conformed to standards of nature esthetics the summer-home community was developed. It was "carefully planned . . . with little or no conflict with other forest uses." Our friend, the recreation chief, believed that, "By quiet insistence on reasonable standards of arrangement, exterior design, color schemes, lot maintenance and sanitation, the natural environment can be maintained."

It hasn't quite worked out that way. There are now 19,000 such residences under special permit. The owners pay the government a minimum amount for the right to build a summer cottage in a sylvan setting. These summer homes, as Edward P. Cliff, Assistant Chief of the Forest Service, has conceded, have grown into a "special king-sized headache." Assuredly, they have brought happy hours to their owners. But a great many have deteriorated into tourist slums and eyesores, far below the lofty standards of design and maintenance conceived years ago. Almost all are located at choice spots, along lake-shores and streamsides, which could be developed as campgrounds—certainly bringing happy hours to far more people.

Summer-home owners, like the old-time ranchers, presume Federal land is theirs forever by right of occupancy and use. I suppose most of us, once installed, would feel the same way and would resist any effort to make us move. The Forest Service has improved its policy considerably, but for the fullest use of National Forests the day of

331

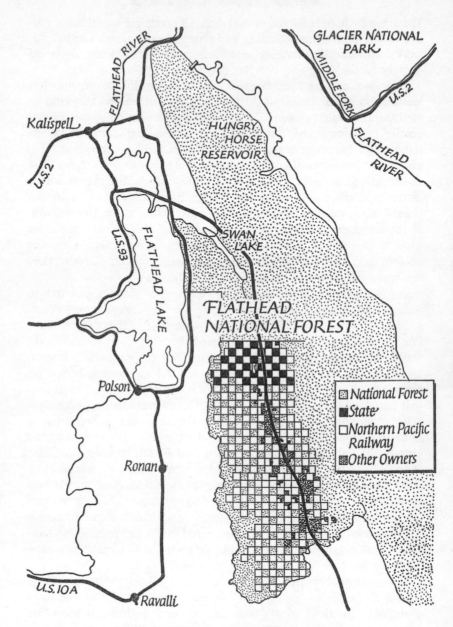

GLACIER NATIONAL PARK

MIDDLE FORK

U.S.2

FLATHEAD RIVER

FLATHEAD RIVER

Kalispell

U.S.2

HUNGRY HORSE RESERVOIR

U.S.93

FLATHEAD LAKE

SWAN LAKE

FLATHEAD NATIONAL FOREST

Polson

National Forest
State
Northern Pacific Railway
Other Owners

Ronan

U.S.10A

Ravalli

A Typical Pattern of Divided Ownership

the summer home should be ended completely. Owners deserve consideration for their investments and should be permitted a reasonable period for amortization, but all the homesites ought to revert ultimately to the public.

Even worse is the checkerboard pattern of private ownership intermingled in our public land. Often it is frightful and disgraceful. In motoring through a National Forest, you are apt to come upon a cluster of faded frame dwellings, or even blighted shanties marring a beautiful parcel of scenery. They are fire hazards and sometimes the starting point of fires that sweep over thousands of acres. Not all "in holdings" are unattractive, but invariably they make land administration difficult and costly.

How did this pattern ever begin? In Montana, as an example, the state was given grants of land, scattered in small tracts, under the Organic Act of the Territory. Homesteaders could go wherever they wished on the public domain, sometimes claiming land that proved unfit for farming or settlement. The Northern Pacific Railway was given alternate sections on a strip forty miles wide paralleling its tracks through Montana. And when the alternate sections were already occupied, the railroad had the privilege of selecting an equal area of land outside the strip. Further complications arose around the beginning of the century, when the railroad sold much of its holdings, bringing many others into the problem of intermeshed ownership. The illustration on page 332, showing the land pattern within one Montana National Forest, could be duplicated scores of times on a national scale.

This situation is not hopeless. Since 1947 the Northern Pacific and the Forest Service have been unscrambling their holdings through exchanges. Land exchange ought to be undertaken on a concerted scale throughout the entire Forest System. Where choice areas are involved, along rivers and lake shores, Congress ought to give the Forest Service money to buy land. It will never make a better investment. Scenic places like Toxaway Falls, North Carolina, and Oak Creek Canyon, Arizona, should have protection for use and enjoyment by all.

The intermingling of private and public ownership gives rise to numerous problems of access. The private owner is free to cross government property to get to his land. But can you—and you may be a hiker, logger or hunter—cross his property to get to your land, that is, to the National Forest?

The "open road" policy is recognized by most landowners, but not by all. About a thousand new rights-of-way are secured each year, through negotiation or condemnation after court hearings. But thousands of cases remain unresolved and new cases are always arising. Why should the Colorado rancher grant access across his land when he can hold a pleasant monopoly over National Forest scenery for the benefit of his guests? Why should the big timber company of the Northwest grant a right-of-way into the National Forest when, by refusing, he can bar his competitor?

In the area of timber production, the consequence is serious. The Forest Service does not open bidding on timber unless there is access for all who want to bid. Consequently, in large-scale areas the timber harvested is far below the level known as "maximum allowable cut." This contributes to hazards of fire and disease in overmature trees. It prevents the nation from getting much-needed timber.

For several years legislation has been pending in Congress which would remedy this condition by establishing right-of-way as a reciprocal arrangement between the government and private landowners.

Another pressing legislative question revolves around land used for mining purposes.

In 1955, Congress took the first positive step in over fifty years to protect the National Forests from mining abuses—or rather from abuses under the guise of mining. Before that time anyone was free to stake out a claim under the ancient mining law of 1872. It was a useful act in its day, when there was far more land than people and the nation could afford to give away portions of it to the hardy prospector who opened the uncharted desert and mountains. But in more recent years, prior to 1955, thousands of mining claims were filed with other purposes in mind: to obtain land for speculation, real-estate development, timber, tourist resorts, filling stations. When Chief Forester McArdle came before a Congressional committee in May, 1955, he warned that mining constituted the most important single problem confronting the Forest Service and was becoming ever more acute.

"Fifty years ago, when the National Forests were established," he said, "mining claims were not the problem they are today. Prospecting was done by a relatively few bona-fide miners. The National Forests were inaccessible to most people. There weren't the conflicting pressures for surface use, and the job of managing the National Forests was largely custodial. Today the situation is entirely different. Population of the West has greatly increased. The highway and the automobile have taken the National Forests out of the hinterlands, and put them in the back yard of metropolitan areas." While Chief McArdle spoke, new claims were being filed on the National Forests at the rate of seven every hour, or 5000 every month. In a single four-week period, 100,000 acres of National Forestland were staked out to mining claims. Many of them were not for valuable metals, but for sand, gravel, cinder, building stone. The claimants could seek patent from the Bureau of Land Management—that is, outright ownership of the land—after performing a minimum amount of development work and making a location survey. The Forest Service had the right to challenge any claim, on grounds of insufficient evidence of minerals, and it did so in thousands of cases.

Nevertheless, in the late 1940's and early fifties, numerous individuals discovered they could stake out claims for building stone in Oak Creek Canyon, one of the nation's most scenic areas. Their clear intention was development of summer cabins and recreation businesses. Finally, a special act of Congress eliminated Oak Creek Canyon from the purview of the mining laws. And in Oregon, in the Al Serena case, the Forest Service fought hard to keep land from going to patent, but was overruled by the highest level of the Federal Government. The question was raised anew by Congressman Michael J. Kirwan, of Ohio, in budget hearings of 1960:

MR. KIRWAN: Have they mined any minerals in that area leased to Al Serena?

MR. CLIFF (Edward P. Cliff, Assistant Chief Forester): You are referring to the Al Serena case in the State of Oregon?

MR. KIRWAN: Yes.

MR. CLIFF: The lands are now privately owned. They went to patent in 1954.

MR. KIRWAN: How about the mining of minerals? They are employing a lot of people?

MR. CLIFF: We have no way of knowing whether or not they are doing any mining underground. Our field men have reported to us that they have seen no exterior evidence of mining activity.

MR. KIRWAN: Of course, the timber is gone, is it not?

MR. CLIFF: No, sir. Part of the timber has been cut but part of it is still there.

MR. KIRWAN: And they are waiting for it to get a little riper.

335

These two tales of Oak Creek Canyon and Al Serena recall the early techniques of obtaining Federal land, which have never quite gone out of vogue.

The historic act of July 23, 1955, known as Public Law 167, closed the gap to some, but not all, abuses. The act eliminated the discovery of common sand, stone, gravel, pumice or cinders as a basis for mining claims. It created a distinction between surface and underground resources before a claim goes to patent; this means the Forest Service has the right to harvest and sell the timber and permit grazing, while prospecting and mining proceed. Another provision has enabled the Forest Service to undertake a vast re-examination of more than 1,000,-000 mining claims, filed over long periods of time, in order to resolve the status of surface rights. Many claims proved abandoned and invalid. In the first four years after passage of the act, the Forest Service surveyed and determined its right to administer the timber and other surface resources of some 35,000,000 acres. This is very painstaking, complicated work undertaken on the ground and through the courts, but a tremendous amount of land is continually being reclaimed for public use.

The 1955 act could not have passed without the co-operation of the American Mining Congress, one of the most powerful of all lobbies in Washington and in the West. Why it should sit in judgment, like a member of the court, in all legislative matters relating to mining is another question. But the truth is that if the mining association had not told Congress that legitimate mining could survive in harmony with timber, grazing and recreation, as provided in the bill, the whole issue would probably still be in the talking stage.

Some energetic citizens have not been discouraged by the 1955 act in their efforts to use the mining law as a means of acquiring property cheaply. In Oregon, for example, one man filed 250 claims on land averaging 60,000 board feet of timber per acre. The total volume on all his claims amounted to 300,000,000 board feet, which he openly planned to cut as soon as the claims were patented. The lands were found to be nonmineral in character, but this involved technical examination of 250 individual claims, followed by proceedings before a hearing examiner and the Bureau of Land Management. There are many similar cases pending and constantly arising.

Regardless of the validity of the claim, should a miner be able to acquire land, which all the people own, as his private property? The Mining Congress feels that he should, because he has always been

336

able to do so. "We believe," declares Raymond B. Holbrook, chairman of the public-lands committee of the Mining Congress, "that the unprecedented development of the mineral resources of this nation and its ability to produce the basic raw materials so essential to our economy and so vital to our national defense is largely due to the basic concepts and principles of our mining laws. They are based on the premises that minerals in public lands should be developed by private enterprise and that, as an incentive and reward for discovery and development of them, title to the lands may be acquired."

There are some of us who feel it is time to change the basic premise. The timber industry cannot patent land, although it provides wood to the nation. Ranchers cannot patent land, although they furnish beef to the nation. There is no longer any patenting of homesteads (except in isolated cases and in Alaska), since passage of the Taylor grazing act nearly thirty years ago. The oil and gas, oil shale, potash, phosphate sodium and coal industries cannot patent land, since passage of the leasing act of 1920.

And yet the miners continue to receive their "reward and incentive." The late Senator Richard L. Neuberger, of Oregon, proposed legislation by which leasing would become the basic premise in mining on public lands. Such a law would not discourage prospecting or mining, where they properly belong, but would assure that lands now in public ownership remain in public ownership, even after they are depleted of their mineral resources. The old concept of the public domain as something to be given away has long ended. And revision of the mining laws, an archaic vestige of the era when grizzled prospectors rustled a grubstake and trekked to the deep recesses of the West, is long overdue.

Mining, ranching, logging—these all involve commercial interests with their special pressures and demands on the National Forests. There is also the classic, historic struggle within the Federal Government. Not over whose woods these are, but over who shall have the privilege and power to administer them.

"Grazing is an agricultural problem. The National Forests are in the main an agricultural problem," insisted an official of the Department of Agriculture in 1901, at a time when Gifford Pinchot and his followers were trying to pry the Forests from the Department of Interior. "Grazing on the National Forests, timber control, insect

337

diseases, predatory animal control are all directly or indirectly agricultural problems."

Consequently Theodore Roosevelt effected the transfer, but the Interior Department has never stopped trying to recapture the Forests, either one at a time, or altogether. And when the Taylor grazing act was passed in the twenties, both departments contested anew jurisdiction over grazing.

"With the administration of all these laws (governing the old open range and the public domain) vested in the Interior Department, it seems only logical and in the interest of good administration that the control and regulation of grazing should also be vested in it," said Secretary Work, speaking for the Interior Department, "and this applies with equal force to the nontimbered grazing areas now included within National Forest limits."

"As to the matter of jurisdiction," responded Secretary of Agriculture Wallace (whose son would fill the same job and fight the same battle twenty years later), "I am not so much concerned about who does the work as I am that it be done, done promptly and done well." Secretary Wallace had more to say about the desirability of placing all grazing lands in the Forest Service; and certainly the Forest Service has fared much better in the grazing field than has the Interior Department's Bureau of Land Management under the domination of the ranching industry.

But I agree with Secretary Wallace. The basic question is not which agency shall manage the land but that it be managed wisely and well, in the enduring interest of the nation. Perhaps Harold L. Ickes, who at one point had virtually completed the transfer of the National Forests, was right in arguing that all Federal lands should be administered by a single department, namely Interior. Or perhaps there is a proper place in the government for a Department of Natural Resources, encompassing all matters relating to fisheries, wildlife, recreation, reclamation, timber, grazing, oil, minerals and Indian affairs, based not on the old public-domain tradition of giving land away, but on conserving it forever. However, regardless of the structural shape of things to come and the recurring proposals for reorganization, we have been considering in these pages the principles and people governing our National Forests, and whether they manage wisely and well, in the enduring interest of the nation.

I have here expressed my own views after spending a considerable amount of time in company with fire fighters, rangers, young foresters, high officials and retired officials who hearken back to Pinchot. But in case I haven't said it before, my lasting reaction is deep pride in having them on our side.

Don't take my word for it. I could be wrong. Go forth from the house in the village. Watch your woods fill up with snow the darkest evening of the year. Or with the glory of the sunlight on the brightest morning. Listen to the sweep of easy wind and the faint fall of flakes. Listen to the many voices of the forest, the soft, serene, the violent, and natural sounds we sometimes hear but cannot understand. Let us share the promise and the joy, each in his own way, of the good and sweet earth, the woods and lake.

# ACKNOWLEDGMENTS

When preparation of this work first began, I doubt that my friends in the United States Forest Service pictured the directions it would ultimately follow. Neither did I at that time. But when I asked for a look at the inside of National Forests and forestry, I was invited to probe as deeply to the core as I wanted to go.

Dr. Richard E. McArdle, the Chief Forester, a tall, firm but soft-spoken Kentuckian, a distinguished career official, had the only delimiting request. "For once," he asked, "please don't call us the 'dedicated men of the Forest Service.'" Nevertheless I am indebted to Chief McArdle for his suggestion that I judge the National Forests not by trees and land alone but by the men who manage them. This stimulated the chapters on Ranger Arthur Woody, Ranger John Hall and Virgil Moss, and helped formulate the general outlook. The Chief also directed me to the trail of Stephen A. Douglas Puter, that celebrated dealer in Oregon land, timber and fraud.

Above all, I appreciate the confidence and encouragement of Clint F. Davis, Director of Information and Education of the Forest Service. Without him this book might never have been written. I am grateful to colleagues of his Division, principally John A. Mattoon, frequently my traveling companion and always my forestry instructor; also, Mary Elizabeth Dale, who facilitated the research; Dr. Matthew Brennan, for his lively reviews of biology and ecology; Leland Prater, the able photographer and forester, and Clifford D. Owsley, who provided the quotation from Mrs. Gifford Pinchot.

Other officials of the Washington office whose counsel and assistance I wish to acknowledge are Clare W. Hendee, Assistant Chief of the Forest Service; Reginald F. DeNio, Director of the Division of Range Management; Merle Lowden, Director of the Division of Fire Control; Axel Lindh, Director of the Division of Land Acquisition; John Sieker, Director of the Division of Recreation and Land Uses; Allen F. Miller, in charge of mineral examinations, William N. Parke, in charge of recreation plans, and Lewis Glover, Division of Engineering.

While expressing deep thanks to the Forest Service, I will say these are not complete or total thanks. Had I relied solely on official sources, this work would have resulted in either a textbook or an apologia, and I hope it is neither. Among others in Washington who furnished valuable points of view were Franklin Bradford, Editorial Director, American Forest Products Industries; Kenneth B. Pomeroy, Forester, and James B. Craig,

340

Editor, American Forestry Association; Ralph D. Hodges, Director, Forestry and Economics Division, and Arthur Z. Nelson, Director, Government Affairs Division, National Lumber Manufacturers Association; Howard Zahniser, Executive Director, the Wilderness Society, and Conrad L. Wirth, Director, National Park Service.

In my traveling about the National Forests, many persons provided guidance and companionship, time-saving arrangements and source material. I express special appreciation to the following, by regions:

NORTHEAST: Theodore C. Fearnow, Assistant Regional Forester, Philadelphia, Pennsylvania; Henry Sipe, staff officer, Monongahela National Forest, Elkins, West Virginia; Gerald S. Wheeler, Supervisor, White Mountain National Forest; Kenneth P. Kenyon, Manager, Waumbek Hotel, Jefferson, New Hampshire; Bruce Sloat, Pinkham Notch Camp of the Appalachian Mountain Club; Paul S. Newcomb, Supervisor, Green Mountain National Forest, Rutland, Vermont; Donald F. Kent, President, Green Mountain Club, Rutland; Diggory Venn, Boston, Massachusetts; Vrest Orton, Weston, Vermont.

SOUTH: James K. Vessey, Regional Forester, Atlanta, Georgia; Edward F. Littlehales, Division of Information and Education, Atlanta; William T. Hardman, Manager, Tourist Division, Georgia State Department of Commerce, Atlanta; Paul Vincent, Supervisor, Chattahoochee National Forest, Blairsville, Georgia; Mrs. Madeleine Anthony, Dahlonega, Georgia; John Olsen, District Ranger, Ocala National Forest, Florida; Victor MacNaughton, Project Manager, Yazoo-Little Tallahatchie Project, Oxford, Mississippi; Ray W. Brandt, Supervisor, Kisatchie National Forest, Alexandria, Louisiana; George W. Tannehill, Jr., District Ranger, Winnville, Louisiana.

Also, Verne C. Rhoades, Asheville, North Carolina, who spoke to me of early forestry as he studied it under Dr. Carl Schenck at Biltmore and practiced it as an early supervisor of Pisgah National Forest; George Stephens, Asheville; Peter Hanlon, Supervisor, North Carolina National Forests; Ted Seely, Ranger of the Pisgah District; Elliott Merrick, Editor, Southeastern Forest Experiment Station, Asheville, and Earl A. Parsons, Ranger of the Robbinsville District, Nantahala National Forest.

LAKE STATES: M. M. Nelson, Regional Forester, Milwaukee, Wisconsin; Richard F. Droege, Assistant Regional Forester; P. Freeman Heim, Division of Information and Education; Anthony J. Quinkert, Ranger of the Eagle River District, Nicolet National Forest, Wisconsin; Lawrence P. Neff, Supervisor, and Ray C. Iverson and J. Wesley White, staff officers, Superior National Forest, Duluth, Minnesota; Leonard J. McDonald, Ely Service Center, and Milton H. Forder, Ranger of the Kawishiwi District, Ely.

INTERMOUNTAIN: James Harrower, mayor of Pinedale, Wyoming;

ACKNOWLEDGMENTS

Kenneth Symes, Bridger National Forest, who taught me to ride the rocky trails; Walt and Nancy Lozier, outfitters of Pinedale; Dr. Roger Keane, Portland, Oregon, a favorite wilderness companion; Charles Schrader, fire-reconnaissance pilot, Lynch Flying Service, Billings, Montana; Robert Johnson, a pioneer of aerial fire fighting, Missoula, Montana; Harry Anderson, Supervisor, Bitterroot National Forest, Hamilton, Montana; John Hall, Ranger of the Sula District; Kenneth Keeney, Assistant Regional Forester, and George Reynolds, Division of Information and Education, Missoula; Miss Doris Stalker, Montana Highway Commission, Helena, Montana; Dr. Irving Witkind, United States Geological Survey, Denver, Colorado; George Duvendack, Supervisor, and Earl Welton and Anthony Durrell, staff officers, Gallatin National Forest, Bozeman, Montana.

Also, Miss Louise Shadduck, State Department of Commerce and Development, Boise, Idaho; Robert Newcomer, Ranger of the Stanley District of the Challis National Forest, Stanley, Idaho; John L. Sevy, Supervisor of the Sawtooth National Forest, Idaho Falls, Idaho; Howard Ahlskog, Supervisor, Boise National Forest, Boise, Idaho; Jim Parsons, Sandpoint, Idaho, and Quentin Larson, Kaniksu National Forest, Priest Lake, Idaho.

SOUTHWEST: Fred H. Kennedy, Regional Forester, Santa Fe, New Mexico; J. Morgan Smith, Assistant Regional Forester, Santa Fe; Fred Thompson, Santo Domingo Trading Post, Algodones, New Mexico; Joseph F. Arnold, Director, Watershed Management Division, State Land Department, Phoenix, Arizona, and Jay Craven, Supervisor, Coconino National Forest, Flagstaff, Arizona.

NORTHWEST: David James, public-relations director, Simpson Logging Company, Seattle, Washington; Clarence Lockwood, Superintendent, Camp Grisdale, Washington; Lloyd Gillmor, Supervisor, Olympic National Forest, Olympia, Washington; Warren Post, Ranger of the Quinault District; Hubert O. Wilson, staff officer, Mount Baker National Forest, Bellingham, Washington; Jack Wood, Division of Information and Education, Portland, Oregon; Richard Kohnstamm, Timberline Lodge; Carl Jordan, Director, State Travel Information Division, Salem, Oregon, and V. A. McNeil, Chamber of Commerce, Portland.

CALIFORNIA: Grant A. Morse, Assistant Regional Forester, San Francisco; Ernest Draves, Division of Information and Education, San Francisco; John Trotter, Los Padres National Forest, Santa Barbara; Don K. Porter, Angeles National Forest, Pasadena, and Lloyd Britton, San Bernardino National Forest, San Bernardino.

I wish to thank my editor, Samuel S. Vaughan, of Doubleday & Co., Inc., New York, for his considerate guidance; and, finally, my wife, Thelma Seymour Frome, for her constructive thoughts and great help.

342

# SELECTED BIBLIOGRAPHY

Collecting information on the National Forests involved, along with personal experience and reporting, the study of many books, booklets, magazines, reports, letters and diaries. However, rather than list all these written sources, I believe it will be more helpful to outline the following selected list for those who wish to pursue ideas the preceding pages may have suggested.

## General and Historical References

AGRICULTURE, DEPARTMENT OF. *The Use of the National Forests.* Washington, D. C., 1907. The slender book that fitted in the ranger's back pocket and answered his questions and the public's.

AGRICULTURE, DEPARTMENT OF. *Highlights in the History of Forest Conservation.* Washington, D. C., 1952.

AGRICULTURE, DEPARTMENT OF. *Black Hills National Forest Fiftieth Anniversary.* Washington, D. C., 1948. Recalling events leading to the first regulated logging in any National Forest.

AMERICAN FORESTRY ASSOCIATION. *Proceedings of the American Forestry Congress.* Washington, D. C., 1905.

AMERICAN FORESTRY ASSOCIATION. *American Forests.* Washington, D. C., monthly. A periodical devoted to broad coverage of forestry.

CARHART, ARTHUR H. *The National Forests.* Alfred A. Knopf, Inc., New York City, 1959.

FRANK, BERNARD. *Our National Forests.* University of Oklahoma Press, Norman, Okla., 1955.

MC DOUGALL, W. B. *Plant Ecology.* Lea, Philadelphia, Pa., 1949.

PINCHOT, GIFFORD. *Breaking New Ground.* Harcourt, Brace, New York City, 1947. The basic work on the guiding philosophy and early history of the United States Forest Service, told in the autobiography of its first Chief.

PUTER, S. A. D., and STEVENS, HORACE. *Looters of the Public Domain.* Portland Printing House Company, Portland, Oreg., 1908.

ROOSEVELT, THEODORE. *Autobiography.* Charles Scribner's Sons, New York City, 1913.

SHOEMAKER, LEN. *Saga of a Forest Ranger.* University of Colorado Press, Boulder, Colo., 1958. Biography of William Kreutzer, one of the first professionally trained foresters, with adventure amid the range wars.

SMITH, GILBERT M., and colleagues. *A Textbook of General Botany.* The Macmillan Co., New York City, 1947.

WILEY, FARIDA A. *Ernest Thompson Seton's America*. The Devin-Adair Co., New York City, 1954. Inspiring selections from the writings of the artist-naturalist.

WOLFE, LINNIE MARSH. *John of the Mountains*. Houghton Mifflin Co., Boston, Mass., 1938. A synthesis of the writings of John Muir.

## Additional References on New England

APPALACHIAN MOUNTAIN CLUB. *Appalachia*. Boston, Mass., April, 1951. The seventy-fifth anniversary issue of the AMC monthly periodical.

FISHER, DOROTHY CANFIELD. *Vermont Tradition*. Little, Brown and Co., Boston, Mass., 1953.

GREEN MOUNTAIN CLUB. *Guide Book of the Long Trail*. Green Mountain Club, Inc., Rutland, Vt., 1960. The fiftieth anniversary edition of the Vermont tramper's guide.

HOUSE, WILLIAM P. *Forty Years of Forestry*. Concord, N. H., 1941. A sketch of the Society for the Protection of New Hampshire Forests on its fortieth anniversary.

## Additional References on Western North Carolina

BILTMORE ESTATE. *Biltmore House and Gardens*. Biltmore Company, Asheville, N. C., 1959. The handbook to this great estate, referring to Pinchot, Schenck and the contribution of the Vanderbilt family to Pisgah National Forest.

ROOSEVELT, THEODORE. *Message from the President of the United States*. Washington, D. C., 1902. Transmitting to Congress a report of the Secretary of Agriculture in relation to the forests, rivers and mountains of the Southern Appalachians.

SCHENCK, CARL ALWIN. *The Biltmore Story*. The American Forest History Foundation, St. Paul, Minn., 1955. The contentious pioneer forester relates in warm, touching passages his personal rise and fall in the United States and his return to Germany. Edited by Ovid A. Butler.

STUPKA, ARTHUR. *Great Smoky Mountains National Park*. Government Printing Office, Washington, D. C., 1960. Anyone visiting the Southern Highlands today should have this natural history handbook, prepared by the National Park biologist who has spent many years studying and interpreting the region.

## Additional References on the South

CABELL, BRANCH, and HANNA, A. J. *The St. Johns*. Holt, Rinehart & Winston, Inc., New York City, 1943. One of the *Rivers of America* Series.

344

ELLIOTT, CHARLES. Articles on Ranger Woody in the *Atlanta Constitution, Southern Outdoorsman* and *Saga* Magazine.

KERR, ED. *Southerners Who Set the Woods on Fire.* An article in *Harper's Magazine,* July, 1958.

MAC NAUGHTON, VICTOR B. *Forestry Called Desire.* An article in *Southern Lumberman,* Nashville, Tenn., December 15, 1959.

MAC NAUGHTON, VICTOR B. *The Forest Returns to the Yazoo.* An article in *Forest Farmer,* Atlanta, Ga., February, 1959.

RAWLINGS, MARJORIE KINNAN. *The Yearling.* Charles Scribner's Sons, New York City, 1938.

STRODE, DONALD D. *The Ocala Deer Herd.* Tallahassee, Fla., 1954. A study of the deer and their management problems, published by the Florida Game and Fresh Water Fish Commission.

## Additional References on Minnesota Canoe Country

ATWOOD, WALLACE W. *Geography of the Quetico-Superior Country.* Chicago, Ill., 1949. An article reprinted from the *Canadian Geographical Journal* by the President's Quetico-Superior Committee.

BRECKENRIDGE, W. J. *Birds of the Canadian Border Lakes.* President's Quetico-Superior Committee. Chicago, Ill., 1949. A booklet.

COATSWORTH, EMERSON S. *The Indians of Quetico.* University of Toronto Press, Toronto, Can., 1957.

MARTIN, HAROLD H. *Embattled Wilderness.* An article in the *Saturday Evening Post,* Philadelphia, Pa., September 25, 1948.

OLSON, SIGURD F. *The Lonely Land.* Alfred A. Knopf, Inc., New York City, 1960. The most recent book by the writer whose works on the canoe country are basic reading.

OLSON, SIGURD F. *Singing Wilderness.* Alfred A. Knopf, Inc., New York City, 1956.

## Additional References on the Wind River Mountains

DE VOTO, BERNARD. *Across the Wide Missouri.* Houghton Mifflin Co., Boston, Mass., 1947.

NEVINS, ALLAN. *Frémont, The West's Greatest Adventurer.* Harper & Bros., New York City, 1927. Includes description of the General's expedition of 1842 and his ascent of the mountain he mistook for the highest in the Rockies.

ROSS, MARVIN C. *The West of Alfred Jacob Miller.* University of Oklahoma Press, Norman, Okla., 1951. Reproductions of the water colors painted by the Baltimore artist during the era of the fur trappers.

SELECTED BIBLIOGRAPHY

## Additional References on Wilderness

DOUGLAS, WILLIAM O. *My Wilderness*. Doubleday & Co., Inc., New York City, 1960. Personal impressions and philosophy of the Supreme Court justice and wilderness traveler.

NATIONAL PARKS ASSOCIATION. *National Parks* Magazine. Washington, D. C., monthly.

SIERRA CLUB. *Bulletin*. San Francisco, Calif., monthly.

SNYDER, ARNOLD P. *Wilderness Area Management*. California Regional Office, U. S. Forest Service, San Francisco, Calif., 1960. This administrative study (hectographed) of a portion of the High Sierra Wilderness Area is perhaps the first comprehensive study of problems and management needs relating to increasing wilderness use.

UNITED STATES SENATE. *Hearings on the National Wilderness Preservation Act*. Washington, D. C., 1957. The viewpoints of all interested parties, pro and con, presented before the Senate Committee on Interior and Insular Affairs.

WILDERNESS SOCIETY. *The Living Wilderness*. Washington, D. C., quarterly. A source of much material on the lives and thoughts of Aldo Leopold and Robert Marshall.

## Additional References on the Earthquake

MATTHEWS, SAMUEL W. *The Night the Mountains Moved*. An article in the *National Geographic Magazine*. Washington, D. C., March, 1960.

WITKIND, IRVING, DR. *The Night the Earth Quaked*. A report by the geologist on the scene. Prepared for U. S. Forest Service and U. S. Geological Survey, Washington, D. C., 1961.

## Additional References on Forest Fire History

EL HULT, RUBY. *Northwest Disaster*. Binfords & Mort, Portland, Oreg., 1960.

HALM, JOE B. *The Great Fire of 1910*. An article first published in *American Forests and Forest Life*, July, 1930, and reprinted in *Montana* Magazine, Helena, Mont., October, 1960.

KOCH, ELERS. *History of the 1910 Forest Fires in Idaho and Western Montana*. An excellent historical document prepared by an early supervisor of the Lolo National Forest, reissued (hectographed) in 1960 by the Forest Service Regional Office, Missoula, Mont.

PULASKI, E. C. *Surrounded by Forest Fires*. An article in *American Forests*, August, 1923.

SPENCER, BETTY GOODWIN. *The Big Blowup, the Northwest's Great Fire.* The Caxton Printers, Ltd., Caldwell, Idaho, 1956.

## Additional References on the Bitterroot Valley

BOESCH, MARK. *Cross in the West.* Farrar, Straus and Cudahy Inc., New York City, 1956. Tells of the building of St. Mary's Mission at Stevensville, Mont.

DE VOTO, BERNARD. *The Journals of Lewis and Clark.* Houghton Mifflin Co., Boston, Mass., 1953. Traces the explorers' course through Bitterroot Valley.

HAMRE, VERNON O., and WATTS, M. J. *Wildlife Management Plan.* Headquarters, Bitterroot National Forest, Hamilton, Mont., 1957. The District Ranger and District Game Warden detail studies and action to balance populations of livestock and big game animals.

HUTCHINSON, S. BLAIR, and KEMP, PAUL D. *Forest Resources of Montana.* Government Printing Office, Washington, D. C., 1952.

## Additional References on Grazing

BARNES, WILL C. *Story of the Range.* Government Printing Office, Washington, D. C., 1925. By an early Assistant Chief Forester in charge of grazing.

DE VOTO, BERNARD. Articles in *Harper's Magazine*, especially from 1947 to 1953.

DUTTON, WALT L. *Forest Grazing in the United States.* An article in the *Journal of Forestry*, Washington, D. C., 1953. By a former Chief, Division of Range Management.

DUTTON, WALT L. *History of Forest Service Grazing Fees.* Washington, D. C., 1953. Hectographed report.

EVANKO, A. B. *Manipulation of Brush Cover on California National Forests.* San Francisco, Calif., 1959.

FLETCHER, ROBERT H. *Free Grass to Fences*, University Publishers, Inc., New York City, 1960.

FOSS, PHILIP. *Politics and Grass.* University of Washington Press, Seattle, Wash., 1960.

MC ARDLE, RICHARD E. *The Outlook for Livestock on the National Forests.* Phoenix, Ariz., 1958. Speech by the Chief Forester before the National Woolgrowers Association.

## Additional References on White-Pine Blister Rust

MIELKE, JAMES L. *White-Pine Blister Rust in Western North America.*

New Haven, Conn., 1943. An article in the *Bulletin of the School of Forestry*, Yale University.

MOSS, VIRGIL D., and VICHE, HENRY J. *Antibiotic Saves Western White Pine from Blister Rust.* An article in *American Forests*, Washington, D. C., 1960.

MOSS, VIRGIL D., and WELLNER, CHARLES A. *Aiding Blister-Rust Control by Silvicultural Measures in Western White Pine.* Government Printing Office. Washington, D. C., 1953.

UNITED STATES FOREST SERVICE. *White-Pine Blister-Rust Control.* Missoula, Mont. An annual hectographed report issued by the Regional Office.

## Additional References on Water in Arizona

AGRICULTURE, DEPARTMENT OF. *Water, the Yearbook of Agriculture.* Washington, D. C., 1955. An encyclopedia of national water uses, needs and prospects.

ARIZONA, STATE OF. *Proceedings of the Annual Watershed Symposiums.* Phoenix, Ariz., 1958, '59, '60. Reporting the meetings sponsored by the Arizona Water Resources Committee and Watershed Management Division, State Land Department.

ARIZONA, UNIVERSITY OF. *Recovering Rainfall.* Tucson, Ariz., 1956. A study issued by the University's Department of Agricultural Economics for the Arizona Watershed Program.

CARR, WILLIAM H. *Water Street, U. S. A.* Tucson, Ariz., 1959. Description of the Watershed Exposition of the Arizona-Sonora Desert Museum.

KENNEDY, FRED H. *Forests and Water.* Albuquerque, N. M., 1958. Report on National Forest developments by the Southwest Regional Forester.

KENNEDY, FRED H. *National Forest Watershed Projects in Arizona.* Southwest Regional Office, U. S. Forest Service, Albuquerque, N. M., 1959.

## Additional References on the Northwest

EL HULT, RUBY. *Untamed Olympics.* Binfords & Mort, Portland, Oreg., 1954.

FAGERLUND, GUNNAR O. *Olympic National Park.* Government Printing Office, Washington, D. C., 1954. A handbook covering the natural history of the Peninsula.

HOLBROOK, STEWART. *Green Commonwealth.* Dogwood Press, Seattle, Wash., 1945. A lumber company's history of a lumber company, with well-told tales of the rugged days.

SPORTS ILLUSTRATED. *How Timberline Overcame Last Year's Scandal.* An article. New York City, January 23, 1956.

STEVENS, JAMES. *Green Power.* Superior Publishing Company, Seattle, Wash., 1958. Big timber states its case.

## Additional References on Southern California

AUTOMOBILE CLUB OF SOUTHERN CALIFORNIA. *Westways.* Los Angeles, Calif., monthly travel periodical.

BROWN, WILLIAM S., and SNOW, S. B. *California Rural Land Use and Management.* San Francisco, Calif., 1944. Six volumes (hectographed) prepared by the Forest Service Regional Office.

KOFORD, CARL. *The California Condor.* New York City, 1953. A research report published by the National Audubon Society.

ROBINSON, W. W. *The Forest and the People.* Los Angeles, Calif., 1946. The history of the Angeles National Forest, told with authority and affection, published by the Title Insurance and Trust Company.

# INDEX